LATIN AMERICAN ADJUSTMENT: HOW MUCH HAS HAPPENED?

JOHN WILLIAMSON, EDITOR

LATIN AMERICAN ADJUSTMENT: HOW MUCH HAS HAPPENED?

INSTITUTE FOR INTERNATIONAL ECONOMICS
WASHINGTON, DC
April 1990

John Williamson is a Senior Fellow at the Institute for International Economics. He was formerly economics professor at Pontifícia Universidade Católica do Rio de Janeiro, University of Warwick, Massachusetts Institute of Technology, University of York, and Princeton University; Advisor to the International Monetary Fund; and Economic Consultant to Her Majesty's Treasury. Williamson has published numerous studies on international monetary issues, including *IMF Conditionality*, *The Failure of World Monetary Reform 1971–74*, *Political Economy and International Money*, *Voluntary Approaches to Debt Relief*, and *The Progress of Policy Reform in Latin America*.

INSTITUTE FOR INTERNATIONAL ECONOMICS
11 Dupont Circle, NW
Washington, DC 20036
(202) 328-9000
Telex: 261271 IIE UR
Fax: (202) 328-5432

C. Fred Bergsten, *Director*
Linda Griffin Kean, *Director of Publications*

The Institute for International Economics was created by, and receives substantial support from, the German Marshall Fund of the United States.

The views expressed in this publication are those of the author. This publication is part of the overall program of the Institute, as endorsed by its Board of Directors, but does not necessarily reflect the views of individual members of the Board or the Advisory Committee.

Printed in the United States of America
94 93 92   5 4 3 2

Library of Congress Cataloging-in-Publication Data

John Williamson (edited)
Latin American Adjustment: How Much Has Happened?
p. 472 cm.
1. Latin America—Economic policy—Congresses. 2. Economic stabilization—Latin America—Congresses.
I. Williamson, John, 1937-
HC125.L34746 1990   90-33670
338.98-dc20   CIP
ISBN 0–88132–125–7

Contents

Tables

Figures

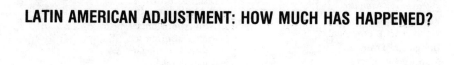

LATIN AMERICAN ADJUSTMENT: HOW MUCH HAS HAPPENED?

Preface

The Institute has addressed the interrelated problems of debt, adjustment, inflation, and development in Latin America on a number of occasions. In 1986, we published a comprehensive set of development proposals in *Toward Renewed Economic Growth in Latin America*. We have conducted several studies on debt, including its impact on the development prospects of the region, the most recent being *Voluntary Approaches to Debt Relief* in 1988 (revised in 1989). We held conferences in 1983 and 1985 to offer interim assessments of the adjustment responses of the largest Latin American countries and their efforts to control inflation.

This volume presents the papers and proceedings of a conference held by the Institute in November 1989 to reassess the course of Latin American adjustment in the wake of profound political and economic changes in a number of Latin countries after mid-1985. Experts from each of eight individual countries in the region and two groups of smaller countries analyze the extent and the results of recent policy reforms. Their analyses focus on three fundamental questions: Is there agreement on what policies are needed to restore growth and overcome the debt crisis? Have the Latin American countries begun to implement such policies effectively? Do the results so far confirm the wisdom of such efforts?

The concluding chapter by John Williamson synthesizes the findings of the conference and offers answers to each of these critical questions. His essay is also published separately in the *Policy Analyses in International Economics* series as *The Progress of Policy Reform in Latin America*.

The Institute for International Economics is a private nonprofit research institution for the study and discussion of international economic policy. Its purpose is to analyze important issues in that area and to develop and communicate practical new approaches for dealing with them. The Institute is completely nonpartisan.

The Institute was created by a generous commitment of funds from the German Marshall Fund of the United States in 1981, and now receives about 15 percent of its support from that source. Major institutional grants are also being received from the Ford Foundation, the William and Flora Hewlett Foundation, and the Alfred P. Sloan Foundation. A number of other foundations and private corporations are contributing to the increasing diversification of the Institute's financial resources. About 10 percent of the Institute resources in its latest fiscal year came from outside the United States, including about 3 percent from Japan.

The Board of Directors bears overall responsibility for the Institute and gives general guidance and approval to its research program—including identification of topics that are likely to become important to policymakers over the medium run (generally one to three years) and which thus should be addressed by the Institute. The Director, working closely with the staff and outside Advisory Committee, is responsible for the development of particular projects and makes the final decision to publish an individual study.

The Institute hopes that its studies and other activities will contribute to building a stronger foundation for international economic policy around the world. We invite readers of these publications to let us know how they think we can best accomplish this objective.

C. FRED BERGSTEN
Director
April 1990

Acknowledgments

The editor acknowledges with gratitude the help and stimulus provided by the authors, discussants, panelists, and floor participants at the conference held on 6–7 November 1989, as well as helpful comments on a draft of chapter 9 by C. Fred Bergsten, William R. Cline, C. David Finch, Felipe Larraín, J. J. Polak, Jeffrey D. Sachs, and William Tyler. He owes a particular debt to the publications and support staff of the Institute, notably Terry Kannofsky and Michael Treadway, and Angela Barnes, Donna Becraft, and Lisa Salaz.

Introduction

John Williamson

Ever since the Third World debt crisis broke in August 1982, debtor countries have been called on to "adjust" as their contribution to resolving the debt problem. The paralysis of Brazilian policy under José Sarney, and the continuing disasters in Argentina and Peru, seem to have nurtured a belief in the industrial countries that Latin America as a whole has failed to respond to the challenge to adjust. The conference reported in this volume was motivated by a concern that this assessment does a serious injustice to many countries in the region, and that continuing acceptance of this erroneous perception could jeopardize the prospects of carrying an ambitious reform program to fruition.

If one wants to establish which countries have tried seriously to adjust, then one needs to start off by specifying what is meant by adjustment. With that end in view I wrote a background paper for the conference, entitled "What Washington Means by Policy Reform" (chapter 2 in this volume), which aimed to lay out the various policy changes that "Washington" had been urging the Latin American countries to make. For these purposes "Washington" meant primarily the International Monetary Fund (IMF), the World Bank, and the US executive branch, although the term was intended to cover also at least the Inter-American Development Bank (IDB), those members of Congress who take an interest in Latin America, and the think tanks concerned with economic policy. It seemed to me that one could identify 9 or 10 policy areas in which "Washington" could muster something like a consensus on what countries ought to be doing, and so I labeled this program the "Washington consensus" or the "Washington agenda." A summary description of the content of this Washington agenda is macroeconomic prudence, outward orientation, and domestic liberalization.

The bulk of the conference (reported in chapters 3 through 6) was devoted to discussion of a series of country papers, all by Latin Americans from the countries themselves. One of the questions posed to the authors was the extent to which the "Washington consensus" also commanded local support. The general answer seemed to be that "consensus" might be too strong a term, but that there is a great deal of convergence—especially among economists but spilling over also, at least on the macroeconomic issues, to most policymakers.

My appraisal of the outcome of the conference (chapter 9) suggests that "universal convergence" might have been a more accurate, if less memorable, title for the "Washington consensus."

The main issue taken up in the country papers is the extent of the policy reforms that have been implemented. These vary a great deal by country, but the papers by and large confirmed that quite a lot has been happening.

The natural next question is whether these policy reforms have been well conceived and are now producing positive results. The papers provide a basis for trying to answer that question, inasmuch as all of them describe economic developments and to a greater or lesser extent relate these to the policies that have been pursued. Such assessments surely provide a better basis for judging the quality of the policy advice embodied in IMF (and/or World Bank) conditionality than the sort of statistical comparisons of program and nonprogram countries on two or three measures of performance that have proliferated in the literature (see Goldstein and Montiel 1986 for a description and criticism of the genre).

My attempt in chapter 9 to distill some conclusions about the success of policy reform in reigniting growth is to be regarded as very much a first attempt to extract systematic lessons from a series of case studies, as an alternative approach to assessing whether the Fund and the Bank are giving good advice. An essential difference between the two approaches is that mine is two-stage: one first asks whether the countries have implemented the reforms being urged on them, and one then goes on to ask whether economic performance in those countries that have reformed has brought the expected benefits. There must be ample scope for making such comparisons in a more sophisticated way than is done in chapter 9, but perhaps that effort will help to redirect examination of this topic in a more productive direction.

Apart from the country papers and my background and synthesizing chapters, the volume includes the conference's concluding panel discussion (chapter 7) and an after-dinner speech by Enrique Iglesias (chapter 8). The latter offers a broad-brush picture of how the adjustment process has been evolving in Latin America as seen by someone who has been at its center, first as the Executive Secretary of the Economic Commission for Latin America and the Caribbean, then as Foreign Minister of Uruguay, and currently as President of the IDB. It is particularly valuable inasmuch as it brought to our conference a taste of the conclusions of the IDB's own conference held 10 days earlier.

It remains to record that my view of what Latin American adjustment is all about evolved drastically between the time the conference was held in early November 1989 and the time when I finished revising chapter 9 as the 1990s dawned. The catalyst for the change was the liberation of Eastern Europe. In those few weeks no fewer than four countries threw off their authoritarian shackles. In each case the political liberalization was accompanied by clear indications that the new leaders anticipated a parallel move toward a market economy.

As one who first got involved in Latin America at a time when the cause of economic liberalism was associated with a clutch of singularly unpleasant dictators in the Southern Cone, I had previously tended to regard the relationship between political and economic liberalism as essentially orthogonal.[1] Events in Eastern Europe made me ask whether it was really a coincidence that Latin America was engaged in its hesitant, controversial, patchy, incomplete, but nonetheless rather widespread attempt to move from statism to a market economy in the same decade that democracy had triumphed. Chapter 9 does not contain anything like a complete exploration of that possible link, but it does reflect a perception that Latin American adjustment is about something much more significant than returning to business as usual while also satisfying the bankers. If the adjustment succeeds, the region should over the next quarter century be absorbed into the comfortable world of the free-market democracies. If it fails, Argentina's decline of the last half-century is all too likely to be a portent.

---

1. I use the term "liberalism" in its historic or European sense rather than that prevalent in US political discourse. These two usages do strike me as essentially orthogonal.

2

What Washington Means by
Policy Reform

What Washington Means by Policy Reform

John Williamson

No statement about how to deal with the debt crisis in Latin America would be complete without a call for the debtors to fulfill their part of the proposed bargain by "setting their houses in order," "undertaking policy reforms," or "submitting to strong conditionality." The question posed in this paper is what such phrases mean, and especially what they are generally interpreted as meaning in Washington. Thus the paper aims to set out what would be regarded in Washington as constituting a desirable set of economic policy reforms. An important purpose in doing this is to establish a baseline against which to measure the extent to which various countries have implemented the reforms being urged on them.

The paper identifies and discusses 10 policy instruments about whose proper deployment Washington can muster a reasonable degree of consensus. In each case an attempt is made to suggest the breadth of the consensus, and in some cases I suggest ways in which I would wish to see the consensus view modified. The paper is intended to elicit comment on both the extent to which the views identified *do* indeed command a consensus and on whether they *deserve* to command it. It is hoped that the country studies to be guided by this background paper will comment on the extent to which the Washington consensus is shared in the country in question, as well as on the extent to which that consensus has been implemented and the results of its implementation (or nonimplementation).

The Washington of this paper is both the political Washington of Congress and senior members of the administration and the technocratic Washington of the international financial institutions, the economic agencies of the US government, the Federal Reserve Board, and the think tanks. The Institute for International Economics made a contribution to codifying and propagating several aspects of the Washington consensus in its publication *Toward Renewed Economic Growth in Latin America* (Balassa et al. 1986). Washington does not, of course, always practice what it preaches to foreigners.

The 10 topics around which the paper is organized deal with *policy instruments* rather than objectives or outcomes. They are economic policy instruments that

7

I perceive "Washington" to think important, as well as on which some consensus exists. It is generally assumed, at least in technocratic Washington, that the standard economic objectives of growth, low inflation, a viable balance of payments, and an equitable income distribution should determine the disposition of such policy instruments.

There is at least some awareness of the need to take into account the impact that some of the policy instruments in question can have on the extent of corruption. Corruption is perceived to be pervasive in Latin America and a major cause of the region's poor performance in terms of both low growth and inegalitarian income distribution. These implications will be mentioned below where they seem to be important.

Washington certainly has a number of other concerns in its relationship with its Latin neighbors (and, for that matter, with other countries) besides furthering their economic well-being. These include the promotion of democracy and human rights, suppression of the drug trade, preservation of the environment, and control of population growth. For better or worse, however, these broader objectives play little role in determining Washington's attitude toward the economic policies it urges on Latin America. Limited sums of money may be offered to countries in return for specific acts to combat drugs, to save tropical forests, or (at least prior to the Reagan administration) to promote birth control, and sanctions may occasionally be imposed in support of democracy or human rights, but there is little perception that the policies discussed below have important implications for any of those objectives. Political Washington is also, of course, concerned about the strategic and commercial interests of the United States, but the general belief is that these are best furthered by prosperity in the Latin countries. The most obvious possible exception to this perceived harmony of interests concerns the US national interest in continued receipt of debt service from Latin America. Some (but not all) believe this consideration to have been important in motivating Washington's support for policies of austerity in Latin America during the 1980s.

Fiscal Deficits

Washington believes in fiscal discipline. Congress enacted Gramm-Rudman-Hollings with a view to restoring a balanced budget by 1993. Presidential candidates deplore budget deficits before and after being elected. The International Monetary Fund (IMF) has long made the restoration of fiscal discipline a central element of the high-conditionality programs it negotiates with its members that wish to borrow. Among right-wing think tanks there may be a few believers in Ricardian equivalence—the notion that individuals adjust their saving behavior to anticipate future taxation, so that whether public expenditure is financed by taxation or bonds has no impact on aggregate demand—who are prepared to deny the danger of large fiscal deficits, but they clearly stand outside the Washington consensus. Left-wing believers in "Keynesian" stimulation via large budget deficits are almost an extinct species.

Differences of view exist, however, as to whether fiscal discipline need necessarily imply a balanced budget. One view is that a deficit is acceptable as long as it does not result in the debt–GNP ratio rising. An even more relaxed criterion would net off that part of the increased debt that has a counterpart in productive public capital formation and simply seek to prevent an increase in the net liabilities of the public sector relative to GNP. Another modification, which I find persuasive although much of Washington regards it as too "Keynesian" to endorse explicitly, argues that a balanced budget (or at least a nonincreasing debt–GNP ratio) should be a minimal medium-run norm, but that short-run deficits and surpluses around that norm should be welcomed insofar as they contribute to macroeconomic stabilization. (Note that Gramm-Rudman-Hollings is automatically suspended if the US economy goes into recession.) A variant of that view, held in some quarters where "Keynesian" is regarded as a term of abuse, is that progress toward the medium-term goal of a balanced budget should be sufficiently cautious to avoid the risk of precipitating a recession.

The budget deficit has traditionally been measured in nominal terms, as the excess of government expenditures over receipts. In 1982 Brazil argued with the IMF that this way of measuring the deficit is seriously misleading in a high-inflation country, where most of the nominal interest payments on government debt are really accelerated amortization of principal. The IMF has accepted this argument (Tanzi 1989), if initially with some reluctance, and hence it sometimes now pays attention to the "operational deficit," which includes in expenditure only the real component of interest paid on government debt. (Political Washington has not yet discovered this sensible innovation, which thus remains to be exploited as a means of relaxing the Gramm-Rudman-Hollings constraints when these threaten to bite.) Indeed, Tanzi (1989) also indicates that in formulating programs the Fund has increasingly been using the "primary deficit," which excludes *all* interest payments from the deficit, on the ground that this includes only items that are in principle directly controllable by the authorities. (That goes too far for my taste, since real interest payments certainly have implications for aggregate demand and the evolution of the real debt of the public sector.)

The exaggeration of budget deficits by inclusion of the inflationary component of interest on government debt is not the only inadequacy of public-sector accounting. Most of the other questionable practices seem to involve understatement of the true deficit:

- Contingent expenditures, such as the guarantees given to savings and loan institutions in the United States, are rarely included in reported budget outlays.

- Interest subsidies and some other expenditures are sometimes provided by the central bank rather than from the budget.

- Privatization proceeds are sometimes recorded as revenues rather than as a means of financing a fiscal deficit.

- The buildup of future liabilities of the social security system is not included in budget outlays.

Despite the significant differences in the interpretation of fiscal discipline, I would maintain that there is very broad agreement in Washington that large and sustained fiscal deficits are a primary source of macroeconomic dislocation in the forms of inflation, payments deficits, and capital flight. They result not from any rational calculation of expected economic benefits, but from a lack of the political courage or honesty to match public expenditures and the resources available to finance them. Unless the excess is being used to finance productive infrastructure investment, an operational budget deficit in excess of around 1 to 2 percent of GNP[1] is *prima facie* evidence of policy failure. Moreover, a smaller deficit, or even a surplus, is not necessarily evidence of fiscal discipline: its adequacy needs to be examined in the light of the strength of demand and the availability of private savings.

Public Expenditure Priorities

When a fiscal deficit needs to be cut, a choice arises as to whether this should be accomplished by increasing revenues or by reducing expenditures. One of the legacies of the Reagan administration and its "supply-side" allies has been to create a preference in Washington for reducing expenditures rather than increasing tax revenues, although it is not clear that this preference is very strong outside of right-wing political circles (including the right-wing think tanks).

Much stronger views are held, especially in the international institutions, about the composition of public expenditures. Military expenditures are sometimes privately deplored, but in general they are regarded as the ultimate

---

1. This figure assumes a desire to stabilize the debt–GNP ratio, D/Y, at no more than 0.4. Assume a real growth rate, $\hat{Y}/Y$, of 0.04. Then $\hat{D}/D - \hat{Y}/Y \leq 0$ implies $\hat{D}/Y \leq \hat{Y}/Y \times \hat{D}/Y = 0.04 \times 0.4 = 0.016$.

prerogative of sovereign governments and accordingly off limits to international technocrats. Expenditures on public administration are recognized as necessary, although sometimes they are believed to be unnecessarily bloated, especially where corruption is out of hand. But there are three major expenditure categories on which views are strongly held: subsidies, education and health, and public investment.

Subsidies, especially indiscriminate subsidies (including subsidies to cover the losses of state enterprises) are regarded as prime candidates for reduction or preferably elimination. Everyone has horror stories about countries where subsidized gasoline is cheaper than drinking water, or where subsidized bread is so cheap that it is fed to pigs, or where telephone calls cost a cent or so because someone forgot (or lacked the courage) to raise prices to keep pace with inflation, or where subsidized "agricultural credit" is designed to buy the support of powerful landowners, who promptly recycle the funds to buy government paper. The result is not just a drain on the budget but also much waste and resource misallocation, with little reason to expect any offset from systematically favorable effects on income distribution, at least where indiscriminate subsidies are concerned.

Education and health, in contrast, are regarded as quintessentially proper objects of government expenditure (Balassa et al. 1986, chapter 4). They have the character of investment (in human capital) as well as consumption. Moreover, they tend to help the disadvantaged. This is an objective that fell under a cloud in the early years of the Reagan administration, but that has recovered its standing of the 1970s ("basic needs") in the late 1980s, aided by the prodding of UNICEF (Cornia, Jolly, and Stewart 1987). Thus, the Managing Director of the IMF, Michel Camdessus, has declared the Fund to have a concern about the impact of its programs on the poor, and more recently Barber Conable, President of the World Bank, has reasserted the Bank's commitment to seeking to end poverty.[2]

Just how much help expenditures on education and health in fact provide to the disadvantaged depends on their composition as well as their level. Primary education is vastly more relevant than university education, and primary health care (especially preventive treatment) more beneficial to the poor than hospitals in the capital city stuffed with all the latest high-tech medical gadgets. This is not to say that there is no need for universities or state-of-the-art hospitals: developing countries need to train and retain an educated elite as well as to raise the standards of the masses and the poorest. But it is to assert that many in Washington believe that expenditures need to be redirected toward education

---

2. See, for example, Camdessus' address to the United Nations Economic and Social Council in Geneva on 26 June 1987 (*IMF Survey*, 29 June 1987) and the interview with Conable in Istanbul on 19 May 1989.

and health in general, and most especially in a way that will benefit the disadvantaged.

The other area of public expenditure that Washington regards as productive is public infrastructure investment. There is of course a view that the public sector tends to be too large (see the section on privatization below). However, that view coexists with the view that spending on infrastructure that is properly within the public sector needs to be large (and also that an industry should not be starved of investment just because it is, however inadvisedly, within the public sector).

Policy reform with regard to public expenditure is thus perceived to consist of switching expenditure from subsidies toward education and health (especially to benefit the disadvantaged) and infrastructure investment. I would add that, for my taste, the hostility toward subsidies tends to be too general. I fully sympathize with the hostility toward *indiscriminate* subsidies, but I also believe that there are circumstances in which carefully targeted subsidies can be a useful instrument. Thus, my own test of a country's policies would not be whether it had abolished all subsidies, but whether it could provide a convincing explicit justification for those that remain in terms of improving either resource allocation or income distribution.

Tax Reform

Increased tax revenues are the alternative to decreased public expenditures as a remedy for a fiscal deficit. Most of political Washington regards them as an inferior alternative. Much of technocratic Washington (with the exception of the right-wing think tanks) finds political Washington's aversion to tax increases irresponsible and incomprehensible.

Despite this contrast in attitudes toward the merits of increasing tax revenue, there is a very wide consensus about the most desirable method of raising whatever level of tax revenue is judged to be needed. The principle is that the tax base should be broad and marginal tax rates should be moderate. This principle, the basis of the 1986 reform of the US income tax, was promoted with equal enthusiasm by the late Joseph A. Pechman of the Brookings Institution and Senator Bill Bradley (D-NJ) and by the "supply-siders" in Congress and the right-wing think tanks.

A particular issue that arises in the Latin American context is whether an attempt should be made to include within the tax base interest income on assets held abroad ("flight capital"). By itself a single country's law subjecting such income to taxation may not have much impact because of the problem of enforcement, but a country is not even in a position to start discussions on enforcement with haven countries until it has legislated to impose taxes on the interest from flight capital (Lessard and Williamson 1987). Achieving effective taxation of the income from flight capital is bound to take a long time, but it would be interesting to know whether any countries have embarked on the effort.

Interest Rates

Two general principles about the level of interest rates would seem to command considerable support in Washington. One is that interest rates should be market-determined. The objective of this is to avoid the resource misallocation that results from bureaucrats rationing credit according to arbitrary criteria (Polak 1989). The other principle is that real interest rates should be positive, so as to discourage capital flight and, according to some, increase savings. Many, including myself, would qualify this statement to say that interest rates should be positive but moderate, so as to promote productive investment and avoid the threat of an explosion in government debt.

The question obviously arises as to whether these two principles are mutually consistent. Under noncrisis conditions, I see little reason to anticipate a contradiction; one expects market-determined interest rates to be positive but moderate in real terms, although high international interest rates may make it difficult to hold rates quite as moderate as might be desired. Under the sort of crisis conditions that much of Latin America has experienced for most of the 1980s, however, it is all too easy to believe that market-determined interest rates may be extremely high. It is then of interest to examine whether either principle has been followed or what sort of compromise between the two may have been achieved. In particular, it is still of interest to examine whether the credit market is segmented and channeling low-cost funds to "priority" sectors and, if so, what those sectors are and whether their selection has any economic rationale. The suspicion is that such segmented credit markets provide a prime environment for corruption to flourish.

The Exchange Rate

Like interest rates, exchange rates may be determined by market forces, or their appropriateness may be judged on the basis of whether their level seems consistent with macroeconomic objectives. Although there is some support in Washington for regarding the former principle as the more important (a view held in particular by those who deny the possibility of estimating equilibrium exchange rates), the dominant view is that achieving a "competitive" exchange rate is more important than how the rate is determined. In particular, there is relatively little support for the notion that liberalization of international capital flows is a priority objective for a country that should be a capital importer and ought to be retaining its own savings for domestic investment.

The test of whether an exchange rate is appropriate is whether it is consistent in the medium run with macroeconomic objectives (as in my concept of the "fundamental equilibrium exchange rate," or FEER; see Williamson 1985). In the case of a developing country, the real exchange rate needs to be sufficiently competitive to promote a rate of export growth that will allow the economy to grow at the maximum rate permitted by its supply-side potential, while keeping the current account deficit to a size that can be financed on a sustainable basis. The exchange rate should not be more competitive than that, because that would produce unnecessary inflationary pressures and also limit the resources available for domestic investment, and hence curb the growth of supply-side potential.

Growth of nontraditional exports is dependent not just on a competitive exchange rate at a particular point in time, but also on private-sector confidence that the rate will remain sufficiently competitive in the future to justify investment in potential export industries (for recent evidence, see Paredes 1989). Thus, it is important to assess the stability of the real exchange rate as well as its level.

A competitive real exchange rate is the first essential element of an "outward-oriented" economic policy, where the balance of payments constraint is overcome primarily by export growth rather than by import substitution. There is a very strongly held conviction in Washington that outward orientation and expanding exports—essentially growth in *nontraditional* exports—are necessary for Latin American recovery (see, for example, Balassa et al. 1986).

Trade Policy

The second element of an outward-oriented economic policy is import liberalization. Access to imports of intermediate inputs at competitive prices is regarded as important to export promotion, while a policy of protecting domestic industries against foreign competition is viewed as creating costly distortions that end up penalizing exports and impoverishing the domestic economy. The ideal is a situation in which the domestic resource cost of generating or saving a unit of foreign exchange is equalized between and among export and import-competing industries.

The worst form of protection is considered to be import licensing, with its massive potential for creating opportunities for corruption. To the extent that there has to be protection, let it be provided by tariffs, so that at least the public purse gets the rents. And keep distortions to a minimum by limiting tariff dispersion and exempting from tariffs imports of intermediate goods needed to produce exports.

The free trade ideal is generally (although perhaps not universally) conceded to be subject to two qualifications. The first concerns infant industries, which may merit substantial but strictly temporary protection. Furthermore, a moderate general tariff (in the range of 10 percent to 20 percent, with little dispersion) might be accepted as a mechanism to provide a bias toward diversifying the industrial base without threatening serious costs. The second qualification concerns timing. A highly protected economy is not expected to dismantle all protection overnight. Views differ, however, on whether import liberalization should proceed according to a predetermined timetable (the World Bank view, embodied in many structural adjustment loans) or whether the speed of liberalization should vary endogenously, depending on how much the state of the balance of payments can tolerate (my own view, based on recollection of how Europe liberalized successfully in the 1950s).

Foreign Direct Investment

As noted above, liberalization of foreign financial flows is not regarded as a high priority. In contrast, a restrictive attitude limiting the entry of foreign direct investment (FDI) is regarded as foolish. Such investment can bring needed capital, skills, and know-how, either producing goods needed for the domestic market[3] or contributing new exports. The main motivation for restricting FDI is economic nationalism, which Washington disapproves of, at least when practiced by countries other than the United States.

FDI can be promoted by debt-equity swaps. Parts of Washington, perhaps most notably the US Treasury, the Institute of International Finance, and the International Finance Corporation, are strongly in favor of debtor countries facilitating debt-equity swaps, on the argument that this can simultaneously further the twin objectives of promoting FDI and reducing debt. Other parts of Washington, notably the IMF, are much more skeptical. They question whether FDI should be subsidized; they ask whether the subsidized investment will be additional; they argue that, if it is not, the debtor loses by having its foreign debt reduced rather than gaining free foreign exchange; and above all they worry about the inflationary implications of adding to domestic monetary expansion.

---

3. An exception to the case for welcoming FDI can arise if the domestic market in question is heavily protected, when the growth produced by foreign investment can be immiserizing: see Brecher and Díaz Alejandro (1977).

Privatization

Debt-equity swaps involve no monetary pressure when the equity purchased by the foreign investor is bought from the government, in the course of an enterprise being privatized. This is one attraction seen in privatization. More generally, privatization may help relieve the pressure on the government budget, both in the short run by the revenue produced by the sale of the enterprise and in the longer run inasmuch as investment need no longer be financed by the government.

However, the main rationale for privatization is the belief that private industry is managed more efficiently than state enterprises, because of the more direct incentives faced by a manager who either has a direct personal stake in the profits of an enterprise or else is accountable to those who do. At the very least, the threat of bankruptcy places a floor under the inefficiency of private enterprises, whereas many state enterprises seem to have unlimited access to subsidies. This belief in the superior efficiency of the private sector has long been an article of faith in Washington (though perhaps not held quite as fervently as in the rest of the United States), but it was only with the enunciation of the Baker Plan in 1985 that it became official US policy to promote foreign privatization. The IMF and the World Bank have duly encouraged privatization in Latin America and elsewhere since.

The lack of a strong indigenous private sector is one reason that has motivated some countries to promote state enterprises. This is again a nationalistic motivation and hence commands little respect in Washington.

My own view is that privatization can be very constructive where it results in increased competition, and useful where it eases fiscal pressures, but I am not persuaded that public service is always inferior to private acquisitiveness as a motivating force. Under certain circumstances, such as where marginal costs are less than average costs (for example, in public transport) or in the presence of environmental spillovers too complex to be easily compensated by regulation (for example, in the case of water supply), I continue to believe public ownership to be preferable to private enterprise. But this view is not typical of Washington.

Deregulation

Another way of promoting competition is by deregulation. This was initiated within the United States by the Carter administration and carried forward by the Reagan administration. It is generally judged to have been successful within the

United States, and it is generally assumed that it could bring similar benefits to other countries.

The potential payoff from deregulation would seem to be much greater in Latin America, to judge from the assessment in Balassa et al. (1986, 130):

> Most of the larger Latin American countries are among the world's most regulated market economies, at least on paper. Among the most important economic regulatory mechanisms are controls on the establishment of firms and on new investments, restrictions on inflows of foreign investment and outflows of profit remittance, price controls, import barriers, discriminatory credit allocation, high corporate income tax rates combined with discretionary tax-reduction mechanisms, as well as limits on firing of employees. . . . In a number of Latin American countries, the web of regulation is administered by underpaid administrators. The potential for corruption is therefore great.
>
> Productive activity may be regulated by legislation, by government decrees, and case-by-case decision making. This latter practice is widespread and pernicious in Latin America as it creates considerable uncertainty and provides opportunities for corruption. It also discriminates against small and medium-sized businesses which, although important creators of employment, seldom have access to the higher reaches of the bureaucracy.

Property Rights

In the United States property rights are so well entrenched that their fundamental importance for the satisfactory operation of the capitalist system is easily overlooked. I suspect, however, that when Washington brings itself to think about the subject, there is general acceptance that property rights do indeed matter. There is also a general perception that property rights are highly insecure in Latin America (see, for example, Balassa et al. 1986, chapter 4).

Washington's Practice

Washington does not always practice what it preaches, as a moment's reflection on the most embarrassing subject mentioned above—corruption—will surely reveal. This paper was, after all, written during the weeks when a massive scandal at the US Department of Housing and Urban Development came to light—a case involving fraud and irresponsibility on a scale large enough to erode the credibility of Washington's preaching.

That would be true, at least, if Washington's advice were a moral admonition to purity. But that is not in fact the way it is generally perceived. Rather, the advice is intended to further the self-interest of the countries to whom it is directed (although not necessarily with a weighting of the interests of the constituent classes identical to that of the ruling elite in those countries). The fact that the United States also suffers from fraud and corruption does not make those practices any less detrimental in Latin countries, especially to those excluded from the elite. On the contrary, the greater pervasiveness of corruption in many Latin countries suggests that the damage it does is much greater.

Washington's record is likewise imperfect in other areas discussed above. On the first criterion, that of controlling the fiscal deficit, the US record of the 1980s is poor. It is true that the federal deficit has been falling since 1985, especially as a proportion of GNP, and that the operational deficit is now only some 1 percent of GNP, which is within the range consistent with continued solvency of the public sector. However, the fiscal deficit remains too large for macroeconomic balance, given the low private saving rate in the United States. The excessively high fiscal deficit results in the maintenance of high real interest rates and an unsustainably large current account deficit, with consequential burdens on debtors, discouragement of investment, nurturing of protectionist sentiment, and the continuing threat of a "hard landing."

The other areas where Washington's practice leaves much to be desired are exchange rate policy, where the ill effects of the dollar's vast overvaluation of the mid-1980s still linger even though the misalignment itself has been largely corrected, and trade policy, which has made discouraging lurches toward protection despite all the pledges to the contrary. In most of the microeconomic areas—notably tax reform, FDI (so far, at least), deregulation, and property rights—Washington's actions are consistent with its rhetoric.

Concluding Remarks

The economic policies that Washington urges on the rest of the world may be summarized as prudent macroeconomic policies, outward orientation, and free-market capitalism. It practices the last of these with more consistency than the first two, but that should not be taken to imply that they are less important. Most of technocratic Washington believes that the failure to practice what is preached hurts the United States as well as the rest of the world.

It is not at all clear that the policy reforms currently sought by Washington adequately address all of the critical current problems of Latin America. Consider, for example, the transitional problems of inflation stabilization. Fiscal discipline is certainly a precondition for mastering inflation. But some would argue that it needs to be supplemented by price and wage freezes and a fixed exchange rate (on the Mexican model), whereas others might well wish to add price liberalization to the list of policy initiatives that Washington should be urging on Latin America. There is no consensus view on this topic, even though some policy on price control (perhaps differing by country) may be critical to successful stabilization.

As a second example, Dornbusch (1989a) has recently raised the question of whether the Washington agenda described above can be relied on to restore growth once stabilization has been achieved. He points to the disappointing experiences of Bolivia and Mexico, where determined and effective stabilization has not yet resulted in a resumption of growth. If he is right in his contention that entrepreneurs may adopt a wait-and-see policy after stabilization rather than promptly committing themselves to the risks involved in new investment, the important question arises as to what must be added to Washington's policy advice in order to restore growth.

A third important issue concerns capital flight. Fiscal discipline, positive real interest rates, a competitive exchange rate, and more secure property rights are all important for reversing capital flight. But it is doubtful whether all those reforms together would lead to a prompt return of flight capital. Elimination of the current tax incentive to keep money abroad would surely help too (Lessard and Williamson 1987), but this is certainly not a policy on which Washington has yet reached a consensus, nor is it clear that adding it would be enough to do the trick.[4]

Even though the Washington consensus may not be sufficient to resolve all the major Latin problems, it is surely of interest to ask:

- Is the consensus shared in Latin America?

- Have the recommended policies been implemented in Latin America?

- What results have been achieved where the recommended policies have been implemented?

Those are the questions that the country studies are being asked to address. Answering them will at least help to clear the ground for examining what additional policies may be needed to limit the transitional costs of inflation stabilization, to restore growth, and to reverse capital flight.

One final reflection: A striking fact about the list of policies on which Washington does have a collective view is that they all stem from classical mainstream economic theory, at least if one is allowed to count Keynes as a classic by now. None of the ideas spawned by the development literature—such as the big push, balanced or unbalanced growth, surplus labor, or even the

---

4. Some might want to add the debt issue as a fourth topic on which it is not clear that the Washington agenda suffices to resolve the current problem, but this seems to me unfair. The Brady Plan is based on the premise that official help in achieving debt reduction should be given to those countries that have "put their houses in order," which implies that the latter alone is *not* expected to achieve a resolution of the debt problem.

two-gap model—plays any essential role in motivating the Washington consensus (although I would fortify my preference for varying the pace of import liberalization depending on the availability of foreign exchange by appeal to the two-gap model). This raises the question as to whether Washington is correct in its implicit dismissal of the development literature as a diversion from the harsh realities of the dismal science.[5] Or is the Washington consensus, or my interpretation of it, missing something?

---

5. Ironically, Washington seems to have reached this position just as Chicago theorists have rediscovered the old ideas of externalities that underlay the development literature: see Shleifer (1989) for a survey of the new literature on the theory of development.

Comment

Richard E. Feinberg

John Williamson has taken on a tough task, that of aggregating views across a wide spectrum of institutions and personalities. It is an effort to mate some unlikely bedfellows: from Jesse Helms to Jesse Jackson, from Michel Camdessus to John Sununu. He has done this without an apparent methodology, using only his well-informed impressions as a guide.

Williamson obtains his consensus by lopping off first the right and then the left wing of the Washington political spectrum. That leaves about half of the Brookings Institution and maybe one-third of the Institute for International Economics; it eliminates a good portion of the US Treasury, maybe half of the IMF staff (I leave it to the reader to decide whether to the right or the left), about one-third of the World Bank, and one-third of the US Congress. After all, a little less than half the Congress would eliminate the international financial institutions (IFIs) altogether if the matter came to a vote.

Has there in fact been movement toward a centrist consensus on an appropriate adjustment strategy for Latin America? In the region itself the old structuralists have sobered, as have their pale liberal reflections in Washington. There is less faith in the state and more respect for the market. Appreciation of the benefits of international trade is becoming more widespread. Andrés Bianchi noted at an October 1989 conference at the Inter-American Development Bank that exporting is now considered "progressive."

Meanwhile, as Edmar Bacha noted at the same conference, the Latin American right and to a degree their counterparts in Washington have learned a few things as well. They now acknowledge that Washington's initial call for adjustment was one-sided, aimed only at the debtors. The current formula, "reform plus debt reduction," implies a recognition that creditors and debtors alike have made mistakes and that both need to adjust. There is also a new awareness and concern on the right about continuing negative net resource transfers; this is a concept that the region's creditors at first rejected but that now may be found incorporated in the official reports of the IFIs. There is also a growing acknowledgment of the relationship between the external debt burden and the internal fiscal deficit and inflation, and there is a growing if perhaps

Richard E. Feinberg is Executive Vice President and Director of Studies at the Overseas Development Council. He served on the Policy Planning Staff of the US Department of State and as an international economist at the US Department of the Treasury and with the House Banking Committee. He has written widely on US foreign policy, Latin American politics, and international economics; his most recent edited volume is Pulling Together: The International Monetary Fund in a Multipolar World.

reluctant acceptance of heterodox elements in the adjustment package, including wage and price guidelines, where needed to speed adjustment of expectations to conform to new monetary policies.

This narrowing of the debate, in Latin America and in Washington, is good for democracy in the region and is good for US–Latin America relations. It heralds a future of less conflict and more constructive dialogue on the remaining areas of disagreement. Still, although there is convergence at a high level of abstraction, the more one delves into the details of policy, the more disagreements emerge. That is why I prefer to talk of "convergence," a term that allows for some remaining differences of view, rather than "consensus."

An example is the role of the state. We are agreed that there should be some trimming and streamlining. But do we want the final product to be a sleek, high-performance Jaguar or a minimalist Yugo? Washington contains at least two schools of thought on this issue. On one side are those who favor the restrictive Reaganite model: provide for national defense, set the appropriate macro conditions, and walk away. On the other side is the more activist school, which includes the proponents of industrial policy and strategic trade theory. This faction is strong in the Democratic Party, parts of the US executive branch (such as the Commerce Department), and parts of the World Bank. This issue is still the dividing line between Democrats and Republicans, and their disagreement reflects different beliefs in the capacity of the state to act efficiently and equitably. Interestingly, both schools interpret the experience of the Asian newly industrializing countries as supportive of their ideas.

Washington was not a participant in the monetarist-structuralist debates that Latin America witnessed in earlier decades. Washington did appropriate the language of structuralism but turned it on its head. Whereas in Latin America "structural flaws" meant market failures and "structural change" meant government action, in contemporary Washington it is government interventions that are the structural distortions, and liberalization and deregulation that are the corresponding necessary structural reforms. This transformation is an example of one of Washington's greatest strengths, namely, the clever co-optation of language.

With regard to fiscal policy, we see in the Washington consensus a reassertion of the old puritan ethic: yes, deficits and monetary emissions do matter. But there is less convergence on how to measure the fiscal deficit and on how much of a deficit is tolerable and under what conditions. Nor is there a consensus on whether to close fiscal deficits by tax increases or by expenditure reduction. Expenditure cutting is preferred, as Williamson notes, among right-wingers, but also at the IFIs (although their preference is in part tactical, since expenditure cuts often can be enacted more quickly than efficient, nondistorting new taxes can be raised). At home the United States clearly shows a revealed preference for low savings, high consumption (two VCRs in every home), and hence large fiscal deficits.

There remain major differences over whether fiscal policies should be wielded as an instrument of social justice. Should tax policy be used to improve the distribution of income, or are the efficiency effects more important? This disagreement underlies Washington's present debate over capital gains taxation. There are also important differences on the appropriate composition of tax revenues.

Similar controversy exists with regard to expenditure priorities. Everyone is in favor of more spending on education, just as both Michael Dukakis and George Bush wanted to be the education president. But should the funds go to support public or private schools? secondary schools or universities? Should schools be highly subsidized and open to all, or operated on a cost-recovery basis and therefore more selective in their admissions? Should liberal arts or engineering be promoted? And should the values fostered be indigenous or cosmopolitan?

Discord also persists on the external side. There is agreement that the debt overhang should be reduced, but not on how much it should be reduced. Is the debt a pernicious drag on stabilization and adjustment, or is it a catalyst for change, an external lever that the IFIs can manipulate to force reform? The US Treasury is happy to reduce the debt marginally but wants to retain enough of an overhang to keep the debtors on a short leash. The debate over the size of the discount in the debt-reduction package reflects these different views on the utility of the debt overhang.

The previously dominant development model saw external financing as a critical input for economic growth. The new view is that external financing matters less. In earlier decades, proponents of the two-gap model saw external finance as a critical input to growth. The newly emerging rhetoric demotes the importance of external finance. Cynics will note how convenient it is that with the emergence of a negative net transfer from the debtor nations it is suddenly discovered that they don't really need the money anyway. Incidentally, this downplaying of the value of external savings is dangerous for the IFIs, because it undercuts one of their *raisons d'être*.

There is a consensus that massive capital flight is bad for a country, but disagreements remain as to its causes and significance. One view, fairly common among those who work on the lending side of international finance, is that capital flight is a symptom of unpatriotic corruption among developing-country elites; the contrary view, that capital flight merely represents prudent portfolio diversification and the mature integration of global capital markets, is more common among bankers on the deposit side. A third view is that capital flight is principally the result of bad macroeconomic policies. Each view is partly correct; the first and third are dominant today, but the second may gain adherents as debt conversions proceed and banks' attitudes come to be dictated more by their deposit accounts than by their lending portfolios.

We all can agree in principle on the need for exchange rate competitiveness. However, Williamson is correct in noting that there is an absence of consensus on the nature of the short-term trade-off between exchange rate competitiveness and price stability, and hence on whether it is good policy to sacrifice international competitiveness for the sake of domestic price stability. In Mexico and Argentina the IFIs are backing the use of relatively fixed exchange rates as an anchor to orient expectations; the US Treasury, on the other hand, is more concerned about payments imbalances and debt-servicing capacity, and hence tends to be less tolerant of exchange rate misalignments.

Williamson also notes a difference of opinion on the speed and pacing of trade liberalization. The official rhetoric and policies often are pragmatic and accept gradualism, but the general-equilibrium buffs worry about the contradictions that result when an economy is, to paraphrase Lincoln, half administered and half free. Do piecemeal reforms mean progress or new problems down the road? Is movement on several fronts at once the answer? This question is being debated most openly now in Eastern Europe.

The Washington consensus does not encompass agreement on a theory of economic growth. Neoclassical economics is primarily an exercise in comparative statics; it lacks a robust theory of dynamic growth. The advocates of industrial policy have the elements of a growth strategy. They do not assume that markets and institutions are preexisting or that they kick in automatically once macroeconomic stabilization is achieved; rather, they recognize that markets and institutions must be created. There is no consensus on growth dynamics, although this will be more critical as the countries of Latin America move, we hope, from stabilization to recovery.

Finally, on the topics of poverty and the environment, there is no consensus in Washington either on the importance of the issue or on what should be done. There are those in the US Congress who would make the environment the central foreign policy issue; this position creates discomfort at the World Bank.

To conclude, the range of debate has narrowed. There is convergence on key concepts. We are all internationalists now; we are all capitalists; we all believe in fiscal responsibility and an efficient, streamlined state. Yet there are still important issues that divide us and where there is no convergence; and even on those issues where there is agreement at the highest level of abstraction, there remains plenty to argue about in the details. In Washington, economists need not worry quite yet about facing unemployment.

Comment

Stanley Fischer

As always, John Williamson has given us a good, sensible paper, even if, as always, he cannot resist the temptation to take a few potshots at US fiscal and exchange rate policy in the process. Actually the paper is confused about the meaning of "Washington." In some places it means all the official agencies and think tanks in Washington; in others it means the US government. At least, that is how I interpret Williamson's statement that "Washington does not always practice what it preaches" in fiscal policy, unless Williamson is attacking the food subsidies in the IMF cafeteria.

Basically Williamson has captured the growing Washington consensus on what the developing countries should do. This consensus extends beyond Washington to virtually all the universities and policy institutions in the United States, and to many in the rest of the world. It is not quite universal: the Economic Commission for Africa has criticized the World Bank and the IMF for their approaches to policy reform in Africa, arguing for more interventionist policies, and the Bank and the Fund are frequently taken to task by developing-country governments for pushing reform too fast and for not paying enough attention to poverty. But the key fact is that there are no longer two major competing economic development paradigms: participants in the development debate now speak the same language. Fortunately no one need fear that the debate will end soon, because many questions remain even for those who accept the basic market-oriented approach to development.

I will leave aside most of my small disagreements with Williamson, except for the following:

- His list of policy instruments omits consideration of the environment, which is becoming an increasingly important part of the Washington policy agenda for the developing countries, and one that could become quite divisive, given that most environmental damage that has taken place to date is the result of growth in the industrialized economies.

- Similar disagreements are likely to arise over military spending. Both these areas are marked by important international externalities: in the case of the environment, the problem is that policies in one nation affect the global environment; in the case of military spending, it is that the level of spending

---

Stanley Fischer is Vice President, Development Economics, and Chief Economist at the World Bank and Professor of Economics at the Massachusetts Institute of Technology. He is the coauthor of Indexation, Inflation and Economic Policy: Macroeconomics, *among other works.*

needed for defense depends on the spending of others. In both areas the implication is that international action could help improve welfare.

■ If future social security obligations are to be counted on the outlay side of the budget, as Williamson would have it, then future social security tax receipts should be counted on the revenue side.

■ The general view that budget deficits are acceptable if they finance infrastructure is only partly right. Here's the arithmetic. Suppose the government captures 25 percent of any additional income in taxes. Suppose then that infrastructure improvements yield a real return of 16 percent. Then the government gets back only 4 percent as the yield on its infrastructure investment. Unless it is borrowing at less than a 4 percent real interest rate, this investment will be inflationary—although of course it will be less inflationary than government consumption spending.

■ Washington's emphasis on financial sector reform goes well beyond a concern with real interest rates, to the notion that the banking system and the financial sector in many developing countries need fundamental restructuring.

■ I am less sure than Williamson that Washington regards the freeing up of capital flows as less urgent than the freeing up of goods flows. I fear rather that much of Washington does believe strongly that financial capital flows should not be constrained, but that it simply has not yet focused on the problem.

■ Finally, Williamson places less emphasis on the need to bring back flight capital than does the rest of Washington—parts of Washington are even encouraging debtor countries to find special incentives for that purpose, despite Washington's general preference for a level playing field.

The Consensus in Brief

There are many ways of describing the policy consensus that has emerged. Williamson's 10 points are one way. Another is to subsume the main needs under four broad headings, which apply generally and not only to Latin America.

The first is a sound macroeconomic framework. Fiscal policy gets the main emphasis, as it should. But the exchange rate is a close second in importance: a competitive exchange rate is crucial to export development and industrial growth, and the tendency to overvalue real exchange rates in the battle against inflation is the most important persistent error made by countries in trouble. There is growing and justified support of independent central banks.

The second is an efficient and smaller government. This usually means tax reform; public expenditure reviews along the lines Williamson indicates, with due attention to the need to provide and maintain physical infrastructure; reform of public enterprises; and—extremely important—the creation of what the World Bank refers to as the "enabling environment": the basic system of laws and institutions that facilitate and control economic activity, particularly in the private sector. Institutional development will become an increasingly important component of development strategies in the 1990s.

Third is an efficient and expanding private sector. This typically requires increasing competition within the country as well as introducing it from outside. Here is where outward orientation matters, both in the promotion of exports and in the liberalization of imports. Import liberalization usually first takes the form of the removal of quantitative restrictions, and later the slow reduction of tariffs. (Incidentally, Williamson's characterization of World Bank conditionality on trade reform as imposing a rigid timetable for tariff reduction is not accurate; there is a timetable for up to two years, with future changes to be discussed subsequently.) Over the coming years there will be an increasing emphasis on the need to coordinate external and internal liberalization, to make sure that the potentially beneficial effects of trade liberalization are not wasted and that domestic supply responds to changed price signals. As discussed below, private-sector investment has to revive for growth to return.

The fourth element is poverty-reduction policies. Emphasis on poverty reduction has increased in recent years and will continue to do so. The concern with poverty reduction goes beyond the belief that economic growth will reduce poverty, to the view that specific policies, such as targeted food subsidies as well as the medical and educational programs to which Williamson refers, can reduce the number of poor people in a given country and should be used for that purpose.

The Key Issue: Proactive Policies

The Washington consensus does not go far enough, but not for all the reasons that Williamson gives. For instance, the issues in the debate over heterodox versus orthodox stabilization programs are no longer much in dispute. We have the right answers on this question.

The big question is growth and what the government can do about it. The Washington program tells the government to do less of most things except export promotion, poverty alleviation, and the creation of an enabling environment. One of the most difficult intellectual challenges the Washington consensus faces is how to encourage private-sector development—how to create an enabling environment that is conducive to the development of an efficient private sector. The issue goes well beyond property rights to the creation of legal, accounting, and regulatory systems and the need for efficient government administration.

Growth will not return to stagnating countries until investment increases. Certainly getting the macro environment right is a necessary prerequisite. Beyond that, there are two possible approaches. One, the Chilean or Thatcher approach, requires the government to set the right policies and incentives, to behave consistently and credibly, and then to step out of the way in the expectation that, eventually, growth will return. This approach seems to work, eventually, at least in those countries that have the institutional capacity to support it.

The alternative, East Asian approach is one in which the government takes a more active and ongoing role, in some interpretations operating an industrial policy. The East Asian experience proves that small government, consistent policies, an undervalued currency, export promotion and explicitly time-limited import protection through tariffs, and an educated and disciplined labor force, combined with entrepreneurial skills, create economic growth.

Does an active industrial policy contribute to growth? The record establishes that industrial policy on balance helped in parts of East Asia, despite the well-known major failures, such as the attempt to promote the chemicals industry in Korea. Nonetheless, we should not advise most developing countries to attempt to run an industrial policy that picks the winners, as opposed to setting a generally favorable economic environment for industry and for investment. The reason is that many governments do not have the ability to run a pick-the-winners industrial policy, nor do the international agencies that advise them. Although development policies should embody a set of general principles involving market orientation and integration into the world economy, they must also be tailored to the histories and structures of individual countries.

Comment

Allan H. Meltzer

John Williamson's paper is a commendable effort to summarize the policy consensus in Washington on the reforms required to bring Latin America toward stable, noninflationary growth. Any effort of this kind runs the risk that some of the participants will decide to disagree upon seeing that they have been included in a consensus.

Williamson lists 10 principles or policy rules on which he finds that some consensus has been reached. The list is remarkable as much for what it omits as for what it includes. A decade or more ago, I believe, there would have been much more about policy activism, discretionary judgment on a case-by-case basis, trade-offs between inflation and unemployment, and development planning. Still earlier, a vociferous group would have favored import substitution. I am not a Washington insider, so I do not know whether Williamson has captured the consensus. If he has, the Washington policy community has come a long way toward rules, private property, reliance on the market system, avoidance of deficits and inflation, and an open economy operating in a competitive world marketplace.

Before commenting on some of the paper's specific proposals and suggesting alternatives, I digress to comment on some of the rhetoric and to mention an omission. I would prefer fewer references in the paper to unnamed right-wing deviationists. The audience would be better served if the paper had stayed on the issues. Also, I was surprised to see no references to the left-wing deviationists and the more rabid environmentalists. Are these groups inconsequential, with no effect on the consensus? Do they offer no relevant alternatives? I find that difficult to believe, particularly about the environmental activists.

Williamson hints at a preference for a cyclically balanced budget, but he thinks the consensus favors an annually balanced budget or at most small deficits. I would have preferred to combine the first two items on his list, budgetary discipline and public spending priorities, so as to emphasize the use of resources and the method of financing. Budget deficits are neither wrong nor harmful if they finance spending that increases efficiency, have a real return in excess of the resource cost, and are not financed by inflation. A rule that keeps

Allan H. Meltzer is University Professor and John M. Olin Professor of Political Economy and Public Policy at Carnegie-Mellon University. He has been a visiting professor at Harvard University, the University of Chicago, the Getúlio Vargas Foundation, and other institutions. He has served as a consultant to the Council of Economic Advisers, the US Department of the Treasury, and the Federal Reserve and is the author of numerous books and articles on monetary economics.

the debt–GNP ratio fixed or balances the budget annually or cyclically pays no attention to resource use.

Of course, the government may use resources badly, turning productive opportunities into wasteful projects, or increasing corruption. In that case it is not deficit reduction but privatization that is required to improve efficiency. Here I join the Washington consensus, but would restate and combine rules for budget policy and spending to emphasize efficiency. My rule would be: Allow the government to spend only where spending does not reduce the efficiency of resource use, and finance the spending in a noninflationary way.

Missing from the consensus is any explicit statement about price controls and other interventions that distort relative prices. Deregulation is mentioned, but that may be too broad a term to cover these distortions. The efficiency rule serves in this context as well.

The Washington consensus, Williamson says, would like real interest rates to be positive and moderate. The word "moderate" is vague and raises the issue of how policy can change real interest rates. One way is to reduce risk and uncertainty in the economy toward the minimum inherent in nature. Credible rules, stable medium-term policies, secure property rights, a commercial code, a legal framework, and a standardized accounting system all lower risks and reduce the risk premiums in real interest rates. I would therefore state the rule in terms of actions to reduce risk and eliminate avoidable uncertainty.

This brings me to the exchange rate. I understand the case for fixed exchange rates and the case for flexible exchange rates and domestic price stability. I do not understand the rationale for the in-between cases that are so prevalent. My solution for Latin America would be to replace the central banks with currency boards. The boards would not be permitted to monetize debt or change the exchange rate. The exchange rate would be fixed. The currency board would issue money in exchange for convertible currencies and would be required to keep the shares of those currencies in its portfolio equal to the trade weights of the country's exports and imports.

Central banks have provided no net benefit to the Latin American countries. Inflation, much of the region's capital flight, and high risk premiums in interest rates are evidence of the cost. Currency boards have worked well in Hong Kong and Singapore and have contributed far more to the welfare of the citizens of those countries than the central banks of Latin America have to theirs.

My proposals, if adopted, would promptly lower real rates by reducing risk premiums; the result would be lower internal debt-service costs and reduced budget expenditure. Further, abolishing the central bank would enhance credibility and encourage the return of flight capital. However, inflation is not the only way to tax assets: fear of confiscatory taxation and outright confiscation would remain as reasons for capital flight.

I do not believe that my proposal is part of the Washington consensus or that it will be soon. I offer it to suggest that the consensus has not thought very deeply about ways of institutionalizing reform to increase credibility. Institutional reform does not guarantee that the public will believe the policymaker, but it works to reduce the lag between policy announcements and beneficial results.

I agree with most of the points Williamson makes about commercial policy. I would further propose that those countries that have not already done so join the General Agreement on Tariffs and Trade. Also, since 1982 I have advocated debt-equity swaps if accompanied by privatization, so I am glad to see the consensus has formed on this issue. And no one will be surprised to learn that I favor secure property rights where these promote efficiency, as they usually do. I would add, as mentioned above, the desirability of a sound legal framework, a commercial code, and removal of exchange controls.

To sum up, my list would be shorter than Williamson's and would differ in a few places. I would:

- Promote efficient use of resources and avoid distortions

- Reduce risk to a minimum and avoid policies that redistribute risks

- Abolish the central bank, establish a currency board or monetary authority, and fix the exchange rate

- Establish or strengthen property rights, a commercial code, and a legal framework. With the possible exception of the currency board, this would be a good list for any country, whether it be the Soviet Union, Poland, Argentina, or, yes, even the United States.

Where I suspect Williamson and I disagree most is on implementation. He talks about finding the fundamental equilibrium exchange rate, using counter-cyclical fiscal policy, and maintaining moderate interest rates, presumably by judgment or possibly by policy mix. I prefer to set rules or medium-term objectives to lower risk and reduce uncertainty.

Yet prior to the problem of implementation is the serious problem of getting the Washington consensus adopted. Public choice theory suggests that governments do not typically act out of goodwill. We have to take the next step and ask what incentives are required to get policymakers to adopt and implement the consensus. Years of experience with conditional lending suggest that this is not an easy problem or one that we know how to solve. Does Williamson agree that there should be no additional assistance forthcoming unless countries implement rules like those called for by the consensus? How do we monitor compliance?

Recent research considers these questions as part of the problem of establishing credibility. Credibility is a stock that, once built up, speeds the adjustment to policy changes. In most of Latin America the credibility stock has been depleted. Some concern for rebuilding credibility is a necessary part of implementation of reforms.

One purpose in describing the consensus is to put restrictions or conditions on aid. This raises some questions. Is there evidence that foreign aid helps its recipients? If so, what kind of aid? Do the benefits to the recipients outweigh the costs to the donors? Or is aid simply a type of charity?

A common answer is that aid encourages adjustments that local governments would not undertake on their own. If this is so, we must face the problem of implementation, of enforcing the rules. Otherwise, the resources provided are likely to permit countries to maintain the policies that the consensus wants to eliminate.

Finally, it might be useful to recall that the consensus in 1983 favored additional lending after the initial crisis had been overcome. Let me suggest that we would now be nearer a solution if the debtors and creditors instead had been encouraged to change policies in 1983. The Washington consensus did not help then. Would it help now? Or would all parties gain if Washington stood aside and let the debtors and creditors work out the solution?

Comment

Patricio Meller

This excellent paper is a good starting point for a fruitful discussion of the policy issues being debated in Washington and Latin America. These comments are intended to provide a Latin American perspective on these issues.

At the most general level, there is agreement on the appropriateness of consistent, responsible fiscal and monetary policies leading to low inflation, and an outward-oriented economy with exports as the engine of growth; the objectives of eradication of poverty and reduction of income inequality are considered equally important. Achieving these three objectives simultaneously is not an easy enterprise, and this is what leads to internal and external disequilibria. It is easy to suggest responsible policies; if instead the outcome is

Patricio Meller is a research economist at the Corporación de Investigaciones Económicas para Latinoamérica (CIEPLAN). He is the author of several articles on the Chilean economy and is the Director of the Editorial Committee of Colección Estudios CIEPLAN.

uncontrollable disequilibrium, it is usually not because Latin economists "like" irresponsible policies.

Fiscal Policies

The distinction between the size of the central government and that of the public sector is an important one. The Washington view often fails to consider the differences in size and composition between the US public sector and that in the typical Latin American country. Most Latin countries do not have a social safety net; the welfare state does not exist. Therefore, it is not inconsistent to promote a reduction of the size of the US government while at the same time favoring an increase in the social safety net in Latin America. The state-owned enterprises (SOEs) are a completely different matter, discussed below.

There is concern in Latin America about the size of fiscal deficits. Again using the US government as the model, most of the Washington recommendations stress the reduction of government expenditures in Latin America. However, two types of expenditure cannot be touched: expenditures on arms and external debt service. This leads to a crowding out and contraction of social expenditures and a reduction of the government wage bill.

Most Latin economists feel that it is important to get advice from Washington in implementing tax reforms that will lead to an efficient and equitable tax structure. Here again, the Washington view mechanically transposes the US model onto Latin America: if it is correct to press for lower taxes in the United States, one should do the same in Latin America. However, the level of taxation in Latin America is already relatively low: there is widespread evasion, the tax structure is very inequitable, there are many loopholes in the tax code, and some economic sectors and high-income groups do not pay any taxes.

Williamson's suggestion to tax Latin American assets held abroad is a very interesting one, but if individual Latin countries attempted such a tax, the response would likely be unfavorable. If, however, the IMF or the World Bank openly promoted such a measure, the results would be different, and it could help to improve the image of those two institutions in the region. But other practical questions remain. Would US banks cooperate in collecting the tax? What could be done about tax havens?

External Sector Policies

Even though there is a consensus in Latin America on promoting an outward-oriented strategy, import liberalization is not considered a prerequisite for export expansion. Moreover, where a highly protective tariff structure still exists, gradual tariff reduction is recommended. An abrupt dismantling of the tariff structure could produce serious imbalances in the trade account; imports could increase very rapidly while exports remain very slow to expand. Therefore, if a country needs to maintain a certain trade surplus, the rate of growth of exports should set the upper bound that should constrain the pace of import liberalization.

The first stage of trade reform should be a simplification of the complex structures prevailing in most Latin American countries; everyone is in favor of reducing endless bureaucratic procedures. Maintenance of a competitive exchange rate is a necessary condition for export expansion. Other, complementary measures are important in countries that have to increase their exports from a very small base: for example, a government agency to provide technology and market information, special credit lines, and tax rebates for small exporters.

The level of the real exchange rate should be determined by the needed current account balance. This implies that the presence of large debt-service obligations requires a real exchange rate as much as 20 percent higher than would otherwise be the case, to generate the necessary real transfer; a more competitive real exchange rate implies lower real wages—this in a region where consumption per capita is 10 percent lower on average in 1990 than in 1980.

Foreign Investment

There has been a clear change of attitude with respect to foreign investment in Latin America from that which prevailed in the 1960s and 1970s. In general, foreign investment is welcome where it fills a void—for example, when it brings in new technology, new machinery, or new know-how, or opens new export markets. The Latin countries now compete in providing incentives to foreign investment; moreover, there is a significant trend toward nondiscrimination between foreign and domestic investors. There are very few areas in which foreign investment is restricted. A special case in this respect is that of foreign investment in previously nationalized companies. Also, the above generalizations apply only to foreign investment as it is traditionally understood, that is, expansion of existing productive capacity; investment through debt-equity swaps obviously does not fit in that category.

Deregulation and Privatization

There is agreement on the need to eliminate red tape. However, the Southern Cone has had a bad experience with unregulated financial markets. Moreover, there is very little experience in Latin America in privatizing SOEs that are natural monopolies. There should be public discussion of which SOEs should be privatized and why. It is important that divestiture procedures be open and transparent, so that there are no giveaways to the already privileged. Also, some regulatory procedures should be established with respect to divested SOEs to ensure that they are not operated recklessly. One reason for privatization is often to prevent loss-making SOEs from being bailed out by the central government, but in Latin America even bankrupt private firms are often able to transfer their losses to the public sector.

On the broader issue of public- versus private-sector behavior, in most Latin American countries the private sector adopts a very cautious, "wait and see" attitude, switching very easily from productive to speculative to fugitive (capital flight) behavior. A key issue is how to inculcate a long-run mindset in this sector. Political stability is a key factor, yet in weak societies like those in many Latin countries, established groups can come to monopolize political and economic power; in such cases the government has to act as a countervailing force.

Omissions

There are certain things not included in the Washington consensus. One is the magnitude of the required adjustment. It took the United States seven years to reduce its fiscal deficit from 6 percent of GNP to below 4 percent. IMF stand-bys, meanwhile, can require lowering a 6 percent fiscal deficit to 3 percent in only one year. Is it logical to ask others to do what one is unwilling to do oneself? A second omission of the Washington consensus is how to achieve the income distribution it professes to desire. Here the concerns of Latin Americans are twofold. First, during an adjustment program, how does one put a floor under the poor, who are already living close to the subsistence level? Second, how does one structure the adjustment program so that sacrifices are shared equally across income groups? All too often it is the labor market that serves as the residual through which almost all the adjustment is achieved. It would be good to see inclusion of these issues in the next formulation of the Washington policy consensus.

Discussion

In his capacity as chairman, C. Fred Bergsten urged that the discussion focus on the problem of adjustment and policy reform in debtor countries rather than on that of debt. The first speaker, Arnold Harberger, proceeded to violate this injunction in the guise of supporting it. He argued that there is no inherent reason why there should be a positive resource transfer to developing countries. For any country there is an equilibrium debt–GDP ratio. The question is, therefore, in which direction does maintenance of that ratio imply that resources will flow? If the real interest rate exceeds the rate of economic growth, the resource transfer will be negative, and vice versa. Since the international real interest rate is currently around 4 percent to 5 percent per year and seems unlikely to fall, and since developing countries in general are unlikely to grow that fast, one should expect negative resource transfers to persist (and this would remain true even if the debt were halved). However, provided the investment financed by the debt yields a return higher than the rate of interest, servicing the debt involves no burden. Policy should concentrate on ensuring that debt is contracted only to undertake productive investment.

Colin Bradford agreed that there had been a substantial convergence in economic thinking during the 1980s, along the lines that John Williamson had described as the "Washington consensus." But, he argued, this convergence carries with it the danger of solidifying into ideology,[6] which may generate a reaction involving rejection of the whole package rather than a constructive search to manage problems in distinctive ways. It is important to emphasize the range of choice that is still possible within the degree of professional convergence that currently exists: what is the point of democracy if those who achieve power by democratic means are left with nothing to decide?

Bradford went on to mention an article by Hirschman (1965) about the frequent disjunction between intellectual ideas and policy practice, citing the way in which the Latin American governments and the Alliance for Progress had finally got around in the 1960s to gearing up to exploit increased capital inflows when those capital flows were cut off by Washington's preoccupation with the Vietnam War. Bradford speculated as to whether the current convergence on outward orientation, macroeconomic stability, and markets might suffer a similar fate, as internal pressures overwhelm external issues. The real challenges to policymakers in the 1990s may involve social issues like income distribution, poverty, and unemployment rather than harmonizing relations

---

6. My own definition of an ideologue, as someone who knows the answer before he has heard the context of the problem, seems to fit perfectly with the speaker's concerns—Editor.

with the external world. Could such pressures even push the present consensus in a more inward direction again?

Jessica Einhorn remarked that John Williamson's paper was straight economics, whereas the morning's discussion had emphasized the centrality of the politics of economic adjustment. Stanley Fischer had noted in his comment that the enabling environment differed among countries. Indeed, the political capacity to implement economic reform is a key element of successful adjustment. We need to factor in the role of the state in the promotion of growth. On another point, military spending, which for years had been politely ignored as a sovereignty issue beyond the competence of international technocrats, is coming under scrutiny. Perhaps the easing in East-West tensions, along with the shortage of capital in the wake of the debt crisis, is leading to a climate where this spending can be looked at in the context of resource allocation and what can be afforded.

Einhorn also touched on two aspects of the question of whether there is likely to be convergence on the environmental issue. Fischer had suggested that raising environmental concerns could backfire on the industrial countries, but Einhorn observed that if the environment turned out to be an important vehicle for regime building and resource transfer, everyone might benefit. Also, as a development issue in Latin America, environmental deterioration is primarily of concern in relation to the poorest of the poor. But at the global level the issue of sustainable development (with sensitivity to environmental concerns) could be considered like trade theory, with explicit recognition of interdependence.

In replying to the debate, Richard Feinberg made two points. The first concerned resource transfer. He agreed that there was no practical possibility of restoring a positive transfer in the foreseeable future. Rhetorical calls for a positive transfer should be interpreted as demands for a reduction in the size of the negative transfer. His second point concerned the politics of adjustment. Drawing on Nelson (1989), he emphasized that what is equitable is not necessarily the same as what is politically sustainable. The World Bank's emphasis on targeting directed to maintaining the income of the poorest may be an answer to equity concerns, but "IMF riots" typically originate among the lower middle class, not the truly poor. Dealing with the political problems of adjustment involves compensation to the classes most prone to riot, and the Bank is mistaken to argue that targeting help to the poorest is likely to help resolve the political problems of adjustment.

John Williamson accepted that "convergence" (which the discussion suggested was a reality) might have been a better description of the state of the policy debate than "consensus." His use of that word had precluded him from including some issues that he personally thought important, but which did not seem to command a consensus. He agreed that the lack of total consensus was not undesirable, because of the danger that a consensus could become frozen into an ideology that would be discredited *en bloc* as soon as one element proved inadequate to the situation. He conceded to Stanley Fischer that his discussion of interest rate policy would have been better phrased in terms of financial liberalization. With regard to Allan Meltzer's contention that central banks should be replaced by currency boards, he agreed that with the benefit of hindsight one would not recommend the establishment of central banks where they did not already exist. But he argued that the important issue was that of establishing a rational exchange rate policy, which was perfectly possible without abolishing central banks.

On the question of equity, Williamson stated that he wished he had been able to include a relevant, agreed policy variable in the Washington consensus. But he did not believe that there was an agreed way of dealing with equity issues, which had indeed been shamelessly neglected in the 1980s (and not just in Latin America). He argued that, when concern again began to focus on poverty, it was crucial that the convergence that has been achieved on issues of efficiency be maintained. A failure to heed the lessons learned through bitter experience in the 1980s would threaten to undermine any renewed assault on poverty.

3

Three Policy Experiments

Three Policy Experiments

Bolivia

Juan L. Cariaga

In May 1989, almost four years after the Bolivian government had embarked on an orthodox adjustment program as the only viable solution to the country's critical economic situation, Bolivians went to the polls to pass judgment on the new plan. In a climate of peace and calm remarkable in a country historically known for political and social violence, 65.4 percent of the electorate favored those parties pledged to continue the economic stabilization measures put in place by the previous administration. The voters sent a clear message to politicians throughout Latin America who for years had been advocating populist measures and rejecting economic adjustment as impracticable.

Although introduced on an emergency basis, the Bolivian adjustment program led, however inadvertently, to implementation of what might be called, following John Williamson (chapter 2), the Washington consensus—a blueprint of economic reforms considered by senior officials of international organizations, financial institutions, and major research centers, as well as the US government, to be appropriate for achieving the objectives of growth, low inflation, a viable balance of payments, and an equitable distribution of income. By adopting the Washington approach, Bolivia became a candidate for assistance under the Baker Plan. The new program opened the way to external financing from the international lending organizations, although not, as it turned out, from foreign commercial banks as the Baker Plan had originally envisioned.

This paper summarizes the actions taken by the Bolivian government along the lines of the Washington consensus (for more detailed treatment see Sachs 1986, Morales 1988, and Cariaga 1988, 1989a, and 1989b) and assesses the

Juan L. Cariaga is the Executive Director of the Inter-American Development Bank for Bolivia, Paraguay, and Uruguay. He was formerly the Finance Minister of Bolivia and a professor at two of Bolivia's major universities. He has written five books and numerous articles on economics in Bolivia and in the United States. The views presented are those of the author and do not necessarily reflect the views of the Inter-American Development Bank.

results of those actions to date. By 1986, the measures had achieved their objective of a net flow of funds to the country, and it was under these circumstances that a consensus in political terms was reached at home and later confirmed in the May 1989 elections.

The Washington Consensus and Bolivian Adjustment Measures

With the reluctance of one who has no alternative—*sin querer queriendo* (wanting yet not wanting to), as the popular Mexican refrain goes—the Bolivian government in August 1985 launched an orthodox adjustment program in response to the serious problem of hyperinflation, which reached an annualized rate of 24,000 percent in September of that year. The program consisted of a series of eclectic emergency measures that stressed a high degree of common sense in the management of the country's public finances, an area in which common sense has traditionally been in short supply. These measures were taken with a view not so much to obtain resources under the Baker Plan as to encourage self-sacrifice on the part of the Bolivian people, so that the country could extricate itself from the impasse through its own efforts. At the time the measures were implemented, Bolivia had lost credibility abroad to such an extent that the decision to carry out a drastic adjustment program was not taken seriously by some of the international financial organizations.[1] It was the credibility earned at home through the implementation of the adjustment measures (described in Cariaga 1989b) that induced the repatriation of capital needed to ensure the success of the stabilization program until credibility could be restored with the international organizations.

---

1. This was the perception of the group in charge of drafting the stabilization measures (G. Sánchez de Lozada, F. Romero, F. Prado, G. Bedregal, R. Gisbert, and the author), after meeting with missions from the International Monetary Fund and the US Agency for International Development in mid-August 1985. After the decree implementing the adjustment program was approved, the group (or at least some of its members) discussed the adjustment measures with other international financial institutions. At that time, both the Inter-American Development Bank and the Andean Development Corporation provided only limited financing to Bolivia but showed great interest in the outcome of the measures. The World Bank announced its full support, although a whole year elapsed before its first loan was disbursed. This is very important, since it is usually assumed that the reaction of the international financial institutions—so essential for the continuity of the program—would be *ipso facto* a supportive one. This was not so in the case of Bolivia, although the response is to a certain extent understandable given that the country had lacked credibility for so many years.

Fiscal Deficits and Fiscal Discipline

At the time the adjustment package was put into effect, it had become clear to the Bolivian government that hyperinflation was not a structural problem, as a number of old-school economists claimed. Rather it could be traced to massive deficits incurred by the central government and public-sector agencies, financed by the central bank through the printing of money (Cariaga 1985, 16). The new financial authorities grasped that the only way to bring this vicious circle to an end was to declare zero tolerance of the deficits of both the central government and the state-owned enterprises. To put this into practice, the Bolivian government adopted three major initiatives:

■ On the revenue side, the budgets of the central government and the state-owned enterprises were balanced basically through the imposition of an indirect tax on fuel, together with a devaluation of the currency to a realistic level and an increase in the rates charged by the state-owned enterprises to the level of their international counterparts. In the wake of these measures a tax reform was implemented. This measure replaced a complex system of taxes directed primarily at income, which brought in little or no revenue, with a simpler system of taxes levied on consumption and property.

■ On the expenditure side, all subsidies were eliminated, including those on food and foodstuffs, as well as those in the guise of low rates and fares charged by the state-owned companies. All illegal bonuses paid in cash and in kind to their employees were eliminated. At the same time the salaries of all public-sector employees were frozen.

■ In addition, the government pursued a policy of tight fiscal discipline under which spending was not to exceed revenue, thus compelling institutions to operate on the basis of a zero-based budget system.

Under the adjustment program, debt-service payments would be made to multilateral and bilateral organizations only; interest payments on obligations to foreign commercial banks were suspended. This was done in anticipation of more favorable negotiations with the international commercial banks, based on the repurchase of the bank debt on the secondary market. By this time, the foreign commercial banks had already suspended lending to Bolivia, including lines of credit for trade financing and direct loans for trade transactions. There was little likelihood that these operations would resume, and commercial bank credits to Bolivia were not expected to be reactivated in the near future.

Table 3.1 shows the dramatic effect these actions had on the financial condition of the central government and the state-owned enterprises in 1986.

Table 3.1 Bolivia: income and expenditures of the nonfinancial public sector, 1981–87 (percentages of GDP)

	1981	1982	1983	1984	1985	1986	1987
Current income	34.7	31.7	23.4	22.0	27.6	31.2	27.0
Tax revenues	9.1	4.7	3.3	2.3	3.1	6.6	8.7
Sales of goods and services							
Domestic	11.2	8.5	6.5	4.1	10.6	12.9	10.3
International	12.3	16.3	12.3	14.6	11.7	10.6	6.7
Other	2.1	2.2	1.3	1.0	2.2	1.1	1.3
Current expenditures	35.4	32.6	30.8	34.4	31.5	29.6	28.9
Salaries	11.3	9.2	8.4	14.8	10.3	7.8	8.7
Purchases of goods and services	15.0	14.6	13.1	11.4	11.0	10.6	9.0
Interest owed	2.8	3.7	4.2	3.6	7.3	6.5	4.7
Other	6.3	5.2	5.1	4.6	2.8	4.6	6.6
Current surplus	−0.8	−0.9	−7.5	−12.4	−3.9	−1.6	2.0
Capital income	0.6	0.1	0.2	0.2	0.2	1.3	0.2
Capital expenditures	6.1	5.9	4.4	4.8	4.5	6.0	7.4
Unidentified expenditures	1.3	7.5	6.7	9.7	2.5	0.0	0.0
Overall balance	−7.5	−14.2	18.4	−26.7	−10.7	−3.2	−9.1
Financed internally	3.6	13.5	19.7	23.9	8.5	−2.1	5.0

Source: Unidad de Estudios de Política Económica and data from the World Bank.

The overall fiscal deficit dropped from 26.7 percent of GDP in 1984 to 10.7 percent in 1985 and to only 3.2 percent in 1986. Regrettably, this "miraculous" turnaround in the condition of public finances was cut short in 1987 and 1988 by two major external shocks. First, the already weak tin and nonferrous ore prices collapsed on international markets at the end of 1985, causing mining operations in Bolivia to be shut down.[2] As a result, over $60 million in social benefits was paid out in 1987 to the laid-off miners. Maintaining operation of the mines would have been incompatible with continuance of the stabilization program. Comibol, the state-owned mining company, incurred losses exceeding $258 million in 1985 alone (Nogales 1989, 116). With international prices after

2. The price of tin collapsed on international markets at the end of 1985. Bolivian mining operations continued during 1986, although at a much reduced pace. After 21,000 mine workers were laid off in late December 1986 and early 1987, most of the operations were shut down.

1985 about one-half what they were before the collapse, the situation would have been much worse.

Second, depressed oil prices and the failure of Argentina to keep current on its payments for gas imported from Bolivia led to further unavoidable expenditure by the Bolivian government. Sales of natural gas to Argentina represent about 40 percent of Bolivia's total export revenues and one-half of the annual income of the state oil company. The company's earmarked contributions also represent approximately one-third of the Bolivian treasury's revenue as well as the most important share of the revenues of two major regional governments. Under Bolivian law these contributions are paid in the form of royalties on wellhead gas production. As a result of Argentina's failure to keep current on its payments, the Bolivian government was forced to transfer resources both to the oil company in the form of working capital and to the regional governments in the form of subsidies for the royalties not received.

It is estimated that the combined losses from these external shocks exceeded $150 million in 1987, which explains why the deficit widened in that year. Fortunately, credibility at home, which had been boosted by the stabilization measures, led to the repatriation of more than $260 million in flight capital (Nogales 1989, 32), which the government used to offset the effects of the external shocks. Without the repatriation of this capital, any attempt at stabilization would have been abortive. In 1988, payment arrears on gas sales continued to have a negative effect on public finances, although their overall impact was less than in 1987, since mining operations had virtually ceased by then. Nonetheless, inflation was kept to a relatively low rate through continued efforts at economic stabilization within the initial scope of the 1985 program. Table 3.2 shows the dramatic decrease in inflation from 1985 to 1987 (calculated from the La Paz price index, the only retail price index available in Bolivia).

Tax Reform

Complementing the fiscal and exchange rate measures taken initially in 1985 was a tax reform bill introduced in the Bolivian congress for the purpose of permanently strengthening the central government's revenue base. This reform dismantled an outmoded system of over 450 taxes directed primarily at income, which accounted for revenues of approximately 2 percent of GDP in 1984, and replaced it with a regime based on nine new taxes levied on consumption and wealth. This measure increased tax revenue to approximately 9 percent of GDP by 1987 (table 3.1). The new system was more realistic in the sense that in a highly informal economy such as Bolivia's, as in other economies in the developing world, it is pointless to tax profits and income when there are no clear guidelines for determining them. In conjunction with this reform, the indirect tax on gas,

Table 3.2 La Paz: rate of inflation, 1983–88 (percentages)

Year	Inflation rate[a]
1983	328.5
1984	2,177.2
1985	8,170.5
1986	65.9
1987	10.6
1988	21.5

a. Annual change in the La Paz price index.

Source: For 1983–87, Banco Central de Bolivia, *Boletín Estadístico* 260, 99 (March 1988). For 1988, Departamento de Estadísticas Económicas, Instituto Nacional de Estadísticas.

originally introduced as an emergency measure, was naturally retained because the government was no longer receiving its royalty payments (from taxes on ore production) because of the slump in tin and nonferrous ore prices.

The new tax system was based mainly on a value-added tax, which, like the indirect tax on gasoline, has the advantage of being capable of transferring resources very rapidly to the central government as transactions occur. This helped to streamline tax collection by avoiding the troublesome process of collecting taxes once or twice a year. Hence, with every purchase of gasoline, resources were actually being transferred directly to the central government without the full awareness of the purchaser.

Reductions in Spending

Of course, fiscal deficit reduction can be achieved not only through the instruments of tax policy described above, but also by means of spending cuts. The August 1985 measures eliminated all government subsidies—not only those on bread and other foodstuffs, but also the subsidized rates and fares charged by public services and utilities. In 1984, gasoline cost as little as one cent a liter, and air and railway fares were as little as one-tenth of what they would have been in an internationally competitive market. Similar subsidies on electricity rates and international telephone calls were also removed. Following the August 1985 measures, leaded gasoline rose in price to 30 cents a liter, and the rates and fares of the state-owned companies were brought in line with international price levels through a more realistic exchange rate set by the Bolivian central bank through currency auctions.

At the same time, the Bolivian government eliminated the illegal bonuses in cash and in kind that were being paid to the employees of the state-owned enterprises. Until then, Bolivian mine workers had benefited from an absurdly subsidized commissariat system that represented one-half of Comibol's 1984 operational deficit (Cariaga 1985, 6).[3] Employees of the state oil company received 400 liters of gasoline a month free of charge, representing another major drain on the company's finances. All public companies paid bonuses and additional wages that amounted in some cases to as much as 21 months' wages in a single year. All these benefits were eliminated. Taken at their value before the measures were implemented, the amounts were combined and added to the annual balance, which was then divided into 12 monthly payments and a Christmas bonus (Christmas bonuses had been paid for many years to all employees in Bolivia in compliance with the General Labor Act of 1939).

By these means the government has effectively curbed its current expenditures since 1986 (see table 3.1). This is one of the few instances in which the public sector has achieved such restraint in practice, given the universally accepted maxim that it is easier to increase revenue than to reduce expenditure. Meanwhile, capital expenditures rose substantially, mainly as a result of the renewed availability of international resources. These resources, coming particularly from multilateral and bilateral organizations, created a net positive flow of funds to Bolivia, reversing the negative trend that had persisted before 1986.

Exchange Rate Policy

The Bolivian government set a realistic exchange rate that was determined by the central bank through a daily currency auction. Although this system brings market forces actively into play (Cariaga 1988, 9), there is much debate as to whether it is producing a sufficiently competitive exchange rate (see, for example, Morales 1988, 16). It is not possible to resolve this issue here or to go into the computations involved in determining the exchange lag, but it should be noted that since 1987 the official exchange rate and the black market rate have never been more than 1 percent apart.

The major advantage of this system lies in the fact that exchange rate policy ceases in essence to be politicized, thus precluding the permanent lags and disruptive effects caused by politically motivated decisions regarding exchange rate levels. By the same token, it also avoids the corruption and political favoritism associated with granting foreign exchange at an official rate, usually

---

3. On 10 March 1985, *Presencia* (La Paz) published a report on subsidized goods received each month by miners through Comibol's commissaries. Miners were entitled to receive 450 units of bread at 0.15 pesos (US$0.00033) per unit, 24 kilograms of sugar at 1.22 pesos (US$0.00271) per kilogram, 16 kilograms of rice at 1.41 pesos (US$0.00313) per kilogram, and 30 kilograms of meat at 2.80 pesos (US$0.00622) per kilogram. At the time this report was published, the official exchange rate was one-third the black market rate.

below parity, and is generally conducive to a more efficient allocation of economic resources.

Trade Policy

Under the Bolivian program, a single uniform tariff was established for all imports, with no exceptions whatsoever. The advantage of a uniform tariff is that all imports are given equal treatment, while effective protection is provided for domestically produced goods with high added value. Until 1985, Bolivia was a classic example of an economy with a high level of effective import protection, which resulted in the proliferation of certain artificial industries. These industries imported inputs under preferential tariffs, and the finished goods were protected by import restrictions or prohibitively high tariffs. In the case of Bolivia, the uniform tariff also had a favorable impact on tax revenues, because the previous, differentiated tariff regime lacked adequate controls and frequently allowed goods subject to high tariffs to be imported at low rates. The elimination of import restrictions gave Bolivia an extremely open trading regime, consistent with its position as a country in which trade accounts for a large share of GDP.

Interest Rate Policy

The Bolivian program provided for interest rates to be set freely in the financial markets for transactions in both Bolivian pesos and foreign currency. The purpose of this decision was to allow real interest rates to be determined by market forces. Banks were also allowed to accept foreign-currency deposits from both Bolivian residents and foreign nationals. This amounted to a tacit acknowledgment that foreign currency was an acceptable medium of exchange for economic transactions. This decision had the extremely favorable effect of inducing the repatriation of a substantial amount of flight capital, which not only increased central bank reserves (Cariaga 1989b, 9) but also made it possible for the stabilization program to proceed until the flow of funds from international organizations turned in Bolivia's favor. Moreover, the repatriation of capital was absolutely essential to cushion the external effects of plummeting tin and nonferrous ore prices and to tide the country over while payments on gas sold to Argentina remained in arrears.

As expected, interest rates dropped sharply from the levels prevailing during the hyperinflationary period (table 3.3), although not as much as would have been desirable. As indicated earlier, Bolivia was deprived of both credits from foreign commercial banks and resources for trade financing, which severely restricted the availability of credit in the country.

Table 3.3 Bolivia: interest rates, 1985–89 (percentages per year)[a]

	1985	1986	1987	1988
Deposit rates				
Dollars	11.2	14.9	15.6	14.9
Pesos	110.6	33.4	29.1	24.9
Lending rates				
Dollars	17.8	23.0	26.0	22.6
Pesos	232.1	65.8	39.5	35.0

a. At end of year.

Source: Unidad de Estudios de Política Económica, *Bolivia: Dossier Estadístico,* September 1989.

Elimination of Price Controls and Deregulation

The adjustment program also removed price controls and price regulation, hallmarks of Bolivian economic policy for the previous 50 years. Most affected by this misguided policy were the farmers, who had to bear the brunt of a hidden tax that favored urban areas, and exporters, who were adversely affected by an uncompetitive exchange rate.

The removal of price controls and price regulation was applied uniformly under the adjustment program, with the elimination of restrictions on imports, exchange rates, and interest rates. In opening the economy to trade, the program allowed domestically produced goods to compete with imported goods. A realistic exchange rate provided a frame of reference within which the competitiveness of domestic goods with respect to imported goods could be compared. Interest rates were allowed to float to bring them down in line with international rates. In both cases, these policies served to make domestic goods more competitive and to enhance the efficiency of the financial system.

Direct Investment and Privatization

In the area of privatization the Bolivian adjustment program did not parallel the Washington consensus. During the stabilization process, the financial authorities tended to give a higher priority to putting in order the country's finances than to privatization.

One of the reasons why privatization was not pursued was that the Bolivian authorities feared replicating the unfortunate experience of other Latin American countries in which the privatization process was marred by corruption, delays, and inaction.

Although Bolivia did not make direct efforts toward attracting foreign direct investment, a sincere attempt was made to lay the groundwork for such investment. On this basis, the country signed commitments for investment insurance with a number of bilateral and multilateral organizations, including the Overseas Private Investment Corporation of the United States and its counterparts in the United Kingdom and France and the Multilateral Investment Guarantee Agency of the World Bank. Legislation now in effect in Bolivia allows for free movement of capital. The economy is open to foreign trade, and Bolivians as well as foreign nationals in Bolivia can freely buy or sell foreign exchange.

Bolivia did not choose to experiment with debt-equity swaps, as a number of other Latin American countries have done, because such a program would have entailed a sharp increase in the money supply and would have undermined the fragile stabilization process. Instead, Bolivia opted for opening negotiations on the repurchase of debt; these negotiations culminated in the successful repurchase of three-quarters of the country's debt to foreign commercial banks at 11 cents on the dollar.

The Bolivian Experience, the Baker Plan, and the Washington Consensus

Having worked successfully along the lines of the Washington consensus, the Bolivian government approached the authorities of the United States and the international lending organizations for the purpose of obtaining the assistance announced as part of the Baker Plan. Bolivia had polished its tarnished image abroad, presenting itself as a textbook case of a country that had successfully deregulated its economy, opened its markets to foreign goods, and curbed inflation. Nonetheless, it came as no great surprise to the Bolivian government when it was turned down for assistance under the Baker Plan on the grounds that the foreign commercial banks were not prepared to make fresh financing available and resume lending to the country. The architects of the stabilization program had anticipated such an announcement. Nevertheless it was particularly discouraging that the banks were not interested in acting as partners in development in a country where the authorities, with the support of the citizenry, had made great strides in putting their house in order. Of far greater comfort was the reaction to the adjustment program of the international organizations—the International Monetary Fund, the World Bank, the Inter-American Development Bank, and the Andean Development Corporation. Acting on their own initiative, these institutions agreed to coordinate their efforts in making available the resources Bolivia urgently needed.

Agreements With the International Monetary Fund

Policy reform along the lines of the Washington consensus paved the way to negotiations with the IMF, which for countries in similar straits is the key to gaining access to multilateral and bilateral credits. Agreement with the IMF is known to reestablish credit with other multilateral organizations almost immediately, and it is a *sine qua non* for negotiations with the Paris Club, which in turn open the door to bilateral credits. Since 1986, the Bolivian government has entered into the following agreements with the IMF:

- A standby arrangement in June 1986 for SDR 50 million

- A compensatory facility in December 1986 for SDR 64.1 million

- A structural adjustment facility in December 1986 for SDR 57.6 million

- An enhanced structural adjustment facility in April 1988 for SDR 136.05 million.

Loans From Other Multilateral Agencies

Since 1985, new loans from the World Bank, the Inter-American Development Bank, the Andean Development Corporation, and other international lending institutions have resulted in a net flow of funds to Bolivia, mainly on concessionary terms. This followed a period of many years during which no lending operations were approved for Bolivia. Since 1985, the World Bank has granted a total of $188.7 million in loans, of which $176.8 million had already been disbursed as of late 1989.[4] This funding was provided on the terms of the International Development Association, the World Bank's soft-loan window. Unlike the World Bank, the Inter-American Development Bank, in keeping with its philosophy of continuity, had kept up its operations in Bolivia even during the years of hyperinflation. However, since 1985 its operations have grown substantially, with a total of $401.5 million having been approved, of which $366.7 million has been disbursed, with a major portion of this financing being granted on soft terms. Likewise, there was a steady increase in the Andean Development Corporation's volume of operations, although concessionary terms did not apply to these loans. Since 1985, loans for $140.3 million have been approved, and $166.7 million has been disbursed.

---

4. In all cases disbursements include loans approved by international financial institutions before 1985.

Table 3.4 Bolivia: net inflow of resources, 1984–88 (millions of dollars)

	1984	1985	1986	1987	1988
Disbursements	159.8	108.7	230.1	238.2	235.6
Repayments of principal	141.9	159.3	139.0	81.8	139.1
Interest payments	201.4	88.8	71.0	85.4	99.8
Net resource transfer	−183.5	−139.4	20.1	71.0	−3.3

Source: Banco Central de Bolivia.

The Paris Club negotiations in 1986 and 1988 and subsequent meetings of the Consultative Group have resulted in disbursements of $215.8 million from various bilateral agencies since 1985, with the lion's share coming from Germany and Japan. Here, too, most of the lending was granted on concessionary terms.

These multilateral and bilateral operations together helped to bring about the positive net flow of resources to Bolivia shown in table 3.4. Since 1986, resources have begun to trickle back to Bolivia as the objectives of the Washington consensus began to be met. The positive net flow was the effective response of the international organizations to the appeal from the Bolivian authorities for capital needed to reactivate the economy.

Consensus Within Bolivia

The measures implemented in 1985 were aimed at coming to grips with Bolivia's critical economic situation and served as the starting point from which the country eventually fulfilled most of the conditions of the Washington consensus. At the same time they helped Bolivia to build a national consensus on acceptance of the structural adjustment program: contrary to the predictions of many politicians, the Bolivian people welcomed the measures and expressed their approval of them in three ways:

- In a country with a tradition of political and social violence, there have been no riots in the streets, no attacks on persons, and no property damage stemming from the adjustment measures themselves. As expected, however, when the stabilization measures were announced in August 1985, the unions, which had enjoyed considerable political clout during the previous administration, called a general strike. Faced with this situation, the government was forced to declare a state of siege as provided for under the Bolivian constitution and was effectively able to put an end to the strike and all resistance to the adjustment measures. This marked the beginning of a passive acceptance of the government's decisions within the country, in the understanding that hyperinflation not only shrunk the economy but caused a sharp decline in real income. (It is estimated that between 1980 and 1985 Bolivian GDP fell by 20 percent and per capita income by 32 percent.)

- In a country that has traditionally experienced problems with tax collection, support for the measures was expressed by the fact that taxpayers showed themselves prepared to queue up, sometimes even in the dark, to pay their taxes.[5] This was the response of a people subjected for several years to the painful experience of inflationary taxation, which adversely affects all individuals on fixed incomes, and therefore most Bolivians.

- In a country where political conflict has traditionally been commonplace, the 1989 election amounted to a plebiscite on the stabilization measures: the parties running on a platform of continuing with the economic program won 65.4 percent of the popular vote. This overwhelming response on the part of the voters showed their desire for economic as well as political and social stability.

This series of credible, coherent, and comprehensive measures, through which Bolivia became eligible for desperately needed external resources, was also the basis of the national consensus in support of the adjustment measures. In its break from traditional political patterns, the recent Bolivian experience serves as a historic lesson, demonstrating that—demagoguery and populist slogans notwithstanding—a people can determine what is best for them.

The adjustment measures described in this paper enabled Bolivia to break the phenomenon of hyperinflation, which had spiraled to an annualized rate of 24,000 percent by September 1985. With the help of multilateral and bilateral organizations, the country achieved a positive net flow of resources that contributed to reversing the trends of negative growth that had persisted from 1980 to 1985. Bolivia returned to a period of growth only in 1987, recording a modest 2.2 percent growth that year and 2.8 percent in 1988. For 1989, a 3 percent growth rate is expected. Had it not been for the external shocks that reduced Bolivia's exports to about one-half of their 1989 levels, economic growth would have resumed in 1986 and might have been much higher thereafter.

Through the adjustment program, a consensus was also reached among the Bolivian people on major structural changes, such as tax reform, tariff reform, and other far-reaching measures. These structural changes may also help to bring about one day a more equitable distribution of income and provide an effective stimulus to production and better employment opportunities for all Bolivians.

---

5. "Long lines formed at the tax collection locations, beginning in the early dawn hours this morning." *Ultima Hora* (La Paz), 15 September 1986.

Chile

Patricio Meller

Almost all of the economic reforms recommended to highly indebted countries after the onset of the debt crisis in 1982 were implemented in Chile during the 1970s. Reprivatization, decontrol of prices, and deregulation were begun shortly after the 1973 military coup; fiscal reform and liberalization of trade and financial markets were accomplished over a short span of time thereafter (table 3.5).[6] Consequently, by the beginning of the 1980s Chile had an open, free-market economy, with a homogeneous 10 percent tariff, free domestic interest rates, a relatively liberalized capital market, and a disciplined, nondisruptive labor force.

When the debt shock came, however, Chile experienced adjustment difficulties similar to those in other Latin American countries; the prior implementation of basic structural reforms neither provided a better shelter from external shocks nor reduced adjustment costs. Nevertheless, seven years later, Chile has apparently overcome the external debt crisis while retaining the main features of its economic model.

Comparison of the precrisis year 1981 with 1987 and 1988 (table 3.6) shows economic growth actually higher and unemployment lower than before the crisis. Inflation, although higher than in 1981, remains low by Latin American standards. The external accounts show similar improvement: a trade deficit equal to 70 percent of current exports in 1981 was converted to surpluses of 23.5 percent and 31.5 percent of current exports in 1987 and 1988, respectively. Meanwhile the current account deficit was reduced sharply. The ratio of net interest payments to exports has been reduced from near 40 percent in 1981 to around 30 percent in 1987 and 1988.

How did the adjustment process affect the Chilean economy? What were the policies used to manage the adjustment? How great were the costs? These questions will be examined in this paper.

---

6. For a more detailed discussion of these reforms see Foxley (1982), Ffrench-Davis (1982), Corbo (1985), and Edwards and Cox-Edwards (1987).

Patricio Meller is a research economist at the Corporación de Investigaciones Económicas para Latinoamérica (CIEPLAN). He is the author of several articles on the Chilean economy and is the Director of the Editorial Committee of Colección Estudios CIEPLAN.

Table 3.5 Chile: major structural reforms of the 1970s

Situation in 1972–73	Post–1973
Privatization	
More than 500 commercial firms and banks controlled by the state	By 1980, only 25 firms (including one bank) remaining in the public sector
Prices	
Price controls	Market-determined prices except wages and exchange rate
Trade and exchange rates	
Multiple exchange rate system Prohibitions and quotas on imports High tariffs[a] Prior deposits for imports	Homogeneous, unified exchange rate. Flat import tariff of 10 percent (excluding automobiles) Absence of other trade barriers
Fiscal regime	
"Cascade" sales tax Large public payroll Large fiscal deficits	Value-added tax of 20 percent Public employment reduced Fiscal surpluses in 1979–81
Domestic financial markets	
Controlled interest rates State ownership of banks Control of credit	Market-determined interest rates Reprivatization of banks Liberalization of capital markets
Capital mobility	
Total control of capital movements Government was the main external borrower	Gradual liberalization of the capital account[b] Private sector is the main external borrower
Labor regime	
Unions played a large role and had considerable bargaining power Worker dismissals prohibited Mandatory wage increases High and increasing nonwage labor costs (40 percent of wages)	No unions and no collective bargaining power Relaxation of prohibition on dismissals Relaxation of mandatory wage adjustments and severe cuts in real wages Reduction of nonwage labor costs (to 30 percent of wages)

a. The average tariff was 94 percent and the maximum was 220 percent.

b. Movements of long-term capital were liberalized in 1981, and those of short-term capital in 1982.

Table 3.6 Chile: summary economic data, selected years

Year	GDP growth (percentages per year)	Inflation (percentages per year)	Unemployment (percentages)	Trade balance[a] (millions of dollars)	Current account balance (millions of dollars)	Interest payments as percentage of exports
1981	5.5	9.5	15.1	−2,677	−4,733	38.1
1987	5.7	21.5	13.1	1,229	−808	32.5
1988	7.4	12.7	11.0	2,219	−167	27.2

a. On f.o.b. basis.

Sources: Central Bank of Chile; Jadresic (1986), updated by University of Chile, unemployment surveys, various years.

Principal Features of the Chilean Adjustment Process

Stages of Adjustment

The Chilean adjustment process was neither smooth nor without reversals. GDP fell 15 percent during 1982–83 before increasing in 1984 (table 3.7). This was in turn followed by a slowdown in 1985 before robust growth resumed in 1986 and 1987. The current account deficit followed a similarly bumpy course.

During 1981, amid clear signals of a world recession—the London interbank offer rate (LIBOR) reached 16.8 percent, and the world price of copper dropped from 99 US cents per pound in 1980 to 79 cents[7]—the economists in the Chilean government explicitly advised a "do nothing" policy. They argued that the recession would be a short one and that with the basic structural reforms having already been implemented, the Chilean economy was well equipped to solve any problems that might arise. The monetary approach to the balance of payments favored by the government's economic team held that, given a fixed nominal exchange rate, the Chilean economy had an automatic mechanism—namely, the interest rate—that would automatically adjust to generate the financial flows required to close any external disequilibrium. The international commercial banks had provided relatively large amounts of external credit in the years up to 1981 and had highly praised Chile's economic reforms. Thus, the sudden inelasticity in the supply of financial capital in 1982 came as a real surprise.

---

7. A 10-cent fall in the world price of copper represents a loss in the value of Chilean copper exports of about $300 million.

Table 3.7 Chile: economic growth and current account deficits, 1982–86

	1982	1983	1984	1985	1986
Economic growth (percentages per year)	−14.1	−0.7	6.3	2.4	5.7
Current account deficit (millions of dollars)	2,304	1,073	2,060	1,329	1,137

Source: Central Bank of Chile.

Three stages can be distinguished in the Chilean adjustment process[8] (see tables 3.6 and 3.7): the period 1982–83 was one of recessionary adjustment aimed at closing the expenditure-income gap; 1984 saw economic reactivation to close the internal gap; after 1985 structural adjustment became the focus, as the Chilean authorities realized that the external disequilibrium was a long-run problem.

During 1982–83, doing its best to close the expenditure-income gap, Chile went through its worst recession since the 1930s: besides the sharp drop in GDP, industrial output and construction also fell by more than 20 percent during 1982, and the effective unemployment rate[9] peaked at over 30 percent. The number of commercial bankruptcies tripled during 1982, contributing to domestic bank losses that for the average bank were twice as large as equity (the two main commercial banks suffered losses of up to three or four times equity). Meanwhile, the Chilean central bank lost more than 45 percent of its international reserves.[10]

Chile subscribed to International Monetary Fund standby programs for the years 1983 and 1984. The first priority of these standbys was to ensure full external debt service (interest plus scheduled amortization); in fact, the need to service the debt has been considered, over most of the period since rescheduling, to be the main constraint on the Chilean adjustment program.

In 1984 an exception was made to the rule that debt service should be given priority. The deep and prolonged recession of 1982–83 put pressure on the government to implement reactivation measures to reduce the heavy adjustment costs. A new economic team was also in charge. Domestic debtors had

---

8. This classification differs from that of Barandiarán (1988), which begins with macroeconomic stabilization (output contraction), followed by recovery (GDP regaining its preadjustment level), and eventually steady growth. In Barandiarán's approach, the stages are distinguished by levels of GDP, whereas in the approach used here, changes in the policy environment differentiate the stages of adjustment.

9. Including as unemployed those participating in special public relief programs that paid some fraction of the minimum wage.

10. For a more detailed discussion of the 1982–83 collapse see Edwards and Cox-Edwards(1987), Morandé and Schmidt-Hebbel (1988), and Meller (1989).

already received some government support to alleviate their financial situation; however, public opinion felt that an expanding economy would provide a more definitive solution to the internal debt problem and reduce the social costs being paid by the large numbers of unemployed. Moreover, since the absorption-output gap had been closed (see table 3.14) and the required devaluation measure had been implemented,[11] the main policy prescriptions for stabilization and structural adjustment were in place, and it was assumed that the Chilean economy was ready to start growing again. Expansionary policies generated a 1984 GDP growth rate of 6.3 percent[12] and an expansion of industrial output of almost 10 percent; effective unemployment was reduced from 31.1 percent in 1983 to less than 25 percent.

The counterpart of the expansion was a rapid deterioration of the external accounts: the trade surplus of $986 million in 1983 was reduced to $283 million in 1984, and the current account deficit nearly doubled (table 3.7). This highly vulnerable external situation provided the rationale for a change of focus: external adjustment was going to be a long-run process, during which austerity would have to be maintained. In 1985, another new economic team was put in charge, whose main objective became the progressive reduction of external credit requirements. To meet this goal a new real devaluation was considered necessary, as the previous one, which had overcompensated for the loss of international competitiveness during the three years of fixed nominal exchange rates (1979–82), was now deemed insufficient to generate the real transfer required to service the external debt. It was decided that exports should become the main engine of growth for economic expansion; additional measures were implemented, as will be seen below.

An external financial package provided key support for the new program. Somewhat paradoxically after the previous year's worsening of the current account deficit, in 1985 Chile succeeded in obtaining almost the same amount of "new money" from the international commercial banks as in 1984 (Rosende 1987). Moreover, Chile subscribed to a three-year extended Fund facility (EFF)

---

11. Almost three years of fixed nominal exchange rates ended on 14 June 1982. After some chaotic experiments and a few changes of finance ministers, a crawling-peg regime was established at the end of 1982, with a real exchange rate level that compensated for the previous loss of international competitiveness; for details on the exchange rate and monetary policies of 1982 and 1983 see Meller (1989).

12. According to official statistics; alternative measures show GDP growth rates of 8.3 percent for 1984 and 1.1 percent for 1985, industrial-sector growth rates of 11.9 percent and 1.6 percent, and construction-sector growth rates of 19.3 percent and −0.5 percent. See Arrau (1986).

loan from the IMF and a three-year structural adjustment loan (SAL) from the World Bank.[13] Table 3.7 presents the outcome of the 1985 program.

The Public-Sector Deficit and the Current Account Deficit

Large public-sector deficits have been one of the main elements present in the Latin American external deficits of the 1980s (see Barandiarán 1988). A large and unsustainable current account deficit has been assumed to be causally associated with a large and unsustainable public-sector deficit.

The recent Chilean experience would seem to be an exception to this rule. Chile's relatively large current account deficit in 1981 was associated with and preceded by surpluses of the central government and of the overall nonfinancial public sector. In fact, the central government had surpluses of over 2 percent of GDP throughout the 1978–81 period (table 3.8).[14] Moreover, the fiscal deficits that appeared during the 1982–86 period (table 3.8) would have been almost nonexistent had a major social security reform not been implemented in 1981 (discussed below). In addition, the public sector, including the state-owned enterprises (SOEs), was subject to many domestic constraints in its foreign borrowing prior to 1981. Table 3.9 traces the external borrowing of the public and private sectors for the 1978–81 period, demonstrating that the severe external disequilibrium of 1981 was related to a private-sector income-expenditure imbalance and not to public-sector deficits.

The standard procedure of measuring the current account deficit as a percentage of current GDP (converted into dollars at current exchange rates; third column in table 3.8) presents a distorted picture of the adjustment effort in Chile's case. Given that it was overvaluation of the exchange rate that generated the current account disequilibrium, and that a real devaluation was implemented later, GDP figures expressed in current dollars are overstated prior to the devaluation, and therefore generate a relatively lower current account deficit measured as a percentage of GDP. Table 3.8 provides revised current account figures for the 1980–83 period, using the postdevaluation real exchange rate of

---

13. "New money" from the commercial banks for 1985–86 amounted to $1.1 billion, including $300 million with World Bank guarantees. The 1983–84 IMF standby provided credits to Chile of SDR 500 million plus SDR 295 million through the compensatory financing facility (CFF). The 1985–87 EFF provided credits of SDR 750 million plus SDR 70.6 million through a CFF. The World Bank SAL programs provided a total of $750 million for the three years.

14. The fiscal surpluses were 2.2 percent and 5.1 percent of GDP in 1978 and 1979, respectively; see Larraín (1988) and Larrañaga (1989). The consolidated nonfinancial public-sector surpluses in the same years were 1.4 percent and 4.6 percent of GDP, respectively.

Table 3.8 Chile: public-sector and current account balances, 1980–87

(percentages of GDP except where noted)

	Public-sector balance		Current account balance		
Year	Central government	Non-financial public sector	As percentage of current measured GDP[a]	As percentage of corrected GDP[b]	As percentage of exports
1980	5.5	5.4	−7.1	−12.4	−41.9
1981	2.9	0.4	−14.5	−25.5	−123.4
1982	−2.3	−3.9	−9.5	−13.6	−62.2
1983	−3.1	−3.5	−5.7	−6.4	−29.6
1984	−3.5	−4.5	−10.7	−10.7	−57.8
1985	−3.6	−2.9	−8.3	−6.5	−34.9
1986	−1.0	−1.5	−6.5	−5.2	−27.1
1987	0.2	0.3	−4.3	−3.4	−15.4

a. GDP in dollars is calculated by dividing current-year GDP in pesos by the current-year official exchange rate.

b. The 1984 official exchange rate is used to calculate 1984 GDP in dollars. Thereafter GDP growth rates are used to calculate GDP in 1984 dollars. The US Wholesale Price Index is then used to calculate GDP in current dollars.

Sources: Larraín (1988); Larrañaga (1989); Central Bank of Chile.

1984. The corrected current account figures demonstrate, first, that overvaluation of the exchange rate was hiding an increasing external disequilibrium. Second, when the 1981 deficit is used as the benchmark, the reduction in the deficit after 1981 is seen to have been more pronounced than standard measurements indicate. Third, the trend in the corrected current account figures more closely matches that in the current account measured as a percentage of current exports (last column in table 3.8), a measure that is not distorted by real exchange rate changes.

The External Adjustment

From 1981 to 1988 the Chilean current account deficit was reduced from 123 percent of exports to approximately 2 percent. Table 3.10, which presents the main components of the Chilean balance of payments for the 1980–88 period (in current dollars), shows how this external adjustment was achieved. It is evident from the table that the elimination of the deficit in trade in goods and nonfactor services (i.e., the nonfinancial part of the current account) after 1981, followed by increasing surpluses after 1985, was the main contributor to the

Table 3.9 Chile: public and private foreign debt, 1978–81 (millions of dollars)

Foreign debt	1978	1979	1980	1981
Public sector	5,198	5,369	5,310	5,623
Private sector	1,955	3,421	6,021	10,077

Source: Central Bank of Chile, *Deuda Externa de Chile,* various issues.

reduction of the current account deficit. For the 1982–85 period, the improvement in the trade account is apparently due mostly to the 50 percent decrease in imports from 1981 levels; exports meanwhile showed almost no change in current dollars, although they increased significantly after 1986. Table 3.10 also shows that average annual net financial payments for the 1982–88 period were higher by one-half than the average for 1980–81, and that the average annual inflow of capital was reduced by two-thirds.

The trade balance figures expressed in current dollars underestimate the role of exports and overestimate that of imports during the 1982–85 period. The volume of exports increased by 6 percent to 8 percent per year during the 1982–85 adjustment period, while that of imports experienced a contraction of around 40 percent on average compared with 1981 levels.[15] In other words, the deterioration in the terms of trade during the 1980s made the external adjustment more painful. Using 1980 as the benchmark for estimating the impact of the terms-of-trade deterioration tends to overestimate this effect;[16] when the 1978–81 period is used instead, the annual impact of the terms-of-trade deterioration during 1982–85 is between $300 million and $500 million.

The expansion of exports has been one of the most positive outcomes of the external adjustment process (table 3.10). The average growth rate of exports by volume in the 1982–88 period was 6.5 percent per year (according to Chilean national accounts figures). Exports have increased their share of GDP (in current prices) from 19.4 percent in 1982 to 37.3 percent in 1988. Table 3.11 provides a decomposition of Chilean exports, showing that copper continues to account for around 45 percent of the total, and the mining sector as a whole close to 60 percent. (A breakdown of Chile's main industrial products is given in table 3.12.)

---

15. Comparing the 1981 and 1986 trade balances as percentages of GDP, Fontaine (1987) estimates that 60 percent of the real adjustment was due to import volume reduction, whereas 40 percent corresponds to export volume expansion. On the other hand, comparing the 1980 and 1987 trade balances, Arellano (1988) finds exactly the opposite proportions.

16. The price of copper peaked at 99 cents per pound in 1980, whereas the average price for the 1976–81 period was 75.5 cents.

Table 3.10 Chile: selected balance of payments accounts, 1980–88 (millions of dollars)

Account	1980	1981	1982	1983	1984	1985	1986	1987	1988
Total exports (f.o.b.)	4,705	3,836	3,706	3,831	3,651	3,804	4,199	5,223	7,052
Copper exports	2,125	1,738	1,685	1,875	1,604	1,789	1,757	2,235	3,416
Total imports (f.o.b.)	5,469	6,513	3,643	2,845	3,288	2,955	3,099	3,994	4,833
Current account	−1,971	−4,733	−2,304	−1,117	−2,111	−1,329	−1,137	−808	−167
Nonfinancial current account	−1,154	−3,378	−492	−534	−141	511	652	766	1,576
Interest payments	−930	−1,463	−1,921	−1,748	−2,025	−1,901	−1,887	−1,700	−1,920
Capital account	1,921	4,631	2,380	1,049	1,923	1,332	1,049	899	271
Amortization payments	1,438	1,819	1,259	895	488	420	432	310	649
Capital inflows	4,483	6,257	1,814	1,239	2,318	1,898	2,012	1,055	1,494
Changes in international reserves	1,244	67	−1,165	−541	17	−99	−228	45	732

Source: Central Bank of Chile, *Boletín Mensual,* various issues.

Table 3.11 Chile: components of merchandise exports, 1980–88
(percentages of total)

Year	Mining and mining products		Agriculture and agricultural products	Forestry and wood and paper products	Fishing and related products
	Copper	Total			
1980	46.1	70.9	6.1	12.5	8.4
1981	43.4	67.2	7.7	10.6	9.0
1982	46.7	69.4	8.4	9.3	10.6
1983	47.9	70.6	7.3	8.5	11.5
1984	43.3	64.6	10.9	10.3	11.9
1985	46.1	65.8	12.4	8.5	11.8
1986	41.9	59.2	15.2	9.7	12.3
1987	41.2	58.1	14.2	11.5	12.6
1988	47.9	62.7	11.6	10.4	11.6

Source: Central Bank of Chile, *Boletín Mensual,* various issues.

External adjustment has required the generation of surpluses in the trade account in order to fulfill external debt-service obligations; in other words there has been a net outward transfer of real resources. The total real transfer made by the Chilean economy to maintain external debt service includes the trade surplus plus changes in international reserves.[17] For the 1982–88 period (with the exception of 1984) the average real transfer was about $800 million per year (table 3.13); this figure represents around 40 percent of net financial services and around 4 percent of the total external debt.[18]

The Internal Adjustment

Let Z_t and Y_t be real domestic expenditure and real output (GDP), respectively, in year t. The existence of an excess of expenditures over output (an expenditure-output gap, $Z_t > Y_t$) generates an external account deficit. (In the Chilean case, as already mentioned, it was the private sector that generated the external disequilibrium.) To achieve the required external adjustment, not only must the expenditure-output gap be closed, but output must exceed expenditure ($Z_t < Y_t$) in order to

---

17. This concept of real transfer is in fact a mixture of real resources and of money terms (which have a real purchasing power).

18. Fontaine (1987) has obtained lower figures, but his method uses only the trade surplus to measure the real transfer and uses the entire 1983–86 period without excluding 1984. This year is clearly an outlier; therefore its inclusion in the average distorts the outcome.

Table 3.12 Chile: principal industrial exports, 1980–88 (millions of dollars)

Year	Fish meal	Sawn wood	Cellu-lose	Paper	Oil products	Iron and steel products	Copper products	Wine
1980	233.7	261.9	230.6	34.6	68.1	12.4	69.1	21.4
1981	202.0	149.7	203.7	24.7	80.2	7.4	44.5	16.7
1982	256.0	104.9	172.8	26.7	73.6	47.6	30.0	13.1
1983	307.1	102.8	156.7	33.9	66.5	51.2	24.5	10.8
1984	275.7	74.3	195.9	44.5	53.0	28.3	32.1	13.6
1985	314.3	51.4	140.5	52.6	43.0	34.1	24.9	20.4
1986	333.2	69.0	192.7	56.7	40.8	43.7	31.4	21.5
1987	375.0	92.8	264.8	61.0	52.5	42.6	40.4	33.5
1988	482.1	105.1	309.1	70.4	59.8	49.7	57.4	38.3

Source: Central Bank of Chile, Boletín Mensual, various issues.

produce the real transfer required to service the external debt. This is accomplished by some combination of expenditure-reducing policies (reduction of Z_t) and expenditure-switching policies (increase in Y_t). Because of differences in the lags with which these policies show their effects, most of the initial internal adjustment will be generated by a decrease in Z_t rather than an increase in Y_t.

In short, the reduction of real domestic expenditure or absorption implies inevitable adjustment costs. Let us define *primary adjustment costs* as the reduction of real absorption necessary to close the existing expenditure-output gap and to generate the required real transfer. Let us then define *secondary adjustment costs* as those generated by existing structural rigidities (such as price rigidities, capital-sector specificity, market imperfections, and lags) and by adjustment policies that are more stringent than actually required (overkill). These secondary adjustment costs are generated by an inefficient adjustment process and therefore should be minimized (Corden 1988), whereas the primary adjustment costs are unavoidable.[19]

Let us measure the primary and secondary costs of the Chilean internal adjustment process. The year 1981 will be considered year 0; that is, $\delta_0 = Z_0 - Y_0$ is the expenditure-output gap that has to be closed. Similarly, $\delta_t = Y_t - Z_t$ is the output-expenditure gap in year t of the adjustment period, which corresponds to the real transfer required by external debt payments. Using superscripts T and N to designate tradeable and nontradeable goods, respectively, let us assume that equilibrium in the market for nontradeables is entirely determined by expenditure

---

19. Corden (1988) also refers to primary and secondary adjustment costs but defines the terms differently.

Table 3.13 Chile: real external transfer, 1980–88

	Balance on goods and nonfactor services[a]				Balance on goods and nonfactor services plus changes in international reserves			
		As percentage of:				As percentage of:		
Year	Millions of US dollars	Exports	Net financial payments	External debt	Millions of US dollars	Exports	Net financial payments	External debt
1982	−492	−13.3	25.6	−2.9	673	18.2	−35.0	3.9
1983	534	13.9	−30.5	3.0	1,075	28.1	−61.5	6.0
1984	−141	−3.9	7.0	−0.7	−158	−4.3	7.8	−0.8
1985	511	13.4	−26.9	2.5	610	16.0	−32.1	3.0
1986	652	15.5	−34.6	3.1	880	21.0	−46.6	4.2
1987	766	14.7	−45.1	3.7	721	13.8	−42.4	3.5
1988	1,576	22.3	−82.1	8.3	844	12.0	−44.0	4.4

a. Trade account figures are in c.i.f. terms.

Sources: Central Bank of Chile, *Boletín Mensual* and *Deuda Externa de Chile,* various issues.

on nontradeables (Z^N). Then, total reduction of absorption in any year t of the adjustment period with respect to the base year 0 will be given by:

$$Z_0 - Z_t = (Z_0^T - Z_t^T) + (Z_0^N - Z_t^N)$$

Using the above definitions of δ_0 and δ_t, this becomes:

$$Z_0 - Z_t = (\delta_0 + \delta_t) + (Y_0^T - Y_t^T) + (Y_0^N - Y_t^N)$$

| Total absorption costs | Primary adjustment costs | Tradeable production gap | Nontradeable production gap |

Secondary adjustment costs

Total absorption costs equal primary adjustment costs only when the expansion of tradeables production is equal to the contraction of nontradeables production. This is so in the case of a perfectly flexible and instantaneously transformable (perfectly mobile and malleable productive factors), small, open (dependent) economy; in other words, there is a smooth and instantaneous movement along the economy's transformation curve.

Let us now separate the two components of secondary adjustment costs. One of the main objectives of adjustment is the expansion of tradeables production; at the least, one would expect maintenance of Y_0^T. Therefore, if the adjustment

Table 3.14 Chile: decomposition of adjustment costs, 1981–87
(percentages of GDP)[a]

Year	Primary adjustment costs		Secondary adjustment costs		Total adjustment costs (absorption gap)
	Initial absorption gap (δ_0)	Output-absorption gap (δ_t)	Tradeables gap	Non-tradeables gap	
1982	15.0	0.2	4.7	11.7	31.6
1983	15.1	4.1	4.6	12.6	36.5
1984	14.2	2.2	1.4	8.8	26.7
1985	13.9	6.3	0.5	7.1	27.8
1986	13.1	6.6	−2.0	3.8	21.6
1987	12.4	5.2	−3.3	−0.4	13.9
1988	11.6	3.9	−5.5	−4.8	5.1

a. Measured with respect to 1981.

Source: Calculated from Central Bank of Chile, *Boletín Mensual,* various issues.

policy package generates a positive term $(Y_0^T - Y_t^T;$ i.e., a contraction of tradeables output), it is a clear indicator of a very inefficient adjustment process. Such a result could be produced by a contractionary monetary policy that reduces credit availability to enterprises engaged in tradeables production.[20]

Several factors could result in a contraction of nontradeable goods production. Tight fiscal and monetary policies aimed at a reduction of total absorption could generate Keynesian or demand-constrained excess capacity (and unemployment) in an economy with a large, modern, and formal nontradeable goods sector (Buiter 1988). Alternatively, the production of nontradeable goods (Y^N) could be complementary to domestic expenditure on tradeable goods (Z^T), as in the case of domestic retail trade and distribution of Z^T (Arellano 1986). To minimize these secondary adjustment costs, and given the fact that most nontradeable goods have a relatively low intensity of imported inputs, the use of a government consumption subsidy for nontradeable goods has been suggested, to reduce the high unemployment that could generate a contraction in Y^N (Dornbusch 1974). This is especially valid in a disequilibrium situation such as Chile experienced, where effective unemployment remained above 24 percent for four years (1982–85) and unemployment compensation was practically nonexistent.

20. Within the tradeables category one must also distinguish between those that are exported and those that compete with importables. In the Chilean case, most tradeables producers specialize in one or the other. Even highly efficient firms producing tradeables for the domestic market take time to switch from a contracting local market to a highly elastic world market.

Figure 3.1 Chile: decomposition of adjustment costs, 1982–88

percentages of GDP

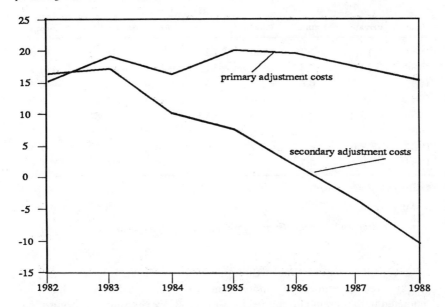

Table 3.14 computes the primary and secondary adjustment costs for the Chilean adjustment process, again taking 1981 as year 0 (these costs are displayed graphically in figure 3.1). As the table makes clear, total adjustment costs have been heavy: real domestic expenditure was lower by more than 30 percent (of the base-year GDP) during the first two years of the adjustment process and by more than 20 percent during the next three years. During the first two years, primary and secondary adjustment costs had roughly equal shares of the total. In 1984–85, secondary adjustment costs fell to about 30 percent of total adjustment costs. The production of tradeable goods decreased by almost 5 percent (of base-year GDP) during the first two years, and was still about 1 percent lower during 1984–85. In spite of the large real devaluation in 1982, it took the tradeables sector four years to recover its real output level of 1981. Most of the contraction in tradeables output was related to production for the domestic market. As pointed out previously, there was a significant expansion of exports, but prior to 1985 this could not compensate for the contraction in output for the overall tradeables sector.

These results in general indicate that the Chilean adjustment process has been excessively costly and prolonged. The adjustment policies have produced a clear overkill.

Within the costs associated with reduction of absorption, it is important to distinguish between present and future costs. Table 3.15 shows that, during

Table 3.15 Chile: changes in consumption and investment, 1981–88
(percentages)

Year	Consumption			Fixed investment			Total absorption
	Private	Public	Total	Private	Public	Total[a]	
1981	12.9	−3.1	10.6	22.7	1.4	16.8	11.6
1982	−24.8	−1.3	−22.0	−37.4	−23.1	−33.9	−24.1
1983	−3.2	−0.6	−2.8	−23.4	6.8	−14.9	−4.6
1984	9.7	1.5	8.4	−4.0	32.8	9.0	8.5
1985	−5.2	−0.3	−4.5	13.0	17.1	14.8	−1.9
1986	6.3	−2.1	5.0	−7.3	25.4[b]	7.1	5.3
1987	7.0	−2.1	5.7	29.0	4.2[b]	16.2	7.3
1988	9.1	4.7	8.5	17.4	2.9[b]	10.7	8.9

a. Gross fixed investment.

b. IMF estimate.

Sources: Central Bank, *Boletín Mensual,* various issues; Solimano and Zucker (1988).

1982–83, total consumption in Chile fell by more than 24 percent and total (gross) fixed investment by more than 50 percent; adjustment has thus generated both present and future costs. By 1988, six years into the adjustment period, gross fixed investment still had not recovered to its 1981 level, while total consumption was still 5 percent below its precrisis level. Most of the contraction of total consumption occurred in the private sector; public consumption shows only small reductions from its 1981 level. However, the public sector has played an important role in the recovery of gross fixed investment. Public gross fixed investment in 1988 was more than 70 percent above its 1981 level, whereas private investment was approximately 25 percent lower in 1981. In each of the years 1984–88, public investment accounted for more than 43 percent of total fixed investment. This increase in public investment is the counterpart of the increase in financing from multilateral organizations.

External Financing

In theoretical terms, a country with an external disequilibrium problem has two apparently distinct options: adjustment or external financing. In practice, the two are interrelated. Even though availability of financing implies a postponement (or reduction) of adjustment, external creditors will provide financing only if they see that the country is implementing policies that will eventually produce the required adjustment.

Table 3.16 Chile: principal sources of external financing, 1983–87
(millions of dollars)

Source	1983	1984	1985	1986	1987
Commercial banks ("new money")	1,300	780	714	370	0
Multilateral and official bilateral organizations (except IMF)	335	448	549	507	519
IMF (net annual credit increment)[a]	600	176	303	243	124
Supplier credit	145	391	207	341	509
Short-term trade credit	−1,339	280	36	129	147
Total capital account surplus[b] plus IMF (net annual increment)	1,041	2,075	1,809	1,590	1,299

a. At the end of 1987, the total Chilean debt to the IMF was $1.45 billion.

b. Excluding amortization payments.

Sources: Fontaine (1987); Central Bank of Chile; IMF.

After the 1982 debt crisis and the sudden decrease in commercial bank credits, two principles guided the Chilean government's attitude. The first may be called the no-confrontation principle: the Chilean government provided public guarantees of nonguaranteed private domestic financial external debt[21] and has maintained full and punctual interest payments on the external debt. Meanwhile, there has been a quiet and orderly rescheduling of a large share of the amortization payments on that debt. The second principle holds that sound macroeconomic policies and serious adjustment efforts "attract foreign financing" (Fontaine 1987). These two principles are based on the notion that Chile's investment in its reputation will lead to its regaining access to voluntary credit (Rosende 1987).

The data in table 3.16 show a clear declining trend in the amount of "new money" (medium and long-term credits) provided by commercial banks from 1983 to 1987. The average annual flow of "new money" (in current dollars) over the 1983–87 period represents around 15 percent of the average annual

---

21. This public guarantee has implied costs. Bad loans of the domestic commercial banking system based on foreign borrowing have been estimated by the World Bank (1985) to amount to at least $3.5 billion. Harberger (1985) put it very neatly: "There can be little doubt that if each foreign creditor bank and each Chilean debtor bank had been left to work out its financial affairs under the applicable laws, a fair share of the foreign debt of the (failed or failing) Chilean banks would have been written off, and Chile's current debt service problems would consequently have been less."

(medium and long-term) credit provided by the commercial banks in the 1979–81 period, exemplifying the standard paradoxical bank behavior of providing less credit when it is most needed and vice versa. The table also shows that multilateral organizations (the World Bank and the Inter-American Development Bank) and official bilateral organizations have been an important source of external financing, providing an average annual flow of credit of $470 million during 1983–87. This has been complemented by an average annual flow of $290 million from the IMF for the same period. Together, multilateral (including the IMF) and official bilateral organizations have provided average annual credits equivalent to 40 percent of net external financial payments.

In short, Chile's investment in its credit reputation has so far met with support only from the multilateral and official bilateral organizations. Ffrench-Davis (1989) has pointed out that this type of credit has an upper bound, and that during the early 1990s scheduled amortization will require net capital flows from Chile to the multilateral organizations. Although almost all the required adjustment measures have been implemented, and there has been a significant expansion of exports, Chile's external debt problem has not disappeared. Access to voluntary credit from the commercial banks remains a key missing input for future economic growth.

Issues and Policies Related to the Adjustment Process

The Financial Crisis

Liberalization of the domestic financial market had produced by 1981 a very fragile financial system. There was practically no control, supervision, or regulation of the commercial banks and *financieras* (finance companies). The domestic real rate of interest for loans was very high, averaging above 35 percent in four years out of the 1976–81 period. Persistently high real interest rates affect the solvency of productive firms, and thus indirectly the solvency of the banks that hold their loans. In addition, close interlocking relationships exist between productive firms and financial institutions in Chile, especially in the two largest Chilean *grupos* (conglomerates), with a high percentage of a given bank's loans going to firms related to the same *grupo*.[22] Finally, the general economic euphoria and the overvaluation of the currency fueled by massive inflows of foreign capital generated a speculative boom; the real index of stock prices

---

22. In 1983 the two largest private domestic banks, Banco Chile and Banco Santiago, which provided 22 percent and 11 percent of total domestic credit, respectively, provided 21 percent and 49.5 percent, respectively, of all bank loans extended to firms related to their own *grupos*.

increased 84 percent in 1980, and that of real estate by almost 120 percent in 1981 (Arellano 1983; Meller and Solimano 1984). High prices of financial and fixed assets encouraged holders of those assets to increase their debt positions.

In 1982 the steep nominal and real devaluation, the sharp contraction of GDP, and the sudden reduction of foreign credit created serious problems for both the real and the financial sector. Many debtors could not service their foreign debts at the new exchange rates, and many could no longer pay the higher interest rates on their domestic-currency debts. The result was an increasing volume of bad loans in the banking system. Domestic indebtedness had become the most critical economic issue by the end of 1982, and the collapse of the whole financial system was only avoided by central bank actions to provide continued liquidity and arrange various types of debtor rescue operations; however, these solutions implied the use of a large sum of public resources.

The measures implemented by the central bank[23] included a subsidized exchange rate or "preferential dollar" for those owing debts in foreign currencies; this dual exchange rate system was maintained during most of the IMF standby and EFF programs. Foreign-currency debtors also benefited from "de-dollarization," or conversion of dollar debts into peso debts, just before the peso was again sharply devalued in September 1984. For peso debtors various internal debt rescheduling programs were implemented offering low real (but positive) subsidized interest rates. In another program, commercial banks were allowed to sell the central bank their bad and risky loans in amounts up to two times the seller's equity, with a repurchase obligation. In return the banks received risk-free central bank bonds paying 7 percent real interest, while their sold-off portfolio was subject to an annual charge of 5 percent (real). Another mechanism used to bail out the commercial banks was that of subsidized interest rates paid on swap operations by the central bank. A commercial bank would open a foreign-exchange deposit account at the central bank and receive LIBOR plus 4 percent (this spread decreased through time); simultaneously it would receive a credit in pesos on which it would pay the domestic savings interest rate. In this swap operation the central bank guaranteed the resale of foreign exchange and absorbed any risks and losses related to a devaluation. Finally, all bank deposits were provided public guarantees, and the central bank together with Banco del Estado, the only Chilean state bank, absorbed the losses of those financial institutions liquidated during the crisis.

Table 3.17 shows some rough figures related to the quasi-fiscal subsidies provided by the central bank. Of these the subsidized exchange rate absorbed the most resources, costing the central bank on average more than $700 million a year in the period 1982–85. Total central bank quasi-fiscal subsidies in those

---

23. For a more detailed discussion see Arellano and Marfán (1986), World Bank (1987), Velasco (1988), and Meller (1989).

Table 3.17   Chile: quasi-fiscal subsidies provided by the central bank, 1982–87

	1982	1983	1984	1985	1986	1987
Exchange rate subsidies (millions of dollars)	906	638	395	932	111	37
Total subsidies (percentages of GDP)	5.3	4.3	4.8	7.3	2.9	1.3

Sources: Exchange rate subsidies: GEMINES (private consulting firm, Santiago) and IMF. Total subsidies: Larrañaga (1989).

years exceeded the registered consolidated nonfinancial public-sector deficits of the same period. According to the IMF, the Chilean treasury had to provide resources (government bonds) amounting to almost $6 billion during 1983–85 in order to recapitalize the central bank.

In its role as lender and bailer-out of last resort, the central bank avoided a collapse of the greater part of the Chilean private financial and productive system; however, these subsidies were not at all neutral in their distributive impact.

The financial crisis had two distinct outcomes. First, the government was prompted to design and implement a new financial surveillance and regulation system. Banks and their customers also learned from the experience and adopted very cautious credit strategies during the years immediately following the crisis. Second, government intervention in the banks and commercial firms of the two largest *grupos* inadvertently created a so-called odd sector (*area rara*) of ambiguous ownership. It was not at all clear who now owned what share of the assets of this intricately interwoven financial and productive structure. (This type of outcome has been called the "monetarist way to statism.") It took quite some time to disentangle and reprivatize this sector.

Exchange Rate Policy

Economic developments in the second half of 1981 led to some sharp disagreements among Chilean economists. One group, focusing on the large current account deficit, believed that the Chilean economy was facing a critical external disequilibrium situation and recommended a devaluation. A second group felt that the external situation was favorable, given that the overall balance of payments was in surplus; this group recommended a revaluation. Yet a third group recommended keeping the nominal exchange rate fixed at 39 pesos to the dollar, the rate that had been maintained for two years; this group argued that

Figure 3.2 Chile: annual nominal devaluation and inflation, 1981–88

percentages

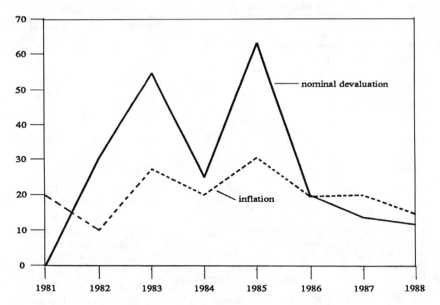

the fixed rate acted as the nominal anchor of the economy and the main mechanism guiding expectations and holding down inflation.

The end of this story is well known. Devaluation was implemented together with wage deindexation in June 1982. By the fourth quarter of 1982, after a 70 percent nominal devaluation, Chile went back to a crawling-peg regime with daily devaluations; the crawl rule was based on the difference between the previous month's rate of domestic inflation and international inflation (estimated to vary between 4 percent and 6 percent per year). There were some further discrete devaluations during 1984 and 1985 followed by a return to the crawling-peg regime. Given that most of the other basic policy reforms had already been implemented, devaluation became the main tool for achieving structural adjustment.

Devaluation increases the price of tradeables in local currency and thus the price of tradeables relative to nontradeables (P_T/P_N). This change in the relative price induces a substitution of production toward tradeables and of expenditure toward nontradeables; both responses clearly help to reduce a current account deficit. However, to prevent a nominal devaluation from being eroded by inflation requires several things. First, fiscal and monetary policies must validate the devaluation. This is considered to be a necessary but not a sufficient

Table 3.18 Chile: tradeable goods and exports as shares of real and nominal GDP, 1980–87 (percentages)

	Tradeable sector[a]		Export sector	
	Share of real GDP	Share of nominal GDP	Share of real GDP	Share of nominal GDP
1980	37.0	37.2	23.7	22.8
1981	36.4	34.2	20.4	16.4
1982	37.6	32.1	24.9	19.4
1983	38.1	36.4	25.2	24.0
1984	38.7	37.8	25.3	24.3
1985	38.7	46.1	26.4	29.1
1986	39.1	47.1	27.5	30.6
1987	38.3	47.5	28.3	33.5
1988	38.2	n.a.	27.9	37.4

n.a. = not available.

a. The tradeables sector includes agriculture and forestry, fishing, mining, and manufacturing. Data for tradeables sector from *Cuentas Nacionales* for 1980–83. For the 1984–87 period a special price index of nontradeable goods was constructed using 120 items from the consumer price index. The price of tradeables was then calculated as the residual between the GDP deflator and the nontradeables price index.

Sources: Central Bank of Chile, *Boletín Mensual* and *Cuentas Nacionales,* various issues.

condition. Second, in the short (and medium) run a real devaluation requires a reduction of real wages; this means deindexation if wages are indexed. Third, the use of a crawling-peg regime after the devaluation has been shown empirically to be the most appropriate means of maintaining the new real value of the exchange rate (Edwards 1989a).

The nominal devaluations in Chile have been successful in achieving a real devaluation. Figure 3.2 shows that nominal devaluations far surpassed the corresponding annual inflation rates in each of the years 1982–85. It can also be seen that the crawl rule has not been a strict one. Instead, the central bank set up an exchange rate reference level with a 2 percent band (later increased to 5 percent), and since 1986 has been able to shift, within a small range, from an endogenous (passive) to a predetermined (active) crawling-peg system.[24]

Real devaluation has induced a significant internal reallocation and transfer of resources toward the tradeables sector. Table 3.18 shows that the export sector has increased its share of real GDP by around 5 percentage points, while the

---

24. This was particularly so during 1988 (the year of the plebiscite): nominal devaluation throughout the year (December to December) amounted to 3.9 percent while the equivalent inflation rate was 12.7 percent.

Table 3.19 Chile: real exchange rate and wage indices, 1980–87
(1980–81 = 100)

	Real exchange rate indices			Relative price of tradeables to nontradeables	Real wage indices	
Year	IMF	World Bank	Central Bank of Chile		Official index	Revised index
1980	106.2	107.4	106.8	105.1	95.7	95.0
1981	93.8	92.6	93.2	94.9	104.3	105.0
1982	132.3	105.7	103.9	81.7	104.0	110.3
1983	124.3	126.0	124.1	96.9	93.0	91.1
1984	141.2	127.8	129.8	100.5	93.1	86.5
1985	180.6	142.7	159.8	141.2	89.0	80.0
1986	195.4	186.8	175.9	144.8	90.9	81.5
1987	n.a.	n.a.	182.0	151.5	90.6	81.2

n.a. = not available.

Sources: Exchange rate indices: the IMF (July 1987) index is a nominal exchange rate index adjusted by a trade-weighted index of consumer prices and exchange rates of Chile's 16 major trading partners (values correspond to December of each year); the World Bank (1987) index is a trade-weighted real exchange rate index (average year values); the Central Bank of Chile's index (Fontaine 1987) is an average real effective exchange rate, computed as the weighted average (import weights) of the wholesale price indices of Chile's major trade partners, converted into pesos at the official rate and deflated by the Chilean consumer price index (CPI).

Relative prices: For 1980–83, Central Bank of Chile, *Cuentas Nacionales.* For the 1984–87 period a special price index of nontradeable goods was constructed using 120 items of the CPI. The price of tradeables was then obtained as the residual between the GDP deflator and the nontradeables price index. The tradeables sector includes agriculture and forestry, fishing, mining, and manufacturing; the nontradeables sector includes the rest. (Values are yearly averages.)

Wage indices: The official index is that of the Chilean Instituto Nacional de Estadística. The revised index was constructed from basic nominal wage data collected by a private consulting firm from a large sample of almost 4,000 firms covering a variety of firm sizes, economic sectors, and regions; the data are weighted by total national sectoral employment figures.

tradeables sector has had an increase of almost 2 percentage points.[25] These increases are related to an increase in the amount of productive factors and to a relatively faster growth in productivity. The export sector and the tradeables sector have increased their share of nominal GDP by more than 12 percentage points, reflecting the relatively larger amount of income perceived by these sectors. One part of this increase is again due to the use of a larger quantity of productive factors; another part is due to a reversal of the internal terms-of-trade

---

25. Arellano (1988) has previously used this procedure for the export sector.

Figure 3.3 Chile: real exchange rate indices, 1982–1986

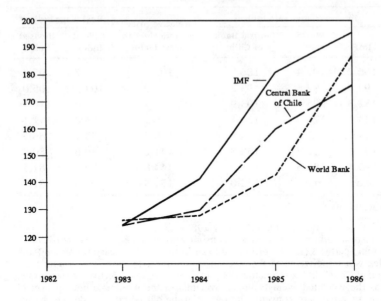

deterioration experienced by the tradeables sector during the period when the exchange rate was fixed in nominal terms. However, an important part corresponds to the large intersectoral income redistribution. Given that the state copper mines account for around 36 percent of total exports, the public sector has captured a significant percentage of this redistribution.

Although there is consensus on the key role that real devaluation plays in any structural adjustment program oriented toward expansion of exports and tradeables in general, there is little agreement on how to measure real exchange rate changes;[26] different indices can produce substantially different results (table 3.19 and figure 3.3). Yet if the level of the real effective exchange rate is not known precisely, how can a consistent adjustment program be designed and evaluated?

Table 3.19 and figure 3.3 trace the Chilean real exchange rate indices calculated by the IMF, the World Bank, and the Chilean central bank. Sizable discrepancies are observed among these indices for the years 1985 and 1986. However, there is greater agreement among the indices for the overall period 1980–86. The real devaluation observed in 1986 with respect to the 1980–81 average was 95 percent by the IMF index, 87 percent by the World Bank index,

---

26. For an excellent discussion of this issue see Edwards (1989a).

and 76 percent by the central bank's index. For the same period, real wages (according to the Chilean Instituto Nacional de Estadística) have fallen by 9 percent to 10 percent (table 3.19, column 5). It is hard to see how a reduction of real wages of 10 percent could generate a real devaluation of 80 percent.[27] Moreover, during the 1980–86 period, average labor productivity has grown by 2.0 percent annually in agriculture and mining and fallen by 2.0 percent annually in the industrial sector (Arellano 1988). How then has the Chilean economy achieved an increase in its level of international competitiveness on the order of 80 percent?

A more consistent relationship between the real exchange rate and the real wage is obtained by using the relative price of tradeables and nontradeables (P_T/P_N) and a revised index of real wages (table 3.19). It is observed that on the alternative concept the real devaluation achieved over the whole of the adjustment process to date has been closer to 50 percent and the contraction of real wages closer to 20 percent. In other words, the greater part of the large real devaluation has been achieved by a significant decrease in the unit cost of production factors, which has come about not through increases in productivity, but through a fall in the incomes of these factors, specifically labor. Up to 1987, the maintenance of depressed real wages[28] was a key factor sustaining the real devaluation.

Public-Sector Policies

As pointed out previously, the central government and the overall public sector were in surplus prior to the adjustment process. These were the outcome of a far-reaching fiscal reform implemented in 1975, consisting of several principal elements (Arellano and Marfán 1987, Larraín 1988). On the revenue side, taxes were fully indexed with respect to inflation (using a monthly CPI indexation and a special unit tax index adjusted by the CPI); this practically eliminated the Olivera-Tanzi effect. A 20 percent value-added tax was applied to almost all goods, including imports. Enforcement of this tax is relatively easy, and this led to a marked reduction in tax evasion. In addition, the tax system was greatly

---

27. Econometric estimation of (markup) price equations for the Chilean economy yields coefficients in a 2:1 ratio for wages and the exchange rate (Jadresic 1985).

28. The unemployment–real wages relationship during the Chilean adjustment process was as follows. The sharp contraction of domestic expenditure in 1982–83 generated a high level of Keynesian unemployment (over 24 percent during 1982–85), which induced a sustained contraction in real wages. The persistence of this depressed situation contributed to lower levels of investment (see table 3.15), thus transforming the Keynesian unemployment into classical unemployment. Then the sustained lower level of real wages contributed in classical fashion to the reduction of unemployment (see table 3.6) through employment growth; for a complete review of these issues see Meller (1989).

Table 3.20 Chile: selected public payroll expenditures as share of total government wage bill, selected years (percentages)

Category	1970	1975	1980	1983
Health	8.9	6.4	7.7	7.9
Education	13.1	12.1	12.8	11.9
Defense	10.2	13.6	15.6	16.0

Source: Scheetz (1987).

simplified, and some special taxes such as the capital gains tax and the wealth tax were eliminated. The previous system had been so complex and the number of special tax cases so great that "the 'general' case was simply another special case" (J. Cauas, cited in Arellano and Marfán 1987).

Meanwhile public expenditures were severely reduced (Larraín 1988) through a sharp reduction of public payroll expenditures from 20 percent of GDP in 1971–72 to 15 percent in 1975 and 12 percent in 1981 (public employment was reduced by 30 percent over this period) and through elimination of subsidies to 260 firms that had been expropriated by the Socialist government and were reprivatized (these subsidies were equivalent to 9.5 percent of GDP in 1973). There were also profound changes in the principles by which the remaining public enterprises were managed: these firms were to become self-financing and profit-maximizing, with great freedom to set their own prices.

During the adjustment process the fiscal deficit increased as a percentage of GDP (table 3.8), but by 1987 there was a surplus. This performance is quite remarkable, since during this period the government had to accommodate the social security reform of 1981, the increase in interest payments related to public absorption of private debts, and the decrease in tax revenues related to the reduction of overall economic activity.[29] The social security reform of 1981 transformed most of the state-administered, pay-as-you-go civil pension fund into a system of privately administered and capitalized pension funds, financed by a 10 percent compulsory tax on wages and salaries, revenues from which are transferred directly to the funds. In this way, the public sector has kept the current pension obligations while losing most of the contributions. This reform has generated an additional annual fiscal deficit of 3 percent to 4 percent of GDP, which will start declining only in the year 2000 (World Bank 1987). Meanwhile there has been a sharp increase in interest payments on the public debt, especially that part related to the external debt, from 0.5 percent of GDP in 1981 to 3.2 percent in 1985 (Larraín 1988). In the Chilean case it could be said that

---

29. A tax reform bill was also passed in 1984 and reduced marginal income tax rates, but its full implementation began only in 1987.

**Table 3.21   Chile: estimates of total defense expenditures, selected
years** (percentages of GDP)

Source	1970	1975	1980	1983
Official sources	n.a.	4.6	3.4	3.6
SIPRI[a]	2.0	3.9	7.4	9.8
Scheetz (1987)	4.4	8.7	7.2	6.8

a. Stockholm International Peace Research Institute.

Sources: See Larraín (1988) for specific references.

the usual causality has been reversed, as it is the current account deficit that has generated the increase in the fiscal deficit.

These extra fiscal expenditures were accommodated by several means. First, the wage bill of the central government was reduced from 7.8 percent of GDP in 1981–82 to 5.8 percent in 1985. Public pensions, which were fully indexed to inflation, were permanently reduced from their 1985 level by 1 percent of GDP. Total public social expenditures (primarily health, education, and housing) have been reduced by around 20 percent in per capita terms. On the other side of the ledger, government revenues were increased by the devaluation and by the privatization process; taxes and transfers to the central government due to operations of public enterprises increased by more than 2 percent of GDP from 1981 to 1985.

Tables 3.20 and 3.21 provide a short breakdown of public-sector expenditures. It is clear that defense expenditures increased during the military regime, whereas health and education outlays fell. Total expenditures on defense (including imports of arms) increased from around 3 percent of GDP in 1970 to around 7 percent to 8 percent in 1983. The official figures may understate actual defense spending; Scheetz (1987) points out that "government reporting has moved many Ministry of Defense–controlled institutions under the accounting responsibility of the Ministry of Hacienda or Public Enterprises, thus making it appear that military expenditures were declining, when in fact the opposite was the case."

The latest (1984) tax reform introduced several measures that have had the effect of moving the tax system about halfway from income taxation toward expenditure taxation (Arellano and Marfán 1987). These measures included tax credits for a wide variety of savings (including deposits and equity shares), reduction of corporate profit taxes, and reduction of marginal income tax rates. All these reforms, however, have produced a trend toward a more regressive revenue base.

Table 3.22 presents data on the changes in composition of Chilean tax revenues. Direct taxes, especially property taxes, have fallen as a share of total

Table 3.22 Chile: composition of tax revenues, selected years
(percentages of total revenues)

	1970	1975	1980	1985
Direct taxes	30.3	34.7	27.9	15.9
Personal and corporate income taxes	15.0	20.6	20.0	12.9
Property taxes	3.1	9.5	0.6	0.7
Indirect taxes[a]	42.4	52.9	51.0	73.6
Goods and services	35.7	42.2	46.7	65.1
International trade	6.7	10.7	7.4	15.7
Social security contributions	27.3	12.4	21.1	10.5

a. From 1976 on a negative component corresponding to rebates on value-added taxes is included in total indirect taxes.

Source: Larraín (1988).

taxation. Income tax revenues in 1985 represented only about 3 percent of GDP. Indirect taxes, on the other hand, have increased their share of the total. The value-added tax collected just under 15 percent of GDP, whereas revenues from taxes on international trade exceeded 3 percent of GDP in 1985. Social security contributions as a share of total taxation have been reduced by nearly two-thirds since 1970.

Privatization

Since 1973 Chile has experienced four separate privatization episodes, two of which involved the reprivatization of entities previously expropriated by the Socialist government.[30] The first reprivatization episode occurred in 1974, when 257 firms and some 3,700 farms that had been illegally seized by the Socialist government or taken over by their workers were quickly returned to their previous owners. These restitutions involved no monetary transactions, and the owners were requested not to initiate legal claims against the new government. The first privatization episode occurred in 1974–78 and included those firms and banks that had been acquired by the Socialist government to constitute the

---

30. The use of the terms "privatization" and "reprivatization" here follows conventional usage in Chile: firms divested after previously being acquired by the state through purchase are said to be "privatized," whereas divested firms that were previously seized by the state without compensation are said to be "reprivatized." For a more detailed review of this subject see Foxley (1982), Hachette and Lüders (1988), Larraín (1988), Morán (1989), and Marcel (1989).

so-called social property sector (*area de propiedad social*). The government received $543 million from the sale of these reprivatized banks and firms (see Larraín 1988 for details); it has been estimated that the public sector provided a 30 percent subsidy on this divestiture (Foxley 1982).[31] Most of these firms were bought with a 10 percent to 20 percent down payment, with CORFO (a public agency) providing credit for the balance. Concentration of property in a relatively small number of hands was encouraged (through the sale of large packages of shares or even 100 percent of a company), on the assumption that in this way the divested firms would command a higher price. Bidding was the main divestiture procedure used. Many of these firms and banks ended up in 1983 as part of the new "odd" sector, and consequently went through a second reprivatization process.

That process was implemented in 1984–86. The net worth of the "odd" sector firms and banks has been estimated at around $1.1 billion (equivalent to approximately 6 percent of annual GDP in that period; Hachette and Lüders 1988), and the public subsidy has been estimated at over 50 percent (see Marcel 1989 for references). In this reprivatization a different set of divestiture procedures was used: "popular capitalism,"[32] stock exchange, and bidding among prequalified buyers. All of these transactions (except those in the "popular capitalism" program) required 100 percent cash down payments. Dissemination of ownership was a clear objective.

The most important privatizations, in terms of total net worth, have been those involving the traditional state-owned enterprises (SOEs). This process was begun in 1986. The list of firms privatized includes most of the public utilities (electricity, telephone, telecommunications) as well as the national airline and others. The total net worth of programmed SOE divestitures is approximately $3.6 billion (Hachette and Lüders 1988).

The usual arguments for divestiture of SOEs are not valid in the Chilean case since, in the wake of the public-sector adjustment measures imposed earlier, the SOEs had surpluses (an indicator of their being efficiently administered) and were transferring resources to the central government. In addition, these firms were structured so as to be self-financing; therefore, in general they could not

---

31. Hachette and Lüders (1988) consider that the low sale prices for these firms and banks relative to their book values corresponded to the relatively high interest rate then prevailing in the domestic capital market.

32. Under "popular capitalism," the government sold the shares of "odd" sector companies at prices below their market value, providing 95 percent of the credit at zero real interest. Buyers could deduct from their income taxes up to 20 percent of the total value of the transaction the following year. Buyers facing a marginal tax rate equal to or higher than 30 percent got a tax credit greater than their down payment. In short, the government paid the buyer to acquire the shares. Given these benefits, there was a limit on the amount of shares one individual could buy.

Table 3.23 Proceeds from divestiture of UK and Chilean state-owned enterprises (percentages)[a]

	Proceeds from divestiture	
Country and period	As percentage of GDP	As percentage of government revenues
United Kingdom (1980–84)	0.21	0.5
United Kingdom (1985–87)	0.85	2.0
Chile (1986–88)	1.87	5.5

a. Average annual flows for the period.

Source: Marcel (1989).

have a negative impact upon the fiscal deficit.[33] The rationale for divestment of the SOEs was that of reducing the size of the public sector.[34] Several different procedures were used: "institutional capitalism," under which the private social security funds were allowed to buy limited quantities of stocks; "workers' capitalism," under which employees of the SOEs were given incentives to buy shares of their companies at subsidized prices and using their severance payment savings; and "traditional capitalism," consisting of offerings of shares on the stock exchange and auctioning to prequalified agents. Sales of the privatized SOEs have reached $1.1 billion, and the subsidy provided by the public sector has been estimated at greater than 50 percent (Marcel 1989). All transactions have required a 100 percent cash down payment, and again a clear objective has been to disseminate property, this time even among foreign investors.

Marcel (1989) has compared the UK and Chilean privatization experiences and shown that, in relative terms, the annual flow of revenues generated by the Chilean SOE divestment process has been more than twice as large and much more rapid than in the United Kingdom (table 3.23). These figures also indicate the key role played by SOE divestiture in balancing the Chilean fiscal budget.

Several criticisms have been leveled at the latest wave of SOE privatizations. Questions have been raised about the manner in which certain operations have been divested; for example, in one SOE the private-sector participation was increased from 16 percent to 49 percent by declaring that part of the public shares had null value. Another SOE transferred its debt to CORFO and was then privatized with a highly attractive debt-equity ratio. It is also claimed that

---

33. Indeed, only if the central government collected more in tax revenues from more efficient privatized SOEs than it had received previously from them would there be a positive impact on the fiscal deficit.

34. As Kay and Thompson have pointed out with respect to the British divestiture process, any goal that could actually be achieved was used as an argument for privatization by its proponents (cited by Marcel 1989).

"popular capitalism" has really been a free gift to high-income groups (those affected by marginal tax rates of at least 30 percent). Critics have asked why these agents were selected as potential buyers and not the unemployed or those who had suffered most severely during the adjustment process. Another suggested alternative would have been to use the proceeds to create an unemployment compensation fund. The decision to allow foreign investors to participate in the divestiture process has also been criticized. Foreigners were allowed to use Chilean external debt certificates, available at a 30 percent to 40 percent discount on the secondary market, which the central bank then redeemed at par value. In this way, it is argued, foreign investors received a double subsidy: on the domestic price of the assets themselves and on the (devalued) exchange rate. Does foreign investment require such large incentives to come to Chile? In fact, there has been relatively active participation by foreign investors, who have acquired, among other assets, 40 percent and 51 percent of the two largest private social security funds. The usual argument for allowing foreign direct investment is that it introduces new technology, new machinery, and new know-how, and opens new export markets. One may well ask which of these is being provided by the foreign buyers in this case.

Another problem is that divestment of the SOEs has been so rapid that there has not been time to establish a regulatory framework within which the natural monopolies among them will operate. Neither is it clear what role the large institutional investors such as the private social security funds will have.

Finally, the fiscal impact of privatization has been insufficiently addressed. Sale of an SOE that is recording surpluses has both present and future effects. The traditional fiscal accounting of classifying SOE sales "above the line" generates a double distortion: it artificially reduces an existing fiscal deficit, and it ignores the long-run economic effects of divestment connected to the reduction of productive government assets. In a country where SOEs were created by the public sector, have belonged to the public sector for 40 years or more, have an image of being efficient, and have been privatized at a 50 percent discount over a very short span of time without any public debate on the matter, some uncertainty about the permanence of the divestitures seems natural. The existence of a few questionable privatization operations generates additional doubts about the whole process. On the other hand, the wide dissemination of ownership (direct and indirect, through pension funds and the like) both of the privatized SOEs and of the reprivatized "odd" sector companies creates a constituency that is likely to be opposed to any reversals.

The main lessons of Chilean privatization seem to be the following. Privatization should not waste national savings through subsidized sales. There should be some controls in place to ensure that divested SOEs keep generating future savings and keep investing. In this way the government can avoid future public losses from intervention in the affairs of bankrupt privatized firms; this will also help avoid a new reprivatization process. The private sector's help in achieving this goal would be useful.

Conclusions

The Chilean experience indicates that it is not desirable to distinguish between good and bad trade gaps on the basis of whether they are generated by the private or the public sector. A large, unsustainable, and nonfinanceable current account deficit, no matter which sector produced it, will lead eventually to an unavoidable adjustment.

The costs of adjustment have been quite heavy. The Chilean experience shows that overly austere adjustment policies in an economy that is neither perfectly flexible nor instantaneously adaptable can generate unnecessary secondary adjustment costs that are as large as the necessary primary costs. Even in the presence of a relatively large real devaluation, export expansion may be slow, and in Chile it took several years for export expansion to compensate for the contraction in nontradeables production generated by the adjustment process.

The key factor in generating an effective and sustained real devaluation is contraction of real wages. The Swedish experience of the 1980s shows that workers will cooperate voluntarily to increase their country's international competitiveness when an appropriate institutional framework exists to ensure that they will participate in the benefits. In the Chilean case, the workers were unable to express their preferences in relation to the real wage contraction process, nor have they shared in the benefits of export expansion.

In the recovery stage of the Chilean adjustment process, domestic private investors have been slower than the public sector to react. Public investment took the lead in the earlier stages of the recovery, foreign investment came later on, and only when the previous GDP peak had been reached did domestic private investment regain its previous importance.

Chile's investment in its international reputation through full and punctual interest payments on its external debt and implementation of a stringent adjustment process has had an effect only on the multilateral organizations. The commercial banks have provided words of praise but no access to medium-run voluntary credit.

In the privatization process, the government should not play the role of Santa Claus to high-income groups and foreigners. Some government regulation is needed to avoid a repetition of the private sector milking the divested SOEs as it previously misused external credit. The process of learning from these past mistakes has been a very costly one for Chilean society.

Acknowledgments

Comments by John Williamson, Barbara Stallings, Francisco Rosende, Manuel Marfán, Esteban Jadresic, and Vittorio Corbo are gratefully acknowledged. The author would also like to acknowledge the highly efficient research assistance provided by Fernando Lefort and the excellent editing by Michael Treadway.

Peru

Pedro-Pablo Kuczynski

The simple answer to the question of how much adjustment has happened in Peru in the 1980s is "not much."[35] Peruvians have suffered dramatically in recent years from an inflation rate that has accelerated to perhaps 3,000 percent annually, and from the related collapse of the economy: according to official statistics, GNP plummeted by over 20 percent in the two years 1987 and 1988. (Table 3.24 summarizes recent economic performance in Peru.) But this misery was not the result of economic adjustment. Rather it was the delayed consequence of the government's attempt in 1986 and 1987 to stimulate the economy through public expenditure and wage increases while freezing prices and neglecting to provide fiscal resources sufficient to match the increase in spending.

Peruvian Economic Policy in the 1980s

The international reserves built up through the at first gradual and then almost total suspension of external debt service, beginning in 1984—a year before the July 1985 inauguration of President Alan García—were enough to finance a consumption and import boom. GNP rebounded, again according to official data, by an average of about 8 percent annually in 1986 and 1987. Eventually, however, the reserves ran out, and inflation intensified because of an increasing fiscal gap as well as domestic capacity bottlenecks: the consumption boom had failed to stimulate investment partly because the economy was operating in an environment of overregulation and low business confidence.

The García government attempted to control inflation in part by keeping the currency overvalued. This policy led to a sharp decline in export earnings and a further erosion of reserves. The government also froze prices, particularly those of fuels, electricity, and basic foodstuffs, all of which are produced or marketed by government-owned companies. By mid-1988 prices of these goods were only one-third their mid-1985 levels in real terms. The result was an increase in the

---

35. See, for example, the description in Crook (1989, 9–10) and Dornbusch and Edwards (1989).

Pedro-Pablo Kuczynski is Chairman of First Boston International and a managing director of the First Boston Corporation. He was formerly Minister of Energy and Mines for Peru and President and Chief Executive Officer of Halco (Mining) Inc.

Table 3.24   Peru: summary economic data, selected years

	1980	1985	1989[a]
GNP per capita (current dollars)	1,716	1,500	1,300
Inflation[b] (percentages)	69	163	2,775
Merchandise exports f.o.b. (billions of dollars)	4.0	3.0	2.6
Merchandise imports c.i.f. (billions of dollars)	2.5	2.0	2.0
Public-sector deficit (percentage of GNP)	4.0	2.4	6.5[c]

a. Estimated.

b. December-to-December change in the consumer price index.

c. For 1988.

Sources: World Bank (1989a); Inter-American Development Bank; IMF, *International Financial Statistics,* various issues.

public-sector deficit equivalent to 7 percent of GNP, on top of the gradual erosion of tax revenues due to rapid inflation. The yawning fiscal gap, together with public expectations of an opening of the price dam (*desembalse*), fueled wage and price escalation.

The fiscal stimulus and its impact on foreign reserves were considerably augmented by the presence of a multiple exchange rate system. This system, in place until 1988, was designed to stimulate some activities and discourage others, according to a mythology developed by the government's economic advisers from theories discredited long ago even in Latin America. Traditional exports, for example, were considered already prosperous enough and were discouraged, whereas basic imports—food, fuel, and basic industrial inputs—had to be kept cheap. The normal tendency of such a system, aided by bureaucratic corruption, was to have more inti payments than receipts at the more depreciated rates. Consequently, by 1987–88 the system was injecting additional liquidity into the economy at a rate of about 3 percent of GNP. This added greatly to inflation and expectations of a massive *desembalse*.

When the *desembalse* came, however, in September 1988, it proved insufficient given the enormous amount of adjustment required. The subsequent rise in domestic prices—about 200 percent in the following two months—triggered a collapse in purchasing power. When the central bank tried to offset the inadequacy of the fiscal measures by keeping an artificial lid on interest rates, there ensued a corresponding collapse in credit. The result was general economic breakdown. Tax revenues also plummeted both because of the sharp contraction in production and because of the lag in tax collections behind inflation, from about 12 percent of GNP to 4 percent or less in mid-1989. As a result, despite the dramatic drop in demand, hyperinflation continued at a rate of about 30 percent monthly.

In late 1989, only the deep economic depression and vastly subsidized public-enterprise prices enabled the government to hold on to an exchange rate that was probably overvalued by a factor of three. International reserves staged a modest recovery earlier in the year (as noted below) only because of the lack of domestic purchasing power, which has brought imports in real terms down to their levels of 15 years ago. On a purely static basis, at the end of September 1989, purchasing power parity would have demanded a further official exchange rate devaluation of 250 percent, whereas at the end of 1987 the official rate was in approximate equilibrium. If the necessary price adjustments are factored in (such as a tenfold increase in utility rates and a fivefold increase in gasoline prices), the change needed in the exchange rate is probably on the order of 400 percent to 500 percent. The big losers under the present disequilibria are the rural areas, where the poorest segments of the population live; the needed adjustments, on the other hand, will obviously impact hard on the urban areas, which are the principal beneficiaries of the present massive subsidies.

How this explosive situation will eventually resolve itself is at present unclear. In late 1989, thanks to the dramatic decline in imports, the central bank has rebuilt its international reserves to about $1 billion. The government used these resources to stimulate another revival of consumption in time for the November 1989 municipal elections; it hopes to carry the stimulus through until April 1990, when presidential elections are scheduled. A possible but by no means certain outcome is a repeat on a smaller scale of the 1986–87 cycle of temporary renewal of modest growth followed by even higher inflation.

Some observers have made much of the apparent link between Peru's enormous economic problems and its external debt. There is indeed a link but its importance is more questionable than some have claimed. At the time of García's inauguration the outstanding debt was about $14 billion, of which about $500 million consisted of interest arrears, against annual export earnings of about $4 billion. That is undoubtedly an unfavorable ratio, but one that is comparable with those of Chile or Brazil at the time, and better than that of Mexico (Kuczynski 1988, 13). Peru has certainly suffered, as has most of the rest of Latin America, from debt-related stagflation, but in Peru's case the problem has been made much worse by the economic path chosen by its government. The buildup of interest arrears—about $6.5 billion since the beginning of the García administration—represents an increase in the debt without Peru getting anything from it. Further, by not servicing its obligations to the World Bank (except for symbolic payments) or to the IMF, Peru has cut itself off from the only possible remaining sources of external credit.

At present the arrears (principal and interest) to the World Bank and the IMF amount to some $1.4 billion; a small additional sum is due to the Inter-American Development Bank. All three institutions have made repeated but unsuccessful efforts to arrive at a settlement in exchange for modest payments from Peru. Arrears to these institutions are expected to reach some $2 billion by July 1990, when a new government is scheduled to take office. That government will inherit a total foreign debt of about $22 billion, of which $8 billion will consist of interest arrears, not counting the approximately $1 billion owed to the IMF. By then Peru might no longer even be a member of the IMF, which was considering its expulsion until a temporary agreement was reached in principle at the end of 1989. Such a move would automatically entail exclusion from the World Bank—an unprecedented step.[36]

The Origins of the Crisis

The real question is not whether there has been adjustment in Peru, but rather how the country got into its present desperate straits. The origins of Peru's predicament go back at least 20 years. The military regime of General Juan Velasco, which had come to power in a coup in October 1968, was seeking a *raison d'être*, as the economy was recovering briskly from the balance of payments crisis of 1967–68 (see Kuczynski 1977, chapter 8). It therefore promptly seized the Peruvian operations of Standard Oil of New Jersey (the present Exxon Corp.). That act set the government's course for the next few years. It actively promoted Marxist unions among the mine workers, teachers, and the existing bank workers' union. Provincial universities created under the first administration of Fernando Belaunde were greatly expanded; this expansion, combined with the lack of jobs for graduates, provided a breeding ground for revolutionary groups, out of which the leadership of the present Sendero Luminoso emerged. Restrictive investment and tax legislation was enacted, and Peru became the nationalist leader of the Andean Pact. Finally, many enterprises, including two of the three large foreign mining companies active in Peru, were taken over by the state without significant compensation. A complex web of regulations and price controls tended to worsen rather than improve the already appalling pattern of income distribution (see Webb 1977).

All of this occurred amid the fawning that business leaders usually reserve for regimes they fear, together with the plaudits of some foreign bankers, who showered the government with loans—the origin of much of the country's

---

36. Cuba was not expelled from the World Bank but left voluntarily in 1960; it stayed in the IMF until 1964.

present debt—until serious financial strains developed in 1973. A second military government in 1975 tried to organize economic recovery, but it was not until drastic fiscal measures were taken in 1978, combined with the commodity boom of the late 1970s, that the reforms succeeded. The state apparatus constructed under the Velasco regime was left untouched, however, and indeed it continued in place into the second Belaunde administration, which was triumphantly elected in 1980. Attempts at the beginning of the second Belaunde government to liberalize the previous pattern—for example, by bringing in foreign investors to develop large new mining projects (e.g., Tintaya), by bringing in new oil companies to explore, and by deregulation—were either quashed or stymied by the entrenched military heirs to the Velasco period and by the lack of resolve and the disorganization of the government majority in the Congress. Much was done to open up foreign trade and payments, but the government was ill prepared to face the twin blows of a sharp drop in export prices in 1983 and the damage from large floods in the north of the country at the same time. As the economy stagnated during the last two years of the Belaunde government, the struggle within the administration to slow inflation and reduce the budget deficit continued unresolved.

It was in this setting that Alan García, a fiery campaigner then only 36 years of age, was elected to the presidency in 1985. Again the plaudits from abroad poured in, this time from academic and media commentators rather than bankers (see, for example, Roett 1985–86), and the private-sector leadership banded together to applaud and win over the young president through a group that came to be known popularly as the "twelve apostles." When Belco, the smaller of the two foreign oil producers operating in Peru, was seized in December 1985, the reaction of the domestic business leadership was, as it had been 15 years earlier, "It can't happen to us." Economic advisers of untested credentials were cheered from the sidelines as they encouraged the new president to spend his way to prosperity, something he was naturally eager to do anyway. The honeymoon ended in July 1987 with the attempt of the García government to take over the banking system. Only massive opposition rallied by well-known author (and now presidential candidate) Mario Vargas Llosa prevented the full application of this measure; even so, the legal ownership of most banks remains unclear and this uncertainty is hampering their operations.

Setting Reform Priorities

If meaningful reform and adjustment are to take place in Peru, history shows us that much more will be needed than a package of legislated adjustment measures. Nevertheless, the first tier of emergency measures is likely to follow a logical, predictable progression, although accompanied by great difficulties at each stage.

The first step must be to curb inflation by decontrolling all prices. Fiscal revenue would then recover, since a large part of it depends on proportional fuel taxes; at the same time, since one-third of government outlays now goes to subsidize low state-enterprise prices for fuel, electricity, and basic foodstuffs, decontrol of prices would free up government expenditure for purposes more productive than subsidies. A substantial devaluation is also likely to be necessary. A major tax simplification will have to be put into effect.[37] It should be designed to raise revenue despite much lower rates by abolishing virtually all exemptions and special so-called promotional regimes. A major but difficult part of the program will be to deflate inflationary expectations and speculation through a large-scale program to increase production of foods and other basic products: initially much of the food supply program will have to come from imports if it is going to have a rapid impact on inflation. This will require foreign financing, which obviously will be extremely difficult to obtain. Another complex issue will be wage policy. Should wages be indexed to the dollar? Are adjustments that do not keep pace with inflation politically feasible? Finally, and only after inflation has been controlled, a new monetary unit should be adopted, eliminating the inti of painful memory.

The second priority is to revive investment and eventually growth. Anti-inflationary programs have often failed to rekindle growth, so that in the end wage and fiscal pressures build up again, reviving inflation. High interest rates, a necessary ingredient of the anti-inflation program, need not provoke a recession if credit mechanisms are decontrolled so that available credit is not forcibly channeled to the public sector through reserve requirements and tax-free bonds, as occurs at present in most Latin American countries. Korea, for example, currently has a growth rate of 7 percent despite real interest rates of 10 percent to 12 percent—but Korea also has gross investment equivalent to 35 percent of GNP. The investment ratio in Peru is probably 10 percent or less, which is not enough even to replenish the stock of capital, let alone allow growth. On the other hand, the Peruvian economy has much unused capacity, and therefore the revival of foreign credit could spark an initial burst of activity.

---

37. As outlined in a book in preparation by Felipe Ortiz de Zevallos and the author. At present, for example, despite import tariffs as high as 155 percent, import duties actually collected amounted to only 2 percent of GNP in 1987. A flat tariff of 15 percent or 25 percent would obviously yield far more revenue, even without counting the additional revenue due to the drastic drop in smuggling which could be expected. The same principle applies to income taxes, which also only yielded about 2 percent of GNP in 1987, before their collapse.

Both the startup of some foreign trade-related credit and the beginnings of privatization are fundamental for an initial emergency program. No revival of credit is possible, however, without a settlement of the arrears to the international agencies, the Paris Club creditors, and the commercial banks. In the case of the multilateral agencies, given the unusually large amount of arrears, the standard formulas being applied in cases of relatively small debtors such as Guyana may have to be modified, to permit capitalization initially of a large part of the interest and rescheduling of the principal over a lengthy period. These are principles that have long been accepted by the Paris Club.

There have been a number of proposals offered to other countries for dealing with their commercial bank debts: for example, to repurchase debt at a deep discount and to negotiate forgiveness of part of the loans. Such proposals, if applied to Peru's entire commercial bank debt, are likely to be counterproductive. As an illustration, if Peru tried to repurchase its bank debt at 10 cents on the dollar, following the example of Bolivia, it would in effect be paying one year's interest in advance, using up very scarce foreign exchange and at the same time cutting itself off from any new credit from the banks for a long time to come. It would be cheaper to service the interest on part of the debt, plus eventually the principal, on perhaps 20 to 25 cents per dollar of debt, and at the same time provide a zero-coupon guarantee for the entire remaining principal of 75 cents with a 30-year final maturity, in effect defeasing the whole debt. The initial cash cost to Peru would be less (about 8.5 cents on the dollar in the first year, including the 6 cents to be placed in trust for the zero-coupon guarantee of the whole debt, falling to 2.5 cents of interest only in the second year), and the cost to the banks would also be less, thus increasing the chances of a revival of trade credit.

Given the high opportunity cost of foreign exchange in the highly indebted countries, the costs and benefits of debt relief schemes have to be put on a present-value basis. Such an analysis would in most cases show that the schemes being forcibly negotiated at present make limited economic sense. By focusing on debt reduction rather than debt-*service* reduction, these schemes give the debtors limited present benefits but at great present cost to the banks.

The approximately 200 state enterprises in Peru are mostly in terrible condition and are not candidates for rapid privatization. Yet privatization is essential to mop up excess liquidity and send a clear signal to investors. The place to begin is with the sale of assets: the gasoline stations owned by Petroperu, the branches and buildings of the state-owned banks, the rights to develop long-dormant mineral deposits controlled by the state, and so on. Many of these are attractive, real-property-related assets that would attract domestic buyers. Special rebates could be given for payments made with funds demonstrably being brought back after a long stay abroad. Major legislative

Table 3.25 Peru: profile of public opinion on selected economic issues, 1989 (percentages)

	For	Against
Role of the state		
State enterprises must be sold	49	35
State must help the poor	86	8
External debt must be paid	83	15
Maintain relations with the IMF	85	3
Foreign investment		
Maintain or increase incentives	80	13
Essential for development	62	
Main problems of Peru		
Inflation	61	
Terrorism	59	
Unemployment	49	
Main cause of inflation		
Budget deficit	48	
Speculation	18	
How to reduce the budget deficit		
Improve tax enforcement	60	18
Raise taxes	20	65

Source: "Perfil del Elector." *Apoyo* (September 1988). The sample consisted of about 800 respondents in Lima and the provinces.

changes would be required, but these could be made part of the initial emergency package, as was done recently in Argentina. The few privatization initiatives that have been undertaken by the present Peruvian government, which give the plants to their employees in exchange for loans at interest rates that do not come close to covering inflation, in effect set the workers adrift without management or credit, and do not have a significant favorable impact on investors.

Privatization also has to be understood to include the wholesale elimination of bureaucratic regulation, both by the central government and at the municipal level. These regulations inhibit enterprise, which in Peru more often than not means small enterprise. The *quid pro quo* has to be to bring such small enterprises within the tax system, which they almost entirely avoid at present.

The Missing Component: Regaining Public Confidence

An essential change must take place in Peru if a program of the kind barely outlined here is to succeed: Peruvians have to believe that the state can help them instead of making their lives miserable. The economic crisis, together with the state of virtual civil war that exists in important areas of the country, has clearly changed public attitudes. The most visible proof is the standing in the polls of Mario Vargas Llosa in the runup to the 1990 presidential election (about 50 percent of the expected vote, with about 25 percent undecided); Vargas Llosa has made it clear that his program would emphasize market economics, privatization, working out a debt arrangement and an agreement with the IMF, and other similar measures. These new public attitudes are of course influenced by other factors, including the personal appeal of the candidate. However, the results of other recent polls aimed specifically at sounding public opinion on these issues (table 3.25) are telling, even if somewhat contradictory (as is to be expected in any such poll).

Only if the state uses the current crisis as an opportunity not only to overcome the country's acute financial problems but also to dramatically reorient its own role away from failed commercial ventures and into improving basic services—in education, health, and basic utilities such as water and electricity—will Peru have a chance to overcome the fundamental problems that have burdened the country for several decades. The economic debacle of recent years would not have occurred, at least not to the same degree, had these root problems been tackled sooner.

Comment

Vittorio Corbo

The need for adjustment arises when there are major imbalances on the internal and the external fronts. Internal imbalances manifest themselves as high inflation, and external imbalances as unsustainable current account deficits and balance of payments crises.

The world recession of the early 1980s was accompanied by the highest real interest rates since the Great Depression, and the sudden cutoff of commercial bank lending after August 1982 made the current account deficits that had emerged in many Latin American countries in the late 1970s and early 1980s difficult to finance. Reduction of the current account deficit requires a combination of expenditure-reducing and expenditure-switching policies. However, inappropriate incentives and weak institutions had reduced output in some countries below potential and had created substantial impediments to factor mobility and firm restructuring. In such cases structural reforms aimed at improving efficiency in the use of resources and enhancing incentives to save and invest may help the adjustment process by increasing output and putting the economy on a higher growth path. Although distortions and institutional weakness have existed in many developing countries (as well as in many industrial countries) for a long time, the payoff from reforms is especially large in a situation of reduced external financing. However, in countries with a long history of overregulation, with a small human capital base, and with major impediments to factor mobility, the adjustment program should deal with these impediments and be realistic about the feasible speed of response to reforms.

The three countries discussed in this chapter illustrate three different adjustment styles. At one extreme, Peru has avoided initiating an organized adjustment program and since early 1988 has entered into a major crisis. At the other extreme, Chile undertook a major adjustment effort in the second half of the 1970s but faced some severe macroeconomic imbalances in the early 1980s, which culminated in a major recession. Bolivia started a comprehensive adjustment effort following the hyperinflation of 1985 and was very successful in controlling inflation and laying the basis for sustainable growth despite severe external shocks: a collapse in the price of tin and payments arrears on exports of natural gas to Argentina.

Vittorio Corbo is the Division Chief of the Macroeconomic Adjustment and Growth Division in the Country Economics Department at the World Bank and Professor of Economics at the Universidad Católica de Chile.

The bulk of my remarks will be addressed to the case of Chile. Patricio Meller has presented us with a very provocative account of the Chilean adjustment experience. I find myself in agreement with a substantial part of the paper (his section on privatization in particular) and will concentrate my comments on the points of contention.

Meller is right in asserting that, when the debt crisis set in, Chile had already implemented most of the structural reforms that a large number of countries have been trying to implement in more recent years. These reforms corresponded closely to those described by John Williamson as part of the "Washington consensus." In particular, the major macroeconomic distortions were eliminated and the large public-sector deficit of 1973 (close to 30 percent of GDP) was transformed into a surplus. It therefore appears paradoxical that the country had so much trouble in the early 1980s. However, one should note that Chile, like Argentina, Uruguay, Nigeria, and Mexico, had an extremely distorted macroeconomic situation prior to the debt crisis. These distortions did not result from policies related to Washington consensus. Domestic absorption grew by 10 percent per year in real terms in the period 1979–81, and the Chilean peso appreciated in real terms following a period in which the nominal exchange rate had been fixed to reduce inflation. Wages, financial contracts, and rental payments, meanwhile, were indexed to previous inflation.

With a much-appreciated currency and a large expansion of domestic absorption, the current account deficit reached 14 percent of GDP in 1981. Following the reduction in inflation and the developing appreciation, the Chilean economy was in the middle of a boom by late 1980. However, clear signals were emerging that the economy was overheating and that the macroeconomic situation was unsustainable: in spite of record capital inflows in 1981, the domestic real interest rate took a quantum jump in the first quarter of 1981, going from 8.6 percent per year in the fourth quarter of 1980 to 36.5 percent per year in the first quarter of 1981, and it increased continuously thereafter until the devaluation of June 1982. As capital inflows began to slow in early 1982, expectations of a devaluation set in, and the further increases in the real interest rate were more than enough to start cooling off the economy. In a fully indexed economy with a fixed exchange rate, the reduction in expenditures, combined with a greatly appreciated currency, resulted in an adjustment process that was extremely costly in terms of unemployment. Thus, Chile was already in the midst of a deep recession when the debt crisis began in the last quarter of 1982. It is important to note that this recession started long before the international debt crisis and was due, in large part, to domestic causes. To make matters worse, Chile suffered significant external shocks in 1981–82, with a drop in export prices (especially copper) and a sharp increase in international real interest rates.

A careful analysis of the role of external causes and domestic policies in the Chilean crisis of 1982 clearly shows that the unsustainable expansion in expenditures was much more important than the external shock (Corbo and de Melo 1989). In June 1982, before the sudden cutoff in external borrowing, the unemployment rate had already reached 23 percent, up from only 11 percent in March 1981.

Following Corden's analysis, Meller studies how successful the macroeconomic adjustment was by considering the primary, unavoidable costs of adjustment—those resulting from the reduction in the level of expenditures required to reduce the current account deficit—and the secondary or avoidable costs that occur when adjustment is so inefficient that output drops as a result. The adjustment of 1982 must have been very inefficient, as it resulted in massive unemployment. This was due to the fact that the reduction in expenditures at the existing real exchange rate was not compatible with equilibrium in the market for nontradeables. Surprisingly, Meller does not mention the role of the real exchange rate in making the adjustment inefficient. Indeed, a real exchange rate depreciation to accompany expenditure-reducing policies is a key recommendation of the Washington consensus.

The procedure Meller utilizes to measure avoidable and unavoidable costs of adjustment seems incorrect. He mixes static with dynamic concepts, and he has an index number problem because he needs to add tradeables and nontradeables in a situation where relative prices are changing drastically. Therefore, he needs an index of relative prices to add tradeables and nontradeables in his adjustment cost equation.

To illustrate this point, consider a successful adjustment program in a small, open economy with perfectly flexible prices of nontradeables. When expenditures are reduced, a flexible real exchange rate allows the clearing of the nontradeables market; the improvement in the current account is achieved without unemployment (maintaining internal balance), while tradeable production (Y^T) increases and nontradeables production (Y^N) decreases. In Meller's measure this will result in a cost, as Y^N will drop.[38]

A proper measure requires output to be measured in units of nontradeables using a Paasche aggregator, as we know from theory that a successful adjustment should result in a higher value of output in units of nontradeables at the new real exchange rate (Dornbusch 1980, chapter 6). More important, however, is the fact that when Chile was able to reestablish a real exchange rate compatible with the macroeconomic fundamentals, the reduction in distortions of the late 1970s started to pay off with a period of sustainable growth in spite of a heavy debt burden. Therefore, the Chilean experience confirms the

---

38. The reduction in Y_T that Meller finds may be due simply to the groupings of activities he uses, which include many nontradeables within the tradeables category.

soundness of the policy recommendations of the Washington consensus. The reduction in distortions and limitations to factor mobility has a major payoff in terms of growth when the fundamentals are in place.

Bolivia illustrates the case of a very successful stabilization program based on correcting the fundamentals. Once the fiscal deficit and money growth were reduced to levels compatible with low inflation, Bolivia was able to stabilize without the need for incomes policies. The paper by Juan Cariaga provides a clear example of how to put the fundamentals in place for a successful stabilization effort. The question that remains in the case of Bolivia is where renewed growth will come from. To move to a higher growth path, conditions must exist for private investment to increase. In most adjustment programs, the increase in private investment has taken much longer than originally envisaged, and therefore growth has been disappointing. This is an important area for research.

The case of Peru shows clearly that fiscal and monetary policies have an important role to play both in restoring macroeconomic equilibrium and in creating substantial imbalances. As has been proved over and over again, expenditure expansions not matched by an increase in output are bound to result in a balance of payments crisis. If the crisis is addressed through the use of trade restrictions and multiple exchange rates instead of through expenditure-reducing policies, large inefficiencies will result and the balance of payments crisis is merely postponed.

Comment

Barbara B. Stallings

Adjustment in Latin America cannot be understood simply as an economic phenomenon. The political and social aspects, both domestic and international, must also be taken into account to explain the extent to which adjustment has occurred in a given country. The papers by Meller on Chile, Kuczynski on Peru, and Cariaga on Bolivia provide an opportunity to consider several key socio-political issues facing the adjustment process as we move into the 1990s.

Barbara B. Stallings is Professor of Political Science and former Director of the Latin American Studies Program at the University of Wisconsin-Madison. She is the author of Class Conflict and Economic Development in Chile, 1958–73 and Banker to the Third World: US Portfolio Investment in Latin America, 1900–86; coeditor of Debt and Democracy in Latin America; and a contributor to Economic Crisis and Policy Choice: The Politics of Economic Adjustment in Developing Countries.

A first issue is the relationship between economic policy and the political system or regime. In a recent article, Robert Kaufman and I suggested that there has been a fairly close link between these two sets of variables during the 1980s (Stallings and Kaufman 1989). We discuss three types of political system: authoritarian (Chile and Mexico), established democracies (Colombia, Venezuela, and Costa Rica), and transitional democracies (Brazil, Argentina, Peru, and Uruguay). Only the authoritarian regimes, we found, were able to make substantial progress toward both stabilization and structural reform. The established democracies did about as well as the authoritarian regimes with regard to stabilization but accomplished little structural change, whereas the transitional democracies succeeded at neither. The papers under consideration here enable us to go further in at least two senses: they provide in-depth case studies of the extreme cases on the spectrum, and they add a third case, Bolivia, that does not fit our model.

Patricio Meller's excellent paper points to a number of problems in the Chilean adjustment experience, including policy overkill and regressive distributional consequences. Nevertheless, his data clearly indicate that adjustment has occurred since 1982. The fiscal accounts and the balance of payments are within sustainable equilibrium, inflation is low (by both historical and cross-national standards), and substantial growth is taking place. The question that leaps to mind is whether this adjustment could have taken place under a multiparty democracy, especially a newly reestablished (transitional) one. A key factor in Meller's analysis, which affected various individual components of the stabilization process, is the fall in real wages. Was that a necessary component, or could the adjustment have been financed in another way? If necessary, could the adjustment have been achieved under democratic conditions? If so, how? Even more problematic is the issue of structural reforms. The Chilean liberalizations and privatizations were begun in the 1970s but extended in the period after 1982. These changes had a tremendous negative impact on large parts of the society. Comparative historical analysis suggests that they probably could not have been brought about had the government not had resort to almost total power.

The Peruvian case is the opposite side of the coin. As Pedro-Pablo Kuczynski points out, the government of Alan García achieved very little stabilization other than a brief drop in inflation in 1986. By 1988–89, of course, an automatic form of stabilization had imposed itself. I agree that the domestic policies followed by the García government have been extremely damaging to the economy, including the very groups that the government wanted to help. Inflation in late 1989 was running at about 6,000 percent annually, while GDP was contracting at a 20 percent annual rate. But two other questions need to be raised: why were those policies followed, and why was there no stabilization during the previous government (of which Kuczynski was part)? One answer to the first question, suggested by Kuczynski, is the incompetence of García's economic team. Incompetence there certainly was, but it is not the whole answer. The political setting also needs to be taken into account. The government's perceived need to prove that democracy was responsive to the population's material interests, especially in light of the increasing power of Sendero Luminoso, certainly helped explain the decision to raise wages and government expenditures in 1986–87. Similarly, under the government of Fernando Belaunde in 1980–85, the failure to stabilize or to bring about significant structural reform must be understood in the context of the politics of a multiparty democracy.

This failure to stabilize or to achieve structural reforms under Peruvian democracy, and the success in doing so in authoritarian Chile, suggests a link between political regime and economic policy. It is at this point that the Bolivian case is of special interest. Juan Cariaga points to what he calls a "national consensus" around stabilization, but he does not explain how or why this occurred. He says, "a people can determine what is best for them," but surely most cases suggest that people are more concerned with short-run costs than with possible long-term benefits. We need to know a lot more about this crucial case in which a new democracy was able to stabilize the economy and implement many structural reforms. Two factors suggest themselves as partial explanations in the Bolivian case: the breaking of the miners' union as a result of the fall in tin prices and the closing of many mines, and the cessation of debt payments, which allowed the results of the sacrifices to be legitimately portrayed as going to the Bolivians themselves rather than to foreign bankers (this is Jeffrey Sachs's explanation). What role did these factors play, and what were the other political prerequisites for the success of the stabilization effort? Furthermore, to what extent did hyperinflation make the adjustment process more likely?

In considering the relationship between political regime and success of adjustment, I do not in any way intend to provide a justification for authoritarianism. Quite the contrary, it is clear that authoritarian governments can wreak havoc on their economies as well as on their societies; we need only look at Chile in the 1973–82 period. Furthermore, authoritarianism alone does not guarantee adjustment. Instead my aim is to raise two questions. If certain changes (especially structural reforms) can only be achieved under an authoritarian regime, to what extent does this diminish their desirability? More important, if the changes are considered sufficiently desirable, what can be learned about ways of bringing them about under democratic governments?

A second important sociopolitical aspect of the adjustment process concerns privatization. A key question here is whether there exists a domestic private sector capable of replacing the state in the activities in question, or whether it is necessary to sell public firms to foreign capital, with the additional problems this creates in certain sectors. The three papers also provide some interesting evidence on this topic. Meller says that the private sector in Chile was very slow to invest (except in speculative activities). In fact, the large conglomerates behaved so poorly that the very government that had fostered their development ended up intervening to save them in 1983. Peru tried to privatize under Belaunde but failed. Kuczynski argues that this was because of military interests, but there was also the problem that no one wanted to buy the firms. Cariaga reports that privatization was one area in which the Bolivian government failed to follow the "Washington consensus"; his discussion then proceeds to foreign direct investment, leading one to assume that this is the type of privatization he had in mind.

Privatization is a political as well as economic issue. For example, Meller wonders why Chilean privatization went forward so fast in the late 1980s. The answer is political: to create supporters for pro-government candidates and to reduce the power that any future democratic government would have. The study by Bela Balassa et al. (1986) is much too positive about the benefits of privatization and too lax on the costs. As many participants at this conference pointed out, privatization does not by itself eliminate either subsidies or inefficiencies. At the same time, the inequities produced by privatization cannot be ignored. The regressive redistribution of income under the military government, documented by the recent publication by the Chilean statistics institute (Instituto Nacional de Estadísticas, 1989) is not coincidental.

A third point on the political-economic adjustment, which is highlighted by all three papers, concerns external debt. The three cases present interesting combinations with respect to the behavior of lenders as well as borrowers. Among borrowers, the three have distinct patterns: Chile with stabilization, structural reform, and prompt debt service; Bolivia with stabilization, partial structural reform, cessation of at least some payments, and repurchase of debt at a very deep discount; Peru with neither stabilization nor structural reform (of the type desired by bankers!) and nonpayment of debt service. Nevertheless, despite the differences in debtor behavior, the lenders have reacted in surprisingly similar ways. The multilateral agencies, within their particular perspectives, have tried to be helpful. Both Meller and Cariaga discuss this explicitly. In the Peruvian case, there were multiple efforts to "regain" Peru as a client. In all cases, however, the banks have reacted negatively. This might be expected with respect to Bolivia and especially Peru. But Chile? Meller says Chile's continued growth depends on regaining access to "voluntary" lending. Will this come about for Latin America's "best" debtor, and what are the implications (for Chile as well as other debtor countries) if it does not? What are the politics of the debt crisis?

In general, there is the need to consider these and the rest of John Williamson's policy issues in a broad political-economic context rather than concentrating only on technical issues (for such an analysis see Nelson 1990).

Comment

Richard Webb

My comment will focus on the paper on Peru. My problem, of course, is that I find it hard to disagree with most of what Pedro-Pablo Kuczynski says. I share his basic view of the situation, how it arose, and what has to be done.

Let me begin by returning to John Williamson's introductory paper, which laid out the "Washington consensus," the basic Washington recipe for adjustment. My main reaction to the paper was, "Is this all the help we are going to get from Washington in terms of guidelines?" Washington is, after all, the world's think tank for macroeconomic policy. We are given a list of some policy instruments, together with, in a few cases, some indication of a number—how much real devaluation is needed, for instance—but really very little else in terms of specific numbers. Yet drawing up an adjustment program is essentially a matter of getting down to numbers.

I remember coming to Washington to look for similar guidance some years ago. In July 1980 I had just been appointed to the Peruvian central bank, and since I had spent the years before that wandering around the *favelas* of Rio and the backwoods of northeastern Brazil, I wasn't at all up to date on macroeconomics. So I went to visit some friends at the IMF to get the Washington consensus of that time. The recommendation that I remember most was one given to me forcibly by a friend at the Fund who had a senior position in the Western Hemisphere Department. His advice was to forget about devaluation. Countries can't devalue in real terms, he said. When I hesitated before swallowing this dictum, he summoned a staff econometrician who informed me, politely, that he had proved it.

That particular notion has very little to do with the Washington consensus of today. For that matter, if one looks back at the different consensuses of the last 10 to 20 years, one ends up asking with each new consensus not only, "Is that all?" but, "How long will this one last?" More to the point, "Will it last at least through its application in my own country?"

Since Kuczynski has briefed us on the current situation in Peru, and John Williamson has sketched the broad outline of the kind of consensus program that might be adopted today, I propose a little exercise: let's develop a program for Peru. Let us turn back the clock one year from the time of this conference, to November 1988, and imagine such a program being put in place at that time.

Richard Webb is coauthor of a forthcoming official history of the World Bank. He was Governor of the Central Bank of Peru and previously served as a staff economist at the World Bank.

Let us then compare the objectives of our imaginary program with the actual numbers one year later.

With an inflation rate of 100 percent in September, Peru in late 1988 is experiencing true hyperinflation by at least one definition. Production has fallen in the previous 12 months by over 15 percent. And, as everyone knows, Peru is not paying its debts.

According to the consensus interpretation, the main problem is fiscal. The fiscal deficit, including central bank foreign-exchange and interest subsidies, is around 8 percent of GDP. We probably cannot eliminate the deficit, but we can put a ceiling on borrowing from the central bank of 2 percent of GDP. That leaves a still-substantial deficit, but after all this is only the first stage of our adjustment program. To achieve this reduction in the deficit we will of course raise taxes, but we know that it will take a few months or maybe a year or more for the revenues to begin coming in. Therefore we shall start off by being draconian on expenditures: let us cut them in half.

Meanwhile we have run out of reserves—another important target. In fact, by the usual definition, reserves are negative. Let us therefore determine to increase our reserves by $1 billion, which is equivalent to half our annual imports. That is an ambitious target.

Our interest rates are horribly negative, well below the rate of inflation. Therefore let us set as a target that we will have positive real interest rates. Likewise for the exchange rate: let us go as far as we can and liberalize, say, at least half of the foreign-exchange market.

This of course means that we will have to cut wages severely all around. That includes government wages since there is no other way to cut real government expenditures in half quickly. But other wages will have to be cut as well. Finally, although it is more of an effect of the measures already specified than a policy variable in itself, let us say that we will not accept any increase in inflation but indeed that inflation ought to begin to come down.

If we had put this program in place at the end of 1988, we could look at the numbers for Peru today, roughly one year later, and say, "We have met all our targets." Government expenditures have been cut by half. Public investment has been about 2 percent of GDP in 1989. Public-sector wages are less than half what they were in late 1988 in real terms. The deficit, defined here as public borrowing from the domestic banking system, has been between 2 percent and 3 percent of GDP in 1989. Peru now has about $1 billion worth of reserves. Real interest rates are positive. In fact, they averaged over 100 percent in the first six months of 1989.

We can ask ourselves whether all this amounts to adjustment. True, we met all the targets. And the targets we set are probably a lot more ambitious than any program that the Fund would have set for Peru or anyone else. Even so, we would not want to say that this is adjustment. The main reason is that inflation in late 1989 is still raging at 25 percent to 30 percent a month. On the other hand, the inflation rate has been stable for eight months. In short, Peru has halted the increase in inflation but is a long way from eliminating it. At the same time the deficit has not been eliminated but remains at 2 percent of GDP, and the official exchange rate is clearly overvalued. Above all, the debt is still not being paid. It is this criterion, of course, that looms largest in any Washington consensus definition of adjustment. Certainly that is the way in which Kuczynski defines it.

The point of this exercise is mainly to raise the question, What do we really know about adjustment? Although I am a believer in free markets, in smaller government, in reducing intervention, in privatization—in short, in the Washington consensus—at the same time, looking ahead to what has to be done very soon in Peru, I am very concerned. I am concerned because I have a sense that we do not know enough about what makes or breaks an adjustment program.

We know that the first step has to be to stop inflation. Yet my sense is that we do not really know whether this is something that Peru could pull off in a month or two, as Bolivia did, or whether it will take three or five years. Peru has not had anything like the degree of indexation that Bolivia had. Unlike Bolivia, Peruvians have not experienced the chaos that accompanies a true hyperinflation, so they have not yet been "inoculated" against inflation as Bolivians have been. Therefore I worry about the timing and priorities of the adjustment program. The government may spend a lot of political capital too soon doing things like privatization or coming to an agreement on the foreign debt—things that do not offer a quick payoff toward stopping inflation. That may prove crucial if the government is going to get a second wind after the first three or six months of the program.

It is here that I come to my one disagreement with Kuczynski: I suspect that normalizing the debt relationship is not a priority in that first stage of stabilization. I realize that this may be sacrilegious in Washington. The Washington that Williamson defines is in large part a bureaucracy engaged in financial transfers, so it is not surprising that normalizing the debt relationship and reinserting Peru into the financial world are seen as the first steps in the adjustment process. But the experience of Chile and Bolivia suggests that the extra cash obtained from such normalization or reestablishment of creditor relationships was not crucial to the adjustment that was achieved. Even if it was, I suspect that there is no way that Peru will get similar treatment quickly enough for it to be a key input during those first six months when inflation has to be stopped.

Discussion

Sebastian Edwards underlined Patricio Meller's point that Chile had implemented most of its reforms long before the debt crisis, and before the World Bank had dreamed of "structural adjustment loans" (SALs). This suggests that structural reform needs far longer than the Bank recognizes when it offers SALs for three years. Edwards also argued that what had happened in Peru was not the result of the exotic imagination of Alan García, but was the outcome of a typical and pernicious way of viewing economic problems in Latin America (Dornbusch and Edwards 1989). Not much over a year ago, Rosemary Thorp (1987) and others had been urging that García's policies provided an example that all of Latin America should be following. The lesson from Peru, as from Chile under Salvador Allende, needs to be taken very seriously by Latin Americans.

Sylvia Saborio and Rudolf Hommes pointed out that the Costa Rican and Colombian adjustment programs, both of which were fairly successful, had taken place within the context of democratic systems.

At the end of his oral presentation, Pedro-Pablo Kuczynski had raised the question of whether countries are in fact being rewarded for good adjustment performance by greater access to external finance. He had failed to find any evidence that even the "good boys" got such a reward. Barbara Stallings had reinforced this point during her discussion, at least so far as the commercial banks are concerned. Their position was challenged by Charles Kovacs. He pointed out that Chile had been able to retire half of its long-term debt to the commercial banks through debt-equity conversions, without harming its relations with most of the banks. In the last year or so, Chile has begun to recover access to the international capital market on a voluntary basis: it has trade and interbank lines much above the level called for by past agreements, there have been several voluntary long-term loans to Chilean companies, and maturities have been lengthening. It is a mistake to expect that a country will be able immediately to return to the syndicated market and raise a jumbo loan. Turkey's return to the market also started with extra and longer-term trade credit and a few floating-rate notes. Uruguay and one or two other countries have also begun this process.

Eliana Cardoso expressed her surprise that Barbara Stallings had apparently endorsed the view that dictatorships provide efficient economic management. Had she forgotten that the economic mess of the 1980s had been bequeathed by the dictatorships of the 1970s?

In replying to the debate, Juan Cariaga focused on the question from Barbara Stallings as to how the Bolivian government had succeeded in maintaining public support for its reform program. His answer was that the Bolivian people recognized that hyperinflation was a blind and damaging tax, and that it provided morally and economically disastrous incentives to divert entrepreneurial activity into speculation. This recognition made the people willing to accept sacrifices to overcome hyperinflation. Yet Bolivia still needed leadership like that of Victor Paz Estenssoro, who realized in 1985 that the time had come to act. Political resolve needed to be reinforced by the sort of political skill that Paz had shown in concluding the "Pact for Democracy," to be able to exploit public willingness to make sacrifices for the common good.

Patricio Meller explained that he had not focused primarily on the 1981–82 Chilean adjustment, since this had already been done admirably elsewhere (Edwards and Cox-Edwards 1987). What Meller found miraculous about Chile, which had already implemented the so-called Washington consensus, was that it succeeded in keeping its model intact even while going through a wrenching adjustment. He had in 1982 expected a return of quantitative import restrictions, price and exchange controls, and a differential tariff system, but none of this had happened.

However, since Vittorio Corbo had raised the topic, Meller described the debate that had gone on at that time. One school wished to devalue because there was a current account deficit of 15 percent of GDP, another school wished to revalue because there was an overall surplus, and those who appealed to the monetary approach to the balance of payments argued in favor of leaving the nominal anchor alone. One of the most influential papers supporting the third view, on the ground that the Chilean economy was homogeneous of degree zero, had been written by none other than Vittorio Corbo (1982). Corbo retorted subsequently that his article had explained that in the Chilean economy as it then was, with 100 percent *ex post* wage indexation, devaluation would have been pointless.

Meller went on to ask what we have learned from Chile's recent economic history. We have learned, he argued, that the exchange rate needs to be set at a level that provides sufficient competitiveness to look after the current account, as urged in Williamson's paper. But that paper fails to mention another lesson: that the rate needed to be substantially more competitive than it had been before to achieve the negative transfer that Chile was now called on to make to cover its interest obligations.

Meller concluded by discussing Chile's debt policy, which was one of investing in reputation. This involved both avoiding confrontation with foreign creditors (including taking over $3 billion to $4 billion in debt from insolvent private debtors) and pursuing adjustment irrespective of the cost. Despite what Charles Kovacs had said, Chile had got very little from the commercial banks in return for its investment. It had got a great deal of help from the multilateral development banks, which had in fact financed 40 percent of Chile's interest payments to the commercial banks, but Chile is rapidly approaching the lending ceilings of those institutions, and by 1991 may well face a negative transfer to them. Despite their compliments, the commercial banks do not provide Chile with much cash.

Pedro-Pablo Kuczynski replied to two points made by Richard Webb. He argued that there is really no need to cut government expenditure further in Peru, since it is only 13 percent of GDP. Instead the needs are to restore revenue to where it used to be and to redistribute expenditures away from price subsidies. How could such a small fiscal deficit have led to such a high rate of inflation? Kuczynski speculated that the high inflation rate might have aggravated measurement problems, and he also blamed the policy of the central bank in rechanneling required reserves into government credit. On the debt issue, Kuczynski asserted that the only potential source of external credit was going to be the Washington institutions, and hence the new government would need to reach an agreement with them as soon as possible after it took office.

4

The Three Major Debtors

The Three Major Debtors

Argentina

Juan Carlos de Pablo

Why policy reforms? "To stop negative transfers," say the creditor banks. "To increase domestic welfare," say a growing number of economists in the debtor countries themselves. "For both reasons," says the Washington establishment. Policy reform is clearly an issue with multiple constituencies—and ambiguous content. Williamson's introduction to this volume is a very useful effort toward providing some substance to the issue, by identifying 10 instruments of economic policy that are candidates for inclusion in a reform package.

This paper attempts to answer the questions raised in Williamson's introduction as they apply to Argentina. First, to what degree is there a consensus in Argentina on policy reform? (This issue may be approached in disaggregated fashion, asking what level of consensus exists among economists on the one hand, and among politicians on the other.) Second, to what degree have policy reforms actually been implemented? And third, what have been the results? Before addressing these questions, however, I offer some general remarks on the subject of consensus and reform, and at the end of the paper I sketch the relevant aspects of the program begun in 1989 under the new Argentine president, Carlos Menem.

Some Observations on the "Washington Consensus"

Prescription Versus Practice

As Williamson notes in his introduction, "Washington does not always practice what it preaches. . . . the advice is intended to further the self-interest of the

Juan Carlos de Pablo is Consultant and Professor at the Centro de Estudios Macroeconómicos de Argentina and Editor of Contexto, *a weekly newsletter on economic affairs in Argentina.*

countries to whom it is directed." The first part of this statement is simply a recognition of reality, although one that some economists are reluctant to talk about; the second is an arguable assertion with which I happen to agree.

David Ricardo invented (or discovered) the principle of comparative advantage, which in the case of foodstuffs the European countries (including even Ricardo's Britain) have apparently forgotten. History teaches us that during World War I more Europeans died from hunger than from bullets, which explains why, in the name of reducing risk, today's Europeans have decided to make themselves poorer by producing foodstuffs domestically. Japan, which consumes just four kilograms of meat per inhabitant per year, is another clear example of the reduction in welfare that results from protection.

Washington is right when it recommends that Argentina not model its trade policy on restrictions such as these; the developed countries can afford such "luxuries," which are based on noneconomic considerations, whereas developing countries cannot. I happen to believe that the removal of distortions is in most cases something good for its own sake. In my view, countries like Argentina should make policy reforms and accept as a *gift* any funds that the world makes available contingent on those reforms.

The Consensus Among Economists

"There is a growing consensus among economists," says Edmar Bacha—"particularly about what should not be done," says Andres Bianchi, both speaking at a November 1989 seminar organized by the Inter-American Development Bank. Broadly speaking, I agree with both statements, although I should warn my younger readers about the dangers of a superficial consensus. When an economic policy fails, those who have supported it stop speaking. Their silence, coupled with the new message emanating from the rival camp, should not necessarily be construed as universal agreement with the new gospel.

The growing consensus among economists in Latin America, I believe, largely represents the maturing of the effort to encourage education abroad, from which many of us benefited. This was particularly important during the late 1950s and the 1960s. In those days, the economics learned at American and British universities was taught and applied literally, in open contrast to more historical or legalistic approaches. Twenty years later, the views of Latin professionals are much more balanced, and consequently more inclined toward consensus with each other and with Washington.

The "New Dialogue" Between Economists and Politicians

In 1985, during the honeymoon of the Austral Plan, the candidates of the party of then-President Raúl Alfonsín won the November congressional

Table 4.1 Argentina: the "arithmetic of power," 1854–1983

	5 Mar 1854 to 9 Dec 1983	5 Mar 1854 to 5 Sept 1930	6 Sept 1930 to 9 Dec 1983	20 Sept 1955 to 9 Dec 1983
Number of presidential terms according to the Constitution	22	13	9	5
Actual number of presidents	42	18	24	16
Average period in office (days)	1,139	1,578	810	679
Average portion of term served (percentages)	52	72	37	31
Ministers of economics	106	54	52	34
Average number of ministers per president	2.5	3	2.2	2.1
Average period in office (days)	451	526	374	320

elections. In 1987, having destroyed for political reasons what remained of the Austral Plan, Alfonsín was defeated in the September gubernatorial elections. In 1989, a victim of hyperinflation, Alfonsín's candidate was also defeated in the presidential election. It is not surprising, then, that a "new dialogue" is now developing between economists and politicians. Contrary to what was supposed during the 1950s and 1960s, good economics now goes hand in hand with good politics.

The Importance of Being Credible

The Washington imagination is bounded. Accordingly, the list suggested by Williamson needs to be complemented. It is not a question of adding an eleventh policy instrument—the missing element is one that relates to *all* reforms. I am referring to credibility, which, like pornography, is not easy to define rigorously, but is something that you recognize when it is in front of you. There is a growing academic literature on the issue of governmental credibility and reputation. This literature is surveyed in de Pablo and Broda (1989), who suggest that a new macroeconomic model is necessary for those countries in which labor, capital, technology, and so on are simultaneously in excess supply, and in which the lack of credibility therefore becomes the operative constraint. The point here is that, in what we have called "incredible countries," policy reforms should be tried harder, and periods of adjustments last longer, than in credible countries. Liviatan has appropriately labeled this phenomenon the "credibility trap": the population demands much more of an incredible government (typically a weak one) than of a credible government.

In incredible countries the lag between a policy reform and the emergence of results is explained not so much by inertia (time deposits are made for seven *days* in Argentina) as by credibility arguments. The typical Argentine develops a wait-and-see attitude, to determine whether this time the program is going to be different from the previous ones, before acting.

One important factor in determining credibility is the duration of high officials in office. Table 4.1 illustrates the lack of continuity of presidents and economic ministers in Argentina up to 1983. In that year Alfonsín came to office, inaugurating a democratic *regime* with greater chances of success. Figure 4.1, which shows the expected and actual durations of presidential administrations since adoption of the 1853 Constitution, reveals why the peaceful transfer of presidential power in 1989 was considered a historic event.

Argentina and the "Washington Consensus"

Table 4.2 summarizes Argentina's record on policy reform in terms of Williamson's 10 policy instruments. These can be conveniently grouped into three classes: fiscal reforms, measures affecting relative prices, and deregulation.

Fiscal Reforms

The consensus within the economics profession on the role of fiscal balance in achieving macroeconomic equilibrium is much clearer today than a decade ago. No professional economist would suggest today that there is no relationship between fiscal deficits and inflation. No one in Argentina still points to the US economy as an example of fiscal deficits coexisting with modest inflation; everyone now realizes that the international demand for the US and Argentine currencies is quite different. Public finance is not a popular branch of the economics profession, but the need for fiscal reform—to avoid the distorting effects of promotion schemes, to reorient activity away from the informal economy, to discourage tax evasion, and so on—are more than reasonably clear.

A similar awareness has emerged among politicians. In Argentina as in any other country, the average politician is not as "orthodox" as the average economist, yet even among politicians the consensus has moved toward rationality in the last decade. Even the most laissez-faire politicians still start their list of public-sector budget priorities with those items on which expenditures should be increased, but the extreme "developmentalist" policy proposals have disappeared from the agenda. On the matter of tax reform politicians have become particularly outspoken against tax evasion.

Argentina is a country in which the public sector as a whole has very rarely been in equilibrium since World War II. Accordingly, "correct" fiscal ideas have been implemented at best intermittently, in the form of emergency taxes (for example, export taxes) at the beginning of a stabilization program. The beneficial results of public-sector equilibrium have therefore been likewise transitory. (No measures of public-sector disequilibria are presented here because the existing long-run series are very difficult to update from 1985 on.)

Relative Prices

According to Williamson, Washington's concern about relative prices is focused on interest rates and exchange rates. Both are relevant variables, but I would add public utility rates to the list.

Interest and exchange rate policies are the only area in which important progress can be shown, not only on the level of consensus, but also at that of implementation. Figure 4.2 shows monthly real interest rates on loans over the last three decades (both the regulated and the free market rates are shown, as annual averages). Figure 4.3 shows the black market exchange rate premium as a percentage of the official exchange rate, and the latter as a proportion of the purchasing power parity (PPP) rate.

For Washington as well as for common sense, progress means nonnegative and (to the extent possible) "moderately" positive real interest rates. In this sense figure 4.2 shows progress: there has been less fluctuation of real interest rates during the 1980s than in previous decades. This stability continued in 1989 (not shown), in contrast with the grossly negative real interest rates of the previous hyperinflationary shocks in 1959 and 1975.

Something similar occurs with the exchange rate. In figure 4.3 the extremes in the black market premium, as well as the extreme overvaluations in PPP terms of the official rate, are seen to be phenomena of the 1970s. The recent fluctuations of the real exchange rate would surely make German or Japanese exporters nervous, but they fail to frighten the survivors of past overvaluation experiments in Argentina.

Figure 4.1 Argentina: nominal and effective presidential terms, 1953–1983

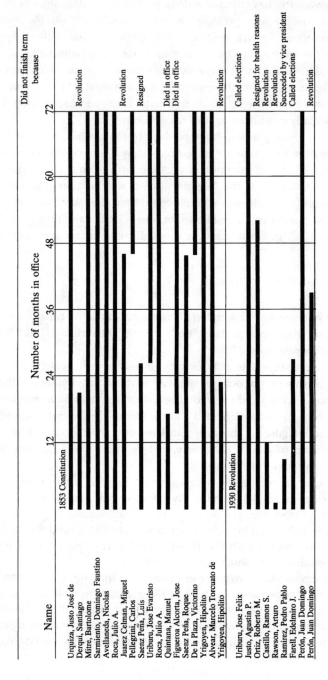

Figure 4.1 **Argentina: nominal and effective presidential terms, 1953–1983** (Continued)

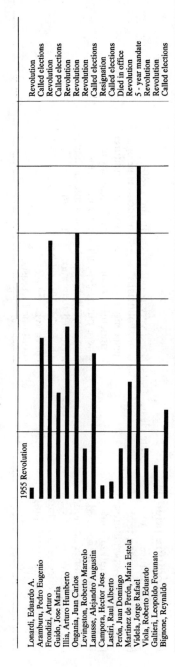

Lonardi, Eduardo A.	Revolution
Aramburu, Pedro Eugenio	Called elections
Frondizi, Arturo	Revolution
Guido, Jose Maria	Called elections
Illia, Arturo Humberto	Revolution
Ongania, Juan Carlos	Revolution
Levingston, Roberto Marcelo	Revolution
Lanusse, Alejandro Augustin	Called elections
Campora, Héctor Jose	Resignation
Lastiri, Raul Alberto	Called elections
Perón, Juan Domingo	Died in office
Martínez de Perón, María Estela	Revolution
Videla, Jorge Rafael	5 - year mandate
Viola, Roberto Eduardo	Revolution
Galtieri, Leopoldo Fortunato	Revolution
Bignone, Reynaldo	Called elections

1955 Revolution

Table 4.2   Adjustment in Argentina: how much has happened?

Issue	Consensus among economists	Consensus among politicians	Degree of implementation	Results
Fiscal deficits				
Large and sustained fiscal deficits are a primary source of macroeconomic dislocation in the form of inflation, payments deficits, and capital flight. They reflect a lack of political courage or honesty to match public expenditures with the resources available to finance them.	Quite clear.	Broad, but by omission. Politicians have stopped arguing that "fiscal deficits are irrelevant" and that inflation has to be attacked by increasing production.	Temporary increases in taxes.	Temporary decline of the fiscal deficit.
Public expenditure priorities				
Cutting expenditures is much better than increasing revenues. Military expenditures, public administration, and subsidies should be reduced, while funding for education and health should be increased. Policy reform thus means expenditure switching.	Quite clear.	Not a very popular issue. Politicians speak more confidently about where public expenditures should be increased than about where they should be cut or where taxes should be increased.	In the 1980s, reductions in operating expenditures and increases in interest payments on domestic and foreign debt.	

Table 4.2 Adjustment in Argentina: how much has happened? (Continued)

Issue	Consensus among economists	Consensus among politicians	Degree of implementation	Results
Tax reform				
The tax base should be broad and marginal tax rates moderate. A country cannot start discussions on enforcement with haven countries until it taxes its own flight capital.	Growing consensus. Not a popular topic among most economists.	Universal condemnation of tax evasion.	Under way, with some difficulties being encountered.	
Interest rates				
Rates should be market determined and positive in real terms. There is a fear that market-determined rates can be too high.	Quite clear since the beginning of the 1970s.	Reasonably clear. One no longer hears about the need to "promote" manufacturing through negative real interest rates.	Rates freely determined since 1977.	Smaller fluctuations in interest rates. Elimination of grossly negative rates. The "institutionalized" financial system has been saved from extinction.
Exchange rate				
Should be "competitive," that is, should promote a rate of growth of exports that will allow the economy to grow at the maximum rate permitted by its supply-side potential.	Reasonably clear. Conflict over use of the exchange rate as an "anchor" during stabilization programs.	Devaluation is a hot political issue. Politicians remain devaluophobics.	Since the *tablita*, gross overvaluation has disappeared.	Smaller fluctuations in the official real exchange rate.

Table 4.2 Adjustment in Argentina: how much has happened? (Continued)

Issue	Consensus among economists	Consensus among politicians	Degree of implementation	Results
Trade policy				
Import liberalization, particularly elimination of import licensing.	Importance varies among economists.	Fear of unemployment.	Programs for reduction of import duties intended from 1976 to 1981, and again since 1987.	Small increase in imports as a share of GDP. Imports compete with service of foreign debt for scarce foreign currency.
Foreign direct investment				
Restrictions are foolish. FDI can be promoted by debt-equity swaps.	Relative importance has declined. Swaps are of disputed value, according to the expected outcome of the debt issue.	Chauvinism is over.	Removal of barriers imposed by legislation.	Poor, given the terrible performance of the economy.
Privatization				
Private industry is managed more efficiently than state-owned industry.	Division within the profession, with most economists more favorably inclined than in the past.	Proponents are no longer labeled "traitors to their country." Popular in opinion polls.	Few actual cases so far, but those have been very successful.	Improvement in quality of goods and services.

Table 4.2 Adjustment in Argentina: how much has happened? (Continued)

Issue	Consensus among economists	Consensus among politicians	Degree of implementation	Results
Deregulation				
The Latin American economies are among the world's most regulated market economies.	Growing consensus on its importance.	Few talk about it.	Little action so far, but great expectations.	
Property rights				
Highly insecure in Latin America.	Some are aware of the need for reforms.	The issue is ignored.	Practical limitations of the judicial system transform justice into injustice.	

Figure 4.2 Argentina: real interest rates on loans, 1955–88

percent per month

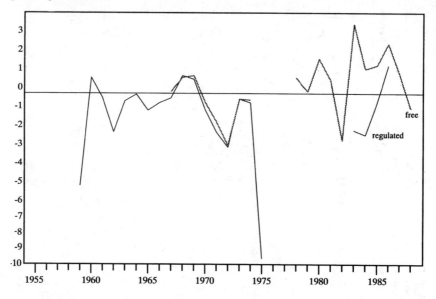

These results, of course, would have been impossible to achieve absent a clear consensus that insisting on absurd price levels in the regulated portions of these markets would have disastrous consequences. Today nobody suggests a policy of inducing investment through "cheap credit," and everybody complains when the exchange rate is used for too long as the anchor of a stabilization program.

Was consensus achieved through discussion, or was it a byproduct of necessity? The answer is that it was a combination of both, but necessity played a crucial role. As then-President of the Central Bank Alfonso César Diz put it, "either in 1977 I freed interest rates, or the whole institutionalized segment of the financial market [would have] disappeared." A similar point can be made for black market premiums greater than about 20 percent; there misinvoicing is the favored mechanism of evasion.

Deregulation

Last but not least, under the general heading of deregulation I include the five remaining items on Williamson's list, namely, trade policy, foreign direct investment, privatization, deregulation proper, and property rights. Deregulation understood in this inclusive sense is a most important issue.

Figure 4.3   Argentina: exchange rate gaps, 1959–88

percent

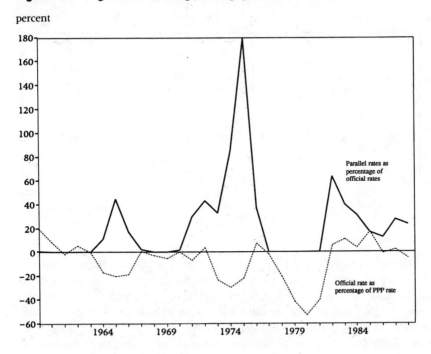

As described in detail in de Pablo and Martínez (1989), the typical day of the Argentine private-sector entrepreneur or executive starts very early in the morning with two hours of news on the radio, supplemented by two or three newspapers. The morning office hours are devoted to meetings with bureaucrats, followed by working lunches with high government officials or with "competitors." Then it is back to the office for still more news on the radio. The typical Argentine entrepreneur is too busy to work!

In 1958 Albert O. Hirschman unveiled his "unbalanced" strategy for economic development. Assuming that in developing countries the binding constraint is the supply of entrepreneurship, Hirschman argued for the concentration of governmental efforts in projects with strong backward and forward linkages with other sectors of the economy. My view of Argentina is different: there is a lot of creative talent in the private sector, but it is aimed in the wrong directions from the point of view of social welfare.

In Argentina, as everywhere in the world, people seek to maximize private profits. As a result of regulations, and the possibility of endogenizing the regulatory process through lobbying, the returns to "being busy" (that is, diagnosing correctly the macro setting within which one's own economic unit

Figure 4.4 Argentina: the closing of the economy, 1900–88

percent of GDP

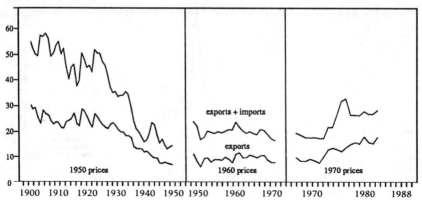

is currently operating and acting accordingly) are much greater than the returns to "working" (putting the right technology in place, choosing the right product specifications, and so on). That is why deregulation, trade policy, privatization, property rights, and the rest are but variations of a single issue: How does one set the rules of the game in a way that will align private and social returns, and what are the corresponding consequences in terms of the overall functioning of the economy?

There were some attempts at reform during the Martínez de Hoz era (the late 1970s) in the area of deregulation as I have broadly defined it. These reforms were aborted under the military regime, although there was a mild—and incredible—effort to revive them during the last years of the Alfonsín period. Figure 4.4 illustrates the structural closing of the Argentine economy during the twentieth century—a process that was only slightly reversed during the 1980s.

The Reform Program of 1989

In July 1989, when the rate of inflation had reached 4 percent per *day*, President Alfonsín handed over the reins of government to Carlos Menem, in the first peaceful transfer of power in Argentina since 1928. It came as a surprise to most Argentines that democracy in Argentina could show itself hyperinflation-proof!

It is helpful in analyzing Menem's program to have some idea of the potential benefits to Argentina of a correctly run economy. Figure 4.5 plots the annual rate of growth of real GDP since the beginning of the century, while figure 4.6 shows the (monthly equivalent of the) annual rate of inflation, as measured by

Figure 4.5 Argentina: changes in real GDP, 1900–88

percent per year

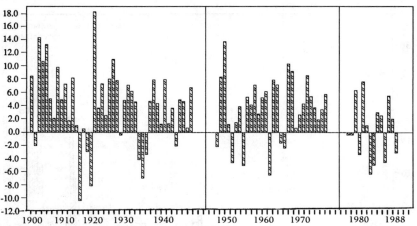

wholesale prices, since 1913. Together these provide a kind of *"curriculum vitae"* of the Argentine economy.

Figure 4.5 divides the century into three periods. The first period, from 1900 to the end of World War II, witnessed sustained high rates of economic growth, except in those years when the economy, which was then very open, suffered external shocks, principally World War I and the Great Depression. From the end of World War II until the mid-1970s there was a reduction in the average rate of growth, but more important was the increase in the fluctuations of the growth rate: years of growth were followed by years of contraction, which cannot be explained by external shocks. From the mid-1970s to the present the story has been one of continued fluctuations, but now around a zero long-run rate of growth.

The average annual rate of growth of per capita GDP for the century as a whole has been about 0.95 percent—today's per capita GDP is just double its level of 1900. However, the average rate of growth for the first three decades of the century (excluding World War I) was 1.8 percent per year—twice the average for the century. A small portion of this difference can be explained by the emergence of the informal sector of the economy, which today represents one third of "true" GDP, according to Guisarri (1989).

Figure 4.6, in turn, shows that inflation in Argentina, as a phenomenon separate from world inflation, started after World War II. Two features are in evidence: a trend increase in the rate of inflation, and from time to time a dip that occurs when a new stabilization plan temporarily reduces the rate of inflation.

Figure 4.6 Argentina: wholesale price inflation, 1914–89

percent per month[a]

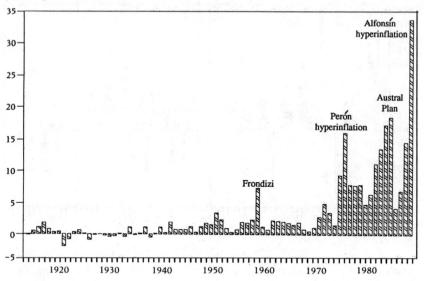

a. Yearly averages.

In the 15 years between 1969 and 1985, Argentina took nine zeros off its currency; the elimination of three more is currently under discussion. Argentina, whose consumer price index (CPI) increased by a mere 0.8 percent per year between 1914 and 1939 (when wholesale prices increased by an average of 1.4 percent), witnessed average rates of inflation (by the CPI) of 19 percent per year during the first administration of Juan Perón (1945–55), 29 percent during the "golden decade" (1964–74), and 220 percent during the following decade, culminating in hyperinflation during the first semester of 1989.

It was against this background that Carlos Menem started his six-year presidential term on 8 July 1989. From an economic point of view it is important to differentiate between Menem's stabilization program on the one hand, and his structural reforms on the other.

During the first half of 1989 Argentina suffered hyperinflation due to technical difficulties related to the Primavera Plan (the stabilization plan launched in September 1988) and the expectation of probable chaos resulting from the electoral victory in the May presidential election of the Peronist candidate—Menem himself. This combination of factors generated a snowball effect, as the technical complications arising from the stabilization plan, as well as the policy responses themselves, increased the probability of Menem winning the election—a prospect that, *ex ante*, was considered disastrous. Foreseeing difficulties ahead, Argentines bought dollars, which increased the probability of such difficulties, which in turn further increased the probability of a Menem victory, which in turn increased the demand for dollars, and on and on.

On 14 May, Menem won the presidential election. That very night, the President-elect began to send signals that surprised everybody. Staying in La Rioja, where he was governor, instead of going to Buenos Aires, conducting rational dialogues with journalists and politicians, and establishing audacious contacts with portions of the establishment, he reversed expectations overnight. Not only has President Menem been better than anyone had a right to expect; he is indeed the president every economic minister dreams of. He makes decisions very quickly: the way in which he replaced two ministers who died suddenly showed him to be a determined man, maintaining continuity by picking new ministers of the same ideological orientation, while providing a political umbrella for necessary reforms. As a result, what is happening today, in terms of stabilization policy as well as in the area of structural reforms, owes much more to technical than to political considerations.

In the wake of the failed stabilization plans of the 1980s,[1] it is well understood that the successful elimination of hyperinflation requires a combination of heterodox measures (some form of freeze of key prices) to break the inflationary inertia and orthodox measures addressing the fundamentals (notably in fiscal policy). A thorough analysis of the Menem stabilization plan is beyond the scope of this paper, but it must be pointed out that the heterodox portion has "worked," the rate of inflation having declined from 200 percent per month in July to 5 percent in October, whereas the orthodox portion is lagging. It is a surprise to no one, then, that in mid-November 1989 the discussion in Argentina is over whether this program is truly different from the previous ones, or whether we are seeing merely the 1989 model of the Austral Plan.

The congress has passed a couple of important pieces of legislation in the area of structural reform. One result has been some action on privatization (starting with two television channels and the telephone company), deregulation (of the petroleum sector), and reduction (labeled "temporary" for the time being) of subsidies.

Menem has demonstrated "political will," a necessary virtue if one is to overcome powerful lobbies, which in Argentina include not just the trade unions but the merchants' and manufacturers' organizations as well. It is still an open question whether or not he will succeed.

---

1. See Bruno et al. (1988) on the experiences of the austral and the cruzado, as well as the more successful programs of Israel and Bolivia.

Conclusion

Through necessity more than through a unilateral change of mind, Argentina finds itself engaged in policy reform. The reforms were started years ago in the area of relative prices (interest and exchange rates), and more recently proceeded to address the fiscal fundamentals. There is new opportunity on the privatization and deregulation fronts, under a president who, miraculously, is providing the political umbrella needed to accomplish real reforms. The key question today is whether the necessary content can be given to this impetus toward reform, so as to transform a good idea into actions that will increase the real welfare of the population.

Acknowledgments

This paper benefited from comments made after its oral presentation by William R. Cline and Sebastian Edwards. Any responsibility for remaining errors is mine.

Brazil

Eliana A. Cardoso and Daniel Dantas

Since 1982 the countries of Latin America have confronted a choice between two paths of achieving sustained resource transfers abroad: inflation and recession. In the end, Brazil chose inflation.

Recession was Brazil's initial response to the 1982 debt crisis. However, this immediate reaction was followed by an export-led recovery in 1984–85. A surge in both investment and consumption in 1986 ended in stagnation in 1988, but by mid-1989 the economy was growing rapidly once again. As table 4.3 shows, Brazil is exceptional among Latin American countries in having had a positive average per capita growth rate for the 1982–88 period; the rest of Latin America experienced a decline. In balance of payments terms as well, the Brazilian response to the debt crisis was the most successful in the region. The dramatic growth of Brazil's trade surplus was the largest in Latin America both in absolute terms and relative to GDP.

Nonetheless, Brazil has not "adjusted" to the debt crisis. Instead the Brazilian government has "accommodated" the disappearance of external sources of finance by printing money and by creating domestic debt. Table 4.4 compares the inflation rate in Brazil with that in the rest of Latin America since 1982. Until 1986 the two rates follow a similar path, but beginning in 1987 the Brazilian inflation rate is approximately four times greater than that in the rest of Latin America.

Between 1980 and 1985, the government's failure to absorb the debt and oil shocks in a noninflationary manner pushed annual inflation up from 50 percent to 220 percent and beyond. On 28 February 1986, with inflation at 400 percent per year, Brazil embarked on a major stabilization effort: the notorious Cruzado Plan. One year later, when the price freeze was removed, prices exploded. The government initiated new attempts to control inflation in mid-1987 under the Bresser Plan and again in January 1989 under the Summer Plan. Once again the government froze prices, squeezed credit, and cut zeros off the face value of the currency. Promises to eliminate the budget deficit were made but not fulfilled. President José Sarney lacked the political will to implement the necessary fiscal consolidation measures. He also lacked credibility, determination, and

Eliana A. Cardoso is Professor of Economics at the Fletcher School of Law and Diplomacy at Tufts University. She has taught at the Universidade de Brasilia and is a former research associate at the Instituto de Pesquisa Econômica e Social in Rio de Janeiro.

Daniel Dantas is a professor at the Fundação Getúlio Vargas and the President of Banco Icatu, Rio de Janeiro.

Table 4.3 Brazil and Latin America: growth in GDP per capita, 1982–88 average[a] (percentages per year)

Country	Growth in GDP per capita
Brazil	0.9
Mexico	−2.4
Argentina	−1.0
Venezuela	−1.6
Colombia	1.5
Peru	−2.1
Chile	0.0
Uruguay	−1.4
Ecuador	−1.1
Guatemala	−2.8
Dominican Republic	0.0
Bolivia	−4.0
El Salvador	−0.9
Paraguay	−1.1
Costa Rica	−0.4
Panama	−3.5
Nicaragua	−4.7
Honduras	−1.8
Haiti	−2.8
Latin America excluding Brazil[b]	−1.4

a. Excluding Cuba. The countries are ordered by their share in regional GDP in 1985.

b. Average of growth rates of the countries in the table, weighted by share in regional GDP (excluding Brazil).

Sources: Banco Central do Brasil and Economic Commission for Latin America and the Caribbean.

allies in the congress. With the budget deficit unscathed and with trade surpluses growing, all three plans amounted to attempts to stop inflation by decree (figure 4.7).

This paper studies Brazil's response to the crisis of the 1980s, concentrating on the policies pursued between 1982 and 1988 and their consequences. First we examine issues related to trade and payments, including the Brazilian law on computer technologies (informatics). We then consider in turn the fiscal budget and privatization, monetary policy and debt-equity swaps, and the impact of the policies of the 1980s on income distribution and poverty. The final section of the paper summarizes our conclusions.

Table 4.4   Brazil and Latin America: inflation rates, 1982–88
(percentages per year)

	Change in consumer prices	
Year	Brazil	Latin America except Brazil
1982	97.9	77.7
1983	179.2	105.9
1984	203.3	175.3
1985	228.0	298.8
1986	58.4	67.6
1987	365.9	112.9
1988[a]	981.0	211.0

a. Preliminary.

Sources: Banco Central do Brasil and Economic Commission for Latin America and the Caribbean.

Trade and Payments

To judge from trade performance alone, Brazilian adjustment to the debt crisis has been nothing short of phenomenal. As table 4.5 shows, the combination of export growth and import substitution has produced large trade surpluses since 1983, in sharp contrast to the trade deficits of the 1970s. Merchandise exports increased from $13 billion per year in 1977–79 to $34 billion in 1988. At the same time, Brazil restrained imports by continuing to expand alternative sources of domestic supply. Imports in 1988 were actually 23 percent lower in volume terms than in 1979, despite the fact that real GDP was 29 percent higher.

In part, these trade flows were a response to the real depreciation of the 1980s: in the 1983–88 period, the average real effective exchange rate was 25 percent above its level in 1977–82. But since the late 1960s Brazil has also been exceptional among the Latin American countries in its successful combination of import substitution and growth as well as diversification of exports. Three factors have played a role in this success. First, the industrial sector, initially established behind protectionist barriers, continues to grow and become more efficient, expanding into intermediate and capital goods. Second, since 1968 a crawling-peg exchange rate policy has kept devaluations in line with the difference between internal and external inflation, thus avoiding long periods of overvaluation. Third, active promotion of manufactured exports through incentives and subsidies has offset the negative effects of import tariffs and controls.

Figure 4.7   Brazil: inflation rates, 1985–89[a]

percent per month (3-month moving average)

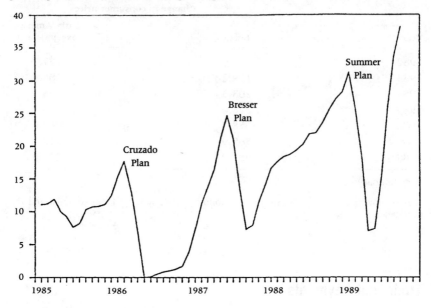

a. As calculated by the general price index of the Fundação Getúlio Vargas.
Source: Conjuntura Economica, various issues.

Import Performance

Import reduction was a central element of the Brazilian balance of payments adjustment to the debt crisis. The relative success of the policy was due not merely to import restrictions but also to an active policy of investment directed toward import substitution in the late 1970s.

Among these import-substituting activities was the ethanol program. Sugar-cane alcohol, known as ethanol, was promoted during the 1970s initially as a supplement to and eventually as a substitute for gasoline. Cane fields prolifer-ated, distilleries were hastily built, and factories were retooled to assemble automobiles that could use the new fuel. In 1988, 90 percent of automobiles coming off Brazilian assembly lines were equipped to run entirely on ethanol. (This figure declined to approximately 65 percent in 1989.) Ethanol is a cleaner, replaceable alternative to oil, but it is not cost competitive at current world oil prices. The World Bank calculates that the Brazilian ethanol program will generate a $2.7 billion deficit in 1989, assuming prices remain constant.

Table 4.5   Brazil: trade balance, real exchange rate, and terms of trade, 1977–88 (billions of dollars except where noted)

Year	Exports	Imports	Trade balance	Real effective exchange rate[a]	Terms of trade[b]
1977–79[c]	13.3	14.6	−1.3	96.2	100
1980–82[c]	21.2	21.5	−0.3	100.0	66
1983	21.9	15.4	6.5	115.7	61
1984	27.0	13.9	13.1	116.7	63
1985	25.6	13.2	12.5	117.4	62
1986	22.3	14.0	8.3	134.4	67
1987	26.2	15.0	11.2	135.9	60
1988	33.8	14.7	19.1	123.6	63[d]

a. 1980–82 = 100. Yearly averages. An increase in the index indicates a depreciation.

b. 1977–79 = 100. Yearly averages.

c. Average of the three years.

d. Preliminary.

Sources: Conjuntura Economica, various issues; Morgan Guaranty Trust Company; Banco Central do Brasil; Inter-American Development Bank.

Despite its limitations, the Brazilian strategy of subsidizing the intermediate and capital goods sectors did make possible a decline in imported inputs without disrupting domestic production. Given the objective of restraining imports, liberalization could not figure high among Brazilian policy priorities during the 1980s. By the mid-1980s, import restrictions were almost the same as at the time of the balance of payments crisis of the early 1960s.

In July 1988, the Comissão de Política Aduaneira approved a project to impose greater rationality on the tariff structure by eliminating special duties, partially eliminating special regimes for imports, and reducing tariffs. Table 4.6 shows that the 1988 reform achieved a reduction in nominal tariffs. However, the comparison between nominal tariffs and implicit tariffs shown in table 4.6 indicates that a redundancy in tariff rates continues to exist. A new round of tariff reductions was expected in the second half of 1989.

Import restriction in Brazil depends on nontariff barriers for its effectiveness. Table 4.7 shows the legal and implemented average tariff rates. The former are considerable, averaging more than 35 percent if one excludes fuel and wheat imports, which are nondutiable, whereas the average implemented rate is only 10 percent. The reason for this difference is straightforward: where imports are permitted at all, they are almost always exempt from tariffs or receive large reductions. The license is the effective binding constraint, not the price. Table 4.8 shows that approximately 20 percent of imports pay the legally stipulated rate.

Table 4.6 Brazil: average tariff rates (percentages)

Type of goods	Implicit rate[a]	Nominal rate Before 1988	Nominal rate After 1988
Capital goods	21.3	62.3	49.6
Intermediate goods	21.4	49.1	31.4
Consumer goods	2.8	72.6	49.8

a. Calculated as $[(P_d/P_i)-1]/100$, where P_d and P_i are actual domestic and international prices, respectively, in 1988.

Table 4.7 Brazil: legal and implemented average tariff rates, 1983–88 (percentages)

Year	All imported goods Legal	All imported goods Implemented[a]	Excluding oil and wheat Legal	Excluding oil and wheat Implemented
1983	21.4	5.0	43.1	11.2
1984	21.4	4.8	40.9	10.4
1985	21.9	5.8	36.6	10.6
1986	30.8	7.4	39.0	9.7
1987	27.4	7.0	37.2	9.8
1988	27.5	7.8	36.0	10.3

a. Tariff revenues divided by value of imports.

Source: Finance Ministry of Brazil.

Others enter as privileged products, such as wheat and oil, or by virtue of special regional trade agreements involving preferential access; still others enter by virtue of their importance as intermediate inputs for export production. Obviously a large degree of administrative discretion exists.

Market Reserve in the Computer Industry

Brazil uses protection to foster its domestic computer industry. Although Brazil continues to allow the importation of large computers, it reserves the small-computer market for local firms, placing legal and administrative barriers against both foreign imports and local manufacture by foreign firms. A law passed on October 1984 extended a system introduced in 1977, which imposed a reserved market in the computer technology area and restricted to Brazilian-owned companies the manufacture and sale of mini- and microcomputers for a period of eight years. The nearly unanimous congressional approval of the

Table 4.8 Brazil: imports by tariff regime, 1983–88 (percentages of total imports)

Year	Paying full tariff	Nondutiable	Drawback	Partial payment under special regime[a]
1983	15.3	70.0	7.4	7.3
1984	15.5	69.9	7.2	7.4
1985	19.1	64.4	10.2	6.3
1986	20.7	50.9	16.2	12.2
1987	19.4	52.8	16.4	11.4
1988	23.7	45.5	16.7	14.1

a. Asociación Latinoamericana de Libre Comercio (ALALC).

Source: Finance Ministry of Brazil.

Special Informatics Secretariat (SEI) bill showed strong, broad-based domestic backing for this policy.

Evans (1989) interprets the informatics law as an attempt at import preemption: "Rather than going through a typical import substitution process—first importing small computers and then trying to convince foreign producers to manufacture them in Brazil and hoping that local firms would eventually become involved in their production—Brazil decided to rely from the beginning on production by locally owned firms."

Between September 1985 and March 1988, the United States threatened retaliation against the informatics law. Despite the restrictions imposed under the law, US computer-related exports to Brazil had grown at essentially the same rapid rate as computer exports worldwide until 1985. However, they stagnated between 1985 and 1988, as shown in table 4.9.

Evans (1989) argues that the trade interests involved in the case were murky. The Brazilian Law of Similars (used systematically to restrict imports since the 1950s) could have been used to restrict imports of computers even in the absence of the informatics law. The novelty of the law is that it also restricted local investment by the multinational computer firms. In the conflict between Brazil and the United States over the informatics law, the United States can claim victory in Brazil's recognition of copyright in software and its recognition of the interests of specific multinationals in Brazil. Yet the informatics law remains in place and is unlikely to change before 1992, when some of its key provisions expire.

The informatics policy has bred complaints about the cost, quality, and servicing of Brazilian computers. High component prices have led to black market deals in imported software, components, and even whole computers.

Table 4.9   United States: growth in computer-related exports (percentages)

Exports to:	Parts 1979–1985	Parts 1985–1988	Integrated circuits 1979–1985	Integrated circuits 1985–1988	Computers 1979–1985	Computers 1985–1988	Total 1979–1985	Total 1985–1988
Brazil	182	−2	280	84	83	−14	143	0.4
World	188	30	119	47	115	26	144	30

Source: United Nations, *International Trade Statistics Yearbook* and US Bureau of the Census.

Pirating of foreign technology is widespread, and software is regularly copied. Some critics also point to a decline in the competitiveness of Brazilian computer products in foreign markets.

Despite the restrictions, foreign and domestic companies in the information industry actively pursue each other as potential partners. The SEI is receptive to proposals that include foreign participation, linking small manufacturers with strong financial institutions, and to projects that propose establishing R & D centers in Brazil or that contribute to a positive trade balance.

Export Performance

On the export side, the 1980s saw the continuation of the decisive changes introduced after the mid-1960s. First, the crawling-peg exchange rate regime survived both a maxi-devaluation in 1983 and the temporary freezes that followed each of the numerous stabilization programs.

Second, export incentives for manufactures remained in place, partly offsetting the anti-export bias of the value-added taxes. Credit subsidies, which had become important in the 1970s, were gradually phased out. Table 4.10 shows the structure of export incentives and subsidies in 1985. By 1988, income tax subsidies had been eliminated and credit subsidies reduced. The current plan is to abolish the remaining subsidies (but not the incentives) in 1989.

The Outlook for Trade Performance

The recent large trade surpluses tend to create an illusory optimism about the ease with which large external transfers of resources can be realized. A more cautious view recognizes that, at low recent levels of investment and imports, Brazilian technological capacity is handicapped vis-à-vis its strengthened competitors among the Asian newly industrializing countries (NICs). The degree of Brazilian competitiveness required for rapid and sustained growth of manufac-

Table 4.10   Brazil: incentives and subsidies to manufactured exports as share of total value, 1985 (percentages)

	Share of total manufactured export value
Incentives	
Drawback	9.1
Exemption from IPI[a]	7.2
Exemption from ICM[b]	20.5
Subsidies	
Income tax reduction	1.6
IPI and ICM premium credit[c]	1.4
Other subsidized credits	1.6

a. The IPI is a value-added tax paid on exports and export sales of industrial goods.

b. The ICM is a value-added tax paid on all manufactured exports and export sales.

c. This credit consists of a subsidy on manufactured exports based on the product's IPI and ICM rates.

Source: Moreira and Baumann (1987).

tured exports can only be achieved in the short term through real devaluation and hence declining real wages. The political feasibility of implementing such measures thus becomes a major factor.

On the import side, there may be a tendency to overestimate the structural reduction in income elasticities owing to import substitution. Artificially low levels of investment, despite the recovery in 1985 and 1986, have helped to keep import demand in check, but such a pattern is not consistent with sustained development. Export growth itself becomes dependent upon access to imports. Brazil's ability to generate large trade surpluses from its existing capital stock should not be exaggerated. Import limitations and emphasis on the internal market could, in the end, worsen rather than improve the balance of payments.

Trade, Debt, and Inflation

The above considerations suggest that Brazilian trade performance and policy are not settled issues. A broader perspective, incorporating the debt as an integral part of the Brazilian development problem, is necessary. As explained below, the link between Brazil's trade surpluses and its high inflation rate is an important one. Trade surpluses have been used to pay the interest on government debt, but the government has financed the purchase of this privately generated foreign exchange by issuing domestic debt and printing money. As a consequence, Brazil experienced extraordinary inflation in the aftermath of the debt shock in 1982.

If the trade surplus is used to pay interest on the external government debt and is not counterbalanced on the revenue side by an increase in taxes, the result will be increased money creation. The inflationary impact of the trade surpluses does not necessarily come from an increase in foreign reserves. Moreover, the need to achieve a real devaluation implies that debt service measured in domestic currency increases; consequently, the budget deficit measured in that currency also increases. This, in turn, increases the required money creation and, hence, inflation.

Soaring debt service is the main component of fiscal deterioration in Brazil, and it has been financed by growing trade surpluses. Ordinary least-squares regression analysis, using seasonally adjusted data from Data Resources, Inc., for the period January 1979 through December 1988, shows a significant response of inflation to trade surpluses in Brazil:

$$\text{Inflation} = 2.16 + 2.05 \text{ trade balance} + 0.67 \text{ lagged inflation}$$
$$(2.59) \qquad\qquad (8.89)$$

$$(120 \text{ observations}; \ r^2 = 0.62; \ \text{Durbin-Watson} = 2.11)$$

Export Performance and Capital Flight

Overinvoicing of imports and underinvoicing of exports are means of accumulating foreign assets surreptitiously. This misinvoicing of trade transactions is subject to conflicting temptations. To avoid import taxes there is a tendency to underinvoice imports, exactly the opposite of what is required to effect capital flight. Which effect dominates depends on the relative size of the duty and the black market exchange premium. Meyer and Bastos (1989) found that since 1977 imports have been systematically underinvoiced in Brazil.

On the export side, both capital flight and evasion of duties work in the same direction (but export subsidies do not). An estimate of the amount of underinvoicing of exports can be obtained by comparing total imports by value reported by all countries for a particular exporting country with that country's own reported exports. Using these data, Cuddington (1986) reports that in the period 1977–83 Brazilian exports were underinvoiced by 12.7 percent. Meyer and Bastos (1989) find similar numbers, with a record of 14 percent reached in 1986. The same authors also calculate capital flight from Brazil according to

Table 4.11 Brazil: foreign direct investment, 1977–88 (billions of dollars)

Year	Direct investment	Total profits	Reinvested profits	Direct investment net of repatriated profits[a]
1977–79[b]	1.22	0.79	0.24	0.67
1980–82[b]	1.55	1.32	0.90	1.13
1983	0.86	1.45	0.70	0.10
1984	1.12	1.30	0.47	0.30
1985	0.80	1.60	0.54	−0.21
1986	−0.12	1.35	0.45	−1.02
1987	2.96	1.53	0.62	2.02
1988	5.45	n.a.	n.a.	3.75[c]

n.a. = not available.

a. Calculated as the difference between new direct investment and repatriated profits.

b. Average for the three years.

c. Preliminary.

Source: Conjuntura Economica, various issues.

various definitions and conclude that in 1988 the stock of flight capital from Brazil was approximately $28 billion.

Foreign Investment

The 1988 Constituent Assembly wrote the new Brazilian constitution in a context of militant nationalism around the question of foreign capital, and even drew some of its ideas directly from the informatics law. The new constitution has yet to be fully implemented in legislation affecting corporate structure, foreign investment, taxation, and interest rates, and indeed these measures may never be implemented, just as some elements of the 1967 constitution never were. Foreign investment in Brazil is now basically governed by legislation passed by the military government in 1964. This law allows repatriated profits of up to 12 percent of a company's liquid capital to be subjected to normal income tax rates. Above that percentage, repatriated profits pay a progressively higher rate. This law will not be fundamentally altered.

Brazil is by far Latin America's biggest recipient of foreign investment. Table 4.11 shows that foreign direct investment net of repatriated profits was negative in 1985 and 1986, but in 1987 and 1988 foreign investment was above its historical level. The central bank predicts that in 1989 foreign direct investment will be much lower than in 1988. The fall is attributed to the suspension of

Table 4.12 Brazil: government revenues, expenditures, and savings[a]
(percentages of GDP)

| | Revenues | | | | | |
Year	Direct taxes	Indirect taxes	Total[b]	Interest on internal debt[c]	Transfers and consumption[d]	Savings
1970–77[e]	10.6	14.8	25.0	0.5	19.4	5.6
1978–80[e]	12.0	13.0	24.0	0.8	21.2	2.8
1981	11.7	12.9	23.5	1.1	21.2	2.3
1982	12.6	12.5	23.8	1.1	22.0	1.8
1983	12.1	12.6	23.2	1.6	22.0	1.2
1984	11.2	10.2	20.7	2.4	19.7	1.0
1985	11.7	10.3	21.2	3.3	21.6	−0.4
1986	13.0	11.6	22.2	3.5	23.7	−1.5
1987[f]	10.2	11.3	19.3	2.4	23.4	−4.1
1988[f]	9.7	10.2	17.2	2.7	24.0	−6.8

a. Includes all levels of government.

b. Includes other revenues minus external debt service.

c. Excludes monetary correction.

d. Includes interest on internal debt.

e. Yearly average.

f. Preliminary.

Source: Resende et al. (1989).

Brazil's debt-equity conversion scheme, which accounted for the bulk of the investment recorded in 1988. The decline in foreign investment also reflects uncertainty preceding the November-December 1989 elections.

Fiscal Policies

In the 1970–77 period, government savings were positive and equal on average to 6 percent of GDP. Since then, they have turned negative. As shown in table 4.12, government dissaving in 1988 was equal to 7 percent of GDP. This is not a true measure of the overall fiscal balance, because it leaves public enterprises out of the picture, but it does show that public finances are deteriorating.

Two factors explain the sharp decline in government savings: growing interest payments on the domestic debt, and a reduction in tax revenues. Total tax revenues fell from 25 percent of GDP on average in 1970–77 to 17 percent in 1988, mainly because of the decline in indirect tax revenues. This in turn was a result of less-than-perfect fiscal indexation and a growing underground economy. The Instituto Brasileiro de Geografia e Estatística (IBGE) calculates that the underground economy is equivalent to at least 15 percent of measured GDP.

Alternative Measures of the Fiscal Deficit

Table 4.13 shows alternative measures of the budget balance. When inflation rises or abruptly falls, these measures are affected in different ways. Inflation in Brazil sharply accelerated in the 1980s, and so did the nominal public-sector borrowing requirement (PSBR), which moves dramatically with inflation because of the inflationary component of nominal interest payments. If inflation were to cease, the PSBR would shrink to the size of the budget deficit corrected for inflation.

The operational deficit (second column in table 4.13) captures the behavior of the budget deficit better than does the total PSBR. It is calculated by subtracting the monetary correction payments from the PSBR. Nonetheless, the operational deficit still is not a proper, inflation-adjusted measure of the budget deficit because the monetary correction index is not always equal to the inflation rate. The difference between the two represents capital gains or losses for the public sector. Moreover, the operational deficit, like the PSBR, excludes the deficit recorded by the monetary authorities (one of whose roles is the distribution of large credit subsidies) and thus may underestimate substantially the actual borrowing needs of the public sector.

One can try to overcome the shortcomings of the operational deficit by correcting for inflation from the available information on the consolidated debt of the public sector. The budget deficit corrected for inflation is defined as:

$$\text{real deficit} = \text{primary deficit} + \begin{array}{c} \text{real interest payments} \\ \text{on the domestic debt} \end{array} + \begin{array}{c} \text{real interest payments} \\ \text{on the external debt} \end{array}$$

This measure (measure A in table 4.13) underestimates the deficit. Consider a situation where prices are rising. By this definition, payments and revenues are deflated using the December price index. When an excess of expenditures over revenues occurs throughout the year, deflating each month's deficit by the December price index grossly underestimates the actual budget deficit if inflation is high. Part of this underestimation can be avoided by using instead the average real debt stock during the year; this is the basis for measure B in table 4.13.

Measure A is relevant if we want to measure whether the real debt stock is growing, but it is not a measure of the deficit as usually defined: the difference between expenditures and revenues. If we believe that the excess of expenditures over revenues for the year as a whole matters, measure B might be a closer

Table 4.13 Brazil: alternative measures of the fiscal deficit, 1981–88
(percentages of GDP)

Year	PSBR[a]	Operational deficit[b]	Deficit corrected for inflation[c]	
			Measure A	Measure B
1981	12.5	5.9		
1982	15.8	6.6	9.1	
1983	19.9	3.0	22.1	19.6
1984	23.3	2.7	9.0	10.2
1985	27.5	4.3	5.0	7.8
1986	11.2	3.6	2.1	−3.4
1987	31.4	5.5	3.3	14.4
1988	48.5	4.3	−0.4	16.2

a. Public-sector borrowing requirement, as defined by the International Monetary Fund.

b. Subtracts monetary correction from the PSBR.

c. Calculated as in tables 4.17–4.19.

Source: Banco Central do Brasil.

approximation. However, none of the measures in table 4.13 is an accurate measure of the budget deficit corrected for inflation, in the sense that none of them deducts exactly the inflation component of interest payments from the budget deficit of the consolidated public sector. Nonetheless, the information conveyed by the different measures helps one to understand what happened in this period. (See Appendix, p. 151, for measurement of the budget deficit corrected for inflation.)

In 1983, as a percentage of GDP, the budget deficit corrected for inflation was extraordinarily large, as both measures A and B indicate. There are at least three major reasons for this large deficit. First, in contrast with the large positive growth rates usually seen in Brazil, output fell by 3.4 percent during 1983. Second, the domestic cost (corrected for inflation) of servicing the external debt greatly increased during 1983 because of the sharp real devaluation experienced in that year (Morgan Guaranty's real exchange rate index declined from 112.9 to 86.4). Third, the interest paid on government bonds included compensation for the 30 percent devaluation of February 1983, because the return on these bonds was linked to the rate of exchange depreciation.

Surprisingly, the deficit corrected for inflation in 1983 is practically the same as the PSBR in column 1 of table 4.13, which one would expect to be larger. Here the reason might well be that subsidies extended through the monetary authorities and excluded from the PSBR were large in 1983, thus counterbalancing the inflation correction in measure B.

In the succeeding years the budget deficit declines. But by 1988, preliminary estimates of measure B place the budget deficit at an extraordinarily high level.

Privatization

Today the popular solution to large deficits, when a government finds itself unable to put in place the needed fiscal reforms, is to sell off public enterprises. Privatization is as fashionable today as direct state intervention in industry was in the 1950s. Hundreds of public enterprises were created in Brazil from the 1960s into the 1980s, finally numbering more than 300. According to the Secretaria de Controle das Empresas Estatais, 62 percent of Brazilian state companies were productive enterprises, and the remaining 38 percent were administrative organs and universities. These companies have been criticized for losing money because of inadequate managerial skills and excessive labor costs, unclear and contradictory objectives, and their privileged access to capital, subsidies, and protection.

So far, however, privatization in Brazil has moved slowly. Since 1980, only 17 publicly owned firms have been privatized. In August 1989 President Sarney sent a bill to the congress calling for the privatization of another 19 companies. The majority of state companies that have been privatized had originally been taken over by the state in bankruptcy. Besides these reprivatized firms, a few companies originally established by the state, or their fixed assets, have also been sold. The procedures for sale of state companies have changed over time. Some firms have been privatized through direct sales, others through the stock exchange. There have also been some instances of semi-privatization, with the sale of some shares to private investors and the state holding the balance.

Privatization in Brazil was motivated by a need to keep the fiscal deficit down, but to date it has not helped much toward this end. In fact, a modest budget impact is exactly what should have been expected. In the simplest theoretical case (assuming perfect substitutability among assets), the sale price of a public company should be equal to the discounted stream of profits the state would have expected had the enterprise remained in the public sector. Of course, different assets are not perfect substitutes, and liquid assets might be more useful to a bankrupt government. On the other hand, if the private sector is more efficient, the government might expect to sell the enterprise for a price greater than the discounted flow of expected future profits.

De Walle (1989) observes that "it is the short time horizon of hard-pressed state officials which has made the fiscal impact of privatization seem so appealing." When the budget is in bad shape, more weight is often given to the prospect of a decrease in expenditures than to the prospect of efficiency gains. In fact, privatization is unlikely to generate major gains in efficiency unless accompanied by other reforms. De Walle (1989) explains that "the incentives to engage in rent seeking, corruption and patronage do not depend on the number of public enterprises in the economy, but rather on the extent to which prevailing prices do not reflect the scarcity value of goods and services." Nonetheless, weak governments might prefer to promote privatization rather than attack economic privilege. Glade (1989) says rightly that, in the case of Brazil, "before the public sector is privatized it might be well to try to privatize the private sector."

Monetary Policy

The Monetary Dilemma

Sargent and Wallace (1981) have called attention to the interrelations between fiscal and monetary policy. They study the inflation path under the following assumptions: the monetary authority is not in a position to influence the government's deficit path, the government runs a persistent deficit, and the real interest rate exceeds the economy's growth rate. These assumptions are relevant for Brazil. The debt crisis in Brazil manifests itself not only in rising inflation, but also in the rapid growth of domestic debt (table 4.14), resulting in part from the domestic financing of external debt service and in part from high real interest rates on existing domestic debt (figure 4.8).

A real rate of return on government securities in excess of the economy's growth rate puts the monetary authorities at an impasse: rolling over a fixed amount of interest-bearing government debt requires raising revenue to pay the interest, so the government must either increase the primary budget surplus, print currency, or issue additional interest-bearing debt. However, this last alternative implies a growing stock of real government interest-bearing debt as a percentage of GDP. Such growth cannot go on forever. A limit will be met well before interest payments equal total GDP. It follows that, without debt relief, fighting current inflation with tight monetary policy alone must eventually lead to higher future inflation or debt repudiation of some kind. In the case of Brazil the situation is made more serious by the extremely short maturity of the debt.

The goal is to maintain a restrictive monetary policy, and in practice this has been translated into very high real interest rates. Nonetheless, the public can effectively write checks on their overnight deposits that are backed by the government debt. This implies that in open market operations money that does not pay interest is merely traded for money that does, and therefore such operations do not affect liquidity. The high interest rate avoids flight into dollars and real assets in the short run, and the government continues to enjoy

Table 4.14   Brazil: domestic debt held by private investors, 1987–89
(billions of dollars)

Period		Domestic debt held by private investors
1987	December	33.8
1988	March	32.4
	June	42.2
	September	43.3
	December	44.7
1989	January	40.9
	February	51.1
	March	62.0
	April	68.0
	May	63.0
	June	58.0

Source: Banco Central do Brasil.

financing for the deficit. Yet when the public finally loses confidence in the government's ability or willingness to pay full indexation, there will be flight to real assets and to the dollar. At that point raising interest rates further would not increase confidence, because it would simply mean even greater budget deficits and a larger debt that is even more unsustainable. The government would then ultimately be forced to pay off the debt by creation of money, financing a further flight into real assets and dollars, thus setting off hyperinflation.

Debt-Equity Swaps

Through an unprecedented proliferation of debt swaps and buybacks, Brazil's external debt was cut by more than $8 billion in 1988, to $112 billion. In sheer volume, it was the largest exercise in debt-equity conversion that Latin America has yet seen. The program's cost, however, was a surge in inflation from the expansion of the money supply caused directly by the conversion of debt paper into local currency. A review of the debt conversion program illustrates why many economists have concluded that the program's risks outweigh its purported benefits.

Rights to relending within Brazil became an active swappable debt. In 1982 foreign banks lent dollars to local banks to be repaid six years later. By 1988 the Brazilian banks did not have the dollars to repay these debts, and foreign banks spotted profits. They bought other banks' maturing loans on the secondary market at a discount and then went to the central bank to be paid off in

Figure 4.8 Brazil: real interest rates on overnight accounts, 1983–89

percent per year

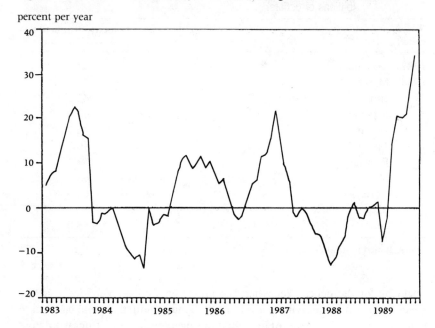

Source: Associação Nacional dos Investidores do Mercado Aberto.

cruzados. They then either sold these to a Brazilian borrower or used them for lending at Brazil's high interest rates.

At auctions of debt for equity investment, banks selling dollar debt for cruzados at Brazil's central bank accepted discounts as low as 1 percent for investment in the northeast region and as high as 50 percent in the year's final auctions. Also common were the so-called informal conversions, which were not expressly authorized by the central bank and which used the black market.

Brazil's agreement with its foreign creditors in August 1988, ending 18 months of conflict over a moratorium on interest payments, stipulated that debt auctions would continue, with a further $1.8 billion of debt to become available for conversion at face value over the next three years. Nevertheless, in October 1988 President Sarney issued a decree closing the door on informal debt conversions for state-owned companies. The Summer Plan to control inflation finally suspended auctions and relending.

Developing countries need foreign investment, and the best argument in favor of swaps is that a debt overhang erodes macroeconomic stability and the profitability of investment. In such circumstances, a debt swap program might improve the investment climate. If the subsidies are large, foreign investment thrives. Foreign investment net of repatriated profits in Brazil was negative in 1985 and 1986, but large subsidies restored positive net flows in 1987 and 1988.

There is no doubt that Brazil should open its doors to foreign investment, but there is no justification for subsidizing it. Meyer and Marques (1989) looked at the impact of debt-equity swaps on the balance of payments. Calculating the reduction in interest payments against the increase in repatriated profits that would result from swaps totaling $15 billion over five years, they projected a net outflow of $1.3 billion in the same period.

A country hard pressed to meet the interest payments due on its debt might find it better to cut its interest bill by carving down the stock of outstanding debt and repaying it at a discount. Creditor governments have also been encouraging the practice. Yet governments have good reasons to resist these swaps because of their impact on inflation, on the budget, and on capital flight. Brazil's case is illustrative. Conversions contribute to inflation by provoking a sharp expansion in the money supply. The Brazilian central bank monetized more than $1.8 billion worth of swaps in 1988, an amount equivalent to one-third of the monetary base.

When the Brazilian monetary authorities issue domestic debt to finance the buyback of external debt, the reduced interest payments on the external debt are offset by increased domestic debt service. There could be a reduction in net interest payments if Brazil could appropriate most of the discount at which the external debt is traded, and if domestic rates (in dollars) are lower than international rates. However, real interest rates in Brazil remain very high. The result then is an increase in total debt service. External debt reduction coupled with large budget deficits, both financed by expensive domestic debt, have evolved into a massive fiscal problem.

One can always argue that as long as the government does not deal with its primary budget deficit, any measure to reduce swaps leaves the cause of inflation untouched. But swaps and capital flight further dramatize Brazil's problems.

Poverty and Income Distribution

Table 4.15 shows the trend in the Gini coefficient (a measure of income distribution) for Brazil between 1960 and 1985, and in selected poverty measures between 1970 and 1985. The Gini coefficient jumped from 0.5 in 1960 to 0.6 in 1970, an unusually large deterioration in only 10 years. Between 1970 and 1980 there was no significant change in income distribution. Sedlacek (1989) shows an increase in the concentration of income and in the Gini coefficient between 1984 and 1987, and attributes this to a redistribution from the middle to the upper classes. Such a redistribution would help to explain the near-tripling in the price differential between luxury and middle-income housing from 1978 to 1988 (figure 4.9).

Table 4.15 Brazil: measures of poverty and income distribution, 1960–85

Data source	Average income[a]	Gini coefficient	Proportion of population below the poverty line[b]	Percentage of national income necessary to overcome poverty[c]
Census 1960	n.a.	0.500	n.a.	n.a.
Census 1970	2.56	0.608	0.422	7.7
Census 1980	4.83	0.597	0.219	1.9
PNAD 1981	4.60	0.584	0.208	2.1
PNAD 1982	4.68	0.587	0.211	2.0
PNAD 1983	3.82	0.589	0.265	3.3
PNAD 1984	4.04	0.588	0.243	2.8
PNAD 1985	4.51	0.592	0.211	2.2

n.a. = not available; PNAD = Pesquisa Nacional por Amostra de Domicilio.

a. In multiples of the minimum wage.

b. The poverty line is defined here as the equivalent of one minimum wage of August 1980.

c. Amount needed to raise the incomes of all persons to the poverty line, as a percentage of national income.

Source: Hoffmann (1989).

By and large, Brazil has seen an improvement in life expectancy, infant mortality, and literacy rates since the debt crisis began. The most common explanation is that progress in these areas has a strong positive inertia. Parents who learn to save a sick child with a simple solution of salt, sugar, and water pass this information on to their children and neighbors. Those who know how to read also realize that it is a skill worth instilling in their children. Technical progress and the self-perpetuating nature of these gains combine to improve welfare indicators even when monetary resources dry up. Superficially, it would seem that progress continues despite the best efforts of society to thwart it.

But how much do the basic indicators really tell us about poverty? Merrick (1989) cautions against relying on aggregate numbers. He asserts the existence of a dual population system in Brazil. He describes a modern urban elite, concentrated in the southeast, passing through the mortality transition and then into controlled natality at a pace similar to that seen in other late-industrializing societies. Coexisting with this population is a mostly rural population, concentrated in the northeast, with the high fertility and mortality rates associated with traditional underdeveloped societies. In other words, the poor enjoy less than their share of the gains recorded by the aggregate welfare indicators.

Table 4.16 shows that poverty increased during the 1983 recession but declined thereafter. In 1986, poverty in the Brazilian metropolitan areas was

Figure 4.9   Rio de Janeiro: ratio of the sale price per room of a luxury apartment to that of a middle-income apartment, 1978–88

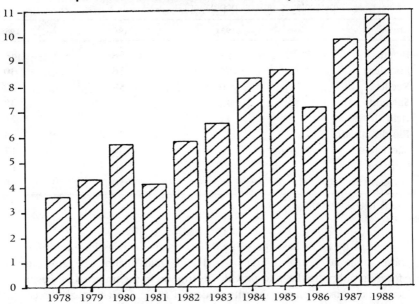

Source: Banco Icatu, calculated from prices reported in *O Globo* and *Jornal do Brasil.*

below its level in 1981. One could argue that, up to 1988, adjustment to the debt crisis had not taken place in Brazil. But if Brazil manages to avoid the hyperinflation that threatens the economy, its response to the debt crisis will have served the poor better than the orthodox approach taken by Mexico.

The Brazilian share of GDP spent on social services is as high as or higher than that of other middle-income developing countries, but Brazilian social welfare indicators are strikingly low. The World Bank (1988a) reports that infant mortality is well above the average for countries in Brazil's income group, and in the northeast it is higher than in much of sub-Saharan Africa. Brazilian children complete fewer years in school than do children in any other Latin American country except El Salvador and Nicaragua. Consequently, the country is characterized by a low literacy rate and a high incidence of chronic diseases.

According to the same World Bank report, the reasons for Brazil's poor social welfare performance are twofold: resources are poorly managed and they are not efficiently targeted. The poorest 19 percent of the population (those receiving less than one-quarter of a minimum wage per household member) receive only 6 percent of all social benefits. An estimated 78 percent of all spending on health is devoted to high-cost, curative hospital services, with only

Table 4.16 Brazil: share of the population living below the poverty line, selected metropolitan areas and years
(percentages of total population)

City	1981	1983	1986
Belém	51	58	46
Fortaleza	54	56	30
Recife	56	57	40
Salvador	43	44	38
Belo Horizonte	31	44	26
Rio de Janeiro	27	35	23
São Paulo	22	34	17
Curitiba	17	30	11
Pôrto Alegre	18	30	16

Source: Rocha (1989).

22 percent going to basic preventive health care such as immunization programs, malaria control, and maternal and child health. The government's education policy has been to provide free tuition in the universities, despite the fact that the cost of each university student is 18 times higher than the cost per student at the primary and secondary levels combined.

Brazilian society continues to be characterized by a large number of people living in extreme poverty and by a notorious inequality in income distribution. Relative shares of income are relevant not only to issues of equity, but to the assessment of policies designed to overcome absolute poverty. Average income per capita in Brazil exceeds that in most African and Asian countries, yet extreme poverty persists as a result of inequitable income distribution. In the Brazilian context it is impossible to look at poverty without considering redistribution as a potential solution.

Conclusions

The major finding of this analysis of Brazil's adjustment is the inadequacy of the public-sector savings effort. What occurred through 1988 can be characterized as an "accommodation" to the disappearance of external sources of finance rather than structural adjustment. The position of the public sector in Brazil continues to be badly compromised by the need to extract resources from the private sector for the service of the external debt. Domestic debt has also grown to finance the budget deficit as well as to pay for large subsidies granted to public enterprises and the private sector. To achieve fiscal consolidation without a major recession, Brazil needs to reduce the transfer of resources abroad. Today that means debt reduction and postponement of debt service. Yet even this will not be enough to restore stability.

Budgetary equilibrium requires major cuts in subsidies and the consolidation of the domestic debt. This could be achieved by privatization, with the proceeds used to retire debt, and by a forced lengthening of the maturity of the remaining instruments. In anticipation of the November-December 1989 elections, the government tried to avoid hyperinflation by raising interest rates and by making mini-adjustments, as it has traditionally done when inflation reaches peak levels. If this course is continued, however, higher and higher inflation is likely to result, simply because the institutional adaptation is irreversible and pushes the economy to ever-higher peaks of inflation. The threat of hyperinflation is real.

Appendix

The budget deficit corrected for inflation at time t is defined as:

$$(G_t - T_t)/P_t + \{[(i_t - \pi_t)/(1 + \pi_t)](B_{t-1}/P_{t-1})\} + \{[(1 + i^*_t)(1 + j_t)/(1 + \pi_t)] - 1\} (E_{t-1}D_{t-1}/P_{t-1})$$

| Primary deficit | Real interest payments on the domestic debt | Real interest payments on the external debt |

where $G - T$ is the primary deficit, P is the price level, π is inflation, i is the nominal interest rate, j is the rate of devaluation of the exchange rate, B is the domestic debt, D is the external debt, and E is the exchange rate.

The budget deficit corrected for inflation can also be measured by:

$$\Delta b_t + \Delta d_t + \Delta h_t + \text{inflation tax}_t$$

where Δb_t is the increase in the real domestic debt, Δd_t is the increase in the real external debt net of foreign reserves, and Δh_t is the increase in the real monetary base.

This can be shown if we start by considering the budget constraint:

(1) $(G_t - T_t) + i_t B_{t-1} + i^*_t E_t D_{t-1} = (K_t - K_{t-1}) + (B_t - B_{t-1}) + E_t(D_t - D_{t-1})$

where $G_t - T_t$ is the nonfinancial component of the budget deficit, $i_t B_{t-1}$ is interest payments on the domestic debt, $i^*_t E_t D_{t-1}$ is interest payments on the external debt, $B_t - B_{t-1}$ is domestic borrowing, $D_t - D_{t-1}$ is external borrowing, and $K_t - K_{t-1}$ is domestic credit creation, which is equal to the change in the monetary base, H, minus the change in foreign reserves, F:

Table 4.17 Brazil: two inflation-corrected measures of the fiscal deficit, 1982–88 (percentages of GDP)

| | Change in real debt[a] | | Inflation tax[b] | | Deficit corrected for inflation | |
| | | | | | Measure A | Measure B |
Year	(1A)	(1B)	(2A)	(2B)	(1A)+(2A)	(1B)+(2B)
1982	7.1	n.a.	2.0	1.5	9.1	n.a.
1983	20.0	18.3	2.1	1.3	22.1	19.6
1984	7.5	7.9	1.5	2.3	9.0	10.2
1985	3.7	5.5	1.3	2.3	5.0	7.8
1986	1.4	−7.0	0.7	3.6	2.1	−3.4
1987	−0.5	11.7	3.8	2.7	3.3	14.4
1988[c]	−2.7	12.8	2.3	3.4	−0.4	16.2

n.a. = not available.

a. From tables 4.18 and 4.19.

b. In column (2A), inflation tax = $\{[\pi/(1+\pi)](H_{t-1}/P_{t-1})\}/GDP$; in column (2B), the share of seignorage in GDP is used to approximate the inflation tax.

c. Preliminary.

Source: Banco Central do Brasil, Brazil Economic Program, various issues.

$$(2) \quad K_t - K_{t-1} = (H_t - H_{t-1}) - E_t(F_t - F_{t-1}).$$

Deflating equation (1) by P_t and using the definitions of inflation (π), of the devaluation rate (j), and of the real interest rate (r), we can write:

$$(3) \quad (G_t - T_t)/P_t + r_t(B_{t-1}/P_{t-1}) + \{[(1 + i^*_t)(1 + j_t)/(1 + \pi_t)] - 1\}(D_{t-1}/P_{t-1})$$
$$= [(K_t - K_{t-1})/P_t] + [(B_t/P_t) - (B_{t-1}/P_{t-1})] + [(R_tD_t) - (R_{t-1}D_{t-1})]$$

Using equation (2) and:

$$(H_t - H_{t-1})/P_t = [(H_t/P_t) - (H_{t-1}/P_{t-1})] + [(H_{t-1}/P_{t-1})(\pi_t/1 + \pi_t)],$$

we can rewrite the righthand side of equation (3) as:

$$\Delta b_t + \Delta d_t + \Delta h_t + \text{inflation tax}_t$$

where:

$$\Delta b_t = B_t/P_t - B_{t-1}/P_{t-1}$$
$$\Delta d_t = R_t D_t - R_{t-1}D_{t-1} - R_t(F_t - F_{t-1})$$
$$\Delta h_t = H_t/P_t - H_{t-1}/P_{t-1}$$
$$\text{inflation tax}_t = (\pi_t/1 + \pi_t)(H_{t-1}/P_{t-1}).$$

Table 4.18 Brazil: consolidated public-sector debt and share in GDP of the change in real debt used in measure A, 1982–88

	Debt stock[a] (millions of NCz)	Consumer price index[a] (1986 = 100)	Change in real debt (millions of 1986 NCz)	Nominal GDP (millions of NCz)	GDP deflator (1986 = 100)	Change in real debt as share of real GDP (percentages)
1981	8.5	1.0		24.6	0.8	
1982	21.7	2.0	222	51.0	1.6	7.1
1983	94.7	5.7	604	118.9	3.9	20.0
1984	334.1	17.5	237	393.7	12.4	7.5
1985	1,242.3	61.2	127	1,413.8	41.0	3.7
1986	2,084.2	100.0	53	3,708.2	100.0	1.4
1987	10,988.0	532.3	−20	11,884.7	309.3	−0.5
1988[b]	115,436.0	5,889.6	−104	92,993.1	2,426.8	−2.7

NCz = new cruzados.

a. December.

b. Preliminary.

Source: Banco Central do Brasil, Brazil Economic Program, various issues.

Table 4.19 Brazil: consolidated public-sector debt and share in GDP of the real debt change used in measure B, 1981–88

	Average debt stock (millions of NCz)	GDP deflator (1986 = 100)	Change in real debt (millions of 1986 NCz)	Nominal GDP (millions of NCz)	Change in real debt as share of real GDP (percentages)
1981		0.8			
1982	15.1	1.6			
1983	58.2	3.9	5.5	118.9	18.3
1984	214.4	12.4	2.5	393.7	7.9
1985	788.2	41.0	1.9	1,413.8	5.5
1986	1,663.3	100.0	−2.6	3,708.2	−7.0
1987	6,536.1	309.3	4.5	11,884.7	11.7
1988[a]	63,212.0	2,426.8	4.9	92,993.1	12.8

NCz = new cruzados.

a. Preliminary.

Source: Banco Central do Brasil, Brazil Economic Program, various issues.

Table 4.17 presents two measures of the inflation-corrected fiscal deficit defined in this manner. The two measures are derived using alternative measures of the change in the real debt, calculated in tables 4.18 and 4.19.

Mexico

Javier Beristain and Ignacio Trigueros

Mexico's adjustment experience since the beginning of the debt crisis has been varied and has provided several lessons for the future. Mexican economic policy in 1981–82 was exactly contrary to what John Williamson has suggested is the "Washington consensus." The public-sector operational deficit was running at about 8 percent of GDP, evidence that there was no concern whatsoever about the level of the fiscal imbalances. Far from moving toward privatization, during 1982 the government nationalized the commercial banks. Trade restrictions, in the form of import permits, were used to tackle the external disequilibrium. Exchange rate stability was regarded more as a symbol of national pride than as something that has to be abandoned once in a while either to achieve consistency among different policy instruments or to face external shocks.

Since 1983 there has been a dramatic turnaround in economic policy in Mexico. Today each of the 10 policy instruments listed by Williamson as forming the basis of the Washington consensus is being applied in a way that promotes adjustment together with low inflation and sustained growth. Nevertheless, the pace and the extent of implementation vary somewhat from instrument to instrument.

Trade liberalization was unthinkable back in 1983, when it was uncertain whether external balance was going to be attained without inducing a collapse in economic activity. Similarly, far-reaching reforms in government finances, which almost certainly would have entailed a reduction in the number of public-sector employees and an increase in tax revenues, were difficult to implement at the beginning of the debt crisis, when the country was experiencing a sharp economic contraction. Thus, economic conditions dictated caution in the implementation of policy reforms. At other times the poor results obtained with certain instruments led to drastic changes in some areas of economic policy. Particularly since mid-1985 what had been more than anything else a forced reaction to the cutoff of foreign funds was converted into a purposeful economic strategy, led by fiscal discipline and the integration of the Mexican economy into world trade and investment flows.

This paper reviews the main features of Mexico's adjustment experience, highlighting those elements that eventually led to the implementation of the

Javier Beristain is Rector of the Instituto Tecnológico Autónomo de México. He has written on income distribution in Mexico and on the economics of education.

Ignacio Trigueros is Chairman of the Department of Economics of the Instituto Tecnológico Autónomo de México. He has written on international economics and on stabilization programs.

so-far-successful Pact for Economic Stability and Growth in 1987. We focus on the process of economic policy reforms, signaling the events that at one time or another played a crucial role. The first section of the paper briefly analyzes the events and policies affecting macroeconomic adjustment up to 1987. The second section deals in more detail with major structural reforms implemented since 1983. The third section explores the current stabilization program in some detail, pointing out its strengths and weaknesses. The concluding section assesses the short- and medium-term outlook for the Mexican economy.

Mexico's Adjustment Program, 1983–1987

At the beginning of the debt crisis the economy bordered on chaos. The annual inflation rate hovered around 100 percent and appeared to be out of control (table 4.20). The dollarization of the economy and speculation on the peso were becoming widespread, the financial system was near collapse, the public-sector deficit was at an all-time high, and the country was forced into a virtual moratorium on its payments abroad. All of this of course was going on in a climate of great uncertainty and little confidence.

The initial adjustment strategy was to induce some order in economic affairs through a fundamentally orthodox program. Through these efforts, the primary public deficit of 7.4 percent of GDP in 1982 was converted into a primary surplus of 4.2 percent in 1983. The urgency of reducing public expenditures and the deficit, however, provoked a sharp decline in public investment, since it is generally easier for the government to reduce capital expenditures than operating expenditures (table 4.21).

In spite of the sharp correction in public finances, the foreign debt could be serviced only by high inflation. During 1983 GDP declined by 4.2 percent. Commitments to the country's foreign creditors required a net transfer of resources abroad, which had to be obtained through a surplus in the trade balance. Between 1983 and 1985 this was accomplished primarily through a contraction in imports. The response of nonoil exports was slow, mainly because of inefficiencies and the decline in productivity stemming from an inward-oriented industrial policy over many years.

Adherence to the initial program was loosened quite a bit from mid-1984 until the first half of 1985, when the second phase of short-term adjustment policy was initiated. Beginning in 1984 a tax incentive scheme was introduced to counteract the sharp recession in which the economy was then immersed. The incentives, which could be applied to the purchase of a wide range of machinery and equipment, had a strong effect on domestic expenditure, especially on automobiles.

Table 4.20 Mexico: summary economic data, 1982–88 (percentages)

Increase in:	1982	1983	1984	1985	1986	1987	1988
Real GDP	−0.6	−4.2	3.6	2.5	−3.7	1.5	1.1
GDP per capita	−2.9	−6.3	1.4	0.4	−5.9	−0.6	−0.8
Consumer price index[a]	98.8	80.8	59.2	63.7	105.7	159.2	51.7
Nonoil exports	−1.9	13.6	38.1	−9.7	37.0	23.7	16.0
Official exchange rate	268.3	49.1	33.8	92.9	148.5	138.2	2.7

a. December to December.

Source: Banco de México, Indicadores Económicos, September 1989.

Table 4.21 Mexico: selected public-sector accounts, 1982–88
(percentages of GDP)

	1982	1983	1984	1985	1986	1987	1988
Nominal deficit	16.3	8.6	8.5	9.6	16.0	16.1	12.3
Operational deficit	5.5	−0.4	0.3	0.8	2.4	−1.8	3.5
Primary deficit	7.4	−4.2	−4.8	−3.4	−1.6	−4.7	−7.4
Total revenue	28.9	32.9	32.2	31.2	30.3	30.6	29.8
Oil exports	8.3	10.8	9.4	8.1	4.9	6.0	3.4
Noninterest expenditures	36.3	28.7	27.4	27.8	28.7	25.9	22.4
Public investment	10.2	7.5	6.7	6.0	6.0	5.6	4.4

Sources: Secretaría de Programación y Presupuesto, Criterios de Política Económica 1990; Banco de México, Indicadores Económicos, September 1989.

Private investment grew considerably and without causing tightness in the domestic capital market because of the accommodating monetary policy that prevailed at the time. It was only in 1985 that the debt crisis at last resulted in a short supply of foreign funds for the public sector. At the same time a deterioration in public finances was seen; the result was strong pressure upon the domestic market for loanable funds. This, along with the incentives for increased private expenditure, should have led to an increase in the domestic cost of loanable funds, which should in turn have halted the increase in private expenditure. Instead, the government took the easy course and financed most of its domestic-currency needs by creation of domestic credit. In this way there was no immediate scarcity of funds but instead a $2.2 billion loss of international reserves, along with an increase in domestic absorption.

By mid-1985 this and other factors had led to a sharp real appreciation of the currency, a decline in nonoil exports, and a widening of the gap between the official and the market exchange rate. Additional adjustment efforts were therefore introduced, and an attempt was made to return to the objective of price stability. However, given the poor performance of the economy over the previous several years, this goal was attempted in a much more gradual manner than before. Public-sector austerity measures were announced to recover what had been lost in terms of fiscal adjustment, and the first stage of a trade liberalization program was implemented. The new trade policy was motivated mainly by the disappointing performance of nonoil exports during 1985 (table 4.20). Greater reliance on market forces in the allocation of loanable funds was to be pursued as well.

The earthquakes of September 1985 and the inevitable reaction of the government and the population caused the administration to abandon its renewed efforts at stabilization. The program of trade liberalization, however, was continued.

At the beginning of 1986, when the country had barely begun to recover from the devastation left by the earthquakes, it was faced with another, even greater economic adversity: the collapse in world oil prices. The oil shock had to be contained and confronted mainly by a nominal and real devaluation of the peso. The real devaluation reached approximately 30 percent by the end of the year. Economic policy during 1986 succeeded in translating this negative shock of nearly 7 percentage points of GDP into a relatively mild recession (GDP fell by 3.7 percent). At the same time a firm commitment to fiscal discipline was crucial in avoiding the slide into hyperinflation. Even more important, the administration continued to go forward with trade liberalization, something that is often put on a back burner under such circumstances. The share of production covered by import permits fell from 46.9 percent in December 1985 to 39.8 percent a year later.

Recovery was experienced in almost all areas in 1987. Only inflation could not be held down. During that year the central bank accumulated almost $7 billion worth of foreign reserves, and the condition of Mexican business was somewhat improved.

Nineteen eighty-seven was a unique year in many respects. At first an attempt was made to maintain the real exchange rate at the high levels achieved in 1986. This effort, which was continued through the first six months of the year, generated strong inflationary pressures, as the authorities tried to prevent the real appreciation of the peso that would have brought the exchange rate to equilibrium. In 1987, the real exchange rate had to be much lower than in the previous year when petroleum income and foreign borrowing had been so low. The obstruction of market forces brought about serious inflationary pressures.

The fact that inflation accelerated during 1987 in spite of a tight fiscal policy led to the official diagnosis that the acceleration was not due to an excess of aggregate demand. This interpretation of events was crucial in justifying the incorporation of heterodox measures into the stabilization program launched in December 1987.

If inflation was not the result of an excess in aggregate demand, it was argued, price controls would have to be imposed. As mentioned earlier, it would have to be determined how much of the inflation really stemmed from inertia and how much from the attempt to maintain an artificially high real exchange rate through nominal devaluations. Given the sound situation of government finances, a lower rate of nominal devaluation was feasible and certainly would have eventually resulted in a decline in the inflation rate.

Some developments in the financial market also contributed to the measures implemented in late 1987. As a result of the increase in inflation registered in 1986–87, there was a significant reduction in the maturity of domestic public debt. This situation created major problems for domestic debt management in that, in the absence of a flexible interest rate policy, any shock to the market for loanable funds could have a rapid and sizable effect on the rate of domestic credit creation.

Two such shocks occurred in the latter part of 1987: the US stock market plummeted in October, downgrading the quality of peso-denominated assets, and there was a sharp increase in the private sector's demand for credit, arising from a unique opportunity to make advantageous prepayments on its foreign debt.[2] These shocks, along with a slow reaction of interest rates, precluded the rollover of public domestic debt on several occasions, forcing the government to print money that would soon be used to buy foreign currency from the central bank.

In the presence of this drain of international reserves, the central bank eventually ceased to intervene in the parallel foreign-currency market. Its withdrawal induced a 40 percent depreciation of the peso. The exchange rate adjustment created tensions with the labor unions, which were dissipated only with the implementation of the Economic Solidarity Pact.

In summary, the economic policy pursued by the Miguel de la Madrid administration was very volatile. It must be recognized, however, that this volatility was largely the result of instability stemming from exogenous factors. Among these, the most important was the 30 percent deterioration in the terms of trade between 1983 and 1988.

---

2. At that time the Mexican government had just signed a rescheduling agreement with its commercial creditors, which was to be extended, with a deadline around the beginning of 1988, to private-sector debt. Some banks preferred prepayments to a generous discount over the grace periods and interest rate conditions implied by the agreement.

In judging the macroeconomic results of the de la Madrid administration's policy, one must also keep in mind that the public sector had to deal with a relative lack of noninflationary financial resources. This factor was particularly important during 1986 when, notwithstanding the clear rationale for foreign financing arising from the collapse in the price of oil, funds from abroad were practically nonexistent.

The most important achievement of economic policy during the de la Madrid administration was that it prepared the economic foundations for growth. Although the aggregate results were rather disappointing—real GDP was no higher in 1988 than in 1982, and inflation turned out to be higher than in previous administrations—it cannot be denied that the country is now stronger in numerous ways. Undoubtedly the most important change has been the economy's exposure to a more open trade environment. This opening has changed the way in which economic policy is made and even the way business is done in Mexico.

Policies for Structural Change

Before going into the details of the Economic Solidarity Pact, it may be worthwhile to describe some of the structural changes carried out in Mexico from 1983 until the Pact was implemented in 1987. First there were the trade liberalization measures implemented in mid-1985 and kept in place despite the external shocks that followed. The process of trade liberalization was deliberate and achieved a depth with few precedents. In 1982 nearly all production was covered by import permits; by the end of 1987 the figure had dropped to 19.7 percent. The weighted-average tariff, around 24 percent in 1982, fell to about 11.8 percent by 1987. By that time, official import prices (a nontariff barrier) had also disappeared.

The outcome of trade liberalization has so far been quite favorable. Very few firms have gone under as a result of foreign competition, and access to imported inputs has had an important effect on domestic costs of production, thus allowing for an extraordinary expansion of nonoil exports. This expansion has played an important role in minimizing the contractionary effects of the decline in oil prices and of the government's latest austerity measures. There is also some evidence that the country is allocating resources more efficiently. For instance, from 1985 to 1988 there was a significant increase in both imports and exports of goods whose production processes are subject to economies of scale, such as chemical products and iron and steel. This pattern indicates greater specialization and therefore more efficient scales of domestic production. Higher levels of investment in textiles and food production indicate a reallocation of resources toward labor-intensive activities.

Other structural changes are related to public finances. The significant reduction in public-sector noninterest expenditures, amounting to almost 14 points of GDP from 1982 to 1988, has changed the way the public sector does business. It is now much more austere, especially at the federal level. This effort, together with a greater flexibility in the prices of goods and services provided by the public sector, has resulted in a correction of public finances, whose balance went from a primary deficit of 7.4 percent of GDP in 1982 to a surplus of 7.4 percent in 1988, despite a decline in oil export revenue equal to 5 percent of GDP.

A related change is the ongoing process of divestiture of state-owned enterprises. This policy is a reflection of a new concept of the state's role in the economy. It is felt that although the government should still exercise its dominance in certain areas, it must be leaner and more agile to accomplish the task with greater efficiency. A more pragmatic line of reasoning running parallel to this concept holds that many of the state-owned enterprises represent burdens that must be reduced to achieve a permanently balanced budget.

Although few individual cases have received much publicity, of the 1,155 entities in government hands at the beginning of 1983, only 496 remain. About 130 of those entities were privatized; the remainder were either liquidated, transferred to state or local governments, or merged with other entities. The recent announcement of the privatization of the telephone company indicates that the present administration of President Carlos Salinas de Gortari will continue efforts in this direction.

Decades of protectionism allowed, and perhaps even provoked, a number of trade practices that eventually became codified in both written and unwritten rules. Although profitable for some, these rules caused inefficiencies in many industries such as trucking, finance, and petrochemicals. Measures to remove barriers to entry and in general to promote a more competitive business framework in these and other areas are now being rapidly introduced, with some impressive results. Deregulation of the trucking industry increased effective capacity by about 10 percent overnight; as a result of a reclassification of petrochemical products, private firms are now allowed to participate in activities previously reserved for the government, and investments on the order of several billion dollars are already being undertaken.

The necessity of making the current price-freeze viable, through cost reduction arising from the elimination of monopolistic rents, has played an important role in accelerating this type of policy reform.

The Economic Solidarity Pact

The unstable situation that prevailed at the end of 1987 convinced the Mexican authorities and many others that a monthly inflation rate of 7 percent was not sustainable. Only a far-reaching stabilization program could do away with inflation and prepare the economy for a period of sustained growth with price stability. The Economic Solidarity Pact was initiated to meet this goal.

The Pact is basically a set of necessarily complex answers to the problem of stabilization. The strategy consists mainly of orthodox elements: tighter spending, monetary and credit controls, and greater efforts at increasing revenues. However, certain heterodox elements, arrived at by negotiation among the major sectors of the economy, are included as well. The orthodox elements are the ones that will result in long-term stability. These make up the fundamental elements of the stabilization program.

The basic idea behind the program is to achieve permanent price stability by reaching a fiscal balance that requires no inflationary financing. The goal for the next few years is to achieve a primary public-sector surplus amounting to between 6 percent and 7 percent of GDP. Assuming reasonable access to foreign funds (i.e., just enough to keep the real value of foreign debt constant), this surplus will give the government the margin it needs to service its foreign and domestic debts without resorting to inflationary financing.

During the first stages of the Pact the exchange rate was kept fixed in order to impose discipline in other areas of public policy, such as minimum wages and fiscal policy. The prices of various goods were also kept under strict control, and at times businesses were actually asked to lower their prices.

Under a new president, Carlos Salinas de Gortari, the administration introduced some flexibility into what at the end of 1988 had become an increasingly tight situation. Thus, while the compromise is still in place to continue with the adjustments necessary to maintain a budget compatible with price stability, some of the lags in public prices and user fees have been corrected, price increases have been authorized for some products, and the peso has been devalued against the dollar at an average rate of 30 pesos per month on a preannounced basis. This will continue in effect until March 1990. Some increases in the minimum wage have also been approved.

The favorable results of the program came about much more quickly than originally expected. Inflation went down from average monthly rates of 7 percent in 1987 to around 1 percent in just a few months, and the expected recession did not occur. Industrial production rose by 3.5 percent in the first half of 1988 compared with the same period in 1987. During the second half of 1988 output was practically stagnant, but a strong recovery was seen during the first seven months of 1989.

The largest output increases have taken place in durable goods, both for consumption and for investment. The increase in the demand for some goods is based on speculation, as some regard the price stability brought about by the Pact as temporary, and on the windfall income arising from high *ex post* real rates of return on government securities.

Speculative demand stemming from uncertainty regarding future prices is also reflected in the behavior of merchandise imports. Here the uncertainty centers on what the exchange rate and trade policy (i.e., the level of liberalization) will be in the near future.

Merchandise imports during 1988 totaled almost $19 billion, up from $12 billion in 1987. The growth in imports has been dominated by capital goods and has resulted in a sharp reduction of the trade surplus to a mere $1.8 billion in 1988. The current account meanwhile went from average monthly surpluses of $300 million to an average monthly deficit of about $430 million in the period from June 1988 to June 1989.

One important effect of the stabilization program was a sharp increase in observed real interest rates. High real interest rates increase the public debt service burden and thus generate a greater fiscal deficit. Either foreign reserves or foreign borrowing must be used to finance this deficit, given that the stabilization program limits the use of inflationary financing. In fact, despite the fact that during 1988 noninterest expenditures were reduced as a percentage of GDP and public-sector income made some progress, the primary surplus was still insufficient to compensate for the real increase in domestic interest payments. The operational deficit thus went from −1.8 percent of GDP in 1987 to 3.5 percent in 1988.

Although such a situation presents some problems in the management of public finances, it is felt that real interest rates will return to normal levels, creating room for structural changes in fiscal policy. However, since mid-September 1989 real interest rates have remained high instead of continuing the downward trend begun in July after the announcement of the foreign debt agreement. Another result has been a real appreciation of the peso of around 20 percent since the beginning of the program. However, during 1989 the real appreciation has stopped.

These results have induced widespread doubts about the feasibility of continuing the program in its present form. Real appreciation, along with a deterioration of the current account balance, has in the past served as a warning sign in other stabilization attempts that were eventually abandoned. However, as we argue below, there is not enough evidence of exchange rate misalignment arising from the current slide of the nominal exchange rate.

The Outlook

Economic growth during the first six months of 1989 surpassed even the most optimistic forecasts, reaching 2.4 percent in annual terms; beginning with the final quarter of 1988, higher rates of growth have been observed in every quarter. Real wages are also starting to show some growth for the first time in four years.

On the supply side, all parts of the economy except agriculture and a few manufacturing industries have experienced growth. The manufacturing sector grew by 7.4 percent, with a 12.3 percent growth rate in metal products and machinery and equipment. Recovery in the construction industry also suggests that the economy has begun a period of expansion.

On the demand side, growth is explained primarily by increases in investment and private consumption. Growth in gross fixed investment reached an annual rate of 13.4 percent during the second quarter of 1989. It is estimated that private consumption grew at an annual rate of more than 7 percent during the second quarter, probably reflecting a higher level of disposable income arising from both the increase in real wages and interest transfers from the government.

This growth during the first six months of 1989 took place under what would conventionally be considered adverse conditions. In particular, the complex foreign debt negotiations going on during this time created considerable uncertainty. The program still faces three major short-term risks. The first relates to the difficulty of fulfilling the fiscal goals, the second relates to the deterioration of the current account observed since the second half of 1988, and the third has to do with the obstacles brought about by the high real interest rates.

Fiscal Goals

For the program to be viable and bring about a permanent stabilization of prices, the adjustment in public finances will have to be deeper than it is at present. For the government to keep from using inflation as a means of financing its deficit and accordingly maintain a low rate of depreciation of the currency, it must first maintain a primary surplus of between 6 percent and 7 percent of GDP, given the current cost of servicing domestic debt. If this is not accomplished, maintenance of the actual rate of depreciation will eventually result in the loss of foreign reserves, which of course cannot be sustained in the medium term. It would indeed be unfortunate if, as in 1985, after having attained some price stability fiscal solvency were not achieved.

It is readily agreed that there has been a great improvement in public finances and that the attainment of some of the program's goals has been hampered by external shocks, such as the decline in the international price of oil. Also, the accord reached between Mexico and the commercial banks on 23 July 1989 marked an important step toward the reduction of the country's foreign debt burden. The incorporation of multiyear financial mechanisms into the agreement does ensure some permanence in the stabilization program.

However, the savings in transfers abroad resulting directly from the agreement do not represent much more than 1 percent of GDP. Thus, the most important way in which the renegotiation of the foreign debt can contribute to stabilization is through the reduction in the risk premium demanded by holders of peso-denominated government paper. This would be the result of a general conviction that the renegotiation has strengthened the solvency of the public sector.

During 1988 real interest payments on public domestic debt were about twice those paid on public foreign debt, even though the former is worth just one-half of the latter. This difference reflects a sizable risk premium on domestic interest rates. A more reasonable risk premium, on the order of 5 percentage points, would give rise to a reduction in domestic real interest payments of about 5 percent of GDP from the amount registered in 1988. During 1989, mainly as a result of a decline in nominal interest rates of between 8 and 13 percentage points since the announcement of the foreign debt agreement, about 40 percent of that reduction will be attained.

Besides the interest rate problem there remain some other questions regarding the maintenance of fiscal solvency over the next few years. Spending will have to be greatly restructured if fiscal equilibrium is to remain permanent. It is obvious that expenditures for investment in health and education will have to be increased sooner or later. The effects of putting off investment in infrastructure can be seen in the deterioration of highways, water systems, telecommunications, ports, and other resources. The results of this neglect will become even more obvious as the level of economic activity increases. If stability is to be maintained, however, increases in public investment will have to be offset by either cuts in other areas or increased public-sector revenues, so that the primary surplus remains unaltered.

On the other hand, many of the reforms implemented in the area of government finances will begin to show an effect during 1990. For example, the divestiture of many state-owned industries that up to now have only represented a drain on revenues will begin to give some relief to the budget. At the same time, many investments traditionally considered to be the responsibility of the government will now be undertaken by the private sector. For example, it is expected that in the next few years the private sector will make important investments in transportation infrastructure and telecommunications. As mentioned above, a recently announced change in the regulations affecting the petrochemical industry will allow the participation of private capital in some activities previously reserved to the state oil monopoly.

Although contributions to fiscal balance from the revenue side have been practically absent throughout the adjustment process, there are prospects of increased tax revenue for the immediate future. From 1982 to 1988 the ratio of public-sector revenue to GDP rose by only 1 percentage point (table 4.21), thus contributing only marginally to the 14-percentage-point correction in the primary balance. During that same period, however, there was a decline of 5 percentage points in government oil export revenues. Hence, other sources of income have already played an important role in fiscal adjustment. Throughout the adjustment period many subsidies in the form of below-market prices on public-sector goods have been reduced. Most recently, the substitution of tariffs for quantitative trade restrictions, the elimination of inflation-induced distortions in the corporate income tax, and reforms in the area of tax administration have also contributed to the goal of fiscal balance.

The most important of these measures is a complementary tax on corporate assets introduced in 1989. This tax, which can be fully credited against corporate income taxes and which therefore only determines a lower bound on tax liabilities, has eliminated some important loopholes, giving rise to an increase of more than 30 percent in corporate income tax revenues during the first half of 1989.

Nevertheless, tax revenues in Mexico are still relatively low compared with those prevailing in other developing countries. This situation is basically attributed to a narrow tax base and is expected to be corrected in the near future. The incorporation of major sectors of the economy, such as agriculture and transportation, into the scheme of the corporate income tax is already being debated in the legislature.

The Current Account and Exchange Rates

Even though nonoil exports have behaved favorably, the current account registered a $2 billion deficit in the first half of 1989. The deficit could well grow to $5 billion for the entire year. The deterioration was at first the result of an accumulation of imported inventories by firms reacting either to the novelty of import liberalization or to the belief that the liberalization measures would not be permanent. The transitory fiscal deficit caused by high domestic real interest rates has also contributed to this situation. More recently the deterioration in the current account is consistent with trends in private investment as well as in private consumption. In fact, the growth in imports of capital and intermediate goods corresponds to the unexpectedly high growth rate of GDP.

The rapid growth of imports in some industries results from deficient domestic supply due to the problems that result from imposing price controls for a prolonged period of time. The public's perception of this phenomenon, however, is sometimes very different. In general it is felt that the well-known conflict between stabilization and trade liberalization is exacting its toll, and that sooner or later an abrupt devaluation will have to take place.

Assessment of the degree of over- or undervaluation of the Mexican peso has become somewhat complicated. As mentioned above, the real exchange rate is now about 20 percent lower than before the implementation of the Pact. However, at that time the real exchange rate was at one of its highest levels since 1982. The sharp real depreciation that accompanied the collapse in the price of oil remained practically intact at the end of 1987. Such a level of the real exchange rate should be considered temporary and necessary to face the abrupt fall in oil revenue, so that the new terms-of-trade situation and trade liberalization can work themselves out to increase the country's nonoil export capacity.

Thus, although some real appreciation was to be expected, it remains to be seen whether 20 percent was the right amount. This amount of real appreciation has remained practically constant during 1989. The behavior of exports does not give a clear-cut answer: although there has been a decline in the rate of growth of nonoil exports, that was to be expected given the increase in their base from 1985 to 1988; on the other hand, value added at the northern-border assembly plants *(maquiladoras)* is still showing 40 percent annual growth. It should also be taken into account that deregulation of the transport and telecommunications industries and the financial system should provide some cost relief for Mexican exporters. More important, the fiscal imbalances, which were the main cause of major exchange rate misalignment in 1976 and 1982, are now entirely absent. Thus, in the absence of a more definite downward trend in nonoil exports, it is reasonable to assert that the exchange rate is not overvalued.

The Interest Rate Problem

Since the unfortunate outcome of the accommodating monetary policy followed during 1984–85 and the failed attempt to administer interest rates after the 1985 earthquakes, there has been an increasing reliance upon the market mechanism in determining interest rates. Even a complicated scheme through which bank reserves were transferred to the government, at a cost somewhat below market interest rates, has been gradually abandoned. In any case, the development of a sophisticated parallel credit market had already nullified its effects. Market-determined interest rates have allowed the normal rollover of domestic public debt, although this has been accomplished at an abnormally high real cost since the beginning of the Pact.

The latent exchange risk mentioned above is one factor causing interest rates to remain high. In this way the Pact has entered into a vicious circle provoked by expectations associated perhaps with the possible overvaluation of the peso, when in fact the current account situation is due to temporary factors. Thus, exchange rate risk does not allow real interest rates to go down, and the consequent high interest payments cause the current account deficit to linger, creating a further fiscal deficit. Although this situation should be temporary, its persistence is turning into a serious problem for the Pact, increasing the short-term risk.

Even though nominal interest rates went down after the announcement of the debt agreement, real interest rates will most likely stay around their present levels. In late 1989 one-month instruments were paying a real rate of about 20 percent per year—a high price for funds. As the exchange rate continues on its present crawl, some exchange rate risk may persist. Although the exchange rate risk is making it difficult to lower real interest rates, the cost of high interest rates must be weighed against the advantages of stabilization.

One extreme response to these difficulties would be to argue that it is impossible to continue the Pact in its present form and that an abrupt devaluation is needed. Public prices and user fees would then also have to be increased, and a new program would have to be announced. Besides being infeasible, this option has a few disadvantages. The financial relief that would come about as a result of the expropriatory effect on the public debt would be short-lived. In the long run, the real cost of debt service would increase because of the devaluation's effect on credibility. The real, albeit temporary, depreciation that normally accompanies a nominal devaluation would be very difficult to achieve in present circumstances as it would be practically impossible to contain the demands for wage increases, which would start at whatever percentage was used for the devaluation.

The continuance of a crawling peg will, on the other hand, provide greater flexibility. The macroeconomic objective of these gradual devaluations would be to facilitate the price adjustments and wage increases necessary to bring about a more efficient resource allocation process.

It is unlikely that price controls will be removed too abruptly. However, prices should gradually be allowed to be determined by the market. Abrupt removal of price controls will generate additional uncertainty about the exchange rate, thus further complicating interest rate management.

The real short-term problem seems to be whether there will be sufficient foreign funds to finance the current boom in economic activity. As mentioned above, the strong recovery of the economy partly explains the deterioration of the current account. However, during the first half of 1989 there were also large capital inflows (about $2 billion), which made the current account deficit easily manageable. In the second half of the year these capital inflows seem to have slowed down, thus bringing about a difficult short-term situation.

An exchange rate adjustment or any other measure aimed at slowing down economic activity would obviously be inappropriate now, after seven years, when things are starting to look normal. On the other hand, financing the deficit with international reserves may trigger additional speculation and make the problem more complex. Perhaps the only option available is to maintain an active interest rate policy until the foreign debt renegotiation is finally completed. Given the sound medium-term policy implemented by the government, once the agreement with the country's creditors is completed, capital should again start to pour in, contributing to the permanence of the current surge in economic activity.

Conclusion

The recent Mexican adjustment experience illustrates the importance of fiscal solvency for successful stabilization. Without it, consensus behind the process of price and wage setting would have been impossible to achieve. The role of price controls is less clear. We have noted that they often give rise to widespread speculation, which may harm economic well-being, if only because of the extraordinary fiscal adjustment necessary to service domestic government obligations. Thus, further analysis of the real contribution of price controls to stabilization is warranted before one can assess their benefits over time.

Acknowledgment

This paper draws heavily upon *The Mexican Economy*, a monthly report published by the Centro de Análisis e Investigación Económica. We wish to thank its staff for their helpful assistance. Comments on a previous draft were given by William R. Cline, Georgina Kessel, Sebastian Edwards, Sweder van Wijnbergen, John Williamson, and the participants of the conference and are gratefully acknowledged.

Comment

William R. Cline

Argentina

Juan Carlos de Pablo has presented a vivid description of the extreme fluctuations and uncertainty that have characterized the economy of Argentina, the only large Latin American country to have experienced hyperinflation in recent times. My one quibble would be with his statement that the real exchange rate has fluctuated less severely in recent years than in the past. Although it is true that the gyrations were larger in the 1970s and early 1980s,[3] Argentina's real exchange rate fluctuations have remained relatively high compared with those of other major countries.[4]

Why did Argentina's successive stabilization plans fail? The Austral Plan of June 1985, the Mini-Austral of March 1987, Austral II in October 1987, and the August 1988 Spring Plan all collapsed for essentially the same reason. The Alfonsín government was unable to close the fiscal gap. The Austral Plan pledged to limit the fiscal deficit to some 2½ percent of GNP, or an amount that could be financed fully from abroad. By the first half of 1989, the nominal fiscal deficit was running at some 15 percent to 20 percent of GNP. Fiscal adjustment typically failed because it relied on temporary, unsustainable expedients—in particular, export taxes. The successive heterodox shocks and price freezes also tended to rely on a fixed exchange rate to stabilize expectations, and overvaluation was the recurrent result.

Structural reform is necessary to close the fiscal gap. Argentina's state firms lose some 2 percent to 3 percent of GNP annually (with the state railroad and oil firms leading sources of deficits). The tax base is weak and evasion rampant.

---

3. For example, a 50 percent real appreciation in 1976, a 33 percent depreciation in 1977, then a 72 percent cumulative appreciation through 1980, followed by a 44 percent depreciation from 1980 to 1982.

4. From 1983 through 1988, the average absolute annual fluctuation around the real exchange rate mean was 11 percent for Argentina but only 4 percent for Brazil (using a trade-weighted, wholesale price–deflated index). And in 1989 Argentina's real exchange rate depreciated by almost 60 percent in the second quarter, with the dramatic collapse of the austral that led to hyperinflation.

William R. Cline is Senior Fellow at the Institute for International Economics. He was formerly Senior Fellow at the Brookings Institution and Assistant Professor at Princeton University. He is the author of 19 books including International Debt: Systemic Risk and Policy Response.

Thus, revenue from taxes on income, profits, and capital gains amounts to less than 3 percent of GNP, compared with 13 percent in the United States (IMF 1988a, 106).

Domestic policies are not the only difficulty. The external debt poses a serious potential burden, as its ratio to exports of goods and services is one of the highest in Latin America. Yet it is revealing that hyperinflation occurred at a time when Argentina had not been paying interest on its foreign debt for more than a year.

The outbreak of hyperinflation in May through July of 1989 did have a key external aspect, nonetheless: a breakdown of support from international agencies as the result of failure to meet domestic economic policy conditions. An expectational explosion on the exchange rate led the hyperinflation, and this explosion occurred after the IMF and the World Bank cut Argentina off in early 1989. With reserves exhausted, the government stopped supporting the austral. It is likely that both the officials of the Alfonsín government and those of the international agencies would have been more willing to compromise if they had known what lay ahead.

The economic program of the new Menem regime is an encouraging break with the past. Far from the populist measures traditionally associated with the Peronist party, it represents a serious program of adjustment and structural reform. The centerpiece of the program is major tax reform based on a broad generalization of the value-added tax at 15 percent (and prison terms for evaders). Extensive privatization is another crucial element. It seems to have taken the trauma of 200 percent inflation in July alone to break down the political barriers to such fundamental change.

It remains to be seen whether interest groups will permit the program to succeed. By early December 1989 there were already worrisome signs. Labor strikes were reviving. Interest rates were back up to 30 percent monthly, and the parallel exchange rate spread was some 50 percent—signs that the government would be unable to hold its pledge of a fixed exchange rate through March 1990.

Brazil

The paper by Cardoso and Dantas contains much with which we can all agree. Brazil did not achieve adjustment, at least not internal adjustment. The government has done little to liberalize imports. The collapse of government savings (from +6 percent of GNP in 1970–77 to −7 percent in 1988) is the key to Brazil's macro destabilization. Interest on the domestic debt is a major burden, and the high real interest rate a serious related problem.

Other themes in the paper raise more doubts. First, an implicit thesis is that the burden of external debt caused much of Brazil's inflationary problem. Here the argument and the evidence are much weaker. The fiscal deficit did not come primarily from foreign debt. From 1980 to 1984–85, government interest on the external debt rose only from 1.8 percent of GNP to 2.5 percent (IMF 1988b; World Bank 1988–89). In contrast, rising domestic spending played a greater role. For example, spending on public administration rose by 2.2 percentage points of GNP from 1983 to 1988, as the new democratic regime engaged in patronage politics.[5]

Did devaluation to deal with the debt problem contribute to inflation? Certainly so. But as the paper on Colombia (Rudolf Hommes, chapter 3) shows, it is possible to carry out devaluation without an inflationary result if the corresponding fiscal and monetary tightening is present. Did debt-equity conversions cause high inflation? A popular view is that the surge of inflation to 1,000 percent in 1988 was caused by the debt-equity swap program. But the Cardoso-Dantas figure of $1.8 billion in monetary expansion as the result of the program should be compared not with the conventionally defined money base but with the entire money supply, including quasi-money in the form of short-term government debt (and the authors correctly point out that this is the proper concept of money in the Brazilian case). This comparison shows money expansion of only about 3 percent from debt-equity swaps, hardly enough to provoke 1,000 percent inflation.

The Cardoso-Dantas regression of inflation on the trade balance is less than persuasive. The same regression for Japan, Germany, or, more directly relevant, Korea, would of course show no such relationship. The equation cries out "simultaneity" and even as a reduced form leaves many macro variables missing (fiscal deficit, indexation rules, etc.). Indeed, a cross-country regression of the same form, including such cases as Chile and Colombia, would be unlikely to show a statistically positive relationship. In short, precisely because cases such as those of Chile and Colombia show that it is possible to manage the external debt without inflationary unraveling, less of the inflationary blame deserves to be attributed to foreign debt than the authors imply. Like the statistical test, this broader thesis in the paper is Brazil-centric.

On the subject of protection, it is surprising that the authors find the tariff equivalents of total protection to be as low as those shown in table 4.6 (around 20 percent for capital and intermediate goods). More broadly, the paper is curiously vague on whether the authors approve or disapprove of Brazil's high level of protection. For example, in the informatics area, I have estimated that the "market reserve" on small computers costs Brazil some $500 million annually, even if one allows some benefit for the saving of scarce foreign exchange (Cline 1987). In the floor discussion at the conference, Cardoso made

---

5. *Veja*, 15 March 1989, 84.

it explicit that the authors indeed endorse Brazilian protection and the use of managed trade (following the Korean example as Cardoso perceives it). Rudiger Dornbusch subsequently emphasized the error he believed Mexico had made by liberalizing trade during adjustment to a stabilization crisis.

Although I am sympathetic to the view that import liberalization should be phased in (perhaps over three or four years) rather than adopted overnight, surely it is wrong to condone the high-protection, import-substituting industrialization model at this juncture. If there is any lesson we should have learned from the more successful adjustment to the debt problem in Asia than in Latin America, it is surely that an inward-oriented development strategy discourages export development and weakens the base for supporting debt service. High protection causes a bias favoring production for the domestic market over the international market, in addition to causing inefficient growth at high capital-output ratios. Mexico, Argentina, and now even Venezuela have learned this lesson. Brazil is simply out of step (perhaps because of its larger domestic market), and Cardoso-Dantas would have Brazil continue so.

Cardoso and Dantas are cautiously skeptical on the feasibility of Brazil's external transfer, and they worry that imports must rebound as growth returns. My projections show that, even using a cyclical elasticity of imports of 2, and assuming a return to 5 percent growth, Brazil's potential trade surplus remains high (in the range of $17 billion or more).

The paper reveals shocking differences in measurements of the real fiscal deficit. Thus, for 1988 the operational deficit is 4.3 percent of GNP, but the authors' measure B of the real deficit is 16 percent. These calculations suggest that policymaking in Brazil is completely in the dark. It seems unlikely that the authors really mean that the government should seek to raise taxes and cut real spending by 16 percent of GNP.

On privatization, I share some of the authors' skepticism and their implicit view that Brazilian state enterprises tend to be relatively efficient. On the matter of high real interest rates, it is certainly correct that levels far above the growth rate of the economy spell disaster ahead. The central problem is that there is a need for major fiscal correction, but until President-elect Collor de Mello takes office with a political mandate the only policy instrument politically feasible is monetary policy. The related issue of substituting high-cost domestic for low-cost foreign debt through debt-equity swaps should be resolved by lowering the domestic real interest rate through fiscal adjustment, not by ruling out debt-equity conversions indefinitely. At lower real domestic interest rates, the trade-off against the discounted retirement of foreign debt begins to look much more attractive.

The paper's findings on income distribution are intriguing, although such data are notoriously shaky. Even so, the absence of a clear loss of income shares at the low end tends to confirm the suspicion that the principal burden of adjustment has been borne by the middle class.

Cardoso and Dantas conclude that the outward transfer of resources must be cut if Brazil is to grow. But they do not offer a convincing demonstration of the resulting growth impact. Even if half of the interest on its bank debt were forgiven (and few proposals would go further), Brazil would save only 1 percent of GNP annually. Assuming greater efficiency than in recent years, a capital-output ratio of 2 would mean increased growth by ½ percent annually—meager in comparison with the collapse of Brazilian growth from some 6 percent or 7 percent annually to near zero.[6] Because the benefits would be relatively modest, Brazil should not expect miracles from debt forgiveness. Correspondingly, although market-related debt reduction (for example, through buybacks using Brady Plan funds) should by all means be pursued, the gains from even deep debt reduction are sufficiently limited that they could fall short of the costs of a more aggressive, confrontational approach that caused a long-term rupture with the banks. Instead, the central means for reestablishing growth in Brazil must be domestic stabilization through fiscal reform, probably coupled with a heterodox shock and deindexation to break inertial inflation (and moderate the severe economic contraction that could result from an attempt to halt inflation without breaking its inertial component).

Mexico

The Beristain-Trigueros paper provides a skillful overview of Mexico's economic adjustment in recent years. The authors correctly stress the extent of fiscal adjustment. The de la Madrid government reduced noninterest government spending from 37 percent of GNP in 1981–82 to 27 percent in 1986–87.[7] Beristain and Trigueros also correctly emphasize the severe blow of lower oil prices in 1986, which aggravated the scope of required adjustment by removing some 6 percent of GNP in fiscal revenue and foreign-exchange earnings. They also properly judge the decision to open the economy as central to the strategy and favorable for the country's long-term growth prospects.

The authors carefully consider the exchange rate debate. Their two main arguments are both correct: the peso did become undervalued from a long-term perspective in the 1986–87 struggle to deal with a collapse in oil earnings; but

---

6. This calculation does not apply a shadow price on foreign exchange, largely because with a trade surplus of $16 billion or more it is difficult to argue that foreign exchange is the key constraint.

7. Based on Secretaria de Hacienda y Crédito Público, *Programa Operativa Anual de Financiamento 1988*, and Banco de México, *Informe Anual*, various issues.

Figure 4.10 Mexico: real exchange rate indices,[a] 1980–88

1985 = 100

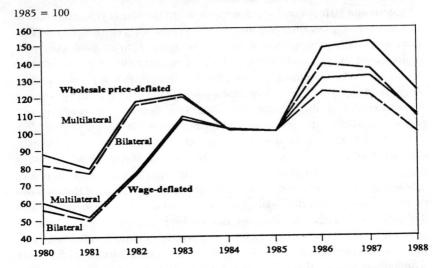

a. Multilateral indices are calculated against the currencies of the six largest industrial countries, bilateral indices against the US dollar alone. An increase in the index represents a devaluation. The wage deflator for Mexico is the average wage in industry.

the exorbitant real interest rates the government still finds it necessary to pay suggest that the public is not persuaded that the real appreciation of the exchange rate in 1988 was compatible with external balance.

The exchange rate debate tends to polarize as follows. Representatives of foreign banks, some foreign official entities, and Mexican exporters stress that there has been a large real appreciation of the peso since 1987, the prospective current account deficit is uncomfortably large, and thus some real depreciation would be advisable. Mexican officials stress instead that when measured by relative wages rather than wholesale prices the real exchange rate remains at historically undervalued levels, and that in any event expectations are so sensitive that any attempt to devalue the peso would trigger a renewed round of increased inflation. There is some merit to both sides of the argument, and the challenge is to identify the prudent strategy.

Figure 4.10 shows the real exchange rate for Mexico during the 1980s. The graph confirms that real depreciation was much sharper over the decade when measured by relative wages than when based on wholesale prices. Nonetheless, the figure also confirms the sizable real appreciation for 1988 as a whole whether one deflates by wholesale prices or by wages. There was further real appreciation by about 5 percent from the 1988 average through the first quarter of 1989, although the real rate remained constant thereafter because of the move to an exchange rate slide by 1 peso daily. On the price-deflated basis, then, the real peso is now about where it was in 1984–85, even though the collapse in oil prices has weakened the external sector compared with that base.

My projections indicate that Mexico's current account deficit can be expected to hover at about $6 billion annually in 1990–91 and a modestly higher level afterward, assuming domestic growth of 5 percent to 6 percent annually.[8] Vigorous expansion of foreign direct investment could make this level feasible, but otherwise the external accounts could be under pressure.

The proper balance in the trade-off between external and internal stability is probably to stick to the current exchange rate slide of 1 peso daily, which is equivalent to about a 14 percent annual depreciation. This pace should hold the real rate against the dollar constant. Continuation of the present policy would avoid any expectational shock in an inflationary direction. In contrast, it would be a dangerous gamble to seek instead to freeze the peso-dollar rate as a new step in the fight against inflation. The result would almost certainly be only temporary relief on the inflation front, followed by destabilization in the future as erosion of the external balance to unsustainable levels precipitated a sizable devaluation. This judgment also means that it is unrealistic for Mexico to aim for inflation in the range of 5 percent, and that consolidating a 15 percent rate should be considered having won the war against high inflation. Beristain and Trigueros would appear to agree with this assessment of exchange rate strategy, and indeed they warn that even the current rate of peso slide will be inadequate unless the government successfully achieves fiscal targets.

In contrast to the leftists and some academics in Mexico (and abroad), the authors approve of the Mexican debt agreement reached in July 1989. Again I agree with them. The banks actually met Mexico two-thirds of the way (35 percent debt or interest reduction versus an original request of 55 percent; or new money refinancing 60 percent of interest versus an original 80 percent). Improved confidence resulting from the tentative agreement enabled a 20 percent reduction in the real domestic interest rate. The additional external interest savings that would have been achieved by holding out for the initial demand would have amounted to only $1 billion annually, or about 3 percent of exports of goods and services. The government was sage not to risk an outright break with the banks, and resulting exchange market chaos and higher rather than lower domestic interest rates, for stakes this small. One issue the paper does not address, however, is whether the emphasis on arm-twisting by

---

8. The projections do not make any special allowance for favorable export growth still in the pipeline as the result of opening of the economy. Because protection creates a price wedge that biases the channeling of production to the domestic rather than the foreign market, liberalization can be expected to reallocate resources toward exports, and some time lags are to be expected in this process.

the official sector may not have done unnecessary damage. Complete use of the $7 billion in collateral resources for the purpose of buybacks could have achieved about the same interest savings while leaving a much larger group of banks in for the long haul rather than inducing them to exit out of frustration.[9]

I do have a few quibbles with the paper. The diagnosis that inflation rose in 1987 because the government failed to let the peso appreciate in real terms despite some oil price recovery is doubtful. The government actually began to lag the exchange rate in the second quarter, and indeed the financial crisis that forced a large devaluation after November was a message from the Mexican public that the rate was no longer credible and that the government had to reorder its priorities and make the control of inflation its primary objective. Only after that message did the government adopt further fiscal adjustment and accept the inevitability of a heterodox shock to break inertial inflation (the Pact for Economic Stability and Growth), an option it had previously opposed.

For the future, Mexico faces the challenges of removing price controls without reviving inflation, of maintaining external balance, and of reducing the real domestic interest rate. An aggressive move into dollar-indexed government bonds might help achieve the last objective, as the exchange risk premium would be absent. The revival of growth to 3 percent or more in 1989 is encouraging and should ameliorate Williamson's disappointment that we have not seen more growth following the adoption of successful adjustment programs. At the most fundamental level, Mexico's strong political leadership and the impressive technical capability at the highest levels of economic policymaking bode well for the country's chances of consolidating adjustment and returning to growth.

Overview

Comparison of adjustment efforts in the three largest Latin American economies suggests, indeed, that political coherence is one of the most important conditions for growth. The contrast is most extreme between the case of Mexico and that of Brazil, where a fragile political system and the bad luck of the death of Tancredo Neves meant five years of vacillation between economic reform and

---

9. With $7 billion in resources available and a secondary market price of 35 cents on the dollar, Mexico could have retired $20 billion in debt. Gross interest savings would have been $2 billion annually, and net savings (after interest on borrowed Brady resources) $1.4 billion—about the same as actually achieved in the negotiation. The authors properly observe that calculations of the interest effects should not deduct interest on Brady *collateral* (as opposed to the buyback option discussed here), because there is an offsetting interest-earning asset. The press has confused this issue and, for example, stated that the package saved Mexico only $800 million annually. *Wall Street Journal*, 6 December 1989.

misguided populist measures. The record of the three countries also highlights the primacy of fiscal adjustment. Strong fiscal correction in Mexico meant achievement of stabilization despite an enormous adverse shock from the fall in oil prices, whereas lack of fiscal adjustment in Brazil meant a march toward four-digit inflation despite the corresponding good luck of lower prices for oil imports. As argued above, the failure of fundamental fiscal reform was also the salient feature of successive Argentine stabilization failures. Finally, the cases of Argentina and Mexico underscore the risk of resorting to an exchange rate freeze as the linchpin of an anti-inflationary program, especially where (as in the Argentine episodes) the fiscal closure is not yet in place.

Comment
Sebastian Edwards

Argentina

It has been argued that the Latin American countries have followed two alternative strategies to deal with the debt crisis: a recessionary strategy and an inflationary strategy. However, Argentina's adjustment under Raúl Alfonsín is the clearest evidence that these two approaches need not be mutually exclusive. In fact, the Argentine experience has shown us how admirably both approaches can be combined: during the period 1983–89 Argentina managed not to make progress on either the inflationary or the growth front.

As Juan Carlos de Pablo points out in his paper, President Carlos Menem surprised most observers by promising to refrain from populist policies and by appointing pragmatic people with a sense of fiscal responsibility to the key economic positions in his cabinet. Two major goals of the Menem administration are to put an end to the pervasive inflationary process and to resume an orderly path of economic growth. These objectives are expected to be achieved through the implementation of sweeping economic reforms aimed at modernizing the productive structure, and with the aid of substantial external funds from the IMF and the World Bank. Additionally, Menem hopes that Argentina will be able to obtain more resources through debt-reduction operations (i.e., debt forgiveness).

Sebastian Edwards is a professor of economics at the University of California, Los Angeles, and a research associate at the National Bureau of Economic Research.

Of course, the key question is, "Can Mr. Menem do it?" I will try to address this issue by commenting on the initial conditions faced by the new government and the basic elements of Menem's reform program.

Initial Conditions

In July 1989, after a disastrous first half-year—the year when Argentina flirted dangerously with hyperinflation—the new Menem administration implemented an emergency package composed of a major devaluation, a wage-price freeze, a deceleration of monetary expansion, and the promise of future reforms. After a brief period of favorable developments, the economy is already showing a number of weak areas. First, in early November 1989, the exchange rate policy seems to be running into serious problems. The reduction in the parallel market premium achieved by the initial devaluation has vanished: the parallel market rate has once again departed from the official parity. The 10 percent premium of the first days of November indicates that confidence in the overall package is eroding rapidly. In fact, I would not be surprised if in less than two months we observe a parallel market rate twice as large as the current one.

Another weak component of the initial situation is the expected behavior of wages. The government's proposal for future wage increases in the following six months turned out to be about one-fifth of what the unions were demanding. The rapid loss of union support that these inconsistent claims might imply would make any attempt to set up a social pact extremely difficult.

The third and perhaps most serious problem faced by the government is the size and composition of the domestic debt, which in November 1989 is slightly over $15 billion, most of it of very short maturity. To persuade the public to hold this debt, the government is paying exceedingly high interest rates: 10 percent monthly as of October 1989. Naturally, this is a highly explosive situation that cannot be maintained in the medium run.

It is clear, then, that the initial conditions faced by the Menem administration are extremely fragile. In fact, they represent a very serious obstacle to the implementation of any type of structural reform.

Menem's Program

President Menem's program for stabilization and growth is based on three main components: a deep fiscal reform; modernization of the productive structure and privatization of public enterprises; and a debt-reduction scheme involving at least a 50 percent forgiveness. The success of this program will depend on a number of important factors, such as the speed of its implementation, the perceived credibility of the private sector, the conditionalities imposed by the international institutions, and the terms of external debt refinancing.

The government, with the aid of the IMF and the World Bank, has already put together a program for fiscal reform. This program contemplates a significant simplification of the tax system, including the elimination of most taxes on exports and the broadening of the base for both the value-added tax and the income tax. It is expected that the medium-run effect of this reform will be to increase tax revenues from approximately 15 percent of GDP in 1989 to 24 percent in the medium term. In my judgment this is an incredibly optimistic program and will probably not work. What has changed to make the Argentine public willing to pay taxes now, when they did not want to pay them before? Why should the private sector think that taxes will now be put to a better use than before? I have no answers to these questions, nor can I find them in de Pablo's paper.

All of this raises the issue of the sequencing of policy, and specifically the sequencing of fiscal reform and modernization measures. The key issue here is the value the public places on government services. It seems to me that in a country like Argentina the appropriate sequencing implies reforming the fiscal side *at the same time* that the modernization, and in particular the privatization process, is being carried out. Unfortunately, all the available evidence indicates that the privatization process in Argentina will be extremely protracted and slow.

The inability to implement these different components of the program simultaneously has important implications for the credibility of the whole package. It is my impression that both Menem's credibility and his ability to defeat inflation are being eroded very rapidly. This suggests that institutional changes geared toward enhancing the credibility of the program should be implemented. In this context the most promising reform—and one that has recently been enacted in neighboring Chile—is to create a completely independent central bank. It should be emphasized, however, that at the very bottom of Argentina's incredible recent economic history with inflation and stagnation is a conflict over income distribution: no segment of society is willing to shoulder its share of the burden of taxation. Only to the extent that we better understand the economic ramifications of this political problem will we progress in our understanding of the possible solutions to the inflation problem in Argentina.

Mexico

Beristain and Trigueros have shown persuasively that Mexico has made considerable progress since the eruption of the debt crisis. The particular features of this experience provide several valuable lessons and raise a number of issues.

I will deal with two important questions implicit in the authors' analysis: the sequencing of structural reforms and stabilization; and the evolution of the real exchange rate, the domestic rate of inflation, and the credibility of the adjustment program.

Recent debates in academia and at the multilateral institutions have asked whether there is an appropriate sequencing of structural reform and stabilization policies. Some economists, most notably Jeffrey D. Sachs, have argued that stabilization, and in particular fiscal balance, should precede those structural reforms aimed at liberalizing the different sectors of the economy. This position coincides, at least in part, with the World Bank view, which holds that because of the high degree of relative price volatility in inflationary environments, structural reforms should be postponed until inflation is under control. Anne O. Krueger, on the other hand, has repeatedly argued that liberalization measures should not wait for stabilization to be completed and that the freeing of markets should proceed rapidly.

The Mexican experience provides an important example of a fairly successful case of "liberalization first." As Beristain and Trigueros show, the Mexican liberalization reforms were initiated in 1985 when inflation was still high and were maintained in place in spite of the severe exogenous shocks of 1986. These measures were indeed dramatic: from 1982 to 1985 virtually 100 percent of imports were subject to prior licenses. In 1987 this proportion was reduced to 19 percent. The liberalization process was accompanied by large devaluations aimed at maintaining the degree of external competitiveness. At the macroeconomic level the most important fiscal measures were adopted in 1987, and these have been reflected in a significant drop in the inflation rate, from 180 percent in 1988 to 17 percent in late 1989.

However, as has happened in other similar episodes, during the last phase of the stabilization effort a serious trade-off between competitiveness and inflation has emerged. Although the maintenance of a pegged exchange rate has become an important element of the anti-inflationary strategy, it has also contributed to a real exchange rate appreciation of around 20 percent to 25 percent in the last few years. This loss of competitiveness is indeed worrying a number of observers.

What is to be done under these circumstances? If the recent economic history of Latin America has taught us one lesson, it is the importance of maintaining a fairly stable real exchange rate. Situations of overvaluation undermine the credibility of the exchange rate regime, and thus encourage capital flight and speculation. It is my judgment that a priority in the case of Mexico should be to avoid a larger appreciation of the real exchange rate. As the experience of Colombia over the last 20 years has shown, it is indeed possible to correct incipient real exchange overvaluations while at the same time keeping inflation at moderate levels, by means of an adequate combination of exchange rate management and fairly conservative fiscal and monetary policies.

Comment

Sweder van Wijnbergen

The paper on Brazil by Cardoso and Dantas presented no direct information that I had not seen before, but seeing it all put together in this way made for a rather astounding picture. Even more astounding is the authors' policy advice to countries to follow Brazil's example. The one characteristic of Brazil's present economic situation that strikes a relative outsider most is that of complete confusion. Such uncertainty persists about the fiscal deficit, for example, that even skillful followers of the economy like Cardoso and Dantas can get results ranging from -0.4 percent to $+16$ percent of GDP. This in itself must be one of the major problems facing any Brazilian stabilization program.

I do not find very convincing the authors' argument that the external surplus rather than the fiscal deficit is relevant to explaining inflation in Brazil. In fact, the explanation of the trade surplus's impact on inflation is best made *through* the fiscal approach to inflation. Brazil is, through its external surplus, effectively prepaying its external debt (at least in real terms) but financing this prepayment by issuing internal debt at extremely high interest rates and by the inflation tax rather than by cutting the primary fiscal deficit. This is really like using your credit card to pay off your mortgage, and it is a good way to achieve fiscal insolvency. This kind of debt strategy sends a very clear signal to the private sector that high inflation will come, today or tomorrow. Therefore I do not see any inconsistency between the need to run a large trade surplus as a factor in Brazil's inflationary process and the fiscal approach to inflation.

We economists have always lamented the fact that we cannot perform controlled laboratory experiments, but the cases of Brazil and Mexico provide something very close. These two countries started in very similar situations, with large terms-of-trade shocks and a cutoff of external capital after an ambitious borrowing program led to a very rapid accumulation of debt. Both countries have had a very uncertain political situation since 1982, and both have seen a dramatic slowdown in growth. Incidentally, I think the measures presented by Cardoso and Dantas showing higher growth in Brazil than in Mexico are a little

Sweder van Wijnbergen is an economist at the World Bank and a former visiting lecturer at Princeton University.

misleading. Mexico lost 6 percent of GDP in oil income between 1982 and 1988. Its nonoil GDP growth appears to be only a little bit less than Brazil's. Initially there was also a substantial increase in inflation in both countries, as both were forced to follow the same credit-card-to-pay-the-mortgage strategy, paying off cheap external debt by issuing expensive internal debt.

The response since the mid-1980s to these similar situations has been dramatically different in the two countries in at least three main areas: the external debt strategy, trade and other structural reforms, and macroeconomic policy. In spite of all the talk about moratoria, Brazil has for practical purposes been following a strategy of prepayment of its external debt at almost face value. It has run very large trade surpluses, and the debt agreement in 1988 included substantial prepayment at face value. Brazil's debt-equity swaps took place at very low discounts. On the other hand, Mexico has just concluded an agreement incorporating a substantial amount of debt relief.

With respect to trade and other structural reforms the differences again could not be greater. Mexico initially introduced reforms gradually, but since 1987 it has gone in head over heels for a dramatic restructuring of the economy, to an extent not seen anywhere except perhaps Chile. The process has in fact gone much further than Beristain and Trigueros point out. The authors overestimate the extent of quantitative restrictions remaining by including those on oil—oil import restrictions are not particularly binding in Mexico. There has also been sweeping deregulation of the transport and industrial sectors as well as extensive financial sector deregulation (which the authors do not highlight), prudently coupled with a substantial strengthening of the supervision apparatus. There has also been a substantial overhaul of the tax structure.

Brazil, on the contrary, has turned sharply inward, in a manner very much in line with the old Cambridge policy advice of targeting the balance of trade using trade policy and focusing fiscal policy on achieving expenditure-induced growth. All this has been done without particular concern for the financing of public expenditure; the consequence has been substantial deficits.

This brings us to the third area of substantial differences, namely, macroeconomic policy. In Brazil, if anything, things got worse during the 1980s: there was no fiscal adjustment, and in fact there were increases in fiscal expenditure at the same time that a price freeze was implemented. Mexico, on the other hand, has transformed a primary deficit of 7 percent of GDP in 1983 into a surplus of 8.4 percent in 1989—quite a dramatic turnaround. The Mexican reform program, rather courageously, was started in an election year, even though it is generally accepted that in an election year one cannot do anything.

A number of other points stand out when one compares these two countries. First, it is very clear, all the talk about inflationary inertia notwithstanding, that fiscal reform is an unavoidable prerequisite for success. The experience of Argentina, which parallels that of Brazil, also makes this point quite strongly.

The unorthodox components in the stabilization program in Mexico have been important, but what has provided lasting success and credibility to the program as a whole is the orthodox part of it. The incomes policy and the price freeze did, I think, help in lowering the unemployment cost of the Mexican program during its first year, but the ultimate explanation of the program's success is the clear fiscal adjustment to the country's decline in wealth and reduced access to foreign capital markets.

A second lesson is that, although fiscal stringency is important, it is not just today's fiscal deficit that matters. True fiscal reform (as opposed to the accounting gimmickry practiced with gusto in the United States) gives a clear signal that this year's fiscal reduction will still be there next year, and that is the signal that is really needed for credibility. Israel and Mexico have done consistently well on this score, although the structural reform program in Mexico is much more coherent and extensive than anything ever implemented in Israel. Brazil, meanwhile, has done unusually poorly in this area. The vehicle that Brazil used to "reduce" its deficits during the Cruzado Plan was asset sales, a mere accounting trick. There really is no difference between selling off an asset and issuing debt. Asset sales should be looked at as a way of financing a given deficit rather than as a means of reducing it.

A third point, related to the issue of restoring fiscal balance, is the importance of debt relief. Debt relief is important for the success of these stabilization programs because it facilitates putting a credible fiscal program together. Dornbusch and Fischer (1986), in a very informative paper about the interwar stabilization programs in Germany and elsewhere, point out that no successful stabilization was achieved in those countries without external support. Similarly, of the countries that have recently implemented stabilization programs, the ones most likely to succeed are those that did or will receive extensive external support: Israel and Mexico. Israel received a huge amount of external support in the form of a unilateral grant equal to 7 percent of GDP—$1.5 billion of reserves courtesy of the US taxpayer. Mexico might soon get some external support as the debt agreement with its commercial bank creditors is concluded.

In Mexico the most important effect of the debt agreement is not so much the direct fiscal impact, although that will certainly help, but the indirect effect on domestic interest rates. Direct evidence from the forward exchange markets shows that the high *ex post* real interest rates in Mexico were mostly due to exchange rate fears. The immediate drop in the cost of forward foreign exchange the day the debt relief package was announced highlights this linkage between debt relief and domestic interest rates.

A fourth noteworthy point is that both Brazil and Mexico clearly demonstrate that the Olivera-Tanzi effect has been greatly overestimated. In a number of cases, countries have supported an exchange rate and price freeze without major fiscal backup by claiming that tax revenue will rise once inflation comes down.

That has not happened, either in Mexico or in Brazil. In fact, in Brazil corporate tax revenues fell just after the Cruzado Plan was implemented.

A breakdown of the tax structures in the two countries indicates why this is so. In both Brazil and Mexico the personal income tax is for the most part a withholding tax on wages—capital income effectively pays no personal income tax. The value-added tax is collected every two weeks or so; hence those revenues are not seriously eroded by inflation either. Finally, corporate taxes in most high-inflation countries are now either indexed or subject to prepayment, so that the Olivera-Tanzi effect if anything works in the other direction. The government gets an interest-free, nonindexed loan when firms prepay their corporate tax liabilities. To top it all off, most countries have indexed tax brackets. So one should expect no magic from reversing the Olivera-Tanzi effect.

What we also get from the Mexican experience is very cautious support for the temporary use of exchange rate policy. Econometric analysis of wage-price dynamics in Mexico suggests that about 60 percent of the reduction in inflation is attributable to exchange rate policy. But what is equally clear is that after about the first six months the use of the exchange rate as an anti-inflation device starts to backfire. High domestic interest rates associated with a fear of substantial devaluation tend to undo the budgetary impact of any fiscal reform. This fiscal erosion in turn feeds back into further exchange rate fears and so on. Therefore, a fixed exchange rate policy may help in the very early phases, but in the medium run it probably does more harm than good to the anti-inflation drive.

A final lesson that has not been mentioned is the importance of a properly functioning central bank. One of the major differences between Brazil and Mexico is that in Mexico there is fiscal policy support for the monetary and exchange rate policy implemented by the central bank. In Brazil of course there is no such support for the central bank's policies.

There is a second problem involving the central bank in Brazil. There the financial sector is so completely in disarray that central bank control over the financial system must be almost nonexistent. This is a major difference between Mexico and Brazil and, in my view, is one of the major reasons for concern in countries like Poland and Hungary, where major reform programs are being put in place in the complete absence of financial sector control.

This is not just a matter of monetary control, for which fiscal support is essential, but also a matter of financial regulation. Countries like Yugoslavia, and to some extent Brazil, have seen a substantial part of their fiscal reforms eroded through what amount to fiscal subsidies extended through the banking system. In the absence of a properly functioning central bank, endowed with regulatory power and supported by a consistent fiscal policy, there would seem to be little chance for stabilization programs to succeed.

I will conclude with some comments on Mexico. At the end of 1987, there was a serious risk of Mexico sliding into hyperinflation. The econometric evidence suggests that the time lags in the wage-price system were rapidly becoming shorter. The lag between wage and price changes was cut almost in half between 1982 and 1987, and we expect to find the same results in the exchange rate adjustment process. Exchange rate policy had switched to one of attempting to protect the real exchange rate from inflation differentials by matching these with nominal devaluations. The time lag was almost zero. As a consequence, any use of the exchange rate as a nominal anchor went out the window, since the authorities were effectively following a real exchange rate rule. In addition, there is an open capital market in Mexico, with money demand determining money supply under anything short of a freely floating exchange rate system. In such circumstances there is nothing to tie down the price level: that is exactly the situation in Brazil now.

The Mexican authorities saw this happening and, in a very tense political situation, implemented what was probably the most skillfully executed stabilization program seen anywhere, including Israel. The Mexicans have clearly made choices that more cautious politicians would try to avoid, especially in an election year. As a consequence, inflation is down, growth is coming back up, and there was no major recession in 1988 or 1989. For the time being, then, the program has been successful.

Four issues remain. One is again exchange rate policy. We have seen that the use of a fixed exchange rate as an anti-inflation device will backfire if adhered to too rigidly and for too long. Mexico has also demonstrated the importance of debt relief for the credibility of exchange rate policy. A related question is the extent to which the issuance of indexed local-currency debt can help resolve the fiscal problems that lack of exchange rate credibility can lead to in the presence of ordinary, nonindexed internal debt. Basically, the public sector in Mexico has been buying exchange rate insurance from the private sector by issuing nonindexed peso-denominated debt. This involves a risk transfer in exactly the wrong direction, from the risk-neutral to the risk-averse. It is not surprising, then, that the government has to pay a very high insurance premium in the form of high real interest rates. It should be selling exchange rate insurance, not buying it, and it could do so by issuing indexed debt. This does not really involve a risk of entrenching indexation; it is easy to get out of such a system once it is not needed anymore, since one can simply refinance the indexed debt with nonindexed debt once inflation has come down.

The second outstanding issue in the Mexican program is the sustainability of the fiscal adjustment. The huge cuts in public-sector investment have been mentioned. Public investment is at its lowest level since before World War II, and anyone who has been to Mexico recently could have seen that it is a serious problem. Infrastructure, anti-poverty programs, social expenditure—all are lagging behind. If this situation is to be remedied without losing the remarkable improvement in the primary surplus, the question Mexico will have to address is a rather unpopular one: should there be tax increases?

I disagree with Beristain and Trigueros that tax rates are high in Mexico. The top marginal rate for the personal income tax is 40 percent, and the corporate tax rate will be 35 percent in 1990. Those are not high by international standards. Revenue from personal income taxes in Mexico is one-third what countries like Chile or Turkey collect, in spite of a similar rate structure. This suggests that the problem in Mexico is the tax base, not the tax rates. As I mentioned, capital income by and large escapes the personal income tax, and agriculture and transport are effectively exempt, creating obvious tax shelters. To solve its fiscal problems in a lasting way without jeopardizing social services, Mexico has to face the issue of taxing its middle class. Unless these loopholes are closed, the fiscal adjustment that has taken place will be jeopardized, and the social consensus supporting the current reform program might well become endangered.

The third issue is trade reform, the speed of which has come under criticism. There is a strong argument to be made for the rapid pace of reform for which Mexico has opted. Mexico is now seeing the emergence of a significant export lobby. The importance of this relates to the political arguments that Sebastian Edwards mentioned. Rapid reform more quickly builds up an export lobby to support trade liberalization, and if lobbying by interest groups is a factor in sustainability, the emergence of a pro-reform export lobby should enhance credibility.

The deterioration in the current account in 1989 had little to do with trade reform per se. Rather it matches very closely the deterioration in agricultural income and net agricultural exports. This suggests a link between the droughts of 1988–89 and the corresponding decline in agricultural income. But theory suggests that one should in fact let temporary declines in income be reflected in the current account. The trade deficit, by the way, is not as big as has been claimed. The Mexican trade figures exclude *maquiladora* revenues, which have been growing rapidly and should be included.

Finally, most observers would probably say that the financial sector liberalization, including effective liberalization of bank deposit rates, that took place in Mexico during the early phases of the program was rather dangerous. I would argue that such a move was less dangerous in Mexico than it would have been elsewhere because Mexico already had an open capital market. It is clear from the forward market data that exist that there is extensive arbitrage between the US and Mexican financial markets. So the usual argument that early financial sector reform opens the door to capital flight does not really hold in Mexico, because that door was open already.

The main thing that financial reform did was to simplify the intermediation process. Instead of Mexican savers putting money abroad and private investors trying to get it back into Mexico, with American banks acting as the intermediary, the money now goes directly from Mexican savers to Mexican investors through the domestic banking system. The issue now that liberalization has been effected is how to control the financial system so as to avoid the kind of crisis that occurred in Chile and Turkey in similar circumstances at the beginning of the 1980s. On that score the Mexicans have done rather well: in cooperation with the World Bank, the system of supervision and regulation of financial institutions has been improved a great deal.

To sum up, I think the Mexican program has been very successful so far and has every chance of ultimately succeeding. It has very few flaws in its policy design. Another reason to believe that it will succeed is the strong political support that the Mexican economic team enjoys. It is difficult to overestimate the importance of that fact, because political support is probably one of the most important signals that the policies are in place to stay, and this enhances credibility. In contrast, the absence of political support for the necessary economic measures may well have been the biggest cause of the credibility problems that have plagued stabilization attempts in Brazil.

Discussion

The three countries were discussed in two separate sessions of the conference.

On *Argentina*, Felipe Larraín drew attention to a dispute about interest rate policy within Carlos Menem's economic team. One camp argues that interest rates should be held as high as is needed to achieve a successful stabilization, while the other group (which is in closer touch with the industrialists) points to the danger of high interest rates killing the economy. The second school seems to be winning, and interest rates are being pushed artificially lower; the result has been a growing premium on the dollar in the parallel exchange market and hence a threat to the stabilization program. Larraín also touched on the topic of privatization, drawing a sharp distinction between a modest program sufficient to demonstrate serious intent and a wholesale program to sell all the state's assets in a year or so regardless of price or anything else; the latter he would regard as highly questionable.

Jessica Einhorn asked Juan Carlos de Pablo to explain the measures that in his view were called for to establish credibility. She also wanted to know whether he agreed with Sebastian Edwards about the importance of sequencing, and the danger that a wrong sequence of policy reforms might leave things worse than the absence of any action.

From the chair, John Williamson had suggested that one of the most constructive things that economists can do is to identify the critical constraint ruling at a particular point in time. He asked whether anyone disagreed with de Pablo's claim that the lack of credibility was the critical constraint currently facing the Argentine government. In response, Arnold Harberger remarked that he had been to Argentina perhaps 30 or 40 times since his first visit in 1956, and that on every single occasion the main problem had been the fiscal deficit. That was his alternative candidate for Argentina's fundamental problem. The failure to close the fiscal deficit is the origin of the lack of credibility.

Juan Carlos de Pablo explained that he had been thinking of the lack of credibility as affecting the viability of the structural reforms more than the stabilization efforts. It is possible to pass a law declaring the central bank to be independent, but a new law could always reverse that; the key to credibility is the record of the minister in charge and, in the longer term, a set of rules that will not arouse expectations of future policy change. The rules of the policy game must, in other words, be time consistent. This need increases the costs of adjustment, but at the present stage there is no alternative but to accept those costs. Argentine policymakers have often succumbed to the temptation to falsify the published outcome to persuade the public that policy is on the right track, but in the long run this simply bred distrust on the part of the public, and has resulted in phenomena like capital flight. There is now no alternative but to implement the right policies and to wait however long may prove to be necessary for them to take effect.

De Pablo also responded to the question from Sebastian Edwards as to why Argentinians are going to start paying taxes this time. He was not relying on a return of social responsibility resulting from the government first providing a more appealing range of government services. Tax revenue is needed before the railways start working again: Argentina needs a balanced budget next quarter. Argentinians will start paying taxes because the new head of the tax collection agency is publicly known to be tough on tax evaders. Tax collections will increase by 3 percent or 4 percent of GDP simply because a serious attempt is being made to collect taxes. An existing law threatening jail for tax evasion was ineffective in the past because the probability of being caught was zero, but that has now changed.

De Pablo told William Cline that fluctuations of the real exchange rate in Argentina had declined: nothing that had happened in 1989 compared with the Martinez de Hoz period. There are undoubtedly still large variations, but this is to be expected in the presence of hyperinflation, and the large misalignments were in any event short-lived.

De Pablo concluded by discussing the origins of the Argentine hyperinflation. It is true that decisions made in Washington may have influenced the result. When the Washington institutions decided to withdraw their financial support because of the likelihood that Menem would win, they contributed to the succession of seven different economic policies that Argentinians endured between 6 February 1989 and election day. But the crucial factor was the Menem that Argentinians thought was coming. The central bank tried to hoard its dollars to be able to cover its dollar liabilities; the suspension of dollar sales led to a sharp depreciation of the austral, which started an economic deterioration, which increased the probability of Menem winning. Since Menem was at that time synonymous with economic chaos, this increased the rush to buy dollars, which increased the probability of Menem winning, and so on in a vicious circle. Thus, Argentina has hyperinflation because of Menem, and now it needs Menem to escape from hyperinflation. Most hyperinflations stem from war; Argentina's is man-made.

Will Peru follow the same path? De Pablo thought not, because Mario Vargas Llosa is likely to be the next president. No one knows what Vargas Llosa is going to do, but he is a sufficiently reassuring figure to convince the Peruvians that all they need to do is wait a bit longer. Brazil? At the time of the conference no one knew who would win or whether either candidate, Collor or Lula, would prove to be another Menem. De Pablo stated that, if his "political" interpretation of the origin of hyperinflation was correct, he judged the danger of hyperinflation to be greater in Brazil than in Peru.

William Cline wondered whether an Argentina that had experienced hyper-inflation during the transition from Alfonsín to Menem might be found to have received an inoculation against inflation comparable to that which Germany received in 1923.

Sebastian Edwards agreed that reforms could not await success in privatization. Perhaps in Argentina it would be best to do everything simultaneously. The World Bank's current conventional wisdom is that one should stabilize before attempting structural reform, but in Argentina both are so urgent that neither should be postponed. He insisted that institutional arrangements do influence credibility: other factors (including psychological ones, and the personalities of those in a particular job) matter, too, but one must pay attention to the design of institutions. Everyone agrees that a fundamental problem in Argentina is the fiscal deficit, but this deficit arises from the country's failure to resolve the political problem of who should contribute how much to close the deficit. If economists refuse to analyze these political and distributional conflicts, we will fail to understand the source of Argentina's difficulties.

The discussion on *Brazil* and *Mexico* started off with Eliana Cardoso responding to the comments of Cline and van Wijnbergen. She commented that she could understand Cline's unhappiness at her regression explaining inflation in terms of the trade balance, since he had long been preaching increased net exports as the solution to the debt problem. Other people had complained that there were many different measures of the budget deficit and that they gave distinctly different results. This is not a uniquely Brazilian problem, but one that inevitably arises in any country with high inflation that lacks consolidated month-by-month budget accounting. The problem is not resolved simply by excluding monetary correction from the public-sector borrowing requirement, as the "operational deficit" does: monetary correction does not always compensate properly for inflation, and it excludes credit subsidies paid by the central bank. For some purposes one can look at what happened to the debt, as the other two measures in the paper do, but this is not a measure of "the deficit" that will serve for all purposes. One must decide on the particular purpose for which a measure is needed before one can decide on the right measure to employ.

Cardoso also emphasized that in her view hyperinflation will not occur in the absence of a collapse in the exchange rate. Even though the fiscal deficit is crucial in understanding the perpetuation of inflation, it is also necessary to take account of the behavior of the exchange rate. At the end of 1988, the operational budget deficit was 3 percent of GDP in Mexico, exactly the same as that in Brazil in the aftermath of the Cruzado Plan. Yet no one expected hyperinflation in Mexico as they did in Brazil. The reason is that the method of financing the deficit is essential in understanding what happens to inflation: Mexico was in recession with high real interest rates and a rundown of reserves, whereas in Brazil real interest rates were negative and the economy was in a boom. Hence the fiscal deficit, important as it is, does not explain how a country gets into hyperinflation.

Cardoso agreed with van Wijnbergen that asset sales in Brazil did little to help finance the public sector: in fact, the government should privatize the private sector before privatizing the public sector. She argued that Cline underestimated the importance of the external transfer problem, since the internal transfer problem derived directly from the need to make an external transfer. She asserted that the one certain effect of trade liberalization is to worsen the current account, and hence Brazil should continue to follow Korea's example in managing its trade. Finally, she remarked that the consensus in Brazil on fiscal policy was very similar to that in Washington: everyone believes that expenditure should be cut or revenue raised at the expense of someone else.

Ignacio Trigueros noted that some real appreciation was to be expected in Mexico in 1988, given that the circumstances of 1986 had produced an exaggerated and therefore temporary real depreciation. He argued that there was no convincing analysis that could determine whether this appreciation had been excessive.

Alain Ize questioned whether speculation against Mexico's ability to maintain trade liberalization was an important cause of the surge of Mexican imports. His own import equations showed no shift in import demand in 1988; the surge in import demand seems to be what should be expected on the basis of trade liberalization and real appreciation. This suggests that imports are unlikely to decline in the future. However, Ize argued that there is still sufficient competitiveness to support major future increases in exports, provided that the necessary investment is undertaken to break bottlenecks in capacity; the critical question is the availability of sufficient foreign exchange to finance the import component of investment. So far as estimates of the Brazilian real fiscal deficit are concerned, Ize argued the necessity of utilizing monthly figures. If one includes the inflation tax as a source of revenue (from both money supply growth and the decline of real interest rates due to the acceleration of inflation), the change in the real value of the debt—and therefore the real deficit—was approximately zero in 1988.

Miguel Kiguel pointed out that it was once fashionable to run regressions in which the trade balance was explained by the rate of inflation, on the theory that high inflation eroded the real wage and thus stimulated net exports. Cardoso had turned this story around; could one reconcile the two hypotheses, and, if not, had anything changed to justify the new interpretation?

Kiguel also asked what could replace the exchange rate (perhaps supported by wage and price controls) as a "nominal anchor" in stabilization programs. He agreed that this often led to overvaluation, and he posed the question as to what the government should do in this situation. If it devalues to improve competitiveness, the stabilization is over. What could then play the role of the nominal anchor?

Answers came from several panelists later in the session. Cardoso noted that use of the exchange rate as a nominal anchor had failed in the Chicago-inspired programs in Argentina and Chile in the late 1970s, and she suggested that the reason was that the fiscal deficit had not been dealt with first. Sebastian Edwards countered that Chile had in fact eliminated its budget deficit before it adopted the exchange rate as a nominal anchor in 1979, yet problems still occurred subsequently. The main one was that wages were indexed to past inflation, thus providing two (inconsistent) nominal anchors. He agreed with Kiguel that the actual exchange rate could get so far out of line with the fundamental equilibrium exchange rate as to dictate abandonment of the exchange rate peg, and he argued that in that event the money stock should become the nominal anchor. The Colombian experience showed how a serious overvaluation could be corrected fairly rapidly by accelerating the rate of crawl, provided it was accompanied by fiscal and monetary discipline. Williamson suggested that an even better nominal anchor than the money stock might be provided by a nominal income target, which offered the possibility of reconciling an exchange rate target with control of a relevant nominal magnitude.

Jacques Polak made a plea to read articles written prior to 1985. This is not the first time in history that the literature had explained how a combination of inertia and what used to be called the inflationary gap could generate a 1,000 percent annual inflation from a budget deficit of 2 percent of GDP. Similarly, distributive conflict had been generally seen as the basic cause of inflation in a conference convened by Felipe Pazos in about 1960. Rudiger Dornbusch subsequently argued that most of the insights were even older and could be found in the literature of the 1920s.

Patricio Meller remarked that in most Latin American countries it was now recognized that stabilization was a necessary condition for the resumption of growth, but that Eliana Cardoso had stated that stabilization would be necessary *and sufficient* in Brazil. What makes Brazil, or specifically the behavior of Brazilian entrepreneurs, different?

Enrique Sánchez noted that on the first day of the conference Cline had criticized de Pablo for underemphasizing the role of the lack of external finance in causing Argentine hyperinflation, but that today he was criticizing Cardoso for blaming high inflation on external problems. Sánchez argued that hyperinflation develops when a highly indebted state is cut off from its sources of finance, be those internal or external, and whatever the original source of the debts. In the Argentine case, external credit was cut off in April 1988, and domestic credit evaporated on the night of 14 May 1989, following the election of Carlos Menem. In the case of Brazil, the same may still happen. External financing has already been cut off, and the only remaining question is whether domestic financing can be sustained, even with the present high interest rates.

In replying to the discussion, Cardoso said that her paper already endorsed the analysis of Ize. She claimed that in Brazil wage indexation prevented inflation from squeezing real wages in a lasting way, thus ruling out Kiguel's reverse causation. She, too, endorsed studying classical authors, like Robert Mundell and Carlos Rodriguez. And she explained to Meller that Brazil was different because it was the only country in Latin America that had not been run into the ground over the previous eight years.

Ignacio Trigueros said that, in Mexico at least, inflation had been an effective mechanism for cutting absorption and thus contributing to an improvement in the trade balance. He conceded to Ize that it was uncertain that speculation had played a major role in generating the import surge, which had started from a very low base.

William Cline denied any inconsistency in his analysis of Argentina and Brazil. Argentina had allowed its reserves to run down to zero, at which point a flight from domestic currency had to lead to hyperinflation. Brazil was in moratorium now to try and escape a similar fate. He argued that Edwards had exaggerated the fall in real wages in Mexico; the *average* real wage had declined about 28 percent (although the minimum wage had indeed fallen more).[10] Finally, he endorsed Polak's explanation of how a small budget deficit could fuel a high inflation, and he added the assertion that the nominal deficit might still be important in driving inflationary expectations even if the operational deficit were all that mattered in driving demand.

Sebastian Edwards challenged the skepticism of Meller and Trigueros regarding the ability to conduct a rational exchange rate policy when different exchange rate indices give different results. Theory does give some guidance as to which are the most relevant measures, and Meller's own paper showed that the relative price of tradeables is a particularly useful concept. This can narrow the range of results. In the case of Mexico, there are serious reasons for concern about the evolution of the real exchange rate, which is now approximately equal to that of 1983–84. Since then major real changes have occurred, including trade liberalization and the decline in the oil price, which create a need for a more competitive rate. He concluded by joining the chorus praising study of the older literature, citing topics like class struggle and distributive conflict that until recently had indeed been neglected by many younger economists working in the neoclassical tradition. Keynes's *Tract* and his article on Poincaré's stabilization include beautiful analyses of topics like the real exchange rate that are strikingly relevant to present-day problems.

---

10. Edwards subsequently confirmed that he was referring to the real minimum wage.

Sweder van Wijnbergen pointed out that the public-sector deficits of Brazil and Mexico are not comparable inasmuch as many Brazilian subsidies are paid by the central bank and escape the measured deficit, whereas Mexico has a consolidated measure that includes the central bank deficit. Cardoso countered subsequently that her real point concerned the *change* in the budget balance, which in Mexico had gone from a surplus in the previous year to a deficit in 1988, as inflation was brought under control, whereas the opposite had happened in Brazil, where the operational deficit declined in late 1986 as inflation was picking up. This emphasized her point about the need to study how the budget deficit was financed.

Van Wijnbergen went on to express surprise at the recrudescence of arguments between balance-of-payments and fiscal explanations of inflation. The public finance approach would recognize that if you start paying off cheap external debt by issuing expensive internal debt you will, in the end, get either a spiraling internal debt ratio or hyperinflation. Thus, the two analyses go in exactly the same direction.

On trade reform, van Wijnbergen asserted that the empirical evidence (especially in Mexico) strongly supports Cardoso's position that trade liberalization worsens the balance of payments. From a theoretical point of view this may seem puzzling, since trade liberalization affects intratemporal trade ("our goods versus their goods") rather than intertemporal trade ("goods today versus goods tomorrow"). One explanation may be that trade adjusts more rapidly on the import side, since a country's residents know about the foreign goods they are lacking, whereas it takes much more effort to sell home-produced goods abroad. Moreover, trade liberalization needs to be accompanied by real depreciation to provide the incentive to sell in export markets the goods that are no longer being bought by domestic consumers. The macroeconomic counterpart is a big increase in stocks, perhaps because of a fear that the reforms will not prove permanent. A liberalization that is perceived as temporary *does* reduce the real interest rate, which leads to a theoretical expectation of a deficit, which may in turn make self-fulfilling the expectation that liberalization will be temporary. How can one implement a trade reform that will minimize these doubts about future reversals? By real depreciation, as mentioned, and by accompanying trade reform with fiscal reform and external support. One hopes that Mexico will be getting this support shortly.

William Cline retorted that it was not obvious that a real depreciation was needed to compensate for liberalization. If that were true, the high protection in Latin America in recent decades should have resulted in strong payments surpluses; instead it had squeezed down both imports and exports. Import liberalization tends to expand exports because it eliminates the wedge that previously favored import production.[11] John Williamson overruled the rest of the panel from his position in the chair to respond that the mechanism that squeezes down exports when imports are protected is precisely a real appreciation, and so a reversal of the protection needs a real depreciation to increase the exports again.

11. In a later continuation of the argument, Cline pointed out that in the two most conspicuous cases where widening trade deficits had been associated with import liberalization—Chile in 1980–81 and Mexico in 1989—the real exchange rate had also appreciated substantially, so that neither offered a good test of the impact of import liberalization per se.

5

Colombia and Venezuela

Colombia and Venezuela

Colombia

Rudolf Hommes
With the collaboration of Claudia Correa

The Crisis of the Early 1980s

After experiencing an unprecedented foreign-exchange boom and high growth rates during the last four years of the previous decade, the Colombian economy began showing signs of trouble in the early 1980s, partly because the government allowed the exchange rate to become overvalued and lost fiscal discipline. Annual GDP growth rates declined from an average of 5.96 percent during the 1977–80 period to 1.99 percent in 1980–84, and the country's industrial product actually decreased in 1981 and 1982. The deficit of the consolidated public sector increased from 3.3 percent of GDP in 1980 to 8.1 percent in 1982. The current account balance went from a surplus of 0.43 percent of GDP in 1980 to a deficit of 11.2 percent in 1982, and the country began losing reserves at a significant rate in that same year and at a much faster rate during 1983. Reflecting the changes in the current account, the investment-saving gap increased from an average 0.6 percent of GDP in current prices during 1970–79 and −0.5 percent in 1980 to 5.4 percent in 1982, at precisely the same time that international commercial credit sources were beginning to dry up. Also during the 1980–82 period, a severe crisis occurred in the financial sector, due in part to incompetence and indelicate practices by bank administrators, but also to the consequences of the severe recession in the industrial sector and the slowdown

Rudolf Hommes is a founder and editor of Estrategia. *He has served the Colombian government on its Monetary Board and as Director of Public Credit. He is currently coordinating economic policy issues for the presidential campaign of César Gaviria in Colombia.*

Claudia Correa has worked as an economist for the Colombian central bank and is in charge of economic planning at the Corporación Financiera del Valle in Bogota.

in growth. Although the unemployment rate did not begin to rise until 1983, employment in the manufacturing sector fell in 1981 and did not return to its 1980 level until 1983.

During the 1980–82 period, the government tried to reverse the recessionary trends by increasing the supply of credit to the private sector, raising levels of industrial protection, increasing export promotion, and undertaking a very ambitious housing construction program for low-income families. These measures proved ineffectual. The severity of the recession and the rapid loss of reserves during 1983 prompted the government to shift strategy: it now aimed additionally to gradually reduce the current account disequilibrium, without sacrificing the expansionary targets. This program, which was also a failure, has been described by two of its advocates (Lora and Ocampo 1988):

In the first semester of 1983, three facts induced a complete modification of the economic strategy. First, the recession had deepened compared with the second semester of 1982, and GDP had fallen for three consecutive quarters. . . . Second, a severe monetary contraction had begun, due to the loss of international reserves. Since the expansion of credit to the private sector did not seem to counteract this effect, it was necessary to use the available primary resources to finance the public sector, or else risk deepening the recession. . . .

A great number of instruments were applied to reinforce the measures taken after 1982. The pace of the crawling-peg devaluation was accelerated, export subsidies and import tariffs were increased, deposits were required prior to exports for some services, exchange controls were reinforced, and import controls were reestablished. The last of these was the most important element of the strategy for the adjustment of the external sector. In April 1983, the government moved to prior licensing of a great number of tariff categories and placed a number of imports on the prohibited list. At the beginning of 1984, a rigid foreign exchange budget was adopted, and import controls became more severe: 83 percent of the tariff categories were subject to prior licensing, 16.5 percent were prohibited, and only 0.5 percent were left free of administrative controls. Although this control system was designed so that it would not hinder industrial production . . . it gave rise to serious delays in the licensing procedures.

Fiscal adjustment followed this process with a lag. [Although public expenditures increased in real terms,] the government adopted an ambitious tax reform in 1983, which modified substantially the income and sales tax structure and reformed departmental (regional) and municipal taxes. . . . [Due to the slow increase in tax revenues] and because external credits and the profits from exchange operations were falling, the government asked the legislature to increase the lines of credit from the central bank to the Treasury in mid-1983 by 60 billion Colombian pesos (equivalent to 2 percent of GDP in that year), of which 60 percent could be used immediately. . . .

Due to the decrease in the external deficit, the net initial effect of the economic policy was expansionary. . . . Import controls were the main tool for reducing the external gap while simultaneously inducing production, without cutting the public deficit. . . .

The most significant element of this strategy was the decision not to use demand-depressive policies to correct the external disequilibrium, in clear contrast with the orthodox policy that followed. . . .

In 1984, since most of the adverse conditions still prevailed, despite some improvements in the trade balance, the government changed the strategy abruptly and removed the minister of finance. Under a new minister, a more orthodox adjustment strategy was adopted, which is described in the following sections.

Policy Reforms Since 1984

In 1984 the government of Colombia started an adjustment program aimed at reducing the public-sector deficit and the current account deficit, promoting exports and export-led growth, and restoring access of the country to international capital markets. To achieve this last target, the government also entered into an agreement with the World Bank to implement a trade liberalization program. The adjustment program involved several major policy areas, which are reviewed below.

Fiscal Deficits

The adjustment efforts of the Colombian public sector during 1984–88 indicate a strong will to maintain fiscal discipline. As shown in table 5.1, the overall deficit of the consolidated nonfinancial public sector was reduced from 6.3 percent of GDP in 1984 to 4 percent in 1985, and further to 0.3 percent in 1986. In 1987 the deficit climbed back up to 1.8 percent and to 2.1 percent in 1988. During 1986 and 1987, when the economy grew by more than 5 percent per year, these deficits were compatible with a nonincreasing debt–GDP ratio (assumed to be about 45 percent). However, when GDP growth receded in 1988 to 3.7 percent, the overall deficit relative to GDP should have fallen below 2 percent, to meet the same criterion. Consequently, the deficit of 2.1 percent of GDP in that year indicates a loss of fiscal discipline compared with the previous years. In 1989 this relapse will become more evident, as the GDP growth rate may fall to near 3 percent and the overall consolidated fiscal deficit may reach 3 percent of GDP.

The reduction of the overall consolidated public-sector deficit was achieved in 1985 and 1986 by actions affecting more the revenue than the expenditure side. During these two years, total revenue of the public sector grew in real terms at rates that were several times those of growth in expenditures (table 5.2). This

Table 5.1 Colombia: consolidated public-sector accounts, 1984–88
(percentages of GDP)

Account	1984	1985	1986	1987[a]	1988[b]
Total revenue	19.2	21.1	23.5	22.2	22.0
Current revenue	18.9	20.8	23.3	21.9	21.7
Tax	12.4	14.1	15.1	14.9	14.6
Nontax[c]	6.9	7.4	9.4	7.5	7.5
Current transfers	0.1	0.0	0.0	0.0	0.1
Adjustment for transfers	−0.5	−0.7	−1.2	−0.6	−0.5
Capital revenue	0.2	0.2	0.2	0.3	0.3
Total expenditure and net lending	25.4	25.1	23.8	24.0	24.1
Current expenditure	15.9	16.4	16.0	16.8	16.6
Wages and salaries	6.9	6.2	5.9	5.7	5.6
Goods and services	1.8	2.8	2.6	2.7	−2.7
Interest	2.4	3.0	3.1	4.4	4.2
On external debt	1.6	2.0	2.2	3.4	3.0
On internal debt	0.8	1.0	0.9	1.1	1.2
Current transfers	4.3	3.9	3.7	3.5	3.6
Other	0.4	0.5	0.7	0.4	0.5
Capital expenditures	9.6	8.6	7.6	7.1	7.5
Fixed capital formation	8.8	7.8	6.7	6.0	6.5
Capital transfers	0.1	0.2	0.2	0.4	0.5
Other	0.7	0.7	0.7	0.7	0.5
Net lending	0.0	0.1	0.3	0.1	0.1
Current account balance	3.1	4.5	7.4	5.1	5.2
Overall balance	−6.3	−4.0	−0.3	−1.8	−2.1
Primary balance[d]	−3.9	−1.0	2.8	2.6	2.0
Overall financing	6.7	4.2	−0.6	1.8	3.0
Foreign	1.9	3.8	2.1	−0.7	2.3
Domestic	4.8	0.5	−2.6	2.5	0.7
Net residual	−0.5	−0.2	0.9	0.1	−0.9

a. Preliminary.

b. Estimated.

c. Property income, operating surpluses, and other revenues.

d. Net of interest payments.

Source: Banco de la República.

Table 5.2 Colombia: real annual growth in consolidated public-sector accounts, 1985–88 (percentages)

Account	1985	1986	1987[a]	1988[b]
Total revenues	14	28	−1	3
Current revenues	14	28	−2	3
Tax	18	23	3	2
Nontax[c]	12	46	−16	5
Capital revenues	10	−12	72	−10
Total expenditures and net lending	2	9	5	4
Current expenditures	7	12	10	3
Wages and salaries	−7	9	3	2
Goods and services	59	9	7	4
Interest	30	18	50	−2
On external debt	29	28	56	−7
On internal debt	34	−1	33	12
Capital expenditures	−6	1	−2	9
Fixed capital formation	−8	−2	−5	13
Current account balance	51	89	−28	5
Overall balance	−34	−91	505	21
Overall financing	−35	−116	418	77

a. Preliminary.

b. Estimated.

c. Property income, operating surpluses, and other revenues.

Sources: Banco de la República; table 5.1.

growth differential occurred even in the face of rapidly increasing interest expenditures. The situation changed after 1986. The real growth rate of expenditures was lower in 1987 and 1988 than during the previous two years, but was higher than the real growth rate of revenue, indicating that the initial thrust of the reforms was lost very rapidly. On the expenditure side, rigidities in wage and salary expenditures, rapidly increasing interest payments, and the inertia of other current spending have shifted the burden of fiscal restraint to the capital budget, where expenditures, particularly for fixed capital formation, decreased in real terms during 1985–87 (table 5.2) and increased in 1988 only to their 1986 level as a proportion of GDP.

Table 5.3 Colombia: composition of central government social spending, 1983–88 (percentages)

	1983	1984	1985	1986	1987[a]	1988[b]
Education	22.0	22.5	19.8	18.8	18.3	16.5
Health	6.0	5.6	4.9	4.8	5.1	4.9
Social security	9.2	8.8	9.3	7.5	8.4	8.0
Housing	2.5	5.3	1.5	1.4	0.6	0.7
Total social expenditures	39.7	42.2	35.5	32.6	32.3	30.1
Investment	24.7	26.7	30.9	26.6	24.8	27.2
Debt service (including interest)[c]	11.3	12.0	12.5	20.6	19.5	20.6
Memoranda:						
Public health and social security expenditures per capita (1987 dollars)			49	44	41	43
Government education expenditures per capita (1987 dollars)[d]			35	33	30	29

a. Preliminary.

b. Estimated.

c. Includes debt amortizations and interest payments.

d. Per capita expenditure in 1980 was $40 (in 1987 dollars).

Sources: Contraloria General de la República, *Informe Financiero;* per capita expenditure data from World Bank, *Public Sector Expenditure Review* (report 7891-CO).

Public Expenditure Priorities

Social Spending

There is evidence that the fiscal discipline derived from the adjustment process begun in 1984 had a more than proportionally adverse effect on social spending. The social expenditures of the central government, including debt service on credits outstanding to the social sector, decreased from 39.7 percent of total expenditures (including debt service) of the central government in 1983 to 30.1 percent in 1988, after a short-lived increase in 1984 (table 5.3). The largest loss in share was suffered by education expenditures, followed by health and housing expenditures (a key program of the 1982–86 administration). Further evidence pointing to a decrease in government social spending is the steady

Table 5.4 Colombia: government spending on education and health, 1983–88 (percentages of total except where noted)

	1983	1984	1985	1986	1987[a]	1988[b]
Education						
Primary[c]	42.8	38.3	38.0	36.8	39.2	39.2
Secondary[d]	25.0	26.6	27.1	27.9	30.0	29.8
Universities	21.1	20.4	20.0	20.5	21.5	21.1
Other	11.1	14.7	14.8	14.8	9.3	9.9
Total (billions of 1987 Colombian pesos)	207.8	234.6	215.8	222.0	218.3	216.2
Health						
Hospitals[e]			58.8	56.7	60.0	53.6
Child care			18.5	17.4	17.8	22.2
Basic health						0.7
Ministry of Health			3.7	3.3	5.3	8.5
Other			18.9	22.6	16.8	15.1
Total (billions of 1987 Colombian pesos)			115.4	130.0	140.2	143

a. Preliminary.

b. Estimated.

c. 90 percent of children ages 7 to 11 years are enrolled.

d. 48 percent of children ages 12 to 18 years are enrolled.

e. Public (including municipal and departmental hospitals).

Source: World Bank, *Public Sector Expenditure Review* (report 7891-CO).

reduction of per capita government expenditures on health, social security, and education during the 1985–88 period. Moreover, government expenditures on education were reduced even as other areas of government expenditure continued to increase in real terms. Health expenditures increased in real terms during the 1985–88 period at a real rate slightly higher than that of total expenditures of the consolidated nonfinancial public sector (table 5.4).

Investment

Public-sector investment, as already indicated, has been adversely affected by the adjustment program. Fixed public investment decreased from 8.8 percent and 9.4 percent of current GDP in 1984 and 1985, respectively, to 6.6 percent in 1987, then rebounded to 8.4 percent in 1988 (table 5.5). However, the

Table 5.5   Colombia: investment and savings, 1983–88
(percentages of GDP)

	1983	1984	1985	1986	1987[a]	1988[b]
Fixed investment (constant prices)[c]	17.7	17.3	15.9	16.2	15.4	15.8
Fixed investment (current prices)	17.2	17.0	17.5	17.7	17.6	18.5
Private	n.a.	8.2	8.1	8.7	11.1	10.1
Public	n.a.	8.8	9.4	9.0	6.6	8.4
Total investment (current prices)	19.8	19.0	19.0	18.0	19.3	19.6
Private	11.0	10.0	9.4	9.5	10.9	11.5
Public	8.8	9.0	9.6	8.5	8.4	8.1
Gross domestic saving	14.6	15.5	17.0	19.6	19.5	18.6
Private	12.1	11.7	12.1	11.3	14.4	15.3
Public	2.5	3.8	4.9	8.3	5.1	3.3
Foreign saving Investment-saving gap	5.2	3.5	2.0	−1.6	−0.2	1.0
Private	−1.1	−1.7	−2.7	−1.8	−3.5	−3.8
Public	6.3	5.2	4.7	0.2	3.3	4.8

a. Preliminary.

b. Estimated.

c. Fixed capital formation at constant 1975 prices.

Source: Banco de la República and Hwa (1989).

increase may be due to a large extent to an increase in the relative prices of capital goods, as shown by the much more moderate increase in fixed investment at constant prices between 1987 and 1988. Furthermore, overall public investment declined steadily as a proportion of GDP between 1984 and 1988, from 9.0 percent to 8.1 percent, indicating further the investment restraint of the public sector in the exercise of fiscal discipline.

Deficits of Public Financial Institutions

The consolidated nonfinancial public-sector deficit does not present the whole picture, however. In Colombia, the central bank also contributes to public expenditure through its interest expenditures related to open market operations, and the net losses of its credit operations. Moreover, other public financial institutions and banks serve as channels for public spending. An indication of

Table 5.6   Colombia: real interest rates, 1983–88 (percentages per year)[a]

Rate	1983	1984	1985	1986	1987	1988
Time deposits[b]	14.6	13.6	10.9	9.3	8.2	3.3
Deposits (all types)	14.7	13.9	10.4	8.6	5.6	4.4
Commercial credit	18.0	14.5	10.7	16.5	13.8	12.3
Directed credit	4.5	1.9	−1.1	1.1	4.9	1.5
Subsidy to directed credit[c]	15.7	15.0	14.5	18.6	11.0	13.8

a. Yearly averages. Deposit rates are stated as effective yields.

b. 90-day time deposits at leading banks.

c. Difference between the average commercial lending rate and the average directed credit rate.

Sources: Banco de la República and Superintendencia Bancaria Bogotá; Hommes (1988).

the fiscal behavior of the public financial institutions, relative to the fiscal restraint of the nonfinancial public sector, is given by the trend in the ratio of total public debt to GDP, which increased from 29.3 percent in 1984 to 33.1 percent in 1985. The increase in this ratio demonstrates that the adjustment measures failed to contain the overall fiscal deterioration in the first two years of the adjustment program. In 1986 and 1988, the same ratio decreased to 32.0 percent of GDP, and in 1987 it fell to 30.4 percent, still above the 1984 level, suggesting the persistence of large deficits in the public financial institutions (Hwa 1989, 35–40).

Interest Rate Subsidies

A portion of the losses incurred by the central bank stems from the extension of subsidized credit to the private sector. At present interest rates, central bank rediscounting of long-term credit by commercial banks and financial corporations implies an interest rate subsidy on the order of 10 percent to 15 percent per year of the outstanding credit of these institutions that is funded by the central bank (directed credit). On average, this subsidy was reduced from 15.7 percent of the outstanding balance per year in 1983 to 11.0 percent in 1987, but it was allowed to increase again to 13.8 percent in 1988 (table 5.6). At the same time, the share of total credit funded by the central bank declined steadily during the 1983–87 period, but increased again in 1988 (table 5.7). The annual value of this subsidy (calculated from tables 5.5 and 5.6) amounted to 0.6 percent of GDP in 1984; it was reduced to about 0.3 percent of GDP by 1987. Despite the significant drop, this subsidy to well-to-do farmers and industrialists remains

Table 5.7 Colombia: credit extended by commercial banks and finance corporations, 1983–88 (percentages of total except where noted)

Total loans and discounts[a]	1983	1984	1985	1986	1987	1988
Commercial banks						
Funded by Banco de la República	9.2	9.7	11.7	6.8	5.4	9.9
Directed credit	27.2	28.6	25.4	25.4	24.8	24.1
Own resources	63.6	61.6	63.0	67.7	69.8	66.0
Total (billions of Colombian pesos)	344.8	415.8	521.7	676.3	907.7	1,102.0
Finance corporations						
Funded by Banco de la República	6.6	9.9	11.1	15.3	13.4.	n.a.
Directed credit	17.0	17.7	17.9	15.1	17.2	n.a.
Own resources	76.4	72.4	71.1	69.7	69.3	n.a.
Total (billions of Colombian pesos)	90.4	99.2	106.6	145.4	208.6	n.a.

n.a. = not available.

a. At end of year.

Source: Revista Banco de la República, various issues.

high. Although there is no evidence that the benefits from this type of subsidized credit extend beyond the private enjoyment of quasi-rents by the borrowers, the government and the central bank are not willing to discontinue the practice because it is regarded (wrongly) as a policy instrument that can induce production and investment, and because it has a strong lobby of beneficiaries. Nevertheless, having shown a willingness to increase interest rates on directed credit and to close the interest gap that gives rise to the subsidy, the government has taken a major step toward the eventual elimination of these subsidies (Hwa 1989, 35–40).

Central Bank Relief for Financial Institutions

Another, less visible expenditure of the government, not recorded in the overall deficit of the nonfinancial public sector (table 5.1), has been the cost of bailing out distressed financial institutions since the 1982 financial crisis. This bailout was accomplished through the central bank and the Fondo de Garantías de las Instituciones Financieras, a deposit insurance institution which in the past charged no insurance premiums and is funded by central bank and public-sector credit. By the end of 1988, this institution had received 45.8 billion pesos in credits from the central bank alone, representing 10 percent of the net credit of the central bank to the Treasury, or about 2.4 percent of the total domestic assets of the central bank. In 1986, the flow of gross credit from the central bank and other public institutions to this fund represented 1.6 percent of GDP. While the financing supplied by the nonfinancial institutions is recorded in the overall deficit as presented in table 5.1, the amount of central bank financing is not detectable from that source.

Tax Reform

In 1983, the government implemented tax reform measures aimed at increasing income tax revenues. The government strengthened its control systems, increased withholding, and broadened the base for presumption of income. During the same year the value-added tax system was reformed. The substance of this reform was to unify tariffs and to extend the application of this tax to retailers (Bernal 1989). In addition, regional and municipal taxes were reformed in an effort to increase their revenues. Also in 1983, the import tax on the c.i.f. (cost plus insurance and freight) value of imports was increased from 1.5 percent to 2 percent. This tax was again increased in 1984 to 8 percent of the c.i.f. value, and in 1986 to 18 percent. During that year another major tax reform was implemented. This set of measures aimed at rationalizing the tax structure at the national level and increasing revenues through the elimination of deductions, exemptions, and tax discounts. The tax exemptions of public enterprises and a wide range of nonprofit organizations also were eliminated. Another salient feature of this reform was the elimination of taxation of dividends; at the same time it made the inflationary component of interest expenses nondeductible and the inflationary component of interest revenues deductible. This reform reduced taxes for the individual taxpayer while broadening the tax base, thus increasing revenues. It failed, however, to introduce tax treatment for interest earned abroad by unregistered depositors. This raises a moral and legal dilemma: on the one hand, it hardly seems proper for government to tax income on funds illegally held abroad; however, refusing to deal with the problem discriminates against depositors in Colombia, since the real interest component of interest earnings is taxable as income.

The results of tax reforms at the central government level may be observed in table 5.8. Income tax revenues increased significantly in 1983 and 1987 as a result of tax amnesties in 1983 and 1986, and increased gradually during the 1982–87 period as a proportion of GDP. Revenues from the value-added tax on local goods showed a steady increase as a proportion of GDP between 1982 and 1985, but this trend seems to be leveling off. As a whole, tax revenues on domestic economic activities increased as a percentage of GDP during the 1982–87 period, and increased very rapidly during the years 1983, 1985, and

Table 5.8 Colombia: changes in central government revenue, 1983–87
(percentages of GDP)

	1983	1984	1985	1986[a]	1987[b]
Overall change in revenues	−0.24	−1.83	1.74	0.72	0.30
Explained by:					
Tax revenues	0.33	0.08	1.34	0.45	0.38
On domestic activities	0.67	0.10	0.52	−0.05	0.25
Income taxes[c]	0.58	−0.15	0.13	0.07	0.36
VAT on local goods	0.10	0.22	0.32	−0.03	0.08
Gas and ACPN tax	0.01	−0.02	−0.03	−0.07	−0.01
Government stamp tax	−0.02	0.05	0.10	−0.02	−0.18
Other taxes[d]	0.00	0.00	0.00	0.00	0.00
On international trade	−0.34	−0.02	0.82	0.50	0.13
Customs duties and charges[e]	−0.21	−0.12	0.07	0.09	0.08
VAT on imported goods	−0.15	−0.03	0.15	0.12	0.10
C.i.f. tax[f]	−0.02	−0.03	0.54	0.12	0.13
Coffee export tax[g]	0.04	0.16	0.06	0.17	−0.18
Nontax revenues[h]	0.00	0.08	0.40	0.27	−0.08
Cuenta Especial de Cambios[i]	−0.57	−1.99	0.00	0.00	0.00

a. Preliminary.

b. Estimated.

c. Tax amnesties in 1982 and 1986 increased income tax revenues in 1983 and 1987.

d. Inheritance tax and grant tax (until 1983), property tax, liquor tax, hotel tax, ticket tax, among others.

e. Cigarette import tax, tonnage tax (until 1983).

f. From 1970 to 1983 this tax was set at 1.5 percent of the c.i.f. value of imports; in 1983 it was raised to 2 percent, in 1984 a surcharge of 8 percent of the c.i.f. value was applied, in 1986, a single 18 percent tax was levied on the c.i.f. value of imports.

g. Initially established at 26 percent of the export price in 1967, this tax has been reduced in seven stages to 6.5 percent in 1987.

h. Fees, fines, and contractual rents.

i. This account with the central bank consists of the interest earnings on international reserves and the "earnings" of the central bank from foreign-exchange transactions. It was eliminated as a source of revenue in 1983.

Source: Bernal (1989), figure 3.7.

1987. Tax revenues on activities related to international trade decreased in 1983 and 1984 as a proportion of GDP but took off in the following three years, mainly because of the value-added tax on imported goods and the surcharge on imports. During 1986, the coffee tax contributed significantly to tax revenues: the increase in revenues from this tax alone represented 0.17 percent of GDP. In the aggregate, revenues of the central government increased substantially after 1984. This is confirmed by the very high real growth rates of current revenues for the consolidated nonfinancial public sector in 1985 and 1986 (table 5.2). Nevertheless, the thrust of the reforms seemed to lose momentum very rapidly, as shown by the negative real growth rate of current revenues in 1987, the modest growth in 1988, and by the leveling off of the increase in revenues compared with that of GDP (tables 5.2 and 5.8).

Interest Rates

The Colombian government has tried from time to time to control interest rates, usually without success. Consequently, interest rates in Colombia are more or less freely determined, with occasional intervention by the government and from a loose but effective lenders' cartel that operates through the country's banking association. Moreover, interest rates in the local markets, despite foreign-exchange controls, are influenced by international rates, particularly at the deposit end of the operation.

The financial sector in Colombia is highly oligopolistic and lacks competition (Ortega 1988, Hommes 1988). Margins are very wide by international standards and real lending rates are moderately high, although they have come down from 18 percent per year in 1983 to 12.3 percent in 1988. Real savings and deposit interest rates have been positive at all times during the 1983–88 period (table 5.6).

As already indicated, average interest rates on directed credit are positive in real terms but far from market levels. The subsidy of these lines of credit adversely affects the distribution of wealth. It is granted mainly to large borrowers, without regard to economic efficiency, because credit is allocated through the commercial financial intermediaries, who bear all the risk and approve credit mainly on the basis of the ability of the borrower to provide collateral. This induces a close correspondence between the distribution of credit and the distribution of wealth. Furthermore, the provision of subsidized directed credit relies on a variety of forced investments of the financial institutions, which induce higher lending margins throughout the system and higher interest rates for ordinary borrowers. The provision of this credit through the central bank adds to the public debt and may produce losses that affect the fiscal deficit.

Table 5.9 Colombia: real trade-weighted exchange rates, 1983–88

	1983	1984	1985	1986	1987	1988
Real exchange rate index (average)[a]	64.4	69.9	80.0	95.0	97.3	97.4
Percentage change from previous year	−2.7	8.5	14.4	18.7	2.5	0.1
Real exchange rate index (December)	67.3	71.9	92.4	100.0	99.7	97.7
Percentage change from previous year	2.7	6.8	28.5	8.2	−0.3	−2.0
Memorandum: terms-of-trade index (1986 = 100)	95	88	98	100	88	99

a. Trade-weighted excluding coffee (December 1986 = 100). An increase in the index represents a devaluation.

Source: Banco de la República.

The main policy challenges posed by the structure of interest rates in Colombia are to increase competition in the financial sector, thereby inducing a narrowing of financial margins, and to eliminate interest rate subsidies and the forced investments that support them. Ideally, directed credit through the central bank or through other public financial institutions should also disappear. The elimination of credit subsidies is an administrative decision that could be implemented at any time. The promotion of competition requires allowing new national and foreign banks to enter the market, privatization of the banks now in the hands of the Fondo de Garantías de Instituciones Financieras, and a willingness on the part of the large public banks to foster market competition and stay away from the cartel agreements that are common in Colombia during the long periods when the government frees interest rates. A bill expected to be approved by the Colombian legislature this year would liberalize regulations on foreign investment in the financial sector (since 1975, foreign banks have been prevented by law from entering the market or increasing their relative shares in the banks they co-own with Colombian shareholders). If the bill is approved, the possibility of new foreign investment in the financial sector raises the odds in favor of increasing competition.

Exchange Rates

During 1985, the Colombian government devalued the peso by nearly 30 percent in real terms against a trade-weighted basket of currencies that represent

Table 5.10 Colombia: money growth and inflation, 1983–88
(percentages)

	1983	1984	1985	1986	1987	1988
Money supply growth[a]						
Monetary base	14	18	26	28	32	27
M1	30	23	28	23	33	26
Net domestic assets	35	28	32	8	32	19
Government	11	13	3	−1	4	n.a.
Private sector	26	18	23	20	25	17
Inflation[b]						
Consumer price index	20	16	24	19	23	28
Wholesale price index	22	18	25	22	25	28

n.a. = not available.

a. Percentage change from December to December.

b. Yearly average of 12 annualized monthly rates.

Sources: Banco de la República and Hwa (1989).

the country's foreign trade composition, with coffee excluded (table 5.9). In the previous two years the government had already been timidly devaluing in real terms, seeking to increase the competitiveness of Colombian exports, which had been lost, among other reasons, through real revaluation of the Colombian peso during the export boom of the late 1970s and the credit boom of the early 1980s.

Surprisingly, Colombia was able to achieve this very large adjustment of the exchange rate without devaluing abruptly. Moreover, the devaluation did not stimulate inflation beyond traditional levels (table 5.10), and the gradual adjustment throughout the year did not cause significant net capital flight, because the speculative outflows were compensated by the return of illegal capital from North American banks (Lora and Ocampo 1988; Garay and Carrasquilla 1987).

This devaluation was a central feature of the adjustment program. Since 1985 the government has been able to increase moderately the competitiveness of the exchange rate vis-à-vis the trade-weighted basket of currencies, maintaining the crawling-peg mechanism and taking advantage of the concurrent devaluation of the dollar (table 5.9). Nevertheless, in both 1987 and 1988 the end-year real exchange rate index was slightly lower than in the previous year, creating a degree of uncertainty about the ability and willingness of the government to prevent the competitiveness of the exchange rate from slipping.

It should also be noted that although Colombia has a successful exchange control regime, the exchange rate movements must obey market signals. The level of the exchange rate is influenced by the border markets with Ecuador and Venezuela, and therefore by the autonomous fiscal, monetary, and exchange rate policies of the governments of these neighboring countries. Furthermore, a very active parallel foreign-exchange market exists in Colombia, linked to the border markets, in which the rates are freely determined by supply and demand. The authorities keep a close watch on this curb market, gauging the movements of the exchange rate to prevent permanent increases in the gap between the official and parallel exchange rates.

The reaction of nontraditional exports to the exchange rate adjustment of 1985 and to the maintenance of its competitiveness has been as expected: these exports have grown by about 14 percent per year in dollar terms between 1984 and 1988 (table 5.11).

Despite the large exchange rate adjustment, the correction of the current account imbalance after 1985 had other causes, and in fact the contribution of the exchange rate adjustment and of fiscal discipline was modest. At the end of 1985, international coffee prices rose above their normal levels, giving way to a coffee export bonanza that extended into 1987. As a result of this boom, coffee export revenues increased by roughly $1 billion in value in 1986 over the previous year (table 5.11).

Increased production of hydrocarbons contributed an additional net increase of $0.5 billion to the current account due to exports and import substitution. Exports of nickel and coal contributed $67 million, so that the net contribution to the current account of exports or import substitutes whose production is relatively price-inelastic amounted to more than $1.5 billion. Adding to this windfall gain in coffee exports, it can be concluded that the very rapid correction of the current account imbalance in 1985 was induced exogenously to a large extent.

This conclusion notwithstanding, it must be noted that the exchange rate adjustment of 1985 allowed the government to liberalize import trade very gradually (and reluctantly), and has created a positive environment for the encouragement of export services and for the increase in net transfers. Together with nontraditional exports, the increase in exports of nonfinancial services and the net increase in transfers contributed $820 million to the current account in 1986, an increment that may be linked directly to the exchange rate adjustment.

Foreign Investment

Colombian treatment of foreign investment is still firmly rooted in the ideology of the Andean Pact, although lip service is paid to a more liberal attitude. With time it can be expected that controls on the entry of foreign investment will be

Table 5.11 Colombia: balance of payments accounts, 1983–88
(millions of dollars)

Account	1983	1984	1985	1986	1987[a]	1988[b]
Current account	−2,826	−2,088	−1,586	462	329	−352
Trade balance	−1,317	−404	109	1,922	1,868	909
Exports	3,147	3,623	3,782	5,331	5,662	5,310
Coffee	1,443	1,734	1,702	2,742	1,633	1,606
Hydrocarbons and minerals	674	790	955	1,226	2,472	1,867
Hydrocarbons	434	445	409	619	1,341	953
Gold	177	245	365	359	792	408
Nickel and coal	63	100	181	248	339	506
Other (nontraditional)	1,030	1,099	1,125	1,363	1,557	1,837
Imports	4,464	4,027	3,673	3,409	3,794	4,401
Consumer goods	487	387	345	380	488	549
Intermediate goods	2,286	2,231	2,163	1,784	1,925	2,329
Hydrocarbons	626	450	466	130	101	139
Others	1,660	1,781	1,697	1,654	1,824	2,190
Capital goods	1,691	1,409	1,165	1,245	1,381	1,523
Services (net)	−1,673	−1,983	−2,156	−2,245	−2,540	−2,151
Credit	1,183	1,104	1,068	1,364	1,360	1,582
Financial	272	108	91	131	176	245
Other	911	996	977	1,233	1,184	1,337
Debit	2,856	3,087	3,224	3,609	3,900	3,733
Financial	1,011	1,178	1,293	1,315	1,399	1,820
Other	1,845	1,909	1,931	2,294	2,501	1,913
Transfers (net)	164	299	461	785	1,001	890
Capital account	1,369	964	2,181	1,130	−327	983
Long-term	1,528	1,822	2,350	2,629	185	876
Investment	512	558	1,015	592	335	187
Debt						
Public sector (net)	943	1,217	1,142	1,848	−91	647
Private sector (net)	73	47	193	189	−59	42
Short-term	−159	−858	−169	−1,499	−512	107
Errors and omissions	−266	−137	−311	−128	−24	−293
Change in net international reserves	−1,723	−1,261	284	1,464	−22	338

a. Preliminary.

b. Estimated.

Sources: for 1983–1987, Banco de la República; for 1988, Hwa (1989).

liberalized. The likely approval of a new, less restrictive regime for foreign investment in the financial sector may initiate a trend in this direction.

The government of Colombia has not adopted any debt-reducing program that would also promote foreign investment. The authorities believe that foreign direct investment is insensitive to artificial inducements and do not foresee that additional investment would flow from debt-equity swaps and similar incentives. Furthermore, these programs are regarded as an obstacle to the present foreign financing strategy of the government, which is based on maintaining the relative exposure of the different types of lenders unchanged, without opening exit doors for the commercial banks to reduce their exposure.

Finally, the widespread belief in Colombia is that these debt-reduction inducements to foreign investment negatively affect "national wealth," because they give market access and transfer national resources to foreign investors at bargain prices, and because it is not clear that either the net initial value or the net present value effect of these programs on international reserves is positive. Most of these positions and beliefs are rooted in moralistic principles or prejudices and do not resist rigorous analysis, but they conform to the ruling ideology and dictate the policy of the present administration.

Privatization

Privatization is not a major issue in Colombia, probably because the government-owned industrial companies do not represent a large share of production or employment. There is a wide consensus that the telecommunications company and the public oil company, ECOPETROL, should not be sold, nor should the water-supply companies or the public utilities. All other government firms may eventually be sold to private stockholders, although the labor unions may oppose these sales, and the government would like to maintain control of a couple of commercial banks that have traditionally been in the public sector. Additionally, local governments are open to the idea of contracting for public services with private firms, rather than setting up costly firms to supply them.

The state development bank, Instituto de Fomento Industrial (IFI), has already sold to Renault its share of the car assembly plant operated in Colombia by that firm, and it has offered its shares of PAPELCOL, a paper mill, on the international equity market. It is seeking also to divest all of its holdings in productive firms. Additionally, the public National Coffee Fund, managed by the federation of coffee growers, will be selling all its holdings of stock in financial or productive firms that have no bearing on the coffee marketing effort.

Finally, regulations have been issued by the government directing the sale of stock of financial institutions held by the Fondo de Garantías de Instituciones

Financieras, opening the possibility for the resale of financial institutions to the private sector.

Deregulation

The prospects for deregulation in Colombia are not bright. The tradition of the country and the relatively large proportion of lawyers in the population pull in the opposite direction. However, the previous administration was able to decentralize some important government functions, and the present administration has successfully simplified tax procedures and practices, bringing down some totems that were thought to be the pillars of the tax system (such as the requirement that both parties to all property transactions obtain certification from the tax authorities that they were not in arrears in their tax payments). These steps open the way for other urgent reforms, of the customs bureaucracy and the financial sector, for example. There is also some discussion of the benefits of reforming the exchange control regime, which has remained unaltered for 22 years, and even of amending the constitution, which dates from 1886.

In this reform-minded environment, if the lawyers get their way, deregulation will not be at the top of the list of priorities, but the private sector and the technocratic bureaucracy may be able to induce some deregulation.

Property Rights

Property rights in Colombia are so well entrenched that their role as obstacles to capitalistic development may be easily overlooked. These rights have stood in the way of successful agrarian reform for decades, and they are a binding restriction on all urban development programs. This is an area in which the concerns should run in the opposite direction: there is a need to introduce property rights legislation in Colombia that would expedite agrarian reform and make it less costly, and make it easier for municipalities to subordinate the private to the public good for the sake of rational urban development. However, laws of this type are not very likely to be adopted in Colombia in the short run, given the wide participation of landowners in the congress.

Trade Policy and Growth

Colombia has a long tradition of reverting to import licensing when current account deficits become large. In the early 1980s, as at other times in the recent

Table 5.12 Colombia: trade liberalization, 1983–88

	1983	1984	1985	1986	1987	1988
Number of tariff categories:						
Prohibited	0	828	69	56	56	50
Prior license required	4,671	4,160	3,602	3,160	3,081	3,131
Free (with import license)[a]	340	23	1,359	1,826	1,905	1,939
Total	5,011	5,011	5,030	5,042	5,042	5,120
Tariff levels (percentages)						
Mean		61		52		30
Standard deviation		29		16		17
Trade-weighted		57		48		27
By stage of production						
Consumer goods						
Durable		87		74		
Nondurable		85		68		
Industrial inputs						
Intermediate and raw materials		34		29		
Capital goods		56		45		
Agricultural inputs						
Intermediate and raw materials		34		29		
Capital goods		37		32		
Average effective rate of protection[b]		61		54		

a. All items imported into Colombia require a license from the Instituto de Comercio Exterior.

b. Calculated for 23 national accounts sectors.

Source: World Bank.

past, the government put an end to the trade liberalization trend that had been under way since the late 1970s and imposed very restrictive administrative controls on imports. In 1985, yielding to pressure from the multilateral credit institutions, the government increased the number of tariff categories that do not require a prior import license (they still require an import license, but it may not be denied if all conditions are met). As a consequence of this liberalization gesture, the number of tariff categories requiring prior license decreased from 4,160 in 1984 to 3,602 in 1985 and 3,081 in 1987. In 1988, however, the number of categories requiring prior license increased again to 3,131; this represents 61 percent of all tariff categories (Table 5.12).

During 1984–88, the mean trade-weighted import tariff was reduced to 27 percent in 1988 from 57 percent in 1984, and the tariff dispersion was reduced by 50 percent. Between 1984 and 1986, the average rate of effective protection, calculated by a World Bank mission for 23 national accounts sectors, also was reduced from 60.8 percent to 53.6 percent (table 5.12).

Although these trends indicate a timid trade liberalization effort, the Colombian economy remains inwardly oriented as a result of an import trade regime beset by effective administrative controls and a very irregular tariff structure. Besides the economic distortions it imposes, this regime encourages administrative corruption and rent-seeking by importers. This regime is expected to be reformed in the near future, and a more liberalized regime has been proposed. The new regime would still grant very high levels of nominal and effective protection to final goods produced in Colombia but would not rely on prior licensing. This reform would introduce a limited degree of competition in all markets. Despite the modest objectives of the liberalization proposal, it has been fiercely opposed by the industrial lobby, and its implementation has been postponed.

It should be noted that although import controls ensure Colombian producers a high level of protection, they are not completely shielded from foreign competition because the borders with neighboring countries are fairly open, and because, with coasts on two oceans and a large surplus of illegal foreign exchange, the country is particularly vulnerable to contraband.

Trade reform is seen as the missing link between the present path of modest growth with moderate inflation and a stable, high-growth alternative way. The reluctance of the government to undertake a serious reform of the foreign trade sector may be the reason behind the failure of otherwise orthodox management to induce reasonable growth rates. There is a growing concern in Colombia and within the multilateral credit agencies that despite the efforts of the government to implement economic policy by the book, development and growth remain elusive.

Growth

The Colombian experience shows that adjustment may be a necessary condition for sustained growth but certainly is not a sufficient one. It was fortunate for the government and the country that the adjustment program was implemented at exactly the same time that an export bonanza began to unfold. This made the adjustment relatively painless and politically palatable. The growth induced by the external sector prevented an increase in unemployment after 1985 and a decline in real wages, except in the public sector, where wages fell as a consequence of the fiscal adjustment (table 5.13). These short-lived induce-

Table 5.13 Colombia: employment and wages, 1983–88

	1983	1984	1985	1986	1987	1988
Unemployment rate[a]	11.1	13.1	14.0	13.0	11.3	10.2
Participation rate[a]	54.4	56.0	55.3	55.9	56.9	57.6
Real wages (1983 = 100)						
Manufacturing	100	106	104	108	108	107
Agriculture	100	99	96	102	105	104
Minimum wage (urban)	100	103	101	104	101	101
Public sector	100	104	93	94	n.a.	n.a.

a. As a percentage of the labor force, measured in September of each year.

Source: Departamento Administrativo Nacional de Estadística.

ments to growth gave oxygen to the adjustment program, which might otherwise have failed because there were no other available sources of growth compatible with the adjustment objectives.

Overall, a serious problem has been the failure of Colombia's orthodox macroeconomic policies to ensure growth. Whereas during the late 1960s and early 1970s the economy grew at acceptably high rates (above 6 percent per year), this growth has not been emulated since 1974, except during the periods of external bonanzas. Capital has grown at a relatively uniform pace in the period from 1945 to 1987, so that fluctuations in rates of capital formation do not explain the differences in growth rates between periods. Differences in productivity growth rates may be more closely related to variations in the growth rate of the economy. Unfortunately, if one discounts the effect of education, productivity has made a negative contribution to growth since 1974, and total productivity has contributed negatively to growth since 1980 (Ocampo 1989a).

Furthermore, there is compelling evidence that the Colombian economy will not become more efficient unless a growth threshold of about 4 percent is surpassed, because growth in productivity, as hypothesized by Kaldor (1967), seems to become negative when the economy grows at a rate below that threshold (Ocampo 1989a). This is not atypical for a late-industrializing economy. In Korea and presumably in other developing countries, productivity is an increasing function of growth, and growth, naturally, also increases with productivity. This virtuous circle is due primarily to three factors: the link between investment and technical change, the realization of economies of scale through market growth, and learning by doing (Amsden 1989).

In the case of Colombia, the record of the postadjustment years offers additional clues to the growth question. Growth appears to be intimately related to exports, and more generally to the current account balance, which seems to

Table 5.14 Colombia: decomposition of economic growth, 1983–88
(percentages)

	1983	1984	1985	1986	1987	1988
Growth rates						
GDP	1.6	3.4	3.1	5.8	5.3	3.7
Public consumption	−0.6	4.1	4.5	1.4	6.1	14.6
Private consumption	0.5	2.9	1.9	3.2	3.8	3.6
Gross capital formation	1.2	1.2	−5.2	7.6	0.0	6.6
Exports	−0.9	10.3	14.4	20.7	8.3	1.0
Imports	−9.1	−4.0	−6.6	4.1	3.9	12.0
Domestic internal demand	−0.2	1.2	−0.1	3.2	4.5	5.6
Decomposition of growth[a]						
Consumption	17	76	60	43	62	108
Households	21	63	44	40	50	67
Public administration	−4	13	16	3	12	41
Gross capital formation	13	7	−29	21	0	27
Changes in inventories	−44	−45	−33	−8	22	9
Domestic internal demand	−14	37	−2	56	84	144
Exports of goods and services	−8	41	65	55	28	5
Total final demand	−22	78	63	111	112	149
Imports of goods and services	−122	−22	−37	11	12	49
Memorandum: net exports (X−M)	114	63	102	44	16	−44
GDP growth	100	100	100	100	100	100
Supply-side contribution						
Agriculture	39	12	12	14	25	19
Mining	12	10	21	24	19	4
Manufacturing (excluding coffee)	8	29	21	20	23	22
Construction	30	8	12	0	−4	1
Infrastructure	40	18	24	18	8	13
Services	−29	23	11	24	29	41

a. Defined as dY = dC + dI + dG + dX − dM.

Source: Banco de la República and Hwa (1989).

be the ultimate constraint (table 5.14). During the period 1983–88, high growth rates, above 5 percent in 1986 and 1987, seem to have been linked to the coffee price and export revenue bonanza. Undoubtedly, growth responded to expanding aggregate demand, and this explains the acceleration in 1986–87. In 1988, however, when export growth slowed and imports reacted with a lag, internal demand was not capable of sustaining growth by itself, and the control exerted by the government on the current account balance may have acted as a deterrent to investment in fixed (mostly imported) capital. The experience of these years suggests that other sources of external demand must be found if Colombia is to replicate the conditions of 1986–87 and remove the obstacles to growth. These sources will be found in the expansion of industrial and other nontraditional exports and in the substitution of selected industrial imports, namely, intermediate goods.

Unfortunately, the present array of policy variables is not particularly geared to vigorous export growth. Although the macroeconomic situation does not inhibit exports, there are other problems that have to be solved: deficiencies in transportation and port infrastructure, government regulation, import controls on raw materials and machinery, lack of technological modernization, and lack of secure, stable access to large industrial markets. On the import substitution side there are also problems to be solved. First, there is a conflict between protection of intermediate goods and promotion of exports. In addition, the instability of trade policies in the past has increased the uncertainty of local producers about future trade policies, and this may prevent investment in import-substituting sectors even under the existing highly protective conditions.

In conclusion, the trade regime chosen for Colombia holds the key to the country's future path of growth. The successful combination of a prudent, rational trade liberalization program that would provide a stable but competitive environment for domestic producers, devoid of abrupt turns or reversals of policies, with an active export promotion program and the traditional Colombian approach to macroeconomic management would ensure a high growth path. The maintenance of excessive protection, administrative import controls, and untargeted export inducements—features that characterize the present regime—will lead to a low growth path, permanently constrained by the restrictions imposed by the current account balance and internal demand, no matter how macroeconomic variables are managed.

If sustained growth is to be achieved, it is clear that the government, in addition to implementing the required trade reform and continuing its orthodox macroeconomic management, must target its priorities correctly. It must avoid the foolish waste of resources in projects such as mass urban transport systems and instead channel public infrastructure and human capital investment in ways that have a direct impact on removing obstacles to exporting. The government must become an active promoter of growth, supplying the private sector with the right mix of carrot-and-stick inducements to accelerate investment.[1] However, these efforts will not be possible without stable access to foreign capital.

Rudiger Dornbusch (chapter 7, this volume) has suggested that what is needed is a Marshall Plan for Latin America that will overcome the private sector's hesitancy and create the dynamics for a return of flight capital. Victor Urquidi has suggested that all that is needed is the repatriation of the interest on Latin American capital that is deposited abroad. To make Dornbusch's proposal or Urquidi's wish a reality, it may be necessary for the international financial community and the governments of the countries in which these deposits are held to collaborate in creating Marshall Plan–like mechanisms to return these deposits. Without this or another source of external finance, the outlook for growth is pessimistic.

Acknowledgment

Armando Montenegro contributed very useful comments on the nature and causes of the Colombian crisis and the government's responsibility therein.

---

1. Amsden (1989) highlights the importance of such a role for governments but does not give any clues to resolving the problem of avoiding distortions and gross inequalities in the process of intervention.

Venezuela

Ricardo Hausmann

For a period of about four decades, until 1983, Venezuela enjoyed a rather stable policy consensus. This stability was both cause and consequence of a very successful overall performance: high and sustained growth (around 6 percent annually) with one of the lowest inflation rates in the world (3.1 percent per year on average for the period 1950–80). The consensus was based on four policy principles: fixed exchange rates, balanced fiscal budgets, fixed interest rates, and protectionism. In a world of low inflation, fixed exchange rates, and stable oil prices this policy mix resulted in a stable real exchange rate, moderately positive real interest rates, and steady growth of demand and output.[2]

Public policy discussions in Venezuela during this era dealt mainly with the structure of government spending. Arguments were usually framed in a populist manner. "The state" was supposed to be the great provider. Citizens had a positive claim on the state to a decent standard of living, but no duties to contribute to collective spending. Oil tax revenue and at most "the rich" were to provide the resources. Populism amounted to entitlements without duties, absolute rights with no trade-offs, redistribution without a budget constraint. In the period of ample oil revenues, this political tradition created an atmosphere of social harmony, but during the 1980s, when fiscal resources dwindled, it prevented a fruitful discussion of the difficult trade-offs ahead.[3]

Problems with the traditional policy approach became obvious during the 1979–82 period when, in spite of the second oil shock, the economy entered a period of zero growth with rising inflation and massive capital flight. Nevertheless, the policy consensus remained basically intact.[4]

---

2. Hausmann (1990, chapter 10) presents a detailed discussion of the economic policy rules in Venezuela during this period.

3. Naím and Piñango (1985) argue that oil income allowed the Venezuelan political system to finance an illusion of harmony that was unaffordable in other Latin American countries.

4. Economists have explained events during this period in very different ways. Rodriguez (1987a) argues that the recession was produced by a contractionary fiscal policy and that capital flight was caused by low domestic interest rates. Elsewhere (Hausmann 1990,

---

Ricardo Hausmann is Professor of Economics at Instituto de Estudios Superiores de Administración (IESA) Caracas. He has been a visiting fellow at CEPREMAP (Paris) and Oxford University. He is the author of a number of articles on the Venezuelan economy and of Exchange Regimes and Fiscal Policy *(1990).*

The Onset of the Crisis

After the reduction in oil exports (from $19.3 billion in 1981 to $13.5 billion in 1983), it became obvious to the financial markets that the prevailing fixed exchange rate could not be maintained. This prompted a massive attack on the bolivar.[5] The balance of payments crisis of 1983 left the country with few international reserves and even fewer ideas of what to do about it. The political elite was facing a situation it had never encountered before.

The closest experience that remained in the collective memory was the mild 1960 balance of payments crisis linked to the end of the oil boom that followed the 1956 Suez Canal crisis.[6] At that time, the stabilization package included the adoption of a multiple exchange rate system, a mild and gradual average devaluation, a cut in fiscal spending, and the adoption of a protectionist trade policy. By early 1964 the crisis was over and the country returned to its traditional fixed exchange rate after a 35 percent cumulative devaluation. The management of this crisis has been regarded ever since as successful. Consequently, in 1983 the political consensus had few other options than to try to repeat this experience.

More than six years have now passed, and Venezuela has failed to return to normal growth. In these years there have been three distinct periods: the first stabilization effort (1983–85), an attempted expansion (1986–88), and the radical adjustment program of 1989. This paper briefly describes the overall policy stance during each of these three periods before going on to analyze in some detail the various policy issues and the changing consensus around them.

The 1983–1985 Stabilization Effort

The first reaction to the crisis was a repetition of the 1960 program. A multiple exchange rate system was adopted with the idea of insulating the real sector from the impact of speculative capital flows. The official exchange rate was

---

chapter 5) I argue that the recession was a reaction to the fiscal overexpansion of the 1976–78 period, which was a consequence of the first oil shock and which produced severe overheating. I support my view by noting that during the 1979–82 recession real wages rose, unemployment went back to its natural rate, and the real exchange rate rose. This pattern is inconsistent with a demand-determined explanation of the recession. Moreover, I argue that capital flight was principally caused by excessive fiscal spending, which crowded out private internal spending and made the nominal exchange rate nonviable given the expected decline in oil revenue. On this period see also Palma (1986).

5. It is estimated that between May 1982 and February 1983 capital flight amounted to $10 billion (Rodríguez 1987b).

6. For an analysis comparing the 1960–64 period with the 1983–88 period see Hausmann (1990, chapter 8).

lowered from 4.30 to 6.00 bolivars to the dollar (table 5.15). A preferential rate of 4.30 bolivars to the dollar was retained, and a free-floating unofficial rate was allowed. Public spending was cut radically, principally affecting investment programs. The regime of import prohibitions and licenses was extended, and access to foreign exchange at the official rate was managed on a case-by-case basis. The price control system was expanded to ensure that the consumer received the benefit of the rationed preferential dollars.

The economy's reaction was to produce a deep recession, relatively low inflation, and huge fiscal and external surpluses (table 5.15). Resources started to move from nontradeables to importables. Even nontraditional exports started to grow significantly, since exporters were allowed to sell the value-added portion of their output at the floating rate (table 5.16).[7] However, the government lost control of the floating rate dollar, which depreciated in real terms by 300 percent in the first six months of the program.

In February 1984 a new official rate depreciation to 7.50 bolivars to the dollar and an additional cut in public spending were introduced. By mid-1985, the results were a rapidly rising level of international reserves, a large fiscal surplus, inflation at around 15 percent, and expanding activity in agriculture, manufacturing, and tourism. A floating rate premium of 100 percent had developed, and the unemployment rate had almost doubled from 7 percent in 1982 to 14 percent in the first semester of 1985.

Under these circumstances austerity seemed unnecessary, and a doubling of public investment from 6 percent to 12 percent of GDP was approved for the following fiscal year. No change was thought necessary in the other policy areas, which had wide support. In particular, the multiple exchange rate system was favored by the trade unions, the import-competing sectors, exporters, the tourism industry, and consumers, among others.

Fiscal Expansion and Oil Crash: 1986–1988

Just as the fiscal expansion started in January 1986, oil income fell by almost half, from an average of $13.9 billion for 1984 and 1985 to $7.6 billion in 1986. For the next three years the government maintained its expansionary policy with increasing difficulty. In 1986, the nonoil economy grew by 7.1 percent, but the floating rate went from 15 bolivars to the dollar in January to 26 bolivars to the dollar in November. The credibility of the official rate, fixed at 7.50 to the dollar, collapsed, and the government was increasingly unable to manage the

---

7. Besides the impact of import controls on the availability of necessary inputs, exports were limited by the control regime necessary to avoid corruption through reexportation of goods imported at the preferential rate.

Table 5.15 Venezuela: summary economic data, 1974–88 (percentages except where noted)

	1974–78	1979–82	1983	1984	1985	1986	1987	1988
GDP growth								
Total	5.8	-0.2	-5.3	-1.1	1.3	6.8	3.0	4.2
Nonoil	8.1	1.0	-4.7	-1.2	3.2	7.1	3.5	4.5
Unemployment rate[a]	4.5	7.2	10.2	13.4	12.1	10.3	8.5	7.0
Oil price (dollars per barrel)	14.2	27.8	25.3	26.7	25.9	12.8	16.3	13.5
Current account balance (billions of dollars)	0.0	1.4	4.4	5.4	3.1	-1.5	-1.1	-4.9
Exchange rates (bolivars per dollar)								
Official	4.3	4.3	6.0	7.5	7.5	7.5	14.5	14.5
Average (imports)	4.3	4.3	5.0	6.6	7.5	8.9	11.8	15.3
Floating[a]	n.a.	n.a.	13.5	14.6	15.2	24.3	31.6	40.5
Relative prices (1974–78 = 100)								
Real exchange rate[b]	100.0	88.4	91.7	105.9	101.4	100.2	96.3	98.7
Importables vs. nontradeables	100.0	86.9	80.7	88.5	89.0	92.8	94.1	92.8
Inflation								
Consumer prices[a]	8.2	13.1	7.0	15.7	9.2	12.7	40.3	35.5
Nonoil GDP deflator	n.a.	n.a.	8.7	13.3	13.4	11.7	27.3	26.3
Growth rate of money supply (M2)	28.0	14.7	28.7	8.8	8.6	16.7	24.4	18.3
Interest rates								
On commercial loans	10.1	16.7	15.8	15.3	12.7	12.7	12.7	12.7
On 90-day deposits	8.0	14.2	13.5	13.0	8.9	9.0	9.0	9.0
Public-sector surplus (as share of GDP)	n.a.	n.a.	-4.5	4.9	3.4	-4.5	-5.9	-7.8
Net internal public spending (as share of GDP)[c]	n.a.	32.6	16.5	9.2	6.3	9.1	14.8	n.a.

n.a. = not available.   a. End of period.   b. Average nominal exchange rate for imports adjusted by inflation differentials.

c. Internal public spending minus internal taxes, where oil taxes are mostly taken as external income, as calculated in Hausmann (1988).

Sources: Banco Central de Venezuela; Hausmann (1988).

Table 5.16 Venezuela: selected balance of payments accounts, 1984–88
(billions of dollars)

Account	1984	1985	1986	1987	1988
Current account	5.4	3.1	−1.5	−1.1	−4.9
Trade balance	8.7	6.8	1.3	1.7	−0.5
Total exports f.o.b.	16.0	14.2	9.1	10.6	10.4
Oil	14.8	12.9	7.6	9.1	8.4
Other	1.2	1.3	1.5	1.5	2.0
Total imports f.o.b.	−7.3	−7.4	−7.9	−8.8	−10.9
Nonfactor services	−1.9	−1.5	−1.3	−1.5	−2.4
Factor income	−1.4	−2.2	−1.5	−1.4	−2.0
Capital account	−3.8	−1.1	−1.4	0.2	−0.1
Net public borrowing	−1.8	−0.8	−1.2	−1.2	−0.7
Foreign direct investment	0.0	0.1	0.0	0.0	0.1
Net private flows	−2.1	−0.4	−0.3	1.5	0.5
Balance of payments	1.6	2.0	−3.0	−0.9	−5.0
Errors and omissions	0.3	−0.2	−0.8	0.2	0.5
Change in net reserves	1.9	1.8	−3.8	−0.7	−4.5

f.o.b. = free on board.

Source: Banco Central de Venezuela.

exchange control mechanism. In December 1986 it was decided to effect a "credible" devaluation of 93 percent, to 14.50 bolivars to the dollar. Inflation accelerated to an all-time high of 42 percent in 1987.

In February 1986 the government had signed a restructuring accord with its commercial bank creditors. This agreement proved nonviable. It had been negotiated prior to the collapse in oil prices and included no new money, a down payment on principal, and no grace period for amortizations. Consequently, in spite of a minor adjustment to the accord in February 1987, during 1986–88 the public sector made net amortizations of $3.1 billion (table 5.16). Given the current account deficits of this period, which totaled $7.5 billion, the government used $9.0 billion in international reserves and forced the private sector to increase its short-term credit lines by $4.8 billion. Thus, long-term public-sector amortizations of cheap foreign debt were paid for with expensive, short-term, private-sector commercial debt and with reserves.

Remembering the political costs of the December 1986 devaluation, and with the December 1988 presidential election approaching, the government felt that it could not carry out a fiscal contraction or increase the fixed nominal interest rates, in spite of rising inflation.

As a result, real interest rates became increasingly negative. This prompted flight from the bolivar and the appearance of a parallel interest rate for the first time in Venezuela. Real money declined and the foreign-exchange premium increased, reaching 200 percent in late 1988, in spite of the 1986 devaluation. Most portfolios had liabilities in bolivars and assets in dollars and benefited from the increasing real depreciation of the floating rate.

To contain the accelerating inflation, the government decided to freeze prices in agriculture and in the public sector. Real public-sector prices fell to half their 1984 levels, accentuating the public-sector deficit, which reached 7.8 percent of GDP in 1988.

The Radical Adjustment Program of 1989

The 1986–88 expansion left the newly elected government of Carlos Andrés Pérez with four major disequilibria. First was an external imbalance evidenced by a very low level of liquid international reserves ($300 million), an exploding foreign-exchange premium (192 percent), short-term central bank dollar liabilities (recognized official rate letters of credit) of $6.3 billion, and no international financing plan for 1989. Second, the fiscal deficit was projected to exceed 12 percent of GDP. Third, repressed inflation was producing serious shortages in basic products, a collapse of supply, and generalized speculative inventory accumulation. Fourth, the financial system was severely repressed and suffering from growing disintermediation.

Constrained in its action by these problems, the new government decided on the following policy package. First, it adopted a unified floating exchange rate system and eliminated the previous exchange control regime. The bolivar went from its previous system of an official rate of 14.5 to the dollar and a floating rate of 42 to the dollar to a single floating rate of 36 to the dollar. It then depreciated back to 43 to the dollar by year's end. Second, prices of public-sector goods and services (gasoline, electricity, telephone, etc.) were raised. Third, price controls were eliminated for all goods except a reduced list of some 10 basic products. Fourth, a trade liberalization policy was adopted, with the elimination of 75 percent of import prohibitions and 70 percent of import licenses, and a 50 percent reduction in the average tariff. Fifth, interest rates were increased to levels close to equilibrium. Maximum rates on loans were raised from 13 percent to 42 percent. Sixth, an international financing strategy based on commercial debt reduction and borrowing from multilateral agencies was put in place.

The economy has reacted with a collapse in GDP (estimated at 10 percent or more), an inflation rate of some 80 percent,[8] a rising level of international reserves, and a balanced public-sector account. (The fiscal results reflect an unwanted overadjustment in spending and better-than-expected receipts.) Interest rates, after peaking at 42 percent, are falling in response to market forces. Unemployment, which had reached 7 percent in late 1988, is likely to jump to 13 percent by the end of 1989.

In 1990, the absence of major new shocks, an increase in fiscal spending, the fall in interest rates, and the adjustment in relative prices should produce healthier conditions for growth. However, the Pérez administration's economic policy has received very little support from most sectors of society, including the government party itself. Relations with the legislature are strained to a degree never experienced before, and many would like to see the "neoliberal" package abandoned.

The Changing Policy Consensus

The preceding section has provided an overview of the economic policy picture in Venezuela as it evolved over the last decade. We examine next in some detail the changing consensus in Venezuela on various specific areas of policy.

Fiscal Deficits

The Venezuelan political consensus has traditionally been against fiscal deficits. Keynesian arguments in favor of deficit spending were very seldom used and never carried much support. This is not to imply that the consensus was not Keynesian. Increased internal spending of oil tax revenue was considered expansionary in the short run. This consensus against deficit spending, embodied in the public credit law (Ley Orgánica de Crédito Público) including its latest revision in 1981, probably has its roots in the 1903 payments crisis that prompted German and Dutch naval intervention. Borrowing by both the central government and the state enterprises requires congressional approval, and the resources must be earmarked for specific development programs. Moreover, the general law governing the public budget (Ley Orgánica de Régimen Presupuestario) requires a balanced budget; under this law amortizations are consid-

---

8. The price level jumped by an accumulated 40 percent over the two months of March and April 1989. Since then the increase has averaged about 3 percent per month.

ered as spending and borrowing as income, but new borrowing is limited by the public credit law.

In spite of this clear political consensus, the public sector somehow managed to accumulate $28 billion in foreign debt, as well as 80 billion bolivars in internal bonds[9] and a significant amount of monetization.[10]

This apparent contradiction between formal consensus and actual behavior is mainly explained by the perverse cycle into which relations between the central government and the state enterprises have fallen. In its typical form, the cycle goes more or less as follows.

At time t_0 there is a political consensus on the need for a given public investment project, which is generally justified on the basis of excess demand on existing capacity or regional development. The project usually includes some foreign borrowing. At time t_1 the investment program starts accumulating cost overruns. Meanwhile the revenues from existing operations deteriorate because the best executives have been assigned to manage the investment program or have been hired by project contractors. The public company starts to have cash-flow problems and incurs some additional unplanned debts.

At time t_2 the company is unable to pay its contractors and suppliers and is accumulating unauthorized short-term debts with them. These groups start to lobby the government for a solution to the problem. Public opinion shifts against the public enterprises. Also at this time, the company finds itself unable to pay its external debt (or uses this as a trick to get more resources from the government). Finance Ministry officials meeting in New York with the Bank Advisory Committee see their negotiating strategy disrupted by the unexpected arrears the public-sector companies have accumulated. When they return home, they pound on tables and demand that payments be made current. But this cannot happen unless the government bails the company out.

At time t_3 the congress passes a debt-reordering public credit law to normalize the "floating debt" accumulated by what by now has become the previous government or the previous company administration. This includes the issue of central government bonds to pay suppliers and contractors, and the takeover of

---

9. The average exchange rate at the time of issue of these bonds was 7 bolivars to the dollar, and the average interest rate was around 13 percent. Consequently, this debt represented the equivalent of some $12 billion, about 22 percent of GDP. With the exchange rate at around 42 to the dollar, interest rates at 42 percent, and the 12-month inflation rate at 95 percent, the real value of this debt has declined in late 1989 to about 7 percent of GDP.

10. Monetization of the fiscal deficit has come about mainly from central bank overestimation of exchange profits during the multiple exchange rate regime in place between February 1983 and March 1989. Using FIFO (first in, first out) accounting rules, the central bank monetized and transferred to the central government the capital gains on its significant foreign-exchange holdings after each of the three official rate devaluations.

the company's external debt. The new administrators demand flexibility so that they can put the company's house in order.

At time t_4 the company uses the bailout funds and the honeymoon of its new managers to propose and initiate a new investment program, and the cycle starts over again.

Through this mechanism, the central government, which itself has only borrowed $8 billion abroad, is now servicing a $23 billion debt. Moreover, to normalize the "floating debt" of the state-owned enterprises it issued internal bonds in the amount of 21 billion bolivars ($6.5 billion) in 1981 and 43 billion bolivars ($7 billion) in 1984. Another law of this type is currently being proposed by the Chamber of Construction, the contractors' lobby group.

The accumulation of external debt by the central government has constrained its ability to perform the primary tasks under its responsibility, namely, justice, health, education, and provision of infrastructure. Moreover, the fact that public awareness is concentrated on the central government budget, whereas most problems occur in the decentralized companies and become an issue only every third year (at time t_3), has made congressional budget discussions irrelevant. Thus, in 1984 and 1988 the central government had a balanced budget in traditional Venezuelan terms, but the consolidated public sector had a surplus equal to 4.9 percent of GDP in 1984 and a deficit of 7.8 percent of GDP in 1988 (by standard IMF accounting).

Finally, the traditional Venezuelan economic definition of a balanced budget has become unworkable given the burgeoning size of the central government debt, which obviously must be rolled over. As a result, IMF-type targets for fiscal policy are becoming the only reasonable criteria for planning purposes, even though these are hard to reconcile with existing legislation. The general feeling is that a 7 percent deficit is too much and a 3 percent deficit is about right, but no economic rationale has been developed for any particular budget target. It may very well be that price stability and politically tolerable interest rates require a small fiscal surplus.

Public Expenditure Priorities

Public expenditure priorities have changed since the first oil boom in the 1920s. Up to the 1940s, defense, police, and road building took the lion's share of the budget. Then development took over as first priority, and channeling of financial resources in the form of loans to the private sector became acceptable. Also, some large public-sector enterprises (steel, electricity, petrochemicals) were established in the 1950s. By 1957, the combined budget of the education and health ministries did not reach 10 percent of central government spending (Hausmann 1981).

With the establishment of democracy in 1958, social spending and private-sector development financing became the new established consensus. Over the next 20 years, student enrollment increased more than threefold, and the number of teachers rose fivefold. This caused the illiteracy rate to fall from 48 percent of the population in 1960 to 14 percent in 1980. During the same period the number of university graduates rose from 1.8 percent of the population to 6.3 percent (Hung and Piñango 1985).

However, after the 1973 oil shock, these items of government spending were unable to channel the increase in public resources. In addition, they had lost political support. Trade unions were perceived to be in control of the health and education institutions and engaging in wasteful featherbedding. Public financial development institutions were perceived as corrupt agencies that never recovered their loans. Current spending became anathema, while investment spending came to be seen as the supreme good (just as in the old days), since it appeared to fulfill the traditional Venezuelan aspiration of "sowing the oil." Consequently, public-sector enterprises became fashionable. These were supposed to transform the oil shock revenues into a sustained source of income for the years ahead when the oil reserves would be depleted.[11]

By the early 1980s, cost overruns, startup problems, and financial losses had done away with the political support for large state enterprises, and infrastructural spending was back in fashion. The 1983–85 period was characterized by a general cut in government spending, with special emphasis on investment, which fell in 1984 to a quarter of its 1981 level. Public-sector nominal wages were allowed to drag not only behind inflation but, more importantly, behind those of the private sector. No strategic criteria were established to redirect spending: cuts were made in those areas where they were easy to achieve.

The 1986–88 fiscal expansion was concentrated in investment spending. At the time, the dominant thinking considered "current spending" (on education, health, maintenance of infrastructure, administration of justice, etc.) as unproductive and inflationary, whereas "investment spending" was seen as productive and noninflationary. Consequently, when the Planning Ministry decided to concentrate investment on social projects that were almost finished and thus required little additional spending, the other ministers objected because such projects would increase future "current spending." Better to start a new hospital project.

A new criterion now also appeared for the first time: the government should invest in production projects for export. This was meant to justify further investment in the aluminum sector, which had become profitable (in private accounting terms) in part because of the devaluation, but also because of the

---

11. At the time, the reserves-to-production ratio was below 10 years. Conservative estimates put it now at 95 years.

distortions caused by the multiple exchange rate system and the pricing of electricity.[12] An $11 billion investment program was designed and implemented in order to build new aluminum smelting capacity, enlarge the alumina plant, increase bauxite mining, and build a new hydroelectric dam.[13] In the meantime, the quality of government services declined significantly as a significant brain drain from the government to the private sector occurred, further reducing the government's capacity to design and administer public policy.

At present, the "neoliberal wing" of the government recognizes the need to radically restructure public spending to concentrate resources in the provision of public goods and social services, leaving productive activity to the private sector. To achieve this, privatization and foreign investment are required. (Progress in these areas is discussed later in this paper.)

This position is currently opposed by the ministers in charge of the state-owned companies (aluminum, steel, electricity, oil, and petrochemicals). Investment projects in these areas are projected to absorb 80 percent of the total public investment budget for the next five-year plan and are therefore being reconsidered. The congress and public opinion have as yet little awareness of the real allocation dilemmas the economy now faces. However, the tide is moving in favor of investment cuts in these areas. Moreover, the congress, which has not been particularly fond of the new government policy, has been approving populist laws, such as a subsidy to high-income mortgage borrowers costing the equivalent of about 2 percent of GDP.

Tax Policy and Public-Sector Prices

Historically, the ample resources provided by oil revenue allowed the government to pay little attention to taxation. The prevailing tax structure has the defects typically found in Latin American countries, including high marginal rates, generalized evasion, little effort at enforcement, and double taxation of capital. Little progress has been made since 1983 in this area. The fiscal surpluses of 1984–85 caused tax policy to be perceived as unimportant. Consequently, the real value of personal tax receipts has declined by half since 1984.

---

12. In 1986 the aluminum companies could import goods and service their foreign debt at the preferential rate of 7.50 bolivars to the dollar, while their export revenue was exchanged at a rate of over 20 bolivars to the dollar. In that same year, electricity was priced at 0.6 US cents per kilowatt-hour, whereas long-run marginal cost estimates vary from 1.4 to 3.2 cents.

13. In spite of the large real depreciation of 1989, the fact that the exchange rate was unified, and the fact that a debt-equity swap that implied a 60 percent subsidy on investment was eliminated, the expansion projects have been curtailed and are requiring an infusion of central government resources, thought unnecessary at the time.

The government plans to reform the tax structure through the revision of the income tax and the adoption of a value-added tax. These two projects incorporate the IMF–World Bank–Washington consensus on good taxation, since they were designed with significant technical assistance from these agencies. The projects were presented to the congress in October 1989, but it is difficult to predict how much of the reforms, if any, will be approved.

Two other areas of policy are having a positive effect on fiscal revenue: the substitution of tariffs for import quotas, and real exchange rate depreciation. The latter redistributes income in favor of the public sector, which is a net exporter.

The government also intends to align the prices of public-sector goods with their social opportunity cost over a period of three years; this means border prices for tradeables such as gasoline, and long-run marginal cost for nontradeables. This policy criterion was established as part of the structural adjustment loan agreement with the World Bank. The disbursement of the second tranche of this loan, due in February 1990, is conditioned on adjusting public-sector prices to 40 percent of their shadow levels. However, political support for these measures is low.

Privatization

Privatization is a new subject in Venezuela. During the 1970s, the issue was nationalization, and major areas of economic activity were transferred to the public sector, including oil, iron ore, electricity, and the airlines. Between 1983 and 1988 little was done except for a failed attempt at selling assets that had fallen into public-sector hands because of private-sector bankruptcies.

At present, however, the attempt to restructure public spending in order to free resources for public goods and social services is forcing the government to adopt a new policy with respect to its large state-owned enterprises. A new privatization fund is being created with the initial task of selling off commercial banks, cement companies, sugar mills, hotels, and other public-sector assets. Privatization of other large concerns such as the airline companies, steel mills, the telephone company, and electricity and water distribution has been discussed but has not been acted upon. Meanwhile, new expansions in aluminum, steel, and petrochemicals are being carried out through joint ventures with minority public participation. However, these projects will require heavy new investments in areas such as electricity, gas, alumina, and bauxite, which are currently supplied through public-sector companies. Since this would affect the public sector's investment plan, the issue of private participation at this level is also being discussed.

Foreign Direct Investment

Venezuela restricted foreign investment for a very long time. Foreign ownership of oil and iron ore companies was traditionally seen as contrary to the national interest, and these companies were finally nationalized in the 1970s. After the adoption of the import-substitution model in the early 1960s, foreign enterprises were established to produce locally those goods that previously had been imported. These firms were seen by the domestic private sector as unfair competition—profitable opportunities were supposed to be left to the locals. This concept was extended to banking services in 1977.

Since 1983, public opinion has moved in favor of a freer foreign investment policy. Multinationals are now seen as a source of technology, management, international marketing opportunities, and capital. Consequently, some regulatory progress was made, and foreign investment picked up from ridiculously low to merely very low levels.[14] However, exchange controls, the multiple exchange rate system, and other regulations have acted to hinder foreign investment.

Current government thinking is decidedly in favor of foreign investment, and many new projects have been registered. Much of the new interest has been directed toward resource sectors such as steel and aluminum, and some to tourism. The government has announced a debt-equity swap scheme, which calls for a yearly total of $600 million in swaps with auctions every other month. Applications worth close to $4 billion have been received, and pressure is being applied to expand the program. The first auction took place in November 1989, after many delays, and yielded an average discount of 43 percent.

Some people are starting to take seriously the argument advanced by Pedro Aspe that debt-equity swaps can act as a drag on foreign investment. Investment can always be postponed, and therefore prospective investors are willing to wait until their best opportunity comes up in the swap auction. At the same time the fiscal and monetary implications of swaps demand that the amounts be limited in any given period. As a result, debt-equity swaps can actually slow down the inflow of foreign investment.

Interest Rates

Interest rates have traditionally been fixed by the central bank. During the 1950s and 1960s interest rates on deposits were moderately high in real terms (3 percent to 5 percent), above international rates in nominal terms, and stable. During the 1970s, nominal rates remained fixed at their historical levels, while

---

14. Foreign direct investment flows rose from $16 million in 1986 to $83 million in 1988. Even this last figure is barely noticeable in table 5.16.

rising inflation produced small negative real interest rates. By 1979, nominal interest rate differentials with international markets had become negative, and they remained so until August 1981. By that time, massive capital flight and falling international reserves had become a serious policy concern, and the government decided to free interest rates.

This measure, taken by the 1979–84 Christian Democratic government, stopped capital flight for a few months but created serious political opposition, led mainly by the construction lobby and the weakest elements of the financial sector (small commercial banks, mortgage banks, and savings and loan associations afraid of competition). In 1982, when oil income declined, capital flight resumed and the government adopted an expansionary domestic credit policy to avoid a monetary contraction. Massive capital flight ensued until the collapse of the exchange regime in 1983. This made the general public feel that freeing interest rates had been a costly and useless exercise.

The Social Democratic government that came to power in 1984 implemented its electoral promise to reestablish administrative control of interest rates, to the satisfaction of most. During 1984–85 the controls did not have much bite and were basically accommodated through a greater foreign-exchange premium and some credit rationing. However, when inflation accelerated in the 1986–88 period, serious distortions appeared in the credit and floating rate markets. It became common practice for the middle class to borrow in bolivars in order to buy dollars or to purchase import-intensive durables with consumer credit. The number of credit cards in the market increased violently as each bank tried to outbid the other.

At one point a parallel interest rate appeared, and during 1988 banks violated the regulations, charging rates of 30 percent when the official limit was 13 percent. Given that deposit rates were then around 8 percent to 10 percent, this made bank profits huge and increased support for an increase in interest rates on deposits.

The situation deteriorated until the Pérez government took over in February 1989. Interest rates were increased initially (from 13 percent to 28 percent) and then freed; they soon rose to 42 percent. However, the freeing of interest rates created a major political backlash. The political opposition undertook two legal actions through the Supreme Court. The first of these challenged the legality of a floating interest rate regime, arguing that the law forced the central bank to fix rates. The second argued against the legality of raising interest rates on previously contracted variable-rate mortgages.

The Supreme Court ruled in favor of the opposition in the first case and forced the central bank to set limits on interest rates. The bank decided to set as wide a margin as possible without offending the court and put the maximum rate on loans at 42 percent and the minimum rate on deposits at 27 percent. In the case of mortgage rates, the Court ruled in favor of the government, upholding the legality of the rise in rates on old variable-rate loans. However, this produced such a political uproar that an act of congress was passed in order to subsidize the mortgages of some 70,000 families for the difference between the market rate and 19 percent. This law was blocked initially by the president, but the congress overrode his veto. The cost of this highly regressive and distortionary subsidy may reach 2 percent of GDP in 1990.

The rise in interest rates has been followed by major new trends in the banking system. Profits, which were abnormally high in 1988, have collapsed. The parallel rate has disappeared, and for the first time in a few years banks are having trouble finding clients to whom to lend their funds. Companies that had built up massive stockpiles of inventories (given negative real interest rates and devaluation expectations) have been canceling their credit lines. Other companies and individuals have been canceling loans used to purchase dollar-denominated deposits (left as collateral for the loans in the foreign subsidiaries of Venezuelan banks). Also, the general market feeling is that the expected rate of devaluation is less than the interest rate differential, and companies have been unwilling to accept bank coverage for their exchange rate risk.

The degree of support for the current interest rate policy is weak. If the stabilization process advances quickly, inflation will come down and so will interest rates. This creates the feeling that the current high rates are a temporary phenomenon. However, if rates go up again, or if banks find the new reduced 10 percent spread unbearable, then political difficulties may lie ahead.

Exchange Rate Policy

Venezuela traditionally has had a fixed exchange rate regime and very low inflation, which translated into a stable real exchange rate. As noted earlier, on two occasions (1960 and 1983) the country faced balance of payments crises, which prompted the adoption of a multiple exchange rate regime. However, capital flows have always been free.

The idea behind the adoption of multiple exchange rates is to implement a gradual real depreciation in isolation from the destabilizing influence of capital flows. The standard justification for devaluation is that the currency suffers from "real appreciation," which even in the outward-looking literature is usually blamed on exchange rate policy (Balassa et al. 1986). The multiple exchange rate regime is supposed to permit a change in those relative prices that affect the real allocation of resources while at the same time avoiding overreaction due to capital flight.

This approach worked well in 1960, and after three and a half years the exchange rate was reunified with an accumulated nominal depreciation of 35 percent. However, in the current crisis, after six years of attempted stabilization and a nominal official rate devaluation of 240 percent, the foreign-exchange premium remained at 200 percent. Massive corruption in administration of official rate transactions finally led to the gathering of political support for abandonment of the system and adoption of a managed float.

It is interesting to study in some detail the political economy and macroeconomics of the multiple exchange rate regime of the 1980s, since it appears that the exchange regime that caused this disastrous experience was not altogether incompatible with the Washington consensus. As presented by Williamson in chapter 2, this consensus stresses two points: first, the important thing is the real exchange rate and not the process that determines it, and second, capital controls are sometimes justified in a developing country.

The point I will make here is that capital controls will lead to a multiple exchange rate regime. If the government loses control of the parallel rate, the exchange rate policy that emerges becomes highly distortionary and allows for a dangerous political economy that reduces the short-run costs of fiscal and monetary largesse and ends up producing an inflationary and destabilizing vicious circle.

First, there is a question of diagnostics. Is real appreciation a consequence of bad exchange rate policy? In the Venezuelan case, I would argue that the real appreciation that occurred between 1976 and 1982 was the standard general-equilibrium result of an unsterilized oil boom. The balance of payments crisis was the consequence of actual and expected fiscal deficits due to a (current or expected) reduced oil income and insufficient spending cuts or tax increases. Adjustment requires reduced fiscal deficits, a cut in absorption, and a real depreciation.

However, if the exchange rate policy is blamed for the crisis, a devaluation in an oil-exporting economy will drastically reduce or eliminate the fiscal deficit in the short run, and the congress will then attach little importance to tax reform. Instead, subsidies to those affected by the devaluation will tend to receive more attention. Since nominal prices do not affect real long-run equilibria, the balance of payments problem will reappear once internal prices adjust to the devaluation. In this context, fixing the real exchange rate through a crawling peg will simply transform bad fiscal policy into higher inflation.

Second, since the principal short-run effects of a devaluation are a tax on wages and on monetary wealth, it is to be expected that behavior will change in order to avoid the tax. Money demand will fall through capital flight, and wage contracts will be indexed or negotiated more frequently, following the Pazos-Simonsen mechanism (Pazos 1978, Dornbusch and Simonsen 1988).

Third, under a multiple exchange rate system, imports must go through a complex, costly, and highly distortive administrative system designed to avoid overinvoicing. Exports and foreign investment are likewise disrupted by regulations designed to avoid exchange rate abuses. Under such a regime, import controls can be used to defend the level of international reserves,[15] thus becoming the principal instrument of trade policy. This changes completely the political economy of fiscal and monetary policy.

Since there is excess demand at the official rate, importers receive a quota rent. This rent, as well as the real price of nonoil tradeables and nontradeables, increases with an expansionary fiscal policy. Reserves are not affected by this expansion, and consequently there are no short-run balance of payments risks for the central bank. The floating exchange rate falls, but that is good news for many: tourism booms, and profits on overinvoicing of imports, underinvoicing of exports, and borrowing locally to hold dollars go up significantly.

An expansionary monetary policy has the same effect: the real side works as a floating exchange rate regime where the proceeds of the depreciation are appropriated by those who receive the import quotas, while the free rate allows for all sorts of income transfers. Inflation is not seen as linked to expansionary demand policies, but instead is blamed on the lack of resolve of those who administer the price control system that is put in place to make sure that the consumer gets the exchange rate subsidy.

When the exchange rate differential reaches extreme levels, the control system collapses and the government is forced to make a credible maxi-devaluation. The system ends up working not as a crawling peg, but as a two-to-three-year leaping peg. These official devaluations happened in 1984 and in 1986, and the stage was set for a new devaluation in early 1989.

After the devaluation, internal prices rise while oil taxes remain linked to the official rate, which is fixed. Relative prices move against the government, increasing the initially reduced fiscal deficit and accentuating the instability.

Faced with the prospect of repeating the 1986 maxi-devaluation, in March 1989 the government decided to abandon the system and float the exchange rate. Given the existing exchange rate differential of over 150 percent, this constituted a major shock to the economy but had the advantage of avoiding the need to determine a new fixed exchange rate that would be believed by the market.

The macroeconomic effects of this measure have already been commented on. However, one further lesson may be learned: under a multiple exchange rate regime, the internal price of tradeables is not equal to the world price calculated at the floating rate. This can be seen by the fact that, in spite of a nominal

---

15. Most multiple exchange rate models assume that imports are demand-determined (de Macedo 1982, Dornbusch 1986). This creates a stabilizing transmission mechanism that works through the level of reserves, the money supply, and aggregate demand. This mechanism vanishes when imports are quantitatively rationed.

appreciation of the floating rate, after the exchange rate was unified the internal price of tradeables rose significantly (over 50 percent in two months).

At present, there is little consensus on how the floating exchange rate system should be managed. The central bank seems to make decisions as if it had four independent policy variables: the exchange rate, the reserve target (and consequently its supply of dollars to the market), the monetary target, and the interest rate. This clearly overdetermines a system that has only two degrees of freedom.

The IMF has proposed fixing the reserve and monetary targets and letting the exchange rate and the interest rate adjust. I favor fixing the volume of intervention and establishing an exchange rate band while using interest rate policy to make the two compatible. Given the structural changes that are occurring in the economy and the fact that dollar holdings by residents amount to five times M2, quantitative monetary targets seem absolutely arbitrary.

Trade Policy

In 1960 Venezuelan trade policy turned protectionist. Directly competing imports were either prohibited or taxed at very high rates. However, a system of tariff exonerations was adopted that in fact acted as a quota system. If the import was not exonerated, the high tariffs ensured that it would not be purchased. Investment projects in new import-substituting fields could ask for and were usually granted import protection. A "supplied market policy" discouraged new projects in already existing sectors, thus introducing an important official barrier to entry.

Noncompeting imports were allowed in on very liberal terms. Given the volume of oil exports, the economy remained fairly open in aggregate terms, with imports averaging in excess of 30 percent of GDP from 1974 to 1982. Substitution effects between imports and domestic manufactures created sufficient competition so that this sector behaved more like a tradeable than a nontradeable sector: in spite of its official rate of protection, manufacturing was adversely affected by the real appreciation that followed the two oil shocks.

By 1982, the tariff system was a complicated mess, where isolated decisions had produced a spread in rates that even at the six-digit level could exceed 300 percent. However, tariff exonerations amounted to 80 percent to 90 percent of accrued receipts. This complicated system had an excellent political economy. Investment risk could be reduced, trade unions could get a share of the protection rents, and the political system could develop clientistic relations with the business community. Amazingly, consumer interests were seldom heard from.

The 1983 crisis made the system more complex and changed the focus of policy action. First, import prohibitions were expanded to include many industrial inputs. A new system of import quotas (*delegaciones*) covered over 50 percent of imports, and the purchase of official rate dollars was controlled on an *ex ante* case-by-case basis.

In this process, little attention was given to the tariff and exoneration system, which had become irrelevant since the new controls had more bite. In administering foreign exchange, the fact that a good could be produced locally, at some price, was sufficient reason not to allow imports at preferential rates. Agricultural imports were closely controlled to cover the difference between supply (affected by guaranteed prices) and demand (determined by fixed administered prices).

The industrial sector reacted quickly with vigorous growth of 7 percent annually for the 1985–88 period, while agriculture went through a "miracle" between 1985 and 1987, with growth averaging close to 5 percent. Few complaints were heard at the time, indicating that no constituency had strong feelings against the system. Of course, everybody wanted more official rate dollars, but the chambers of commerce and industry were brought in to participate in the allocation of foreign exchange. The system thus remained rather cozy, but consumers became increasingly vociferous against what they termed "speculation."

In 1989, the abandonment of the multiple exchange rate regime eliminated the core of the evolving protectionist system. Fiscal arguments favored the abandonment of the exoneration mechanism, and consequently the arbitrariness of the existing tariff structure was uncovered. Moreover, the need to obtain multilateral financing and the World Bank's offer of a trade policy loan helped redefine the role of commercial policy. Finally, the sharp rise in prices that followed the elimination of most price controls in March 1989 caused a public outcry against the industrial sector, which was suddenly seen as a group of inefficient monopolists living off the consumer. Making them compete with imports became a popular idea.

The Pérez government has adopted what must be considered by any standard a radical trade-liberalization policy. Import prohibitions were basically eliminated except on some symbolic luxury goods. The system of *delegaciones* was cut by 70 percent. A program of tariff reduction was adopted. In June 1989, maximum tariff rates were reduced to 80 percent for consumer goods and 50 percent for industrial inputs. Those items subject to rates lower than the maximum had their rates reduced in proportion to the average exoneration previously received. In March 1990, maximum tariff rates are to be reduced to 30 percent for industrial inputs and 50 percent for consumer goods. Also, the tariff system is supposed to be restructured by that date, increasing its clarity and simplicity. Agriculture is being excluded from this process, but some liberalization has occurred, especially in wheat and cotton.

So far, the new trade policy has had little bite. The depth of the recession and the size of the devaluation have both forced and allowed producers to keep prices competitive, so that imports have in fact declined from close to $900 million a month in the first quarter of 1989 to some $500 million in the June-August period. At present, the process seems to be going smoothly, but many people are waiting for the March 1990 deadline to see if the government really means business.

Venezuelan Adjustment: How Much Has Happened?

In the 1983–88 period, Washington-style adjustment was basically absent, in part because of the regulatory and political economy implications of the multiple exchange rate policy that had been adopted. During the 1984–85 period, the economy adjusted in an inward-looking manner to the 1982–83 fall in oil income and financial flows. However, the government never adjusted to the 1986 fall in oil income. In fact, the government did not even adjust in terms of its financial relations with the commercial banks; instead it signed a nonviable agreement in February 1986, which had been designed before the collapse in oil prices.

The multiple exchange rate system adopted in 1983 required such a complicated regulatory regime that it distorted trade policy, thwarted efforts to promote exports and foreign investment, and freed the government from the short-run balance of payments costs of fiscal and monetary largesse, thus creating a constituency in favor of inflationary growth. Interest rates were controlled and lowered, little effort was made on tax reform, and public spending was not restructured but simply cut (between 1982 and 1985) and then expanded (from 1986 to 1988).

In 1989, on the contrary, Washington-style adjustment is happening at an astonishing rate on nearly all fronts, including exchange rate policy, trade policy, public spending, tax reform, interest rate liberalization, privatization, and foreign direct investment. This reversal is due in part to the fact that the new administration faces few degrees of freedom as a consequence of the 1986–88 expansion. Political support for the adjustment policy is very low, however, given that GDP is falling at a record rate (more than 10 percent in 1989) and inflation will exceed 80 percent, double its previous 1987 record. The political survival of the process will depend in large measure on the speed with which the economy starts to show some recovery.

Acknowledgments

I would like to acknowledge the comments made on an earlier draft of this paper by Sterie T. Beza, Felipe Larraín, John Williamson, and other participants at the conference on which this volume is based.

Comment

Sterie T. Beza

For much of the postwar period one would not have asked the question of how well Colombia and Venezuela had adjusted. From 1950 to 1980 these two countries followed fairly conservative macroeconomic policies and delivered quite good per capita growth. There were, nevertheless, shortcomings in microeconomic policies and what we now call structural reforms, and by the end of the period foreign borrowing was proceeding at a pace that clearly could not be sustained.

Ricardo Hausmann summarizes the record on Venezuela very simply, saying that in the 1983–88 period adjustment of the kind we are discussing was virtually absent, but that such adjustment is now occurring at an astonishing rate on practically all fronts. I would have described the 1983–88 period somewhat differently, putting more emphasis on year-to-year changes within the period, but it is also evident that by 1989 the financial situation of the country was in a parlous state, with all the danger signals in full view.

Hausmann attributes much of the problem to the multiple exchange rate regime adopted in 1983. He makes an important point, but I think the issues were somewhat broader. There were, I believe, some misunderstandings about what was needed to respond to the drop in oil exports and the loss of access to external credits in order to set the stage for a return to growth. Immediately after the developments of 1983 the authorities may have been led to believe that the job was easier than it really was. The rapid recovery of international reserves in the period 1983–85—a period in which some adjustment was made, even if it was less comprehensive than needed—certainly led the authorities to think that the arrangement of external finance was less pressing for Venezuela than for many other countries of the region. There was also the expectation that voluntary external credits would return soon.

I differ with Hausmann concerning his view that the multiple exchange rate regime chosen was similar to the Washington consensus, according to which capital controls are justified for a developing country. I would first note that a multiple rate system such as the one Venezuela had involves far more than capital controls. More important in terms of the record, I do not know whether I am part of the Washington consensus, but I can make it clear that I objected to the multiple rate system when it was established. The IMF thereafter continued to advocate termination of the multiple rate regime. Indeed, I would

Sterie T. Beza is Counsellor and Director of the Western Hemisphere Department of the International Monetary Fund and is a former assistant professor at Princeton University.

go further than Hausmann in my criticism of the multiple rate regime as it operated in Venezuela, drawing attention to the hidden fiscal costs and credit expansion resulting from the central bank's losses and to the regressive effect on income distribution of the subsidies implicit in a multiple rate system.

As Hausmann notes, the Venezuelan authorities are well embarked on a program of major reforms, and the multilateral institutions are committed to supporting their efforts. In addition to the need to follow through on these reforms there is the task of completing the financing of the program, including the critical element of commercial bank financing through a combination of elements including debt reduction features.

Hausmann implies that he would favor a different exchange rate policy from that preferred by the IMF. I would note that the policy is that of the authorities and that the particular form of exchange rate policy is less important than the basic fiscal, credit, and wage policies pursued by the authorities. (In his oral presentation at the conference Hausmann appeared to drop his objection to the present floating exchange rate policy.) I would also note that the program takes account of the fact that Venezuelan residents hold large claims abroad, and it envisages adjustments to credit policy to correct deviations in growth of the monetary base from the program projections in the face of unplanned capital reflows.

As Rudolf Hommes noted in his comprehensive paper, Colombia embarked on an adjustment program in 1984. Although his evaluation of the program is not clear, Hommes makes the important point that the trade regime chosen will have important consequences for the growth prospects of the economy. There have been some advances in this area, but it is clear—and the present authorities would surely agree—that a great deal more needs to be done. Hommes also refers to the likely approval of a new regime for foreign investment in the financial sector, and this can be expected to have significant consequences for competitiveness and efficiency in that sector.

Prudent macroeconomic management has been traditional in Colombia, and together with the realistic exchange rate policy that has been pursued for a number of years, it provides a good setting for the implementation of reforms aimed at changing the pattern of resource allocation. There is also a need to continue to raise domestic saving; this is one of the tasks of fiscal policy and will also be promoted by improvements in the functioning of the financial system. My own discussions with the relevant authorities in both Colombia and Venezuela provide assurance that they subscribe in broad terms to the view that economic growth is most successfully pursued under a macroeconomic management that promotes saving, reduces inflation, limits external financing to manageable amounts, and is accompanied by market-oriented reforms.

Comment

Felipe Larraín

Rudolf Hommes and Ricardo Hausmann have written two informative and interesting papers on the adjustment cases of Colombia and Venezuela. The more dramatic experience of Venezuela will tilt the discussion that follows toward that case, although a comparative analysis will be stressed.

Contrasting Initial Conditions

Hommes and Hausmann describe two countries that were, as of the beginning of 1989, at very different levels of adjustment. Whereas Venezuela had yet to start a decisive adjustment effort, Colombia had been undergoing substantial adjustment since 1984. The situation changed in the course of 1989.

Since the inauguration of the Pérez administration in early 1989, Venezuela has undertaken one of the most aggressive adjustment programs in Latin America. The program includes unification of a system of multiple exchange rates; sharp increases in the prices charged by public enterprises, especially in the energy sector; elimination of price controls; trade liberalization; and relaxation of interest ceilings. Thus, Venezuela has moved quickly to implement the so-called Washington agenda in one big step.

Colombia's adjustment program, begun in 1983–84, included fiscal restraint, tax reform, and some trade liberalization. According to Hommes, the principal remaining issues are three: further liberalization of trade; tighter control over the quasi-fiscal spending of the central bank, particularly spending on interest rate subsidies and on bailing out the commercial banks; and liberalization of foreign investment.

The contrast between the two countries is quite marked. Whereas Venezuela is in the midst of a radical adjustment program, Colombia faces relatively modest further policy adjustments. This difference in adjustment reflects, to some extent, diverse initial conditions in the two economies, but also, to a large extent, differences in the policies pursued in the late 1970s and early 1980s.

Felipe Larraín is Associate Professor of Economics at Pontifícia Universidad Católica de Chile and a visiting professor at Harvard University. He is the editor of several books, including Desarrollo Económico en Democracia: Proposiciones para una Sociedad Libre y Solidaria, *and is co-author of* Debt, Adjustment and Recovery: Latin America's Prospects for Growth and Development.

Venezuela presents a major paradox. Its economy stagnated in the aftermath of the second oil boom, when the country was profiting handsomely from a major improvement in its terms of trade. Venezuela accumulated a massive foreign debt, at a time when the public budget and the current account enjoyed significant cumulative surpluses. How did the external debt problem develop? It was the counterpart of massive capital flight, which resulted mainly from two factors: exchange rate overvaluation and the artificial maintenance of nominal interest rates at very low levels (even below world levels), at a time when the currency remained convertible. The private sector responded by all but wiping out the country's international reserves at the central bank (for a detailed analysis see Rodriguez 1990). Thus, Venezuela is largely a case of self-inflicted damage in the late 1970s and early 1980s. In contrast, Colombia pursued a policy of flexible exchange rate management that avoided substantial overvaluation and allowed interest rates to remain close to equilibrium levels, thereby avoiding substantial capital flight (for an analysis of the Colombian reforms see, e.g., Ocampo 1989b).

In spite of these divergent policies, both countries were affected by the debt crisis. Yet they differed fundamentally in their willingness (or ability) to adjust. Whereas Colombia chose early on to pursue a comprehensive adjustment package, Venezuela avoided appropriate adjustment until the situation was virtually unsustainable.[16] Here lies an important lesson: failure to adjust adequately and promptly means that, in the end, the adjustment will have to be much greater and thus the medicine that has to be swallowed will be much more bitter. Ricardo Hausmann reports that GDP was expected to fall by about 10 percent in Venezuela during 1989, whereas inflation will be about 90 percent (mostly coming from corrective price increases).

An interesting question is whether Venezuela had a viable alternative to the sharp adjustment implemented in 1989. From what we know of the Venezuelan situation combined with Hausmann's description, the answer seems to be no. Liquid international reserves were at very low levels (less than 15 days of imports), the parallel market premium was on the order of 200 percent, and the fiscal deficit was well over 10 percent of GDP; repressed inflation was substantial, and the financial system, restricted by widespread interest rate controls, was in very poor shape. The need for decisive action was urgent.

---

16. The 1983–85 package was unnecessarily harsh on the fiscal front and ill-conceived overall. It included substantial additional restrictions on trade, multiple exchange rates, and widespread price controls.

The Political Economy of Adjustment

Although Venezuela's adjustment program is coherent and headed in the right direction, Hausmann reports that the program "has received very little support from most sectors of society, including the government party." This statement underscores the difficult political economy of adjustment, as the measures have hurt many influential groups, among them the recipients of import licenses and quotas and those with access to cheap foreign exchange. The public at large has been hurt by the drastic reduction of subsidies on controlled prices (including those of public enterprises).

The problem in Venezuela was that the needed adjustments were extremely large, yet the population was not experiencing a crisis because the huge subsidies were being financed by the use of international reserves. This path was clearly unsustainable, as reserves were fast depleting, but the absence of an open crisis made it harder for the people to accept the program. The benefits of reform seemed mostly concentrated in the medium to long run, whereas the costs were felt in the short run. The question is then how to engineer support for reform so that the adjustment program can be maintained. In a less dramatic way, this question also applies to Colombia, if Hommes's suggestion of further trade liberalization is heeded.

A first important effort should be to mount a public relations campaign to explain the adjustment measures, emphasizing that the short-term pain is a necessary price to pay for significant long-term rewards. Public relations, often overlooked and not a strong suit among economists, can be of substantial help. Second, and more important, it will be necessary to show some results relatively early in the program. This applies clearly to Venezuela and potentially to Colombia. There are at least two areas where such early progress can be achieved: trade liberalization and debt reduction.

The beneficial effects of trade liberalization in the short term are increased competition in the tradeable goods sector, which could check price increases in the economy. This is an obvious benefit to consumers. The problem is that consumers are rarely organized as efficiently as the groups who suffer from the liberalization (e.g., industrialists and importers). In the case of Venezuela, this limitation is compounded by the fact that trade liberalization was implemented simultaneously with increases in various subsidized prices, and the net effect was to make the consumption basket more expensive in the short term. Nevertheless, this is an area worth exploring.

Debt reduction is being actively pursued by Venezuela, the secondary market price of whose foreign commercial bank debt had fallen to 33 cents on the dollar as of late November 1989. Balance of payments projections, made with the cooperation of IMF staff and assuming moderate economic growth, show the need for significant debt reduction. After the slump expected for 1989, Venezuela cannot be expected to resume timely service of its debt, as the cost would be a continued depression, which would surely provoke renewed social unrest and a collapse of the reform program. On the other hand, the achievement of substantial debt reduction in the near future would provide clear benefits for the impoverished Venezuelan people. Reaching such an accord will not be easy, but the prospects look better in the wake of the Costa Rican agreement. Colombia's debt, meanwhile, is traded at 65 cents on the dollar. Although this is the highest for any Latin American country, a discount of 35 percent signals a debt-service problem here as well. Yet Hommes does not mention a specific Colombian policy on external debt (other than to say that the strategy is to maintain the relative exposures of the different creditors). Perhaps the government does not have a clear policy agenda on this front.

Specific Reforms

The Need for Tax Reform

Venezuela is an extreme case of "tax disease" arising from public-sector wealth. For many years, oil revenues were used to pay for public expenditures (at the height of the oil boom, oil contributed close to 80 percent of government revenue), and thus no effort was made on the tax front. As a result, the country was left with serious deficiencies in its tax system, including lax enforcement. In essence, the country lacks a tax culture.

Now that the situation has changed and oil cannot be counted on to cover public-sector needs, it is necessary to develop a modern tax system. The new Venezuelan government has recognized this reality, and a tax reform proposal has been submitted for legislative approval. Most successful tax reforms elsewhere have focused on a few taxes, allowing as few exceptions as possible. Efficient tax schemes are generally based on two pillars: a value-added tax with as flat a rate as possible, and a progressive income tax with moderate rates for corporations and individuals.

Colombia has already made much progress on this front. This 1983 reform moved toward the elimination of tax exemptions and discounts. It broadened the tax base and reduced the rates yet at the same time increased tax revenues. Tax reforms along these lines have been implemented in Bolivia and Chile, and a similar program is currently under study in Ecuador.

It is likely, however, that the Venezuelan government's tax reform proposals will face resistance even if they lower tax rates. (In Ecuador, the proposal to reduce the top income tax rate from 60 percent to 30 percent did not meet an enthusiastic reaction in several quarters.) One reason is that various groups stand to lose the privileges they enjoyed under the old tax system. Another is that under the old system many people did not bother to pay taxes, even if they were not legally exempted; for them, a reduction in tax rates coupled with increased compliance means an increase in the tax burden. The success of tax reform hinges on not giving in to pressures from these groups.

For the future, it is necessary to stabilize the tax structure. This raises the important issue of devising mechanisms that can resist the pressure of favorable terms-of-trade shocks and, in general, of windfall gains for the public budget.

It is interesting that Hommes rather than Hausmann raises the issue of taxing income on flight capital, since Venezuela has much more to gain than Colombia if this should materialize. It is impossible to disagree with the taxation of flight capital on equity grounds. The question is one of feasibility. It would require the ratification of tax treaties with the countries that host the most important financial centers. Even though isolated agreements with one or a few countries may help, they would be likely to result in significant shifts of funds from these countries to others that have not agreed to the treaty. A global approach, although difficult, is required.

Public Expenditure Policy

A common experience of Colombia, Venezuela, and most other Latin American countries during the 1980s was a cut in domestic government spending. This was felt especially in the areas of public investment and social welfare spending. At the same time, pressures mounted on the central banks of the region to come to ·the assistance of domestic debtors through interest rate and exchange rate subsidies. These forms of quasi-fiscal spending have generally proven to be quite regressive.

There is a fundamental consensus emerging that fiscal resources should be used primarily on two types of programs, in addition to the traditional functions of government (defense, administration of justice, etc.). The first consists of the so-called social sectors—education, health, housing, nutrition, and social security—which are to be addressed primarily through programs directly targeted to the poor as opposed to generalized price subsidies. The second is infrastructure investment, which is clearly complementary to private investment efforts. This is not a matter of ideology, but rather a crude reality. It is based on the fact that the government has limited resources and limited administrative capacity.

Privatization

Privatization seems today to be more of an issue in Venezuela than in Colombia. It undoubtedly has the potential to complement other economic reforms. Rather than analyze the advantages of privatization I shall focus on some of the dangers involved. If privatization is not handled well, it can become discredited and can end in failure.

Many of the dangers of privatization stem from a sense of urgency that rushes the process. It might be useful to divest a limited number of small state companies quickly, to indicate that the government is serious about the program. However, the bulk of the privatization program cannot be rushed. To increase their attractiveness to private investors, it may be necessary to make some reforms in public enterprises prior to divestiture (for example, converting them into corporations).

Common problems of privatization that can and should be avoided are:

- A lack of transparency in the process

- Concentration of ownership of the privatized firms in a few hands that have the financial muscle to bid for them

- Privatization of natural monopolies in the absence of an appropriate regulatory framework

- Selling public companies too cheaply.

Sales of public enterprises below their market value not only make fiscal adjustment more difficult but also raise issues of national patrimony. This is a bigger problem the greater the concentration of ownership in the new company. In the extreme case where one share of the firm is given away to each national of the country, there of course will be no gain in revenue but the equity problem is avoided.

Foreign Investment

Both Colombia and Venezuela have restrictive foreign investment legislation based on the criteria of the Andean Pact. However, the tide is moving toward liberalization of foreign investment rules in both countries. This change, which is part of a generalized world trend, is highly welcome.

A question that emerges in both papers is the role of a debt-equity swap program in the promotion of foreign investment. Both authors are skeptical about such schemes, and correctly so. They point out some of the flaws of these programs, among them their delaying effect on foreign investment and their perceived lack of additionality. Two additional problems of debt-equity swaps are their fiscal and monetary consequences and the distribution of debt discounts.

It is generally the case that the foreign liabilities being swapped are public, whereas the equity is private. This poses a delicate macroeconomic problem: the government has to exchange its debt for domestic assets, which will then be invested in a private venture. The options for the public sector are basically two: it can monetize the foreign debt, or it can exchange it for domestic debt. The first alternative risks increased inflation and/or losses of international reserves, both bad outcomes for economies that are struggling to maintain stability. The second option implies an exchange of foreign debt at international rates for domestic debt that normally carries much higher real interest rates; this will likely provoke a deterioration of the budget.

The other issue is how debt discounts are distributed. Normally debt-equity swap programs carry a vast subsidy to foreign investors (either the commercial bank creditors themselves or other foreign companies). That is, a large fraction of the discount on the country's debt in secondary markets is appropriated by the investor, and little stays in the country.

Debt-equity swaps as part of a program of privatization can avoid the undesirable macroeconomic effects, since then the public sector may offer equity directly in exchange for the debt. The question that remains is how the discounts are distributed between the debtor and the foreign investor.

6

The Smaller Countries

6

The Smaller Countries

The Caribbean

DeLisle Worrell

The countries chosen for this analysis are five of the larger Caribbean nations: Barbados, the Dominican Republic, Guyana, Jamaica, and Trinidad and Tobago. They range in size from 441 square kilometers to 215,000 square kilometers (or, 170 square miles to 83,000 square miles), in population from 250,000 to 7.5 million, and in GDP from US$800 million to US$10 billion. All have governments chosen in multiparty elections, although the legitimacy of the polls has been seriously questioned in the Guyanese elections. The countries are trade oriented; they export minerals, sugar, tourist services, business services, and light manufactures, and import the equivalent of 30 percent to 60 percent of their national incomes. Most of these countries' trade is with the United States, with which there are also strong financial links through migrants' remittances, investments, foreign asset holdings by locals, and trade-related finance. Income per capita ranges from about US$400 for Guyana to US$5,000 for Barbados and Trinidad and Tobago.

Currently all five of these economies are experiencing some economic difficulty, mild in some cases and acute in others. The Barbadian economy has grown at an average annual rate of 2 percent to 3 percent in the 1980s, and inflation has been held to international levels, but the balance of payments has been sustained by medium-term borrowing, and the unemployment rate remains high. The Dominican economy has expanded in recent years, but the rates of inflation and unemployment are high, income distribution may have worsened, and the country is considerably in arrears on its international payments. All indices of economic performance in Guyana are negative: output is in decline, inflation is high, unemployment and underemployment are rife,

DeLisle Worrell is Director of Research and Information at the Central Bank of Barbados. He was a visiting fellow at the Institute for International Economics in the fall of 1989. He has authored several articles and books including Small Island Economies: Structure and Performance in the English-speaking Caribbean Since 1970.

257

and external payments arrears are larger than the GDP. Output in Jamaica seems to have stabilized, inflation rates are in line with international rates, and balance of payments arrears have been mostly cleared, but unemployment remains high and income very unequally distributed. Output has fallen in Trinidad and Tobago throughout the 1980s, unemployment has risen, and the foreign-exchange reserves built up during the 1970s have been exhausted.

All five countries enjoyed resource-based growth in the 1960s, because of the buoyancy of markets in bauxite, alumina, sugar, and tourism. The fruits of economic growth were not well distributed in the Dominican Republic and Jamaica, but in the other countries income distribution was not markedly uneven. There was little attempt at deliberate economic management in those years; the burden of the temporary adjustments required from time to time, principally because of terms-of-trade shifts, fell immediately and directly on current incomes and spending.

Prices began to be pushed upward by international inflation around 1971, then accelerated with the 1973 oil crisis and stagflation in the industrial world. Exports of goods and tourism services were depressed, arresting the growth of incomes. (Trinidad and Tobago, the only oil-exporting country among the five, countered the trend, experiencing an economic boom after 1973.) A temporary increase in agricultural prices softened the initial impact of the oil shock, but the terms of trade quickly turned against the Caribbean. The Dominican Republic and Barbados adjusted relatively successfully to the diminished export prospects, with new investment in tourism, mineral extraction, and manufacturing, and the use of conservative fiscal policies. Jamaica and Guyana failed to adjust and entered the 1980s with output declining, foreign-exchange shortages, high inflation, and high rates of unemployment.[1]

Economic Performance in the 1980s

Table 6.1 compares the economic performance of these five countries. The second oil crisis and the subsequent recession in the industrial countries exposed the fragile basis of economic growth in the Dominican Republic and Barbados, stalled aggressive adjustment measures then under way in Guyana, and aggravated the economic disequilibrium in Jamaica. The fall in oil prices during the mid-1980s created severe adjustment problems for Trinidad and Tobago.

Barbados adjusted to the second oil shock, but much less successfully than to the earlier episode. Growth was much slower, and foreign spending was largely

---

1. My analysis of the economies of the English-speaking Caribbean since 1970 appears in Worrell (1987); for a recent economic survey of the Dominican Republic see Ceara-Hatton (1989).

Table 6.1   The Caribbean: summary economic data, 1980–88

(percentages except where noted)

	1980–84	1985	1986	1987	1988
Barbados					
Annual change in:					
Real GDP	0.3	1.0	4.7	2.7	2.3
Retail prices	9.9	4.9	0.2	3.6	6.0
International reserves[a]	9.4	40.9	−10.5	−3.5	25.0
Nominal exchange rate[b]	n.a.	n.a.	n.a.	n.a.	n.a.
Fiscal deficit as share of GDP[c]	5.6	5.7	7.0	7.3	5.3
Dominican Republic					
Annual change in:					
Real GDP	3.2	−2.2	3.2	8.1	0.9
Retail prices	12.7	37.5	9.8	15.9	44.4
International reserves[a]	−25.0	13.6	28.9	−202.0	75.0
Nominal exchange rate[b]	24.0	42.6	53.1	51.2	57.9
Fiscal deficit as share of GDP[c]	6.3	1.0	6.0	4.5	n.a.
Guyana					
Annual change in:					
Real GDP	−3.4	0.1	0.2	0.6	−3.0
Retail prices	19.5	15.0	7.8	28.7	40.1
International reserves[a]	3.6	−5.0	−62.4	−74.5	−21.0
Nominal exchange rate[b]	8.9	11.0	4.8	28.3	2.0
Fiscal deficit as share of GDP[c]	45.0	53.6	53.8	51.0	37.0
Jamaica					
Annual change in:					
Real GDP	0.0	−5.2	1.9	5.2	1.9
Retail prices	17.2	27.5	15.1	6.7	8.2
International reserves[a]	−57.4	−4.2	−40.9	74.2	177.7
Nominal exchange rate[b]	22.5	41.0	−1.5	n.a.	n.a.
Fiscal deficit as share of GDP[c]	16.0	17.8	9.8	6.8	10.6
Trinidad and Tobago					
Annual change in:					
Real GDP	−1.6	−5.6	−3.3	−7.4	−4.0
Retail prices	14.6	7.6	7.7	10.7	7.8
International reserves[a]	−156.7	−228.2	−654.8	−258.1	−87.1
Nominal exchange rate[b]	n.a.	2.1	46.9	n.a.	8.3
Fiscal deficit as share of GDP[c]	−6.8	−5.6	−6.5	−6.6	−5.8

n.a. = not available.

a. In millions of US dollars.   b. Official rate.   c. In nominal GDP terms.

Sources: For Barbados, Barbados Statistical Services and Central Bank of Barbados; for Guyana, Inter-American Development Bank, *Economic and Social Progress Report*, various years; for other countries, *International Financial Statistics*, various issues; Inter-American Development Bank; Planning Institute of Jamaica.

financed by medium-term external borrowing, which did not increase the country's exports. A recession may be in prospect for 1990. The Dominican Republic fell into crisis in the 1980s partly because of adverse terms of trade and declining agricultural exports, and partly because of an upsurge in demand among wage earners, whose expectations had been repressed in the previous decade. Between 1979 and 1981 the Guyanese government devalued the currency and tried to shrink public-sector deficits, but the increase in import prices jeopardized the program. Government reaction was slow and inadequate, and the economy deteriorated. In 1981 the Jamaican government instituted what was for those days an orthodox adjustment program, and followed through with subsequent efforts, all supported by the international financial institutions (IFIs). These efforts seem to have stabilized the external payments and arrested the decline in output, but without restoring real incomes from their depreciated level. The Trinidad and Tobago economy contracted as the price of oil declined during the first half of the decade, and the government is still in the process of implementing an adjustment program.

Barbados

Barbados experienced an economic recession in 1981 and 1982: output declined, inflation accelerated, and there was a balance of payments deficit in 1981. Strong fiscal action was taken, resulting in a contraction of the deficit in 1982–83. An IMF standby and foreign medium-term market borrowings were secured to add to foreign-exchange reserves. A gradual revival of tourism served as the basis for renewed growth, although manufacturing output declined because of economic recession in Trinidad, Barbados's principal regional market, and because Barbados was becoming increasingly less competitive with its less prosperous neighbors in low-skill operations.

Between 1984 and 1986 output was pumped up by fiscal expansion, supported by foreign borrowing at medium term, but little impression was made on the unemployment rate. The fiscal deficit was reduced somewhat from 1987 onward, but foreign borrowing was needed every year in order to finance balance of payments deficits, and the debt-service ratio rose sharply. Inflation was contained, but the rate of unemployment remained around 18 percent. Tourism continued to expand at a modest rate, but agricultural and manufacturing exports in 1989 were less than two-thirds their 1980 levels. Foreign loans and money creation financed a boom in construction and retailing, with no improvement in the external position.

The Dominican Republic

By the time of the second oil shock the Dominican economy was already running out of steam, and by 1982 a major disequilibrium had emerged, with the exhaustion of foreign-exchange reserves. The immediate causes included terms-of-trade losses (a rise in sugar prices was too small and too fleeting to compensate for inflation in import prices), increases in international interest rates which drove up the cost of external debt servicing, substantial principal repayments on the external debt in 1981, a failure to diversify exports away from sugar, and an overemphasis on foreign-exchange-dependent import substitutes (Coutts et al. 1986; F. Rodriguez 1987). It has also been suggested that there was considerable capital flight at the time of the 1982 presidential election (Ceara-Hatton 1989).

Sugar production fell drastically after its peak in 1981, and the situation was later aggravated by the reduction in the country's quota for sugar exports to the United States. Ferronickel production ceased temporarily in 1982 as a result of disputes between the government and the mining company over taxation, but was resumed afterward. Demand-management policies limited the output of nontradeables and import substitutes.

Fiscal policies were tightened, but large deficits registered by the state corporations limited the improvement. Determined efforts were made to bring down the external debt-service burden by improving the terms of service and reducing the amount outstanding over time. The persistence of high international interest rates was a major handicap, however. The government's exchange rate policies during this period must be accounted a failure, and a downward spiral of exchange rate depreciation and inflation developed.

There has been some economic growth since 1985, mainly due to the dramatic expansion in tourism capacity and investment in free trade zones. Investment in these areas has been mainly foreign, attracted by the failure to sustain the US dollar value of the average wage. These investors are not affected by the foreign-exchange scarcities and exchange rate uncertainties to which domestic investors are subject. There has been domestic investment in significant amounts only in construction, and not in those sectors that have an ongoing capacity to generate output. The fiscal deficit was contained, but fiscal policy could not stabilize the economy in the absence of complementary exchange rate policy.

Guyana

Guyana began the 1980s in economic crisis. A 1979 extended agreement with the IMF had been suspended by the end of that year. Because of the terms-of-trade shock, a new agreement was drawn up in 1980, with larger credits and a World Bank structural adjustment loan in addition. However, the programs were aborted because the fiscal deficit could not be contained. The government also failed to carry out its announced intention to manage the exchange rate flexibly; a multicurrency basket was set up as a benchmark, but the US dollar value of the Guyanese dollar remained unchanged. Transactions were diverted to the parallel markets for foreign exchange, imports, and some easily portable exports such as gold and agricultural products.

The failure of the 1980 IMF agreement was followed by an interval of policy inertia and economic decline. Export supply contracted for lack of essential inputs, external payments arrears built up, income contracted, and inflation rates were high on informal markets, which had become the only sources of many consumer goods. The rate of emigration increased.

In 1984 the official exchange rate was devalued by 28 percent, and four unprofitable state corporations were shut down. The economy continued to stagnate, however. External arrears continued to build up, and no additional trade credits were made available to Guyana. Essential commodities such as fuel were often in short supply, as all imports had to be paid for in cash or barter. Power outages and fuel shortages became common, roads and sea defenses fell into disrepair, and health and educational indicators fell.

January 1987 marked the beginning of a long period of draconian policies to secure external adjustment, renew the country's creditworthiness, and restore investor confidence. The ideological commitment to a state-directed economy was completely abandoned.

In mid-1989 the government entered into a so-called shadow program with the IMF, under which it agreed to meet fiscal, monetary, and balance of payments targets. Even though the Fund is providing no financing in return for these measures, the program affords Guyana the IMF "seal of approval" essential for obtaining official bilateral assistance. If the targets are met, assistance from the IFIs is contemplated in 1990. Meanwhile, Guyana is negotiating a rescheduling of its arrears and financing for a program to "ameliorate" the social impact of the adjustment.

Jamaica

On the whole, real output in Jamaica stabilized in the 1980s, but the trend has not yet turned upward. The fastest growth rate in any year was 5.2 percent in 1987, and years of economic contraction interrupted growth throughout the decade. Inflation was held in check except in the years of sharp devaluation (1984 and 1985). External payments were in balance most years, in spite of a debt-service ratio approaching 50 percent of earnings from exports of goods and services. External arrears were wound down but not entirely eliminated.

The administration headed by Edward Seaga, elected in 1980, inclined to the liberalization of the tightly controlled economy, and an easing of controls began in 1981 along with a reduction in government spending. In April 1981 Jamaica concluded a three-year extended arrangement with the IMF, under which SDR 403 million (of an agreed SDR 478 million) was drawn over the life of the agreement. Although the economy began to expand and inflation fell, there remained an excess demand for foreign exchange. In February 1983 the Jamaican dollar was devalued and a multiple exchange rate system was set up. Reserve and liquidity ratios for the commercial banks were increased in an effort to contain the supply of credit to the private sector. The actual result of these and other monetary strictures, however, was to encourage the growth of near-banks and other financial institutions, which were not covered by successive amendments to financial legislation.

In June 1983 Jamaica entered into a one-year standby agreement with the IMF, for SDR 64 million, which was fully drawn. In November the exchange rates were reunified, and a twice-weekly foreign-exchange auction was introduced. The shortage of foreign exchange continued, however, driving the exchange rate down at an ever-increasing rate for the next two years. As a result, inflation rose to the 30 percent range in 1984 and 1985.

In July 1985 a 21-month standby was agreed upon, and reserve and liquidity ratios were tightened once more. However, the program targets could not be met, and only SDR 42 million of the agreed SDR 115 million was drawn. In November 1985 the Bank of Jamaica was finally able to supply enough to the foreign-exchange auction to stabilize the exchange rate at 5.5 Jamaican dollars to the US dollar, where it remained until the first quarter of 1989. As the exchange rate stabilized, inflation fell to single digits.

In March 1987 an IMF standby arrangement was approved for SDR 85 million, with an additional SDR 40.9 million from the compensatory financing facility. The amounts were fully drawn. A 14-month standby for SDR 82 million was approved in September 1988, but it was revised and the amount raised after Hurricane Gilbert passed through in the same month. An additional SDR 36.4 million of emergency assistance was provided, and the program was extended to May 1990.

Loans from Paris Club members and the international commercial banks were rescheduled in May 1987, with principal payments deferred to March 1990. There was a further Paris Club rescheduling in October 1988.

Trinidad and Tobago

Falling oil prices brought a reduction in national income in Trinidad and Tobago beginning in 1982. Loss of oil revenues meant a large fiscal imbalance, a balance of payments deficit, and a contraction in domestic demand for import substitutes and nontradeables. The fiscal deficit was worsened by a retroactive wage award to government workers in 1982, the result of protracted negotiations based on high inflation rates in the previous decade.

Early attempts to reduce aggregate demand were too feeble to produce external balance, and in December 1985 the exchange rate was devalued by one-third. The adjustment effort was intensified after a change of administration in 1986. In January 1987 a National Recovery Levy was imposed, followed by a 15 percent devaluation in August 1988. That year also saw the beginning of a three-year program of fiscal and other reforms.

Real output in Trinidad and Tobago declined from 1982 to 1988, the rate of unemployment rose, and an excess demand for foreign exchange exhausted the country's considerable stock of international reserves. However, external payments have been kept current, and inflation has been held below 10 percent per year. It is too early to say whether the latest measures have stabilized the balance of payments. The near-term prospects depend heavily on trends in oil prices, the results of current exploration for oil and natural gas, and the success of a campaign to market the products of energy-based industries in international markets.

Caribbean Policies and the "Washington Consensus"

Economic policies in the English-speaking Caribbean have converged on the "Washington consensus," in John Williamson's phrase, but from different starting points and at different rates. Even some of the more dubious elements—for example with regard to interest rate policy—have appeared on the Caribbean policy menu. There have been considerable differences in emphasis, especially on issues such as privatization and deregulation, on which "Washington" really has no clearly articulated guidelines. There has been insufficient attention paid to the nonquantifiable determinants of investment, a failing that "Washington" shares.

The Dominican Republic is currently the exception to the convergence on "Washington" policies; up to 1986 the Dominican Republic had moved rapidly in line with the Washington consensus, but since then its exchange rate policies have been at variance with that position.

Barbados

Barbados agreed with the IFIs on the need for a small fiscal deficit, defined in the way these institutions conventionally define it. Recently the government also agreed on the need to reduce the ratio of external debt to GDP. But there was sharp disagreement on the timing of adjustment to the fiscal target: the IFIs have called for a sharper contraction from 1984 onward than actually occurred, in view of the fixed exchange rate target.

Barbados shares the Washington consensus that infrastructure and human capital development should be the highest priorities for government expenditure, although it might interpret human capital development more widely than the IFIs might. Of current government spending for 1984–88, some 40 percent went for health and education, while infrastructure and the construction of schools, health facilities, and low-cost housing accounted for about half of the capital budget.

Tax reform in Barbados has been an incremental process, beginning in the mid-1970s. There was a major displacement in 1986, and the direction of change was reversed somewhat thereafter. The top marginal rate of personal income tax, which had been lowered twice in the decade to 1985, was reduced to 50 percent in 1986; there are now five bands, but a variety of exemptions have been retained. The base of the personal income tax has been narrowed by raising personal exemptions much more quickly than the rise in real incomes on three occasions, most recently in 1986. There is a single rate of corporate income tax; in 1986 it was reduced from 45 percent to 35 percent. There is a general consumption tax, whose rates have been increased gradually since the mid-1970s to compensate for the loss of income tax revenues. The tariff structure conforms to the common external tariff of the Caribbean Economic Community (CARICOM), but imports are subject to an additional stamp tax, introduced in 1982 and raised on two occasions since then.

The financial sector in Barbados is oligopolistic, with six institutions responsible for 75 percent of all financial liabilities (other than insurance claims). Competitive setting of interest rates is not feasible; instead the central bank sets interest rate indicators. Deposit rates have been mildly positive from 1982 to 1987, and loan rates strongly so. However, deposit rates in Barbados drifted below the trend of comparable rates in international dollar markets in 1988, and no corrective action had been taken by the final quarter of 1989.

The IFIs and the Barbadian government agree on the need for a competitive exchange rate, but for the entire decade they have differed on the best means to achieve it. The IFIs have argued for a nominal exchange rate change, but the Barbadian government has preferred to use domestic policies instead. The debate as to which alternative best stimulates investment in the export sector, which both parties see as the goal, remains unresolved. It may also be argued that domestic policies have not in fact maintained competitiveness, as evidenced by the increase in foreign borrowing, even though foreign-exchange reserves were adequate up to the end of 1988.

Studies were under way in 1989 to guide trade liberalization. There is only a weak lobby in favor of quantitative restrictions on imports, but a stronger sentiment exists in favor of tariff protection for infant industries and small business. There are no exchange controls on trade transactions. The proceeds of exports must be repatriated to the country, but they need not be surrendered to the central bank. Deregulation has never surfaced as an issue between the Barbadian government and "Washington"; on the contrary, there is a need to strengthen financial regulation in the wake of the recent collapse of a small financial institution.

The Barbadian government accepts in principle the need to privatize some state corporations, although there is no consensus, either within Barbados or between the Barbadian government and "Washington," on the candidates for privatization. The program has not been pursued with any enthusiasm, but in any case Barbados has very much less state enterprise than does any other country in this survey.

Economic policy in Barbados in the 1980s comes close to agreement with the Washington consensus on the major issues, although it may be argued that implementation has fallen short of its targets. The fiscal deficit has been too large since 1984, in light of spending propensities, the slow growth of export earnings, and the fixed exchange rate target. Tax reforms have tended to shift revenues away from direct toward indirect taxes, rather than to broaden the tax base. (This appears to have been viewed favorably by official Washington.)

The Dominican Republic

The policies of the Dominican administration from about 1980 to 1985 were moving toward the Washington consensus to the extent that it had emerged by that time. Some relatively new emphases were not then given prominence—for example, the importance of social amelioration. By 1985 the Dominican Republic had adopted the Washington agenda in all its major aspects: realistic exchange rates, fiscal reform, liberalization, and privatization. However, these policies aroused considerable internal opposition and were perhaps the deciding factor in the defeat of the Dominican Revolutionary Party in 1986. Since then the Dominican Republic has diverged from the Washington consensus on exchange rate management.

The need for a low fiscal deficit was accepted by all Dominican administrations in the 1980s. Central government deficits were contained, but subsidies to state corporations drove up the deficit in the early 1980s. Measures to reverse this tendency both by reducing the deficits of the state corporations and by raising additional tax revenues were not markedly successful, and the deficit rose to about 6 percent to 7 percent of GDP in 1983, 1984, and 1986. (It fell to 1 percent of GDP in 1985 because of a surge in revenue from a new tax on internationally traded goods.) A deficit equivalent to 4.5 percent of GDP in 1988 was too large in view of private spending propensities, and it may need to be reduced in future years to eliminate an excess demand for foreign exchange.

Government expenditure has not reflected a bias toward infrastructure and the development of human capital. Current expenditure on health and education has grown more slowly than overall spending in the 1980s, and the proportion of infrastructure, schools, and health facilities in capital expenditure has not increased. Schools, hospitals, and transport facilities have run down, and a program was begun in 1989 to repair the damage. However, government subsidies continue to absorb a sizable portion of expenditures, much of it through subventions to state trading corporations.

The introduction of a modified value-added tax was the main element of tax reform undertaken in the Dominican Republic. As a replacement for a miscellany of indirect taxes, it accords with the Washington consensus. There is a case for reform of the income tax, which is narrowly based and not very productive, yielding only about the same amounts of revenue as the tax on alcoholic beverages in 1986 and 1987.

Interest rate policy since 1985 has emphasized positive real rates, without any explicit consideration of how high the real interest rate should be. Real deposit rates were in the vicinity of 10 percent in 1987, but record levels of inflation in 1988 drove the rates down. (To say that real rates were negative in 1989 would be to enter a judgment that the inflation rate in the Dominican Republic is expected to remain over 20 percent.) The IFIs are concerned about the provision of credit at below-market rates for selected activities, on the grounds that this distorts the allocation of finance. However, it should not be assumed that there are no externalities involved and that credit would be allocated in socially optimal ways in the absence of discriminatory interest rates.

Exchange rate policies in line with the Washington consensus were implemented between 1981 and 1986. These included legalization of the parallel market in foreign exchange, unification of the exchange rate regime, and periodic adjustment of the rate. The timing of changes and the administration of the rate were matters of debate, but the principle of an adjustable rate was shared on both sides. This changed with the adoption of a fixed rate and exchange controls in 1987.

The establishment of free trade zones, the most important source of new employment in the Dominican Republic in the second half of the 1980s, has been the main item of trade liberalization. The IFIs are of the view that tariffs and other restrictions should be reduced so as to bring the domestic resource costs of exports and import substitutes closer to each other, but it is questionable whether this would have any significant effect on the allocation of finance or investment in exports.

Foreign direct investment has been mainly determined by the country's low US dollar wage rates compared with some other Caribbean locations, by the island's tourist potential, and by the exemption from tariffs in the free trade zones. Although the IFIs would argue for a more flexible exchange rate policy and the elimination of preferential interest rates, it is doubtful that either of these measures would speed up investment in the export sector.

The Dominican Republic thus has accepted the Washington view over most of the period when that view was evolving to its present content. It therefore reflects that evolution, with an emphasis on adjustment in the early phases followed by greater attention to the supply side. Social amelioration and human capital development were not well integrated in the program, because by the time they had become part of the Washington canon, policies in the Dominican Republic were no longer so sympathetic to the Washington view.

Guyana

Guyana is the most recent of the five countries in this survey to have adopted the Washington consensus. Of the English-speaking countries it is the furthest from having implemented the major items in the program. The present administration seems committed to the program in its entirety, as evidenced by actions already taken, commitments publicly made, and communications with the World Bank and the IMF. However, the liberalization program is slow and time consuming because Guyana begins from a position of extensive state control. One cannot be confident that the program enjoys great conviction with the population as a whole. Some actions already taken have met with industrial unrest and strong political opposition.

The Guyanese government accepted the need to contain the fiscal deficit throughout the 1980s, but the continuing losses of the state enterprises, many of which had been acquired in a wave of nationalizations in the 1970s, frustrated efforts to hold the line on spending. The government has had only limited success with efforts to privatize these companies, and a few have been closed. In addition, employment in the public sector has been reduced, by layoffs as well as by early-retirement schemes, and public-sector wage increases have been held well below the official rate of inflation for the entire decade. Draconian wage restrictions may have impaired efficiency; the wages for public-sector managers and skilled workers are so low that there is a critical shortage, and public servants must find ways of supplementing their pay. With repeated devaluations and the rapid growth of external debt and arrears, interest payments have been a major factor in the widening fiscal deficit. But for the net effects of devaluation on the government's budget (interest payments net of additional receipts from taxation on exports and imports), the fiscal deficit would probably have stabilized in the late 1980s. However, the government will have to achieve fiscal surpluses to meet foreign interest payments for at least a decade, unless relief can be negotiated with the country's creditors. Talks on debt rescheduling have been under way since late 1988, but at the end of 1989 there was as yet no commitment on reduction of interest. However, some creditors have indicated an intention to reschedule principal, if agreement can be reached with all creditors.

Public spending has been cut so severely that even those programs that should have had priority were slashed. A report released in October 1989 found that Guyana's sea defenses were in an alarming state of disrepair. (Most of the settled land in Guyana lies below sea level.) Power outages are chronic; other public utilities, transport, and communications are unreliable; and social services have declined. Programs to repair the infrastructure and to restore social services are being planned.

No plans have been announced for wide-ranging tax reform, although some exemptions on income and consumption taxes were removed in 1988, broadening the base somewhat. Income taxes cover a broad sweep of wage earners, because so much of the labor force is in the state-owned sector, but they are evaded by the informal sector, which is thought to be at least as large as the formal (see estimates in Thomas 1989).

Interest rates were raised sharply in 1989, to 35 percent, in search of a positive real rate given an anticipated rate of inflation in the neighborhood of 30 percent. The rate is determined by the Bank of Guyana, and the government is committed to the IMF to maintain a positive real rate.

The exchange rate has been adjusted on several occasions during the decade. Besides the 1984 devaluation of 28 percent, the Guyanese dollar was devalued by 56 percent in 1987 and again by 70 percent in March 1989. However, only in 1989 was a commitment made to the IFIs to adjust the rate periodically in line with mutually agreed indicators (the parallel market rate and the rate of wage increases). For some years Guyana has had a large competitive wage advantage over the other countries in this survey (and a general 20 percent limit on wage increases was imposed in 1989), but investment was inhibited by poor infrastructure and an acute shortage of skills caused by emigration. The demand for imports has been severely compressed, but with a debt-service ratio that is in excess of 100 percent there is no exchange rate that will yield a balance of external payments. A cap on interest payments and a rescheduling of external debt, under negotiation in 1989, are required before a target for the exchange rate can be set.

In the 1970s Guyana established the most elaborate and counterproductive system of trade, price, and exchange controls in the English-speaking Caribbean. Most of these controls are now being gradually removed: most prices except for basic food items have been freed, the government monopoly on the marketing of rice has been rescinded, and prohibitions and quantitative restrictions on imports have been eased. However, there has been only limited relaxation of exchange controls. Liberalization enjoys the support of all political parties and interest groups, and it may be expected to continue. The country remains a long way from equalizing domestic resource costs for import substitutes and exports, but the investment potential at current relative prices is considerable, if the bottlenecks in energy, producers' goods, skilled labor, and infrastructure can be alleviated.

The Guyanese government, international business companies acting on behalf of the government, and a "support group" of representatives from the industrialized nations have together made considerable effort toward encouraging foreign direct investment. They have offered debt-equity swaps, finance and marketing packages, and joint ventures, but with very little response through 1989.

The government's most radical about-face was the decision to dismantle the network of state corporations that accounted for three-quarters of all economic activity. However, efficiencies had declined so sharply that buyers were few. In the major export areas—agriculture and bauxite—government has arranged or is negotiating management contracts.

Guyana came to accept the Washington consensus fully in 1988–89, and many aspects are yet to be phased in—fiscal reform and deregulation, for example. Acceptance of the Washington program was forced by dire economic circumstances and the government's lack of a coherent alternative to deal with the magnitude of adjustment required. The speed and comprehensiveness with which the new program has been adopted raise some question about the internal tensions it may engender and their impact on its sustainability.

Jamaica

Economic policy in Jamaica mirrors faithfully the evolution of the Washington consensus in the 1980s. The early years saw a focus on adjustment through deficit reduction and exchange rate adjustment. Liberalization was a concern from this time, but only later did it gain equal status with fiscal and exchange rate issues. More recently the social requirements of the program have come to the fore, and even now some would argue that they do not yet enjoy equal status. The economy appears to have stabilized, but there has been no overall growth in the 1980s, social indices have deteriorated, and investment has been insufficient to reduce the level of unemployment. However, open unemployment in Jamaica, on the basis of the usual definition which includes only those actively seeking jobs, is the lowest of the five countries, at 8.3 percent in 1988 (Planning Institute of Jamaica 1989, page 16.1).

The fiscal deficit was reduced slowly over the decade. The ratio of deficits to GDP stayed stubbornly high from 1983 to 1985 because of the combination of interest payments on the foreign debt and devaluation of the exchange rate. In January 1986 the government embarked on a comprehensive reform of the fiscal system based on studies begun in 1985 under a program funded by the US Agency for International Development and coordinated by the Maxwell School at Syracuse University. The reform accords in all major respects with the Washington bias toward a broad tax base, few exemptions, and low marginal rates. A single personal income tax rate of 33⅓ percent was introduced, and allowable credits were reduced to three. A modified value-added tax (to be known as the general consumption tax) is scheduled for 1990.

Government expenditures were also reduced, but because of high debt-service obligations inherited from the 1970s, the cuts fell heavily on social programs. Foreign debt service also required severe constriction of imports, which in turn required a very strong contraction in aggregate demand and an even lower fiscal deficit. The fiscal targets were attained, but the cost in terms of human capital and income distribution may have been excessive.

Subsidies were drastically reduced and human capital enrichment programs cut close to the bone. However, much infrastructure was restored and improved, following a serious decline in the late 1970s. General subsidies were replaced by targeted programs, including a food stamps program, but they were admittedly inadequate, and a social restoration plan was drawn up in 1988.

Sharp interest rate increases were introduced as one of the measures associated with the 1984 IMF standby. The rates were freed from Bank of Jamaica direction, with auctions for government securities and Bank of Jamaica certificates of deposit. The rates remained little changed when the over–30 percent inflation of 1984–85 was tamed, and real deposit rates have been in the region of 15 percent since then. There has been no move to adjust the rates, and no downward market pressure, despite the recognition that high real rates discriminate against investment in new productive capacity. The persistence of high real rates may have diverted potential investors to real estate and speculation, leaving no influential wealth-holders to lobby in favor of rates more suitable for investment in agriculture and manufacturing.

The exchange rate has been managed flexibly since 1983. The main effect has been to depress the demand for imports. By the end of 1983 the exchange rate had fallen to the point where Jamaican wage rates in US dollars were more competitive than those of close competitors such as Puerto Rico, the Dominican Republic, and the eastern Caribbean (except Guyana). On the basis of supply incentives the rate might well have stabilized there. However, import demand remained too high, and subsequent depreciation of the rate helped to reduce it.

Trade liberalization and deregulation have been actively pursued. Quantitative restrictions were eliminated, exchange controls relaxed, and price controls minimized. In January 1987 stamp duties on services were increased and exemptions from customs duty eliminated, and in July 1987 banks were authorized to make current account payments in foreign currencies without first securing central bank permission. In 1988 the combined customs and stamp duty on imports was lowered to the higher of 20 percent or the rate applicable under the CARICOM's common external tariff. Of the countries under review, Jamaica's domestic resource costs for import substitutes are closest to those for exports, but the country's export investment record did not match that of the Dominican Republic.

Official policy throughout the 1980s has been to privatize a range of state corporations. Some of these were deliberately nationalized in the 1970s (sugar estates, for example), and others were acquired to avert collapse (including several hotels), whereas still others were established by government in the first place. (Both major political parties at some stage supported state enterprise in a variety of activities.) Banks and hotels found ready buyers at home and abroad. A private firm was contracted to manage several large state farms, and other state-owned agricultural lands were leased to private companies. However, the government found it necessary to step into some industries to promote exports (in the case of ethanol production) or to arrest a decline in output (in bauxite and alumina).

The Jamaican government tried to attract foreign direct investment by revamping its incentive schemes, establishing free trade zones, and rejuvenating its export promotion agencies. A debt-equity swap program was announced in 1987. The response to these measures was uneven, with strong interest in hotels and substantial activity in the free trade zones, but negligible debt-equity swap activity and no direct investment in agriculture.

The Washington-based institutions seem to have learned from countries such as Jamaica about the importance of explicit social amelioration programs and the need to address supply problems at the microeconomic and institutional levels. Macroeconomic policy such as exchange rate measures loses its effect on supply beyond a certain point. The fully articulated Washington model has been in place in Jamaica for less than one year, if one includes the social amelioration aspects as a central part of that program.

Trinidad and Tobago

The comprehensive adjustment program initiated in 1987 by the government of Trinidad and Tobago, and elaborated in the years since, bears most of the hallmarks of the Washington model. Although the measures appear to have stabilized the external accounts—provided the price of oil does not soften—it is too early to assess its impact on economic growth and social welfare indices.

The fiscal deficit is being cut (as a demand-reducing measure) by a variety of actions. The government payroll is being reduced by 10,000 workers—about 20 percent of the civil service—largely through a voluntary retirement scheme. A health surcharge was introduced on personal income taxes back in 1984, and a cut in the nominal wages of public-sector employees has also been imposed. Other reforms include the introduction of user charges on some services, price increases for public utilities, and reduced transfers to state enterprises.

Tax reform began in 1987. The tax base was broadened through the elimination of most exemptions. The following year the top marginal rate was lowered and the number of tax brackets reduced to four. At the same time corporate tax rates were unified at 45 percent. Stamp duties, originally imposed in 1985, were increased, and a business levy and an income surtax were imposed. Sales taxes were also increased, but they are to be replaced by a value-added tax in January 1990.

Public spending priorities seem to be in line with the Washington consensus. Subsidies have been sharply curtailed, and the declared intention is to protect the poor and maintain infrastructure. The interest rate level is influenced by the central bank's discount rate, but loan and deposit rates are not mandated. The *ex post* real rate has been close to zero since 1987. The exchange rate is managed by the central bank, using relative prices in Trinidad and abroad as the main indicator.

The government has established a timetable for trade liberalization. Quantitative restrictions are to be removed by 1990, and tariffs are to be reduced progressively. There has been some deregulation of the financial markets, allowing more active trading in government securities. Government is seeking private venture partners for large-scale energy-based industrial development. Leases and management contracts have already been arranged for some firms, and others are being negotiated. A government-appointed commission recommended some rationalization, some disinvestment, and some closures.

An Evaluation of the Caribbean Experience

The full-fledged Washington consensus is very new, and although it is well represented in the Caribbean, more time is needed for an adequate assessment of the package as it has been implemented in the region. The earlier incarnations of the consensus have guided policy in Jamaica for all of the 1980s and were seen in action in the Dominican Republic between 1983 and 1985. Those policies proved to be seriously flawed, achieving external stabilization at the expense of social deterioration, which ultimately could derail the program. In both countries the policies have failed to provide a foundation for real economic growth. Barbados, which achieved growth and external balance by banking on its creditworthiness, does not provide good insight into the effects of the Washington consensus either. Although its policies were in line with Washington notions, with the possible exception of its interest rate policy, the government can be faulted on the timing and mix of these policies.

Nevertheless, it seems clear that some elements of the Washington consensus have been essential to the economic adjustment that has occurred in the region. Countries that failed to combine tight fiscal policy with market-clearing exchange rates, that attempted to ration imports and foreign exchange, and that did not provide for a carefully planned and financed social amelioration program found themselves increasingly short of foreign exchange, with output falling and social welfare declining.

The experience of the Dominican Republic suggests that adjustment programs need to be grounded on a sufficiently robust combination of domestic interests (Nelson 1989). Tensions bottled up by the adjustment program contributed to its overthrow as soon as the political process offered a suitable opening. There is a similar danger now in the case of Guyana. A consistent program is not enough for success. The administration must be fully committed, it must have the technical capacity to execute the program, there must be sufficient national consensus to ensure the durability of the program, and the country requires leadership to mold and sustain that consensus.

The timing and coordination of the adjustment measures are quite important. It may be necessary to space out the entire program to allow for the trade-offs necessary to attain general acquiescence, if not enthusiasm. Major economic adjustment takes several years, if only because of the investigation, learning processes, and preparation times involved in such elements as fiscal reform. Guidelines are slowly emerging on the coordination of the elements. For example, it is now felt that current account transactions should be liberalized before the capital account.

The unresolved issue of external debt hangs over all these discussions. Although this study has not analyzed the debt issue, no realistic projection foresees growth in real income for Jamaica or Guyana for the remainder of this century unless debt relief is forthcoming to a far greater degree than is reflected in any scheme currently in effect or under discussion.

Some Observations on the "Washington Consensus"

The Size of the Fiscal Deficit

Ex post the fiscal deficit (DEF) may be defined by the following identity:

$$DEF = dTML - dCRP - dFA - dBP$$

where dTML is the change in monetary liabilities, dCRP the change in bank credit to the private sector, dFA the change in foreign assets of the banking system, and dBP the change in government borrowing from the nonbank domestic private sector. To secure equality between the *planned* deficit and the righthand side variables, government must employ a model of macroeconomic adjustment to measure how these variables respond to proposed policy changes. Differences in the assessment of fiscal policies may reflect differences in the assumed model.

In an open economy a persistent balance of payments deficit indicates that the fiscal deficit ought to be trimmed. In the short run, an excess of external demand must be eliminated by reducing aggregate demand, since supply responses appear only after some time has elapsed. Cutting aggregate demand invariably means fiscal contraction. Looked at another way, a persistent balance of payments deficit indicates that government saving is too low, given the level of private saving. Provided the country has adequate foreign reserves or good external credit ratings, a one-shot balance of payments deficit may be financed, but fiscal correctives must be brought to bear if the external accounts remain in deficit for several periods.

In calculating the fiscal deficit, an adjustment might be made to avoid recognizing in the current year the full impact of an increase in external debt-service costs (in terms of local currency) arising from a devaluation. In principle, government may finance these costs by internal income redistribution in some way that shifts the real effects into the future. For example, if devaluation does not cause government revenues to rise by a compensating amount, the central bank may issue special nonnegotiable securities to cover the remainder.

A multiyear target for the fiscal deficit—and for the fiscal policies that it will involve—is required. A large deficit for a single year does not necessarily create an adjustment problem; it may be desirable to cushion a temporary shock, and it may be inevitable in election years. However, a succession of deficits destabilizes the external accounts. A model-determined fiscal trajectory, incorporating accompanying monetary and exchange rate policies, is advisable.

Public Spending Priorities

The Washington consensus on spending priorities closely resembles the position argued for over many years by many developing countries. The major difference is the reluctance to eliminate subsidies, but this has always been a pragmatic decision. Targeted subsidies are justified in circumstances where their elimination would cause such a severe burden on the poor that the entire adjustment program may be put at risk. The ranking of fiscal priorities is not controversial, but translating them into any single country's circumstances is.

Simple, Broad-based Taxes

One may support tax reform to provide relatively simple, broad-based taxes as a practical means of clearing out an accumulation of anomalies in an existing system. It is naive, however, to suggest that the outcome will be more equitable. Even if we ignore the weakness of the theoretical arguments in favor of such a system, once it is in place economic forces will assert themselves to shift the incidence of the reformed taxes, as they did with the old tax system. Taxes and their incidence are always in a state of flux, due to changes in legislation from year to year, but even more to changes in the institutional arrangements set up in response to the legislative changes. A fresh start is useful from time to time, but one should recognize that, however close the reformed system comes to what was intended, it will begin to deteriorate quite soon afterward.

Interest Rates

In the oligopolistic markets of small developing countries, market-determined interest rates will not promote investment in productive capacity. Financial institutions tend to hold an existing interest rate as long as possible, because of the potentially destabilizing effects of any significant move. When domestic inflation rates are expected to remain in line with international rates, the market will hold the local rate constant for long periods, at a rate close enough to the average of international rates so that external capital flows are not sustained. They will compensate by widening or narrowing their credit-liability margins on the interest rate in accordance with the supply and demand for credit. When inflation is expected to be high, the interest rate tends to rise to a level dictated by the demand for credit of currency or real estate speculators, depending on the source of the inflation and its manifestations. Productive investors usually find these rates prohibitive. Moreover, the rates tend to remain high even when inflation abates, because speculation remains profitable at high real interest rates.

A better operational guide is for officials to manage the rate flexibly, anchoring an indicator rate on the most relevant foreign interest rate. Because of the uncertainty of expected inflation, countries with low inflation are advised to use nominal rates for comparison. Any attempt to anticipate inflation may trigger expectations of higher inflation. Nominal rates above the international trend (by more than the cost of financial transactions) signal that the authorities expect higher domestic inflation. However, in countries with high inflation the comparison must be between real rates of inflation at home and abroad.

Targeting the Exchange Rate

Williamson's definition of the exchange rate target in the introduction to this volume is a useful starting point. However, to set a rate that can be sustained in the medium term involves choices about which opinions may vary widely: pricing strategy and production technology in new export markets, changes in the costs and productivity of competitors, and the evolution of markets and technology. In practice, the same circumstances allow for wide differences of opinion about the desirable exchange rate. In the end the authorities may have little choice but to use the expected demand for foreign exchange as the exchange rate indicator, even though this often produces a demand-contracting rate rather than a demand-switching one.

Trade Liberalization

Trade liberalization is not an important issue for small, open economies that already allow duty-free imports of most producers' goods. The size of the domestic market limits the scale, production technology, and range of activity of firms producing for the local market. At best they will command only a very small proportion of available finance, skills, and entrepreneurship. Production of import substitutes does not draw any substantial resources away from exports, where firms are of a different order of magnitude and use different technologies and organization. Equalizing domestic resource costs may depress the small-business sector, but it will not have a noticeable impact on exports.

Foreign Direct Investment

Foreign direct investment, and in particular new equity, is the only hope for renewed growth before 2000 in the majority of developing countries in the Western Hemisphere. Unfortunately, it seems that noneconomic factors are critical in the investment decision.

Privatization

No easy generalizations are possible with respect to privatization. Economic theory does not provide an unambiguous guide as to what activities ought to be in the private sector, and there is no pattern to be gleaned from experience. Extremes of state inefficiency and private exploitative monopoly are easy to identify in practice, and may be eliminated, but the debate is about the large gray area in between.

Deregulation

Deregulation is called for where there is administrative rationing. Rationing, except by prices, seems to work only as a temporary expedient. If it is maintained, institutional arrangements grow up with the intent to circumvent it. Regulations that provide for orderly, informed markets and offer prudential safeguards may need to be strengthened, especially in foreign-exchange and financial markets.

Debt Relief

It is unlikely that any adjustment program for the heavily indebted countries will be sustained in the absence of much more substantial debt relief than is currently expected. For these countries the most optimistic projections for adjustment are in effect a perpetual holding operation, offering little prospect of an increase in real per capita purchasing power and improved living conditions in the medium term.

Implementation

To be effective, the goals of any adjustment program should be fully endorsed by the administration of the country and be within the competence of its executive, and their implications should be understood and accepted by the population. These requirements are never fully met, and it is a matter of political judgment when there is sufficient capability for the success of the program. Wise leadership is needed to develop a sufficient consensus behind the program, and to prevent that consensus from slipping away.

Central America

Sylvia Saborio

In assessing the extent of economic adjustment that has taken place in Central America in the 1980s, it is important to bear in mind that issues of war and peace, not economic reform, have dominated the agenda in much of the region. Of course, whether or not they were at the top of the political agenda, economic problems had to be addressed. They were addressed, but usually with the greatest reluctance and in ways that were dictated more by domestic political constraints than by sound economic reasoning.

Whereas Washington technocratic circles may view economic reform as an orderly and coherent process, among policymakers in Central America reform has often seemed instead a haphazard exercise in crisis management, fraught with uncertainty and risk, and imposed from abroad to boot. In any case, it is probably unrealistic to expect countries immersed in the worst crisis since the Great Depression, engaged in war and facing a hostile external environment, to be able to tackle the economic crisis, the war, and the longstanding structural rigidities and distortions embedded in their economies all at the same time. If they had such capabilities in the first place, they probably would not have found themselves in such straits. Even so, the 1980s have probably ushered in more economic policy reforms in the region than any other decade in recent history.

In what follows, I focus first on the nature of the advice emanating from Washington and the extent to which it has been followed by countries in the region. Then I examine the results achieved so far and attempt to explain differences in the breadth and depth of reform and performance among the countries.

The Reform Agenda

The "Washington consensus," to use the terminology suggested by John Williamson, is largely transmitted to the region via three channels: the US Agency for International Development (AID), the International Monetary Fund (IMF), and the World Bank, with the Inter-American Development Bank (IDB)

Sylvia Saborio is Senior Fellow at the Overseas Development Council. She has held various positions in the government of Costa Rica, most recently that of Special Financial Representative and Minister Counselor at the Embassy of Costa Rica in Washington. She has written extensively on trade, finance, and development issues.

playing an increasingly supportive role in recent years.[2] If the degree of influence an agency enjoys were commensurate with the amount of financial assistance it provides, the AID's views would surely have prevailed. Whether they have in fact prevailed or not depends on which AID views one has in mind. The economic and technocratic structure within the AID has generally supported the strict conditionality associated with IMF stabilization programs and World Bank structural and sectoral adjustment loans, and indeed has often made its own disbursements contingent upon compliance with them. On the other hand, political and national security concerns within and outside the agency have sometimes overridden economic considerations and resulted in the provision of plentiful financial assistance with virtually no economic conditionality attached. Honduras and El Salvador, the largest recipients of US assistance in the region and the least prone to reform, are cited as prime examples. On the whole, however, dissonance has been minimal, and these institutions have conveyed a relatively coherent and mutually reinforcing message from Washington.

In terms of the broad thrust and direction of reform—prudent macroeconomic management, greater outward orientation beyond the Central American Common Market (CACM), and greater reliance on markets as opposed to government intervention—the Washington view is by now broadly shared, in principle, by most governments and intellectuals in the region. It is also generally recognized that stabilization is a precondition to structural reform. On the other hand, there is considerably less uniformity of views, both among the Washington institutions and in the countries themselves, regarding the pacing and sequencing of the reform package, the resolution of the trade-offs and inconsistencies involved, and the proper mix of internal adjustment and external financial support.

Does this amount to a consensus with Washington's views? Not entirely. Conditionality is still deeply resented, and most countries do tend to wait until they have no other choice before coming to Washington for help. Except in the heady days of a new administration, reform is generally seen not as a desirable goal but as a cross to bear, and policymakers everywhere are painfully aware of the costs. But perhaps this simply reflects the fundamental difference between giving advice and taking it.

A complex array of political and economic factors originating both within and outside the region has made economic management extremely difficult in Central America in the 1980s.

---

2. IDB project lending now typically requires an adequately managed exchange rate, positive real interest rates, nonsubsidized utility rate structures, and other measures that in totality far exceed the conditionality traditionally associated with project loans.

War. All of the countries in the region have suffered, albeit with different intensity, the consequences of war and social unrest (see table 6.2). Nicaragua, El Salvador, and Guatemala have borne the heaviest costs in terms of human lives, damage to infrastructure, destruction and abandonment of productive facilities and activities, and dislocations in factor markets caused by the displacement of workers, conscription, emigration, and capital flight. Last but not least has been the steep cost of the war effort itself. Even countries not directly involved in the armed conflict, such as Costa Rica, have suffered its side effects: a large influx of refugees, disruption of intraregional trade and payments flows, and destabilizing effects on investment, capital movements, and tourism—not to mention the considerable amount of time, energy, and resources dedicated to the pursuit of peace in the region.

External Shocks. Shocks from outside the region also complicated economic management. In the late 1970s and early 1980s all the Central American countries suffered a sharp deterioration in their terms of trade, in the range of 15 percent to 30 percent (table 6.3), due to the rise in oil prices (all but Guatemala are oil importers) and the steep decline in the prices of primary commodities, which constitute the bulk of the region's exports. In the course of the 1980s, adverse movements in the terms of trade coupled with weak export performance (table 6.4) have resulted in declines in the purchasing power of exports of around 50 percent in Nicaragua and El Salvador and nearly 30 percent in Guatemala (table 6.3). The external positions of these countries were further strained by the rise in international interest rates and the virtual suspension of new commercial lending to the region. The severity of these external constraints made it necessary to pursue extremely restrictive domestic policies, which, given recessive trends elsewhere in the economy, resulted in significant output losses.

The Unraveling of the Traditional Model. Beginning in the early 1960s, Central America followed a two-pronged growth strategy: expansion of traditional agricultural exports to world markets and an inward-oriented industrialization process under the protective umbrella of the CACM, which was largely propelled by extraregional exports but had an important regional multiplier effect. The strategy worked quite well in the prosperous 1960s, began to experience serious difficulties in the late 1970s because of instability in international commodity markets and political problems in the region, and ran aground in the 1980s in the face of increasing hostilities and generalized payments problems among the trading partners. Thus, policymakers in the region have been confronted with the dual challenge of restoring macroeconomic balance under uncommonly adverse conditions, while at the same time steering these inefficient and vulnerable economies toward a new, outward-oriented growth model.

Table 6.2 Central America: real-sector indicators, 1983–88

	1983	1984	1985	1986	1987	1988
Real GDP growth (percentages)						
Costa Rica	2.9	8.0	0.7	5.5	5.4	3.8
El Salvador	0.8	2.3	2.0	0.6	2.7	0.5
Guatemala	−2.6	0.5	−0.6	0.1	3.1	3.5
Honduras	−0.2	2.8	3.2	3.1	4.9	4.0
Nicaragua	4.6	−1.6	−4.1	−1.0	−1.1	−8.3
Real GDP per capita (1980 = 100)						
Costa Rica	85.1	89.5	87.7	90.0	92.4	93.4
El Salvador[a]	73.4	74.4	74.9	74.1	74.8	74.4
Guatemala	87.1	85.1	82.0	80.3	80.6	81.2
Honduras[a]	88.8	88.7	88.9	88.9	90.8	91.7
Nicaragua	74.3	94.0	87.1	83.4	79.8	70.7
Investment as share of GDP (percentages)						
Costa Rica	24.2	22.7	25.9	25.2	28.2	27.8
El Salvador	12.1	12.0	10.8	13.3	12.6	12.2
Guatemala	11.1	11.6	11.5	10.3	13.8	14.0
Honduras	14.9	19.0	18.1	14.1	14.7	13.3
Nicaragua	22.5	22.2	23.1	16.9	15.8	31.1
Export volume (1980 = 100)						
Costa Rica	101	105	108	116	118	130
El Salvador	83	88	86	79	86	83
Guatemala	86	87	88	72	83	86
Honduras	90	99	105	104	101	108
Nicaragua	118	91	75	60	70	49
Import volume (1980 = 100)						
Costa Rica	64	70	75	78	86	97
El Salvador	93	97	94	97	98	99
Guatemala	73	83	77	68	99	105
Honduras	67	76	81	84	89	90
Nicaragua	99	111	110	102	109	105
Open unemployment rate (percentages)						
Costa Rica	7.9	6.7	6.2	6.1	5.5	5.6
El Salvador	32.9	32.2	23.8	24.0	24.5	24.0
Guatemala	11.0	10.0	13.7	16.6	12.6	12.6
Honduras	21.0	21.0	22.0	23.0	24.0	24.0
Nicaragua	19.0	21.1	20.9	22.1	24.3	26.0

a. 1978 = 100.

Sources: Concejo Monetario Centroamericano and Economic Commission for Latin America and the Caribbean.

Table 6.3 Central America: price indicators, 1983–88
(1980 = 100 except where noted)

	1983	1984	1985	1986	1987	1988
Change in consumer prices (percentages)[a]						
Costa Rica	33	12	15	12	17	25
El Salvador	13	12	22	32	25	20
Guatemala	6	3	19	37	12	11
Honduras.	8	5	3	4	3	5
Nicaragua	31	35	220	682	1,012	14,316
Real minimum wage						
Costa Rica	95	100	104	106	104	98
El Salvador[b]	97	96	84	72	64	65
Guatemala[c]	118	108	93	76	81	83
Honduras	91	89	86	82	80	76
Nicaragua	49	70	58	18	20	9
Terms of trade						
Costa Rica	88	90	88	106	94	100
El Salvador	82	71	68	87	59	62
Guatemala	84	86	81	104	82	85
Honduras	78	78	82	101	90	100
Nicaragua	83	105	98	103	100	99
Purchasing power of exports						
Costa Rica	92	97	96	116	114	117
El Salvador	68	63	58	68	51	52
Guatemala	73	75	71	75	68	73
Honduras	77	82	83	100	94	103
Nicaragua	97	93	71	59	68	47
Real effective exchange rate[d]						
Costa Rica	n.a.	122	123	137	152	167
El Salvador	n.a.	71	67	81	72	63
Guatemala	n.a.	83	115	118	123	132
Honduras	n.a.	76	72	77	81	82
Nicaragua	n.a.	56	40	34	23	31

n.a. = not available.

a. Annual average.

b. Real average wage, 1976–78 = 100.

c. Real average wage.

d. An increase in the index represents a devaluation.

Sources: Concejo Monetario Centroamericano and Economic Commission for Latin America and the Caribbean, World Bank, 1988. *Adjustment Lending: An Evaluation of Ten Years of Experience.*

Table 6.4 Central America: external-sector indicators, 1983–88

	1983	1984	1985	1986	1987	1988
Trade balance (percentages of GDP)						
Costa Rica	−1.5	0.0	−1.8	0.8	−3.1	−1.2
El Salvador	−2.0	−4.6	−5.0	−2.9	−7.2	−6.4
Guatemala	0.4	−0.5	−0.3	2.2	−5.0	−5.0
Honduras	−1.9	−4.6	−2.6	0.5	−1.2	−0.5
Nicaragua	−13.2	−14.6	−20.5	−18.9	−17.9	−19.9
Current account balance (percentages of GDP)[a]						
Costa Rica	−9.1	−4.2	−3.3	−1.8	−5.7	−3.0
El Salvador	−0.9	−1.6	−0.9	3.4	3.0	1.1
Guatemala	−2.5	−4.1	−3.7	−0.3	−6.2	−5.9
Honduras	−7.3	−9.8	−5.9	−3.9	−5.5	−5.2
Nicaragua	−21.1	−22.6	−30.6	−28.0	−24.8	−23.2
Unilateral transfers (percentages of GDP)						
Costa Rica	1.5	3.0	4.5	2.6	2.0	4.0
El Salvador	4.4	6.1	4.9	5.3	8.0	5.4
Guatemala	0.0	0.0	0.0	0.5	1.8	1.6
Honduras	1.1	2.2	3.8	3.8	2.9	2.7
Nicaragua	2.8	3.1	2.8	3.6	3.4	n.a.
Public external debt (percentages of GDP)						
Costa Rica	102.3	96.0	94.6	82.8	86.6	81.8
El Salvador	50.8	46.5	49.8	47.0	37.9	32.9
Guatemala	23.7	27.2	39.4	35.8	37.9	35.2
Honduras	57.4	62.2	62.1	63.5	60.2	56.0
Nicaragua	122.9	154.0	180.9	202.9	226.9	234.8
Debt service as percentage of exports						
Costa Rica	54.8	51.4	52.1	49.8	44.3	43.1
El Salvador	41.1	38.1	41.5	49.1	41.9	42.0
Guatemala	28.3	33.4	40.9	38.2	29.0	30.0
Honduras	23.6	22.8	24.4	22.7	23.8	22.5
Nicaragua	19.7	11.9	14.7	11.1	n.a.	n.a.

n.a. = not available.

a. Inclusive of unilateral transfers.

Source: Concejo Monetario Centroamericano.

The complexity of the situation and the generally adverse, often critical conditions in which policy actions have had to be undertaken have posed serious problems of a technical as well as a political nature. The task of devising and implementing technically sound, consistent, and comprehensive policy packages to deal with the myriad problems afflicting these countries is probably beyond the capabilities of most Central American bureaucracies; creating the political space necessary for such an ambitious undertaking likewise probably far exceeds the abilities of most governments in the region. Instead, authorities have generally taken a minimalist approach to economic reform, tackling problems one at a time and doing as little as necessary in order to muddle through. As a result, policy changes have been somewhat erratic in their timing, sequencing, and calibration, and important policy reversals have occurred as governments have had to yield to opposing pressure groups. Perhaps to reduce risks such as these, reforms have often been circuitous and contrived rather than straightforward and transparent.

Fiscal Reform

As a major culprit in generating inflationary pressures and external imbalances and crowding out private investment, fiscal deficits have been subject to enormous pressure. Yet budget cutting has proved difficult because of structural rigidities in the budget, the automatic escalation of certain items (notably the accrual of interest payment obligations on public internal debt as well as external debt), and, except in Costa Rica, high and rising defense expenditures. Nevertheless, deficits have generally been on the decline, except in Nicaragua where half the budget is absorbed by the war effort and the deficit has hovered at around 20 percent of GDP (40 percent if the total public sector is included) through most of the decade (table 6.5). By far the most notable success has been attained by Costa Rica, where the public-sector deficit has been reduced from 14 percent of GDP in 1982 to 2 percent in 1989. El Salvador cut its deficit by 6 percentage points of GDP, to around 3 percent, and Guatemala and Honduras have each reduced theirs by 3 percentage points, to 1.5 percent and 6 percent of GDP, respectively.

The reduction of fiscal deficits has been accomplished through a mix of expenditure cuts and revenue increases, in varying proportions among countries and over time, although it has generally proved more difficult to raise revenues than to compress expenditures. On the other hand, the pattern of expenditure cuts has been quite similar across countries. A disproportionate share of the cuts has fallen on the capital account, as new investments have been scaled down or postponed and maintenance of existing infrastructure has been neglected. As a result, the ratio of public investment outlays to GDP fell across the board from

Table 6.5 Central America: public finance indicators, 1983–88
(percentages of GDP)

	1983	1984	1985	1986	1987	1988
Current revenues[a]						
Costa Rica	16.6	16.6	16.2	15.4	15.6	15.1
El Salvador	12.4	13.2	13.4	14.4	11.9	10.7
Guatemala	8.2	7.0	7.7	8.9	9.4	10.2
Honduras	13.3	15.1	15.6	15.6	16.4	16.2
Nicaragua	31.2	35.2	32.3	32.4	27.7	21.8
Total expenditures[a]						
Costa Rica	19.9	19.3	18.2	18.8	17.7	17.2
El Salvador	21.2	19.1	17.1	17.4	15.5	13.8
Guatemala	11.2	10.6	9.6	10.8	11.9	12.4
Honduras	23.6	26.5	24.6	23.4	23.3	23.6
Nicaragua	56.4	57.0	54.8	49.6	44.5	48.2
Fiscal deficit[a]						
Costa Rica	3.3	2.7	2.0	3.3	2.1	2.1
El Salvador	3.4	2.6	2.7	1.4	1.3	1.5
Guatemala	3.0	3.5	1.8	1.5	1.3	1.2
Honduras	10.4	11.4	9.0	7.8	7.0	7.4
Nicaragua	24.0	21.0	21.9	16.1	16.2	25.9
Domestic financing as percentage of deficit[a]						
Costa Rica	82	63	n.a.	52	71	90
El Salvador	15	31	30	0	8	40
Guatemala	70	94	61	60	62	58
Honduras	46	25	32	40	59	47
Nicaragua	88	85	97	91	100	94
Public-sector deficit						
Costa Rica	7.5	5.8	6.7	5.4	3.2	3.4
El Salvador	9.7	6.2	4.0	2.4	3.0	2.8
Guatemala	3.4	4.0	5.5	5.6	2.7	2.9
Honduras	12.2	11.3	7.5	6.5	6.1	5.3
Nicaragua	39.9	37.5	48.8	39.9	41.4	n.a.
Central bank losses						
Costa Rica	4.9	4.3	5.2	3.7	2.9	3.5
El Salvador	0	0	0	0.2	0	0
Guatemala	0	0.5	4.2	4.9	1.7	1.5
Honduras	0	0	0	0	0	0
Nicaragua	4.0	5.5	2.8	7.6	5.3	n.a.

n.a. = not available.　　　　　　　　　　　　　　a. Central government only.

Sources: Consejo Monetario Centroamericano and IMF.

a range of 7 percent to 9 percent in 1980 to only about 3 percent to 4 percent in 1989. Among current expenditures, there has been a shift in favor of defense (except in Costa Rica), general administration services, and interest payments (on an accrual basis), at the expense of social and developmental outlays.

On the revenue side, efforts have been made to mobilize resources primarily through increased indirect taxation and through the reduction or elimination of subsidies, both implicit subsidies in the pricing of public utilities as well as direct price subsidies such as those on basic grains. No clear trends are discernible regionwide in terms of the overall tax burden. Where the ratio of tax revenues to GDP has traditionally been low, in the range of 6 percent to 12 percent (i.e., in Guatemala and El Salvador), it has tended to remain that way, although in Guatemala it has risen somewhat in recent years, whereas in El Salvador it has declined. In Honduras and Costa Rica, tax revenues have remained in the neighborhood of 15 percent of GDP. Finally, in Nicaragua, after rising to about 35 percent of GDP in the mid-1980s, tax revenues have plummeted to around 17 percent, largely as a result of the Olivera-Tanzi effect: the erosion, due to hyperinflation, in the real value of receipts between the time taxes accrue and the time they are collected.

The record on tax reform proper is almost universally bad in Central America. A number of factors appear to have conspired against an increase in the tax effort. Most of these countries rely heavily on traditional export taxes, especially on coffee. This form of taxation naturally subjects tax revenues to a boom-bust pattern following the vagaries of international primary commodity prices. It has the additional disadvantage of making fiscal and balance of payments crises go hand in hand. However, the sporadic, temporary fiscal relief that comes about every time there is a surge in primary commodity prices obscures the need and reduces the pressure to switch to more permanent and stable sources of revenue.

Another factor has been the erosion in the tax base due to the decline in GDP, inflation, and the expansion of the informal relative to the formal sector of the economy. But even within the formal economy, numerous loopholes and a patchwork of exemptions, exonerations, and tax holidays linked to various schemes to foster investment, production, and exports provide plenty of opportunities to avoid taxation legally. In addition, deficient tax collection systems and weak enforcement powers probably make tax evasion the rule rather than the exception in most places. The irony is that, although nobody pays them, the tax rates that are on the books are often so high as to constitute a formidable weapon against efforts to increase taxes whenever the subject comes up.

An additional problem is that some of the reforms implemented in recent years as part of the "new model" have also tended to strain the public purse. Export-promotion schemes effectively delink fiscal revenues from the most dynamic sector of the economy or, worse, constitute outright drains on the budget when the incentives also include tax rebates. At the same time, import-liberalization measures in the face of constrained overall import capacity also result in a loss of tariff revenues.

All of these factors make integral tax reform a necessity, but at the same time make it a very risky political proposition and therefore a most unlikely prospect. The power to tax is simply very weak. For instance, in Guatemala and El Salvador, where tax burdens are extremely low (below 10 percent of GDP), tax increases have been decreed only to be later rolled back, and a more recent tax reform package in Guatemala is expected to yield a net reduction of revenues. In Costa Rica it took the legislature a whole year to pass a tax reform bill whose provisions became so complex and confusing along the way that it was practically impossible to assess its impact. If these precedents are any guide to the future, the simple, fair, transparent, and efficient tax system we all profess to want is a long way off.

A separate but related matter is the issue of how fiscal deficits are financed. This is dealt with at some length in the next section, but a general pattern can be discerned. In the early 1980s, as access to foreign credit became increasingly difficult to procure, countries tended to rely rather heavily on financing by the domestic banking system, either through direct loans by the central banks or through the more or less involuntary purchase of government paper by the commercial banks. Over the years, less reliance has been placed on this type of borrowing, and deficits have been increasingly financed through a combination of external credit and grants (where available), domestic borrowing from nonbanking sources, and the accumulation of both external and internal arrears (floating debt).

Several aspects of fiscal management are worth pondering. The overriding concern throughout the 1980s has been to compress fiscal deficits, and in this, as noted, most countries have succeeded to some extent. How this was done is another matter. It is worrisome that macroeconomic balance should have been restored in a way that tends to exacerbate the social cost of adjustment and jeopardizes future growth. In a period of declining incomes, falling wages, and high unemployment, the share of social services in the budget ought at least to have been maintained. Similarly, the decay in physical infrastructure through neglect and, in some cases, war damage is already impairing economic recovery and structural adjustment. To free the resources for this badly needed physical and social investment, fundamental changes will be necessary on both sides of the budget. This will require that hard choices be made regarding the role, size, and efficiency of the public sector and the manner in which it will be financed.

Financial Reform

Financial reform has been another uphill battle. In most of these countries the financial sector is segmented into a formal system of not very efficient, highly regulated, and often state-controlled institutions, alongside a network of informal channels that handle the overflow. In the formal system, interest rates on both loans and deposits have traditionally been set by the central banks, along with guidelines for credit allocation to various categories of borrowers, including the government and state-owned institutions. Like the exchange rate, interest rates have tended to be kept low and fixed in nominal terms, with only occasional adjustments to their level and structure.

In the 1980s, financial systems throughout the region were subjected to a series of shocks. The failure of large numbers of firms and the virtual insolvency of others, victims of the sharp downturn in economic activity, left banks with large, uncollectable debts. Inflationary surges wreaked havoc on the level and structure of domestic real interest rates. Rising international interest rates, coupled with the reluctance of foreign commercial lenders to extend new loans or roll over old ones, put a further squeeze on the banks. Heavy valuation losses accrued to all holders of external liabilities, including the banks, in the face of depreciating currencies. Additional strains were caused by the heavy losses the central banks incurred through their interventions in the foreign-exchange markets and the need to accommodate the sizable borrowing requirements of the nonfinancial public sector, whose external sources of finance had suddenly dried up.

Thus, on top of their traditional, structural deficiencies, financial systems became the catchall for unresolved problems and policy shortcomings in other areas. Money creation has been essentially driven by the financial needs of governments and by the losses of central banks in their defense of overvalued exchange rates and, in some cases, the direct absorption of the external obligations of public—and sometimes even private—debtors. Although this transfer of liabilities to the central banks resulted in deficits for the nonfinancial public sector that were lower than they would otherwise have been, it still did not meet all the financing requirements of the sector, especially since the shortfall in external credit had to be made up with domestic resources. This often put central banks on a collision course with treasuries over whether the remaining public-sector deficit ought to be financed directly by the banking system or whether both should scramble for funds in what had become very short-term money markets. Indeed, inflation and the expectation of continued instability had so enhanced the liquidity preference of prospective lenders that only high-yield, no-risk, highly liquid instruments could hope to be sold on a voluntary basis in the market. How this conflict was resolved has been instrumental in determining the profile of domestic real interest rates, as well as the trade-off between internal and external stability.

As it happened, the treasuries initially won the argument, and there was substantial direct financing of public deficits by the banking system, as reflected in increases in net claims on the public sector as a share of total domestic credit in every country in the region. By the mid-1980s, however, this trend was reversed (except in Nicaragua), and a rising proportion of the banking system's domestic credit went to the private sector. Correspondingly, as noted, governments resorted to other internal and external sources of finance and, when all else failed, to the accumulation of arrears.

The crowding out, first of the private sector and then of the public sector, from access to credit from the banking system has put upward pressure on underlying domestic interest rates. Where these pressures have been repressed, capital has tended to shift from the formal to the informal sector, and often out of the country altogether, while rent-seeking behavior on the part of economic agents with access to subsidized credit is feared to have made the allocation of credit and the distribution of income even worse. Where government intervention in rate setting has been reduced, and interest rates are essentially market-driven (i.e., in Honduras and Costa Rica), real rates have been and remain very high (table 6.6). Although, other things being equal, this discourages capital flight, it also tends to discourage productive investment and aggravates the fiscal deficit.

The abandonment of interest rate setting and credit rationing by the central banks also poses the question of how then to control monetary and credit expansion. In industrial countries this is done mainly through open market operations, but none of these economies have fully developed financial markets. Therefore, money market operations on a large scale would again bring the central bank on a head-on collision course with the treasury, as both would be competing for essentially the same limited pool of funds. Instead, central banks (in Costa Rica and to a lesser degree in Honduras) have resorted to the use of the discount rate and legal reserve requirements to control monetary aggregates. Discount rates have been set at prohibitive levels, not only in real terms but also in relation to commercial lending rates, thus effectively discouraging anyone from even approaching the discount window. At the same time, legal reserve requirements against deposits have been raised to very high levels, in the range of 30 percent to 40 percent. The excessive reliance on reserve requirements to contain credit expansion has unduly increased the cost of financial intermediation and reduced the profitability of banks, thus feeding back into further upward pressure on lending rates.

This suggests that financial liberalization cannot proceed much further without first tackling the fundamental causes of money creation and fiscal imbalances. In the case of Honduras there is room for relieving financial pressures through further budget cuts, since the deficit is still high at around 6 percent of GDP. In Costa Rica the situation is more complex, given that the nonfinancial public sector is already in surplus. True, that surplus could be increased, but it is evidently the losses of the central bank that are causing the problem. Since those losses accrue mainly from the revaluation of the stock of foreign debt every time the currency is devalued (whether the debt is actually

Table 6.6 Central America: monetary indicators, 1983–88

	1983	1984	1985	1986	1987	1988
Total liquidity (percentages of GDP)						
Costa Rica	50.0	46.6	44.3	42.8	44.4	48.5
El Salvador	34.0	36.0	37.4	35.2	32.2	30.7
Guatemala	25.3	27.3	29.7	25.3	25.9	25.1
Honduras	30.4	31.3	30.0	30.1	33.5	35.1
Nicaragua	50.6	64.4	56.1	49.8	55.6	55.4
Net domestic credit (percentages of GDP)						
Costa Rica	44.2	41.0	36.4	36.4	36.9	35.4
El Salvador	51.5	50.3	49.0	39.4	36.5	34.0
Guatemala	34.6	38.6	34.9	23.2	22.9	21.4
Honduras	46.8	48.2	48.8	48.3	51.7	51.4
Nicaragua	101.5	103.9	77.8	54.8	49.7	139.7
Net claims on public sector as percentage of total domestic credit						
Costa Rica	35.7	51.5	47.0	50.8	48.5	50.6
El Salvador	42.1	43.3	40.4	34.5	34.5	32.9
Guatemala	39.8	42.7	43.3	33.2	24.0	19.2
Honduras	30.3	29.6	28.7	28.4	27.9	29.6
Nicaragua	65.9	75.7	78.9	70.4	73.4	85.7
Real interest rates (percentages per year)						
Loans						
Costa Rica	−5.1	12.4	9.7	10.9	5.3	6.8
El Salvador	1.1	1.9	−5.2	−9.4	−3.8	0.7
Guatemala	8.1	8.1	−5.5	−16.7	1.5	4.5
Honduras	9.9	12.6	14.2	12.7	13.1	11.3
Nicaragua	−11.4	−14.9	−51.4	−65.5	−85.5	n.a.
Deposits						
Costa Rica	−8.0	9.9	5.0	6.4	3.2	2.4
El Salvador	−2.7	−1.9	−8.6	−14.2	−8.1	−3.7
Guatemala	5.3	5.2	−8.1	−18.9	−1.2	1.8
Honduras	1.6	5.1	6.3	5.1	6.2	4.2
Nicaragua	−15.6	−16.5	−51.9	−64.5	−85.5	n.a

n.a. = not available.

Source: Consejo Monetario Centroamericano.

paid or not), and the rate of devaluation cannot be slowed down without impairing the export drive, a reduction of the debt overhang is clearly called for.

Exchange Rate Policy

The battle to realign exchange rates has been an intense and difficult one. All of the countries in the region have a longstanding tradition of fixed nominal exchange rates, and keeping them so has long been a matter of national pride. Honduras, for instance, has kept the lempira pegged to the dollar at a rate of two to one since 1918. In some circles currency realignment is still regarded as the ultimate indignity. In others there is the concern that nominal devaluations of the currency in small, undiversified economies, where import dependency is high and supply elasticity low, may simply lead to inflation and trigger a vicious cycle of devaluations negated by price instability that then require further devaluations and so on.

For all of these reasons, by the early 1980s exchange rates in all of the Central American countries were way out of line. Nevertheless, in the face of adversities—the second oil shock, collapsing primary commodity prices, the virtual standstill of the CACM, global recession, high and rising international interest rates, and practically no external finance—one by one the countries had to capitulate. But they did so in circuitous ways, so as to avoid a clear-cut devaluation of the currency. The authorities typically stepped in to create intermediate parallel markets between thriving black markets already in place and the official market, and then proceeded to shift imports and export receipts from the official market to the others until the exchanges stabilized. By managing the flows in this manner they effectively devalued without having to change the official parity. In the process, however, they created an extremely complex web of separate but interconnected markets that has been a nightmare to administer, has provided vast opportunities for rent-seeking and corruption, and ultimately did not avert the need to devalue openly (except in Honduras).

After so much trouble to devise a mechanism for surreptitious devaluation, have currencies actually been realigned? Only Costa Rica and Guatemala have managed both to streamline the foreign-exchange regime and to attain a real effective devaluation of the currency in a sustained fashion (table 6.3). Costa Rica has devalued by some 35 percent to 40 percent, and Guatemala by 20 percent to 25 percent, from 1980 levels. In June 1989 Nicaragua effected a real devaluation of some 30 percent, but it is unclear whether a new overvaluation of the cordoba can be prevented. El Salvador and Honduras are still saddled with cumbersome exchange systems and hopelessly overvalued currencies.

Trade Policy

The need to shift to a more outward-oriented strategy beyond the CACM has been one of the most persistent themes in the policy dialogue between the

Washington institutions, particularly the AID and the World Bank, and the Central American countries, and some tangible results have been achieved. Apart from the realignment of exchange rates, where as noted above the record is mixed, a twofold approach to reducing the bias against exports has been suggested. This approach involves, first, a reduction in the level of effective import protection afforded by the common external tariff (CET), along with the elimination of nontariff barriers to trade; and second, the establishment of specific systems of incentives to promote nontraditional exports to markets outside the CACM.

At any other time during the last two decades, talk of dismantling or weakening the CACM would have drawn fire, but since the virtual collapse of the CACM on its own in the late 1970s, authorities have been more open to considering new options. Even so the degree of commitment to the CACM and its role in the future scheme of things remain matters of some controversy in the region.

The 1980s have witnessed two rounds of cuts in the CET. The first round aimed not only to reduce import protection but also to rationalize the trade regime. It converted specific tariffs into *ad valorem* rates, switched the nomenclature to that of the Brussels code, and eliminated all exemptions under the Central American Agreement on Fiscal Incentives, as well as the existing regional investment incentives and import surcharges under the San Jose protocol. Costa Rica spearheaded the effort, but the other regional partners (Guatemala, El Salvador, and Nicaragua) eventually agreed, and the new regime became effective in January 1986.[3] As a result of this exercise, the maximum tariff was lowered from 220 percent to 100 percent, the mean tariff was halved from 53 percent to 26 percent, and tariff dispersion (as measured by the standard deviation) was reduced from 52 percent to 21 percent.

The second round of tariff cuts was initiated in 1987 by Costa Rica alone, under safeguard provisions of the CACM, as part of the second structural adjustment loan agreement with the World Bank. Other countries in the region are under pressure from the Bank to follow suit, and the subject is being formally discussed at CACM council meetings. Nevertheless, only El Salvador has so far taken concrete steps to lower its tariffs, also under safeguard provisions. If fully implemented, the new regime would lower the maximum tariff to 40 percent, reduce the average tariff to 16 percent, and cut tariff dispersion to 13 percent.

The notion of export promotion was championed by the AID, and export incentive schemes began to be introduced in most of the countries in the mid-1980s. These schemes typically involve duty exemptions on imports of intermediate and capital goods for export production, income tax holidays for a

---

3. Honduras, although not a member of the CACM, subsequently adopted essentially the same measures.

number of years, the establishment of free trade zones and temporary admission regimes, preferential access to credit, licenses to sell all or part of foreign-exchange proceeds from nontraditional exports in the parallel market at favorable rates, and tax rebates linked to the value of exports.

Although nontraditional exports have expanded rapidly, partly as a result of these incentives, so have the problems associated with these schemes. For one thing, the fiscal cost is becoming increasingly burdensome and adds to the inflexibility of the budget through automatic escalation. In Costa Rica, for instance, nontraditional exports have been growing at an average annual rate of 27 percent, but tax rebates in 1989 alone are expected to account for about 7 percent of total central government expenditures. Even the exporters are beginning to realize that a transfer of this magnitude to the export sector is simply not sustainable. Second, the incentives create distortions, whereas the whole thrust of the reform is supposedly to remove them. Moreover, the incentives constitute yet another special-interest regime that, though intended as a temporary measure, once installed is going to prove very difficult to remove. Finally, the incentives are being challenged, through countervailing action, in the very same nontraditional markets that they are designed to help penetrate, notably the United States.

In sum, an inevitable winding down of export promotion schemes cannot be far off. The question then becomes how to maintain export momentum. In those countries where the exchange rate is still overvalued, currency realignment is the obvious place to start. But in Costa Rica and Guatemala, where there has already been a large and sustained real effective devaluation of the currency, it is not obvious that further devaluation is advisable, particularly in view of its implications for central bank losses and domestic inflation. My own view in the case of Costa Rica is that incentives, particularly tax rebates, have been far too generous and could probably be significantly reduced without unduly curtailing export activity, provided the present exchange rate policy is maintained and indirect measures to boost exports such as improvements in port and transportation facilities, customs clearing procedures, and the like are stepped up. Even if export growth suffers in the short run, a change of signals is important to ensure that those exporters that remain or enter the scene are lured by the activity itself and not by the pursuit of fiscal rents.

Privatization and Deregulation

Another item high on the agenda of both the World Bank and the AID has been the need to reduce the size and role of the state through divestiture and deregulation. The sale of public enterprises as well as the privatization of certain activities heretofore performed by the state has been recommended as a way not only to reduce fiscal deficits, but also to reap efficiency gains. This is a sensible idea, but its potential should not be overplayed. Many of these enterprises were in the public sector in the first place because they either were deemed to have strategic value or constituted natural monopolies in the small economies of the region, or required large and lumpy investments with long recovery periods that private firms could not be expected to make. Many of those reasons remain valid today.

Of course, over time governments in the region have also gotten involved in activities that far transcend the scope of the minimalist tradition, such as cement, fertilizers, marketing, and financial intermediation. A case could be made for reassessing the benefits of such involvement given the harsh fiscal realities of the 1980s and 1990s. Still, the zeal for privatization as a cure-all should probably be toned down in favor of a less ideologically motivated efficiency drive in both the public and the private sector: although government inefficiency may be flagrant all around, markets in all of these countries are likewise concentrated, fragmented, and notoriously inefficient allocative tools.

The most ambitious program of privatization in the region so far has been carried out in Costa Rica, where AID funds were used to essentially dismantle the state holding company CODESA. Of over 40 companies held in the early 1980s, all but 2 have been sold, liquidated, or otherwise disposed of. There the process has probably reached its tolerance limit, at least for the time being, but elsewhere in the region further movement can be expected in the years ahead. El Salvador has recently announced its intention to privatize its banking system, along with other public agencies and activities. With far less enthusiasm but a lot of prompting, Honduras has put in place a program to divest 12 public enterprises, as part of its structural adjustment program with the World Bank.

Like state ownership, the tradition of government intervention is well entrenched in Central America, but like elsewhere in the region, the abundant regulation is mostly red tape and does not translate into very effective control. Effective or not, there is tremendous resistance to relinquishing formal controls, and probably more deregulation has occurred by default (i.e., through inability to maintain effective control) than by design. Deliberate deregulation has been largely confined to prices and wages, the financial sector, and the surrender of control implied by privatization. In a similar vein, attempts have been made, if not to deregulate, at least to simplify bureaucratic procedures (e.g., through the creation of one-stop centers for the promotion of foreign investment and exports). On the whole, however, deregulation in Central America has come in isolated, sporadic episodes rather than as a systematic dismantling of state controls. The sea-change mentality required to tackle that task with a vengeance has not yet occurred.

Economic Performance

The 1980s have been struggling, immiserizing years in Central America. Every country in the region is far worse off today than it was 10 years ago. GDP losses have been staggering: in per capita terms, the cumulative GDP decline from 1980 through 1988 has ranged from around 7 percent in Costa Rica and 8 percent in Honduras to 19 percent in Guatemala, 26 percent in El Salvador, and 29 percent in Nicaragua (table 6.2). Meanwhile neither internal nor external balance has been attained anywhere in the region, although all of the countries except Nicaragua have managed to escape the spiraling hyperinflation prevalent elsewhere in Latin America. Within this dismal regional picture, however, there are important differences among countries that derive from disparate initial conditions, the differential impact of exogenous shocks, and the exercise of diverse policy options.

Costa Rica

After three decades of practically uninterrupted economic growth accompanied by social progress and political stability, Costa Rica plunged into a severe recession in 1980–82. Over the years the country had accumulated large internal and external imbalances as it tried to compensate for the income loss imposed by the oil shocks of the 1970s through expansionary domestic policies financed by additional foreign borrowing. The situation became untenable in the face of a sharp decline in the terms of trade, coupled with a steep rise in interest rates (given the large stock of short-term and variable-interest debt) and the withdrawal of virtually all external commercial credit.

At the trough of the recession, per capita income had plunged 15 percent from its 1979 peak; the unemployment rate was nearly 10 percent; inflation reached 100 percent; the public-sector and current account deficits hovered at around 15 percent of GDP; the exchange rate was veering out of control, having multiplied fivefold in a matter of months; foreign reserves were all but depleted; and, having lost access to virtually all sources of credit, the country had to suspend most external payments. The administration of Luis Alberto Monge, which took over in May 1982, immediately adopted a five-point economic stabilization plan aimed at restoring order and stability to the foreign exchanges; drastically reducing the fiscal deficit; ensuring equitable sharing of the adjustment costs through an incomes policy; restructuring all external debt obligations; and renewing orderly financial relations with the multilateral agencies and friendly governments.

This "shock treatment" was remarkably successful. Within two years the foreign-exchange market had been consolidated and stabilized, and a crawling-peg system had been put in place to prevent the overvaluation of the colon. The public-sector deficit had been cut to around 6 percent of GDP. Inflation had receded to an annual rate of 10 percent to 15 percent. The decline in national income had been halted, and the rate of unemployment was diminishing. Within this two-year period, the country also entered into a standby agreement with the IMF, restructured its official bilateral debt at the Paris Club, rescheduled its commercial bank debt, and started preliminary discussions with the World Bank about a possible structural adjustment loan.

In subsequent years progress has been slower and far less spectacular, but there has been progress nonetheless. The main achievements have centered around the consolidation of the stabilization process, the reactivation of economic activity (GDP growth has averaged 4.5 percent per year since 1983), and the outward reorientation of the economy (nontraditional exports have expanded at an average annual rate of 27 percent since 1983 and now account for 40 percent of total exports). It took several years of consciousness-raising and consensus-building, but the country is now fully committed to a process of outward-oriented structural transformation.

Despite all these achievements, the external payments situation remains precarious, and the country has been able to move ahead in recent years in large measure because it has not fully discharged its external financial obligations. Full servicing of the external debt on contractual terms would have absorbed some 45 percent of export earnings and nearly 75 percent of national savings. An outward transfer of that magnitude would almost certainly have precluded any real growth. Unless the country succeeds in significantly reducing the external debt overhang, it will continue to face a sizable financial gap of $150 million to $200 million per year well into the medium term.

The internal debt is also a problem. Indeed, while fiscal deficits have been on the decline, the external resources available to finance those deficits have declined even more, so that deficits are now almost entirely financed domestically through high-yield, short-term bonds (table 6.5). Apart from the crowding out of other potential borrowers and the generalized upward pressure on domestic interest rates that this causes—and that feeds back into the public budget—the extremely short-term structure of the internal debt requires constant refinancing and obstructs the proper use of open market operations by the central bank. A critical review and radical reform of public finances—the amount of resources to be allocated, the purposes to be served, the efficiency with which those resources are used, and how they are financed—will be one of the main challenges for Costa Rica in the 1990s. In the years ahead the country will also have to face up to its social and environmental debts.

El Salvador

Rather than big upheavals, the Salvadoran economy has experienced a long decade of stagnation. Following a sharp decline when the Marxist insurrection first broke out in the late 1970s, real GDP per capita has remained essentially unchanged at a level 25 percent below its peak in 1978. With violence in the countryside undermining the country's agricultural base, the shrinking local and regional markets depressing industrial activity, and sabotage damaging much of the country's infrastructure, El Salvador has suffered a significant drain of its productive resources—human, physical, and financial. The economy appears to have settled into a pattern of low resource utilization (around 25 percent open unemployment, table 6.2) and low output generation.

Large infusions of funds from abroad, mostly in the form of AID grants and remittances from Salvadorans in exile, finance as much as 80 percent of the country's import bill and a similar portion of the fiscal deficit. These inflows have masked the need to adjust the highly overvalued currency (the real effective exchange rate in 1988 was 37 percent below the 1980 level) and the negative real interest rates. As some World Bank officials have pointed out, El Salvador shows signs of suffering from an aid-induced "Dutch disease."

The administration of Alfredo Cristiani has promised a radical change of course. Its recently unveiled Economic and Social Development Program is a blueprint for reform that aims to implement much of the Washington consensus. The strategy aims at redressing macroeconomic imbalances, seeking economic efficiency through greater reliance on market forces, protecting the poor from the adverse impact of adjustment measures, and reducing absolute poverty. In the macroeconomic policy sphere it proposes monetary restraint and positive real interest rates; a two-tier foreign-exchange regime with market forces playing a role in determining the exchange rate; a maximum nominal tariff of 50 percent and elimination of all nontariff barriers; reduction of the public deficit through higher taxes, better tax administration, and expenditure cuts (including a freeze on public employment and wages, an early-retirement program for public-sector employees, and the elimination of subsidies); and liberalization of most prices.

The government has already taken the first steps in this program by raising interest rates, devaluing the currency, reducing some tariffs, deregulating some prices, raising some taxes, and announcing its intention to privatize the banking system and other public activities. Opposition to some of these measures is already gathering momentum, as are inflationary pressures derived therefrom. Thus, there is a risk that the government may have to change the pace if not the path of reform.

Guatemala

After a prolonged period of relatively rapid growth, the Guatemalan economy contracted sharply after 1980. Per capita GDP fell every single year through 1986, for a cumulative decline of 20 percent (table 6.2). To counteract the contractionary impact of the decline in the terms of trade and the precipitous fall in exports (from 1980 to 1985 the purchasing power of exports fell by 30 percent, table 6.3), the authorities pursued an expansionary domestic policy financed by external borrowing. As it happened, the external debt trebled between 1980 and 1985, from $934 million to $2.7 billion, but did not produce the intended reactivation of domestic activity, as political instability and a severely overvalued exchange rate caused most of the inflow to be dissipated in capital flight.

The crisis erupted in 1985 when, unable to continue borrowing abroad, the central bank proved no longer able to support the highly overvalued official exchange rate. A black market developed, and eventually the authorities established a parallel market where the exchange rate was nearly three times the official rate. In response, imports contracted by nearly 30 percent from their 1984 levels, external arrears began to accumulate, and domestic inflation soared from 3 percent in 1984 to over 30 percent in 1986.

The administration of Vinicio Cerezo, which took over in early 1986, launched a Programa de Reordenamiento Económico y Social de Corto Plazo to stabilize the foreign exchanges, cut the fiscal deficit, reduce internal liquidity so as to contain inflationary pressures, and improve the external payments position. The program was a watershed: it restored confidence within Guatemala and, very importantly, helped to secure large amounts of external financing for the country.

Within a year, improvements were evident in several areas. For the first time in seven years the decline in per capita GDP was arrested. Price escalation reverted to an annual rate of around 12 percent, aided by the easing of speculative pressures against the quetzal and the 50 percent increase in imports, which boosted domestic supplies. Even though the deficit of the nonfinancial public sector expanded somewhat, 70 percent of it was externally financed (half of it through grants), so that the pressure on domestic financial markets was actually reduced. Further relief was derived from a sizable reduction in the losses of the central bank due to the stabilization of the foreign-exchange markets and the decision that public agencies, not the central bank, would henceforth absorb the exchange risk on their own external indebtedness.

Despite a large trade deficit, the balance of payments position was eased by large capital inflows in the form of official credits, unilateral transfers, and foreign direct investment, as well as the return of some domestic capital that had previously fled the country. The external payments situation was further helped by the fact that Guatemala was able to reschedule a portion of its external public debt.

These positive trends have generally continued, and Guatemala seems to be well on its way to consolidating its internal balance. Investment, both public and private, has been rising; economic activity is expanding moderately at around 3.5 percent annually; and, through a combination of adroit foreign-exchange management and fiscal incentives, nontraditional exports have been growing at an average annual rate of 18 percent since 1985. Nevertheless, the external payments position remains precarious: the current account deficit is nearly 6 percent of GDP, and Guatemala has come to rely heavily on external concessional resources that may not always materialize in the future. More worrisome still, there are signs of increasing tension between the government and the private sector over the present and future course of economic policy, and the recent wave of political assassinations may yet destroy the climate of confidence painstakingly built over the last few years.

Honduras

Like El Salvador, Honduras has undergone a prolonged period of slow decline or semi-stagnation rather than a severe crisis, and it has likewise settled into a pattern of low savings (5 percent to 6 percent of GDP), low investment (13 percent to 14 percent), low growth (3 percent to 4 percent), low inflation (3 percent to 5 percent), and high unemployment (23 percent to 24 percent) (tables 6.2 and 6.3). Honduras has also relied heavily on external transfers, mostly grants from the AID, to help finance both the fiscal and the current account deficits, each of which amounts to about 6 percent of GDP. At the same time, however, the country has been extremely reluctant to adopt policy reforms in the two areas its principal benefactor has been urging: the fiscal deficit and the exchange rate.

Things are beginning to change, but slowly. Despite the large external transfers the country receives, foreign-exchange scarcities have become increasingly pronounced in recent years, as manifested in the large external arrears that have accumulated (nearly 3 percent of GDP) and in the growing margin between the official and the parallel exchange rates. In early 1988 the government introduced a new instrument to foster nontraditional exports, called *certificados transferables de opción de divisas por exportación*. In a concealed and limited manner this move amounted to an effective devaluation of the lempira. This mechanism is now being extended to other products, so that Honduras is, in effect, abandoning the fixed nominal exchange rate ideal. With respect to the fiscal deficit, certain austerity measures have already been adopted, such as a freeze on public-sector wages and employment and a commitment to the World Bank to privatize a dozen public enterprises.

The measures taken so far have been insufficient to satisfy World Bank and IMF conditionalities; moreover, Honduras was recently declared ineligible for new loans due to the buildup of arrears with those institutions. However, the new President Rafael Leonardo Callejas has announced that his administration will be more prone to reform and that one of his top priorities will be to restore orderly relations with the multilateral financial institutions.

Nicaragua

Throughout the 1980s Nicaragua has been in a virtual state of war. Apart from the heavy toll in human lives, the war has caused profound dislocations in production and population, as well as severe damage to the infrastructure, and the war effort itself has stretched public finances to the breaking point. In addition, the political ramifications of the conflict, such as the barring of Nicaragua from access to multilateral credit sources and the US trade embargo, have seriously compounded the country's internal political and economic difficulties.

Against this background, the impoverishment and disarray that have come to pass are hard to fathom. By 1988, real GDP per capita was 40 percent below its peak (1978) level, real minimum wages stood at only 9 percent of their 1980 level, open unemployment was conservatively put at 26 percent of the labor force, and consumer prices were escalating at an annual rate of over 14,000 percent (tables 6.2 and 6.3). Additional evidence of the magnitude of the imbalances is the fact that, over the last three years, the public-sector deficit (including external arrears and central bank losses) has been in the range of 40 percent to 50 percent of GDP, while the current account deficit has been around 25 percent to 30 percent of GDP (tables 6.4 and 6.5). The country imports four dollars' worth of merchandise for every dollar it exports, and the external debt–exports ratio now exceeds 3,000 percent.

The road Nicaragua took to hyperinflation was a simple and familiar one. The central bank accommodated whatever public deficit was left unfinanced by other sources. As the generous external support Nicaragua received during the initial years of *sandinismo* began to wane, a rising share of the cost of the war, the revolution (i.e., the political commitments of the new regime), subsidies, and other current expenses came to be financed through monetary emission.

Several attempts were made to correct course when it became obvious that things were getting increasingly out of control. Thus, in 1986 and 1987 several large devaluations of the cordoba were effected, and nominal interest rates and reserve requirements were increased. In both cases, however, inflation quickly eroded the nominal adjustments: the exchange rate remained highly overvalued in real terms, and real interest rates stayed very negative at around −80 percent. Similarly, in an attempt to reduce the deficit, expenditures were compressed, indirect taxes were raised, and surcharges were imposed on foreign-exchange transactions. However, the smaller deficit was financed entirely by the central bank, feeding anew the inflationary spiral.

By mid-1988 it was evident that nothing short of an orthodox shock would do. Accordingly, a monetary reform package was put in place that changed the currency base, unified the exchange rate markets (thereby transferring exchange rate risk from the central bank to the users of foreign currencies), and realigned relative prices. Price realignment was achieved through the selective indexation of some key variables (the exchange rate, interest rates, public utility rates, fuels, basic consumer goods, and certain indirect taxes on consumption and imports) and the deregulation of private-sector wages and other prices. At the same time, the reduction in hostilities made possible a significant rollback of public expenditures and the layoff of some 30,000 public employees, half of them from the security forces.

It is too early to judge the total effect of this reform package, but by mid-1989 inflation was down to 800 percent, the fiscal deficit had declined to around 7 percent of GDP, interest rates were positive in real terms, and the real effective exchange rate was 33 percent above its 1985 level.

Concluding Remarks

Central America is in bad shape, but winds of change are blowing everywhere in the region. For the first time in a decade, people are more preoccupied with peace than with war. A lowering of hostilities would not only permit but, indeed, demand that reconstruction and development rather than political survival become the top national priorities. One clear lesson of these troubled years is that, if peace is to be lasting, Central America must begin to service in earnest the massive social debt that it has incurred over many years of indifference and neglect.

The economic crisis likewise has taught some valuable if costly lessons. The first is that there is no real alternative to biting the bullet, but how this is done is instrumental in determining the associated costs and, ultimately, the success of the effort. In order for reform to succeed, a critical mass of mutually reinforcing and compensatory changes appears necessary. But the ability to act on many fronts at once requires both a highly qualified technocratic and bureaucratic elite and a broad base of political support. The latter requires, in turn, that the social costs of adjustment be explicitly factored in and addressed and that alliances be forged with the potential beneficiaries of the changes in order to withstand political pressures from the losers. The case of Costa Rica is illuminating in this regard, precisely because it is atypical. Nowhere else has this combination of forces been mobilized.

Another important lesson that has been relearned is that appropriate domestic policies are not enough. If anything, the process of trade liberalization will make Central America even more vulnerable to external conditions. Thus, even though the response to exogenous shocks may have improved, developments in these nations will continue to be largely dominated by events outside their control.

Acknowledgments

The author wishes to thank all those government officials and colleagues at the World Bank, the International Monetary Fund, the Inter-American Development Bank, and the US Agency for International Development who provided valuable information and insights about the reform process in Central America.

Comment

Susan Collins

Since the papers by Saborio and Worrell cover such a large number of countries, rather than comment on them country by country I will step back and examine some broader issues.

There are good reasons to include the Central American and Caribbean nations in a study of adjustment in Latin America. So often, when one's attention is focused on the larger debtor countries, the issue of inflation tends to dwarf all other concerns. When instead one looks across the varied experiences of a range of countries, including the smaller ones, one sees a number of other questions that come up again and again. Their recurrence suggests that they are truly important and that we do not yet have definitive answers for them.

On the central question posed by this volume, it is very clear from both of these papers that only limited adjustment has taken place in Central America and the Caribbean. Both areas have a long way to go in terms of reviving stable growth. Within this group of countries there is of course a great deal of variation. Costa Rica is in many respects the pedestal country of the region; Jamaica's situation looks relatively good, although it appears to be a long way from achieving stable, sustainable growth; at the other extreme are countries like Trinidad and Tobago, which has had seven years of negative growth. Much progress remains to be made toward restoring sound economic performance in these countries.

A second set of questions posed in this conference is whether there is now a consensus on appropriate policies for adjustment and growth and the extent to which these policies have in fact been implemented. In my view, quite a broad consensus has developed on the basic elements of a sound policy package, some of which is fairly recent. For example, it is surprising how much broader the consensus is now than even a few years ago on the view that controlling fiscal deficits is a critical element of any successful stabilization effort. Other policy elements on which there is consensus include, on the macroeconomic side, maintenance of competitive exchange rates and restrained monetary growth, and, on the structural side, trade and financial liberalization and other market-oriented reforms. In my view, the responsibility for poor economic performance in some developing economies clearly lies to an extent with policymakers in these countries who have failed to implement many of the policies on which there has been agreement.

Susan M. Collins is Associate Professor of Economics at Harvard University and is currently on leave as a senior staff economist at the Council of Economic Advisers.

At the same time, the focus on whether there is consensus over the elements of an appropriate policy package misses an important point: we remain far from a consensus on the appropriate speed for implementing such a package. With the question of timing comes the related issue of proper policy sequencing. In many respects, the feasible speed and sequencing of reform has less to do with the underlying economics of "what should work," and more to do with political and social factors in individual countries. These issues remain a long way from resolution, and are critical areas for future analysis and discussion.

Thus, a key issue that the two papers address from different perspectives is the importance of having social and political consensus on any reforms undertaken. One of the papers goes so far as to suggest that it is futile to attempt comprehensive reform in the absence of such consensus. That raises an obvious question: if you do not have that consensus, yet your need for reform is overwhelming, what do you do? Sylvia Saborio said that effective reform must take into account the many linkages among policy measures, and that therefore a "critical mass" of mutually consistent and reinforcing measures is needed if any of the individual measures are to work. The need for social consensus, however, may require qualification of that statement: perhaps something of a balancing act is called for, selecting for inclusion in the reform package those measures that will help build a country-wide consensus for reform.

Of course, this makes for a very country-specific approach. One lesson that we learn from those countries such as Costa Rica that have implemented successful reforms is that the economic history of a country makes a difference. As Saborio's paper informs us, Costa Rica's crisis of 1980–82 followed two decades of almost uninterrupted growth. One cannot assume that adjustment policies that worked in a country with a long history of stable growth and consistent, sound economic management can be picked up and transplanted to a country that has experienced long-term decline and whose policies have changed from month to month. You cannot change a country's history, but it is worth recognizing that the cold-turkey adjustments that have been successful, in whole or in part, for some countries might have very different effects in others.

Costa Rica serves as an example of yet another important aspect of adjustment, one that I have observed in Korea and other countries as well. Countries trying to return to a path of stable growth often require what I call an economic "time out" in the form of large short-term capital inflows or some other kind of financial adjustment. Very few countries have been able to make the huge structural adjustments needed to reorient resources and turn the trade deficit into a surplus while at the same time servicing massive debt obligations. Costa Rica dealt with this dilemma by accumulating rather large arrears. Korea ran into its problems well before the debt crisis broke in 1982, and so it was able to continue borrowing in order to get itself through its adjustment. The point is that we simply do not observe countries improving their balance of payments, getting their fiscal houses in order, restructuring all of their resources, and at the same time resuming growth overnight.

Despite the emerging consensus on the elements of a sound reform package, complex and controversial questions remain about policy timing and sequencing. The answers are likely to depend on circumstances that will differ over time and across countries, such as social and political factors and the climate in international financial markets. The idea that we can identify—much less implement—a single consensus policy package, appropriate for all countries trying to stabilize and revive growth, is an idea that needs serious rethinking in light of our experiences to date.

Discussion

Alain Thery challenged the contention in much of the Costa Rican literature that the country had hesitated to initiate adjustment. He argued that, on the contrary, fiscal correction had started rather promptly. The earlier terms-of-trade gains had been diffused widely through the population, so that when the crisis hit, everyone shared the blow. Every group was affected in turn by the adjustment, which may help to explain why the process of adjustment was relatively peaceful and successful.

William Cline asked Sylvia Saborio to clarify the nature of the losses suffered by the Central Bank of Costa Rica from the debt crisis. She explained that these consisted of valuation losses from devaluation and losses due to the absorption of debt by the central bank on behalf of the rest of the public sector.

Cline also asked how Costa Rica, which has a lower ratio of interest payments to exports than a number of larger Latin American countries, had managed to get such lenient treatment of its debt. After some debate about the actual figures, John Williamson noted that even if Costa Rica had not been among the most indebted countries, it had been one of the first to take the attitude that, while it would continue servicing its debt as best it could, it was not prepared to give that objective a higher priority than the maintenance of growth. He speculated that this decision had demoralized the bankers, who had then begun selling off Costa Rican debt cheaply on the secondary market, which had in turn produced the opening that permitted the relatively favorable debt reconstruction that had recently been announced.

In replying to the debate, DeLisle Worrell cast doubt on the possibility of predicting *ex ante* the political circumstances that would sustain a successful adjustment program. The one safe generalization was the crucial importance of dynamic and credible political leadership. He agreed that "history matters" and strongly endorsed Susan Collins's emphasis on the need for a "breathing space" with regard to external finance, but he emphasized also that this was not a sufficient condition for successful adjustment, citing the Jamaican experience in 1981–83 as a case in point.

7

Panel Discussion on Latin American Adjustment: The Record and Next Steps

7

Panel Discussion on Latin American Adjustment: The Record and Next Steps

Rodrigo Botero

As the 1990s begin, policymakers in Latin America are rethinking their economic strategies while coping with the still-unresolved problems that caused the regionwide crisis of the 1980s.

The papers presented at this conference as well as the comments and discussions have reminded us of how different the national experiences are, despite the apparent similarities. We tend to speak of a Latin American economy, a Latin American debt problem. Confronted with similar problems, Latin American countries have made policy responses that correspond to their individual political circumstances, historical perceptions, and economic realities. If one were to make a general statement about Latin American economic policy today, it would be that at present there is no commonly accepted adjustment strategy in the region. Likewise there is no single development model that can be described as commanding widespread support.

The different approaches to adjustment and recovery throughout the region allow for cross-country comparisons that contribute significantly to the policy debate. After eight years of economic crisis, much remains to be done in terms of adjustment and restructuring in most of the Latin American countries. Notwithstanding the present difficulties, some progress has been made in several of the large and medium-sized countries in the region. The capacity to diagnose the problem and to formulate comprehensive policy responses has improved. In those countries where there has been adequate political support for adjustment programs, the necessary economic expertise to formulate and implement the programs has been readily available. Some of the policy failures of the past few years can be attributed more to an absence of political will on the part of the governments concerned than to the incompetence of economic policymakers.

Economic policy concerns in Latin America during the 1980s can be grouped into three categories:

Rodrigo Botero is an associate at the Center for International Studies at Harvard University and was formerly Finance Minister of Colombia.

- Restoration of macroeconomic equilibrium

- Management of external shocks

- Redefinition of the development model.

One could describe the first of these as primarily an issue for the short term, the second as a medium-term issue, and the third as a matter for long-term solution. Among Latin American policymakers, one could describe the first category as the one where the largest degree of consensus can be found, the third category as the one where there appears to be the least consensus, and the second category as somewhere in between.

A similar result can be obtained by ranking these categories according to the degree of consensus between Latin American policymakers and the Washington-based policy establishment as defined in John Williamson's background paper (chapter 2). Thus, there is a certain consensus on short-term policy issues, less on medium-term issues (prominent among them the external debt problem), and still less on the long-term issues.

Economic adjustment programs cannot be so easily classified, however; instead they include elements from each of the three categories. In practice, this means that discussions with the international financial community on adjustment programs will reveal disagreement on medium- and long-term issues, even when there is agreement on the short-term agenda.

On the need to restore macroeconomic equilibrium, the emerging consensus among Latin American policymakers is not far removed from what the international financial community would like to see. The need for fiscal discipline is recognized, as is the need for an appropriate exchange rate policy. Although the details of what constitutes the optimum policy are open to debate, an overvalued currency is understood to be highly undesirable. Positive real interest rates are recognized as necessary for a healthy capital market. A high priority is assigned to the search for relative price stability. The need to increase domestic saving, private as well as public, is recognized as a critical factor for stabilization and for growth.

The advantages of an outward orientation of the economy are accepted. The successful experience of several Latin American countries (Brazil, Chile, Colombia, Costa Rica, Mexico, and Uruguay) with export diversification provides sufficient empirical evidence to refute the "export pessimism" that was prevalent in the region some time ago.

In 1985 the principal debtor countries in Latin America came to the conclusion that a unified approach to the debt problem was not in their best interest. In spite of attempts to maintain the appearance of coordination at the political level, in practice each government has managed relations with its creditors in accordance with individual circumstances and in light of what is perceived to be the most advantageous bargaining strategy.

Beyond the questions of stabilization and debt restructuring, Latin American policymakers face the challenge of redefining the development model. The concept of the corporate state, with public spending as the engine of growth, is in crisis. The long-term restructuring of the Latin American economies will require a reassessment of the role of the state and a redefinition of its priorities. The extent of state intervention in the economy and the manner in which that intervention takes place will have to be reviewed. A clear delimitation will be required between the state as arbiter and regulator, and the state as producer of goods and services. If the Latin American countries are to compete internationally and get back on a sustainable growth track, the obsolete structure of the corporate state will have to be dismantled. This is the most difficult long-term policy issue confronting Latin America.

Finally, looking toward the decade of the 1990s, one can identify three topics that will be of concern to Latin American policymakers. The first is the question of what is proper trade policy in a world that appears to be moving toward three large trading blocs. The second is the implications for Latin America of the changes taking place in Eastern Europe. The third is the outlook for financial flows to the region, as Japan becomes the principal creditor nation in the world.

Beyond the problems of stabilization, financial recovery, and restructuring, the Latin American countries need to address explicitly the issue of how they will participate in a rapidly changing international economy. How policymakers respond to this challenge will, in large part, determine Latin America's economic performance in the 1990s.

Rudiger Dornbusch

Latin America is in the throes of extreme instability. For some countries—Brazil and Peru, for example—severe inflation continues to destroy financial institutions, bankrupt the government, and make money useful only as wallpaper. When money dies, economic progress is rolled back by decades, wrecking social achievements and threatening political freedom. For other countries such as Argentina, stabilization remains precarious and might fail in a few months. Still others, notably Mexico and Bolivia, have firmly established stabilization programs yet cannot seem to restore growth. In fact, year after year their per capita income declines. Only Chile and Colombia seem to have escaped from the general deterioration of economic conditions.

In judging the region's economic performance it is essential to adjust for the rapid growth of population. Figure 7.1 therefore shows per capita income for Latin America as a whole in the 1970s and 1980s. Although there may have been some growth in total GDP, real income per capita continues to fall almost everywhere. That real per capita income should be declining in those countries undergoing institutional destruction as a result of hyperinflation may seem plausible. But that this should also be happening in Bolivia or in Mexico where stabilization is more firmly in place is surprising. Even in Chile, with its entrenched reforms, real per capita income in the 1980s has barely increased.

Lessons on Stabilization

The task of price stabilization involves two objectives: stopping inflation fast and avoiding the resurgence of inflationary pressures. Ending inflation through incomes policy is relatively easy, but keeping it down requires fiscal support. The chief mistake in stabilization policy is to rely excessively on incomes policy— fixed exchange rates and wage-price freezes—and insufficiently on fiscal austerity. Such programs quickly lead to repressed inflation and overvaluation, at which stage a tight monetary policy is introduced to sustain the imbalances. Ultimately that does not work, and another inflationary explosion provides the starting point for yet another stabilization. Argentina, with its succession of

Rudiger Dornbusch is Ford International Professor of Economics at the Massachusetts Institute of Technology and Vice President of the International Economic Association. He has written numerous articles and books, including Exchange Rates and Inflation *and* Deuda Externa e Inestabilidad Macroeconómica en la Argentina.

Figure 7.1 Latin America: per capita income, 1970–89

1970 = 100

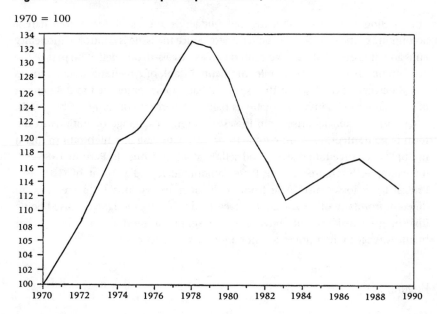

Source: Economic Commission for Latin America and the Caribbean.

failed stabilization programs in the second half of the 1980s, offers a clear example of this process.

Budget Balancing

Fiscal deficits are the ultimate source of inflation. When external sources or the domestic capital market cannot finance the deficit, it must be adjusted. Two questions immediately emerge. First, how large a deficit is consistent with stability? Second, how does one cut the deficit down to the required size?

Brazil, Argentina, and Peru failed to adjust their fiscal deficits in the aftermath of their 1985 heterodox stabilization programs. Wage-price controls and fixed exchange rates provided immediate results in each country in stopping inflation and raising the political popularity of the president. The resulting opportunity for fiscal stabilization was not exploited, however. Instead the deficits persisted and were financed by money creation. The fact that there is scope for some remonetization, once and for all, at best offers a bridge for sound fiscal policies to be implemented; it is definitely not a substitute for such policies.

Quasi-fiscal Deficits

The starting point for balancing the budget is the need for a transparent accounting of the consolidated government. Since the issue is control of monetary emission, it is essential that the central bank's "quasi-fiscal" deficit be part of the accounting. In 1986, for example, the Central Bank of Argentina suffered losses of 1.8 percent of GNP, Costa Rica's central bank losses amounted to 2.8 percent of GDP, and in Uruguay they were as high as 4 percent (Blejer and Chu 1988).

Quasi-fiscal deficits arise from losses on foreign-exchange operations in the form of guarantees, forward contracts, or simply buying at a high rate (under a multiple exchange rate system) and selling at a lower one. In Peru in 1986–87, for example, foreign-exchange losses amounted to 2.3 percent of GDP. But central bank losses also arise from credit operations. Subsidized credit is no different from any other subsidy; in fact, credit subsidies long ago ceased being investment subsidies and have become simply a production subsidy that finances wages when prices are not allowed to reflect costs.

Revenues

The second item on the reform agenda is to achieve a productive tax system. Increasing the yield of the tax system is dictated by the need to eliminate deficits. Tax collection is performing very poorly in all the high-inflation countries and in fact throughout Latin America. Peru's case is, of course, extreme: tax revenues have fallen from around 16 percent of GDP in the late 1970s and early 1980s to an estimated 4 percent in 1989.

It is striking that in periods of economic populism the revenue system invariably deteriorates. One would think that populist governments, with their emphasis on redistribution, would seek to achieve it through the mechanism of the tax system. In fact, however, they use inflation and as a result fail miserably: income distribution deteriorates under their auspices, and they leave behind a wrecked tax system.

Price stabilization makes an immediate contribution to tax revenues because the inflationary erosion of revenues ceases. But the contribution is a small one, perhaps around 2 percent of GNP. The major effort must be the reconstruction of the tax system. Corruption and evasion, which now undermine the collection of taxes, must be stopped. Mechanisms to increase compliance must be introduced and demonstrated to be serious. Just as Spain and Italy during the 1980s finally attacked the issue of compliance, so must all of Latin America. The complacent acceptance of pervasive tax evasion is the most regressive aspect of the Latin American tax system. A good case in point is the Brazilian experience of the 1960s, when revenue was raised from an average of 18.8 percent in 1961–65 to an average of 22.1 percent in 1966–69.

The revenue effort must also concentrate on the elimination of subsidies in public-sector enterprises. In many countries there is now in place a pervasive management of public-sector prices both to control inflation and to try to prevent a decline in real wages. The implied revenue losses are extraordinarily large and cannot be justified by either objective. For example, in Peru control of telephone rates has reduced the real price of the service to one-tenth the 1985 level. It is difficult to argue that controlled telephone rates have an important incidence either on inflation or on the welfare of the poor, but they do contribute to deficits.

Governments should therefore eliminate any and all subsidies. The resulting revenue gains must be applied to eliminating inflation, which in itself raises the welfare of the poor since inflation is a highly regressive tax. Part of the revenues should also be used for targeted food and employment programs for the poorest groups.

Beyond cutting all subsidies and raising revenue under the existing structure, governments should use the opportunity of the crisis, and the resulting consensus on the need for fundamental change, to institute a more efficient tax system that will produce more revenue with fewer distortions. Effectively that means eliminating the pervasive exemptions from direct taxes and raising tax rates. A comprehensive value-added tax of 15 percent, with a 5 percent surcharge for luxuries, might be the starting point for discussion.

Government Spending

For many observers the right way to achieve adjustment is by cutting government spending, not by raising taxes. Inefficiency in government, they believe, is so pervasive that the fiscal problem can be solved right there. They propose massive firing of public-sector employees and privatization as the appropriate remedy.

Inefficiency in government is indeed pervasive, and public-sector employment in many countries is unjustifiably high. But there is no presumption that budget adjustment should fall here primarily rather than on the tax side. There is a need to restructure public-sector spending from consumption to investment and productive services, but the level of spending certainly is not excessive in most Latin American countries. More spending, absolutely and relatively, should be devoted to infrastructure and to health and social services for the poorer groups. The current composition of spending is not only unproductive but probably also regressive.

The example of Mexico makes the point most strikingly (table 7.1). A major decline in oil revenues was offset to a minor extent by increased taxes and

Table 7.1   Mexico: fiscal adjustment, 1982–88 (percentages of GDP)

	Average 1982–85	1986	1987	1988
Revenues	31.3	30.3	30.6	29.8
Oil	12.2	9.0	9.8	7.5
Taxes	10.2	11.2	10.7	11.9
Outlays	41.0	44.8	45.0	39.0
Noninterest	30.0	28.3	25.2	22.4
Investment	9.5[a]	5.8	5.0	4.5
Interest	11.0	16.5	19.8	16.6

a. 1980–85.

Source: Banco de México.

primarily by a dramatic cut in government spending other than interest in 1988. Much of the spending cut has fallen on public investment, health, and education. Certainly more infrastructure investment could be undertaken by the private sector—for example, for telephone services, but also for public transport and even the road system. Mexico is now exploring such options. But the fact remains that cutting infrastructure spending should not be the priority in balancing the budget.

Privatization

No doubt privatization can play a role in resolving the fiscal crisis. In any area where the private sector can plausibly take over, state assets should be sold as quickly as possible. There ought to be a reasonable process of public tender to avoid corruption, but beyond that due haste is appropriate. Telephone companies, national airlines, and hotel chains, among others, should be sold without delay. And the list is far longer.

There are three reasons why governments should sell these operations. First, when there is a fiscal crisis, any current resources command a very special attraction. Second, the government's ability to manage is stretched unreasonably by these operations. Third, liquidating or even closing loss-making public-sector enterprises may be a powerful way to reduce the deficit.

When the economy is in crisis, the prices at which public-sector firms will sell are low. Is that an argument against privatization? Unless inflation is brought under control by better public finance, the price will never be right, and that means privatization must be one of the revenue sources. But there is a need for caution. Selling public-sector enterprises should be a source of financing; this is not the same as using privatization as a way of reducing the external debt.

Incomes Policy

Fiscal austerity is the *sine qua non* of stabilization, but incomes policy is an important, desirable component. Without budget balancing a stabilization will not last, without incomes policy it may not even start.

Incomes policy is designed to bring about a rapid, coordinated end to inflation. In a hyperinflation, incomes policy amounts to fixing the exchange rate. Because price setting is geared to the movements of the dollar, the move to a fixed exchange rate is enough to break the inflation and the expectation of inflation.

However, when inflation is only 100 percent or 200 percent per year, incomes policy is both more essential and more complicated. Without incomes policy, use of demand management alone to end inflation would create an extraordinary depression. Inflationary inertia represented by cost increases that are due to explicit or implicit indexation implies that current inflation cannot get away from past inflation unless the government breaks the process by means of incomes policy. Incomes policy here means both fixing the exchange rate and stopping wage inflation. The government will have to intervene in loan contracts to reduce excessive real interest burdens that otherwise would result from the unanticipated decline in inflation. Also, because wage contracts provide for periodic adjustments for inflationary erosion, a sudden ending of inflation requires intervention here as well. Some wage contracts will have to be rolled back, and others will need to receive an upward adjustment.

Exchange Rate Policy

Exchange rate policy assumes a strategic role in stabilization, as does public-sector pricing.

The starting point of a program is invariably a fixed exchange rate. But the next issue is when to give in. If inflation does not end completely, sooner or later an adjustment in the exchange rate and in public-sector prices is called for. The decision to abandon the fixed rate is a difficult one because it signals the government's acceptance of inflation as inevitable. As a result there is a temptation to postpone exchange rate adjustment until a significant overvaluation has developed.

Overvaluation in turn creates the expectation of a devaluation, and very high real interest rates become necessary to ward off a speculative attack. High real interest rates in turn increase domestic debt service and worsen the budget

Figure 7.2 Argentina: real exchange rate, 1970–90

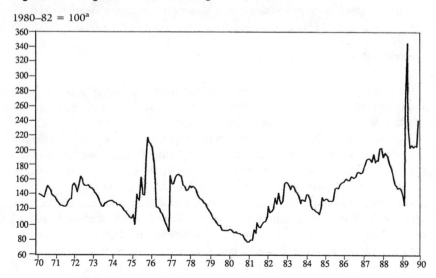

1980–82 = 100[a]

a. An increase in the index signifies a depreciation.
Source: Morgan Guaranty Trust Company.

situation. Ultimately the exchange rate adjustment does have to come, but often the overvaluation has gone so far that an outright exchange crisis and collapse are the end of the abortive attempt to practice a fixed exchange rate.

The pragmatic answer is to move after two or three months to a crawling peg, depreciating the exchange rate at a pace that maintains external competitiveness. Figure 7.2 shows the Argentine real exchange rate. The Primavera Plan of 1988 is shown as a major real appreciation, followed by the collapse of early 1989. The stabilization undertaken by Carlos Menem started with an extremely competitive real exchange rate, but the process of real appreciation is once again under way.

The risk of an overvaluation keeps economic horizons short and stands in the way of recovery. The right time for a crawling peg is very early, because the government should try to preserve maximum competitiveness. Holding onto a fixed exchange rate for too long may yield an extra month of low inflation, but it also sacrifices competitiveness and therefore prejudices the return of growth.

Indexation

A major stabilization decision regards indexation. The common view is that indexation is responsible for the inflation and, accordingly, that it should be abolished. Moreover, governments should declare a target of zero inflation rather than create mechanisms that make it easier to live with inflation.

The view that without indexation there will be price stability represents wishful thinking. It assumes that any inflationary shocks such as public-sector price increases and depreciation are fully absorbed into lower real wages. Of course, that does not happen easily. Without explicit indexation the government becomes the judge of what wage increases to grant. Two consequences immediately result. First, wages become politicized, and that invariably means larger rather than smaller wage increases. Second, wage increases come sooner rather than later. In fact, when a government seeks to avoid explicit indexation, as Brazil did after 1985, inflation soon becomes more unstable and prone to a far more rapid escalation than had ever been experienced under indexation.

Indexation is a mechanism that preserves inflationary inertia and hence avoids a rapid acceleration of inflation. Reintroducing half-yearly indexation may therefore be a key step in establishing the expectation of low inflation. Once the wage is locked there will not be the expectation of a very rapid resumption of inflation. As a result, horizons can lengthen far more effectively than is the case under threshold provisions or in the absence of any kind of formal indexation.

Monetary Policy

Monetary policy does not play an independent role in stabilization; rather it is dictated by the budget and by exchange rate policy. There are two possible concerns. One is that following stabilization real interest rates are too high. The argument might be made that to resume growth the economy needs reliquification. There is very limited room for reliquification, but it is best done by monetizing reserve inflows rather than by deficit finance or domestic credit creation.

The alternative is an overly firm commitment to a zero inflation target. Policymakers might be tempted to make monetary policy (and the exchange rate) do what fiscal policy has not achieved. The risk is that of a long period of extraordinarily high real interest rates and possibly an exchange overvaluation. These might stop inflation, but they will also destroy the real economy.

The best and only lasting way to bring about low real interest rates is by a balanced budget and a supercompetitive real exchange rate. It is also the only way to moderate inflation.

Whether inflation is zero or 20 percent is ultimately irrelevant. The policy of committing oneself to zero inflation is a luxury that developing countries can really not afford. Inflation should be as low as the fiscal situation and incomes policy allow, preferably below 20 percent and, certainly below 40 percent.

Policies for Growth

To promote growth, the government must go beyond budget stabilization and improve the economy's supply side. Along with efforts to make the public sector more efficient, there ought to be significant deregulation of economic activity. All the industrialized countries have taken steps to deregulate in the past decade, and there is every reason for poor countries to seek productivity gains in this direction. Beyond this general presumption, five areas need comment in particular: the trade regime, the financial sector, external debt, foreign direct investment, and the return of capital flight.

Trade Policy

Trade liberalization has been preached to Latin America for a long time. The region's economies, in search of industrialization, are overly closed, and they are closed in a very inefficient fashion. But to open them overnight is not the answer.

A sensible trade strategy involves three steps. The first is to move without delay from quotas and licenses to a high, uniform tariff. A tariff is preferable to licenses and quotas because it is more transparent. Equally important, it yields revenue.

The second step is to begin a transition to a more moderate protectionist stance. Here it is dangerous to move too fast. The example of Mexico makes the point. In the belief that trade opening would create competitive pressures in support of the disinflation program, Mexico opened up very rapidly and brought tariffs down to very low levels. Within two years the level of imports doubled even though the economy was stagnating. The import liberalization may have helped Mexico disinflate (although there is really no evidence available to support this proposition), but it created a serious problem in turn. The doubling of imports wiped out the trade surplus and thus made the exchange rate seem overvalued. High interest rates are now supporting the exchange rate, with a major adverse impact on the budget.

The argument that import liberalization very rapidly translates into export growth is simply not borne out by the evidence. This is especially the case when imports take the form of consumer goods. The lesson must be that if a country cannot devalue to adjust to an import liberalization, and if a major increase in imports cannot be financed, then liberalization must wait.

Financial Sector Reform

Imprudent, eager reform of the financial sector is as dangerous as imprudent trade reform. The presence of government deposit guarantees creates the basis for moral hazard problems that can very rapidly assume major proportions. This is not the case only in developing countries, as the US savings and loan crisis demonstrates so well.

Two areas in need of reform are commonly identified. One is financial repression, meaning regulated interest rates that often translate into substantially negative real interest rates. It is argued that a shift to positive deposit and lending rates would better mobilize national saving and lead to more productive investment. There is substantial evidence that persistently negative real interest rates do divert national saving and translate ultimately into poor growth performance. But there is no evidence whatsoever that deposit rates should be positive and high. The evidence in support of this proposition presented by the World Bank (1989b) or by Polak (1989) does not stand up to close scrutiny (Dornbusch 1989b).

Reforms to increase competition are also needed, although they present the following risk. After a major macroeconomic disruption, existing financial institutions often have particularly weak balance sheets. Meanwhile new institutions start with a clean slate and therefore can afford to lure away the best customers with favorable interest rates. The existing institutions therefore find that their loan customer pool deteriorates and their loss ratios rise. The process intensifies until the older institutions go bankrupt and are taken over by the government.

There is a strong case for more competition, but the process should not be started until existing institutions' balance sheets, one way or another, are put into a position where they can compete. It may be cheaper for the government to do the sanitation at the outset rather than allow bad debts to grow.

External Debt Strategy

Commercial bank creditors and the financial sector in debtor countries invariably emphasize that poor relations with creditors—disrupted debt service and absence of significant debt conversion programs—are a major part of a country's lack of confidence and lack of growth. They argue that along with fiscal and supply-side programs, a better debtor-creditor relationship is essential for the return of confidence.

There is little merit to the claim. The more concessions are made to commercial bank creditors, the more strained the budget will be, the more precarious the exchange rate, and the poorer the profit opportunities in the domestic market. A good debt strategy is essential for the return of growth. One such strategy is to postpone all debt service until reconstruction is accomplished.

Two examples make the point. The low prices of debt in the secondary market encourage the view that a debtor country can take advantage of bargains. Buybacks or debt-equity swap programs seem to afford the opportunity for banks to get out and for debtors to pay off their debt on terms far less onerous than the face value of the contract.

The basic point, though, is that a country that is in the midst of a fiscal crisis, and possibly a hyperinflation, has an extraordinarily high shadow price of resources. Printing money to retire debt is bad business. The same applies to a buyback operation where scarce foreign-exchange reserves are sacrificed to reduce debt burdens. For a brief time the operation may seem successful, but soon the lack of foreign exchange becomes apparent and starts exerting its own price in the budget via high domestic real interest rates.

Governments should also be reluctant to use privatization as a means of debt reduction. If there are attractive assets to be sold, the government should use the opportunity to raise cash, not to reduce the external debt. Interest rates on external debt are in the neighborhood of 10 percent per year, whereas those on domestic debt may be as high as 100 percent. For example, if Argentina were to privatize its national railroads, it would be a major blunder to allow commercial banks to participate on a debt-reduction basis. The government should use the resources from the sale to reduce domestic debt, not foreign debt.

Foreign Direct Investment

Latin America will have to rely on saving for capital formation except for the support that can be derived from foreign direct investment. In the past, intellectuals in Latin America have developed powerful propaganda against foreign direct investment, an important argument being that it creates "dependence." It is ironic that, following this thinking, Latin America plunged into debt financing, with the result that dependence on foreign creditors and treasuries is now more extreme than at any time since the colonial era. Today no Latin American government undertakes significant economic change without checking first in Washington.

It is well to remember just how wrong Latin American intellectuals have been on this point and that their error makes them in no small part responsible for the sharp decline in living standards in their countries. Foreign direct investment is a powerful source of growth. It brings money, technology, and market access, none of which can be derided in current state of crisis. Needless to say, the same message must be spread in the United States, where attitudes toward foreign direct investment are very unhealthy. Throughout the hemisphere, foreign direct investment should be seen as providing "good jobs at good wages."

Table 7.2 Estimates of cumulative capital flight, selected countries
(billions of dollars)

Country	1976–82	1983–87
Argentina	22.4	6.8
Brazil	5.8	24.8
Mexico	25.3	35.3
Peru	n.a.	3.3
Venezuela	20.7	18.9

n.a. = not available.

Source: Cumby and Levich (1987), updated by the author.

Return of Capital Flight

A common problem in the aftermath of stabilization is the lack of a stabilizing capital reflow.[1] Foreign direct investment is slow to come, and Latin America's own assets are even slower (table 7.2).

Investors have the option of postponing the return of flight capital, and they will wait until the front loading of investment returns is sufficient to compensate for the risk of relinquishing the liquidity option of a wait-and-see position. How can governments reassure investors? The common answer is to bring about a "credible" stabilization. Credibility is a buzzword used to explain vacuously why programs fail or succeed. In practice credibility comes down to high interest rates and an exchange rate so competitive that further depreciation is not expected. But high interest rates tend to restrain growth because they lead to holding of paper assets rather than real investment. A low real exchange rate cuts the standard of living and thus reduces domestic demand and profitability for all investments except in the traded-goods sector.

If real depreciation is not sufficient to bring about investment, the government faces a very awkward situation: income has been shifted from labor to capital, but because the real depreciation is not sufficient, the increased profits are taken out as capital flight. Labor will obviously insist that the policy be reversed. This uncertainty is an important feature in understanding the relationships between the real exchange rate and capital flight and the poststabilization difficulties some countries have faced.

Stabilization by itself is not enough to trigger a virtuous circle of investment and growth. There is a need for a coordination mechanism that overcomes the market's tendency to wait. What markets would consider a sufficient policy action may be beyond the political scope of democratic governments to

---

1. This topic is modeled in detail in Dornbusch (1989b).

implement. In fact, even if a government went so far as to create the incentives that would motivate a return of capital and the resumption of investment on an exclusively economic calculation, the size of the implied real wage cuts might be so extreme that asset holders would now consider the country too politically perilous for investment.

In the aftermath of a major macroeconomic shock there may simply be no equilibrium that is politically safe and economically rewarding on a scale that induces the return of growth as the response of competitive markets. Without the leverage afforded by external capital—1920s' style or in the form of the Marshall Plan—there may be little prospect of reconstruction.

Did Washington Malpractice?

Most of the discussion about Latin America's poor performance focuses on what has or has not been done by the governments in the region. But occasionally we should reflect on how much of the responsibility must be shouldered by Washington, specifically the US Treasury and the IMF. Their advice and their actions have helped shaped policy. In four areas their advice and policy have been very poor:

- The IMF took almost a decade to come to grips with the concept of inertial inflation and the resulting need for incomes policy. Better understanding of the inflation process and a less dogmatic adherence to received wisdom would have allowed more sensible discussions with Brazil, for example, in the early 1980s.

- Washington has been desperately slow in recognizing the need for comprehensive fiscal reform. The most striking evidence is that even today no manual on how to do a tax reform is available. There are no case studies that are routinely distributed in the way that Hernando de Soto's *The Other Path* has been marketed.

- Washington has been obscene in advocating debt-equity swaps and in insisting that they be part of the debt strategy. The US Treasury has made this dogma, and the IMF and the World Bank, against their staffs' professional advice and judgment, have simply caved in. When Assistant Treasury Secretary David Mulford barks, all of Washington falls to its knees.

- Washington has failed to recognize that stabilization and supply-side economics are not enough. Even today the IMF has no research available on how to proceed from stabilization to growth (see Khan and Knight 1985 and the discussion in Dornbusch 1989a).

The belief in bootstrapping Latin America into prosperity continues because anything else would be too big. Even today Washington is debating how much debt to collect, rather than focusing on the need for a Marshall Plan.

No one should take the blame from Alan García and José Sarney for destroying their economies; neither Washington nor the debt crisis in the end is responsible for what happened in Brazil or Peru. But the Washington record has been poor, and learning has been slow. Two expressions are routine inside the Beltway: "political reality" and "genuine signs of progress." The former is used to explain why one is not doing what plain common sense would suggest. The latter is handy when describing a situation that is hopelessly out of control. Washington has clearly abdicated its role in providing viable solutions for reconstruction.

Conclusion

The 1980s are seen as a lost decade for Latin America, and one fears the 1990s may go the same way. Income per capita declined by 8.3 percent (figure 7.1), and low investment in infrastructure, education, and productive capital throws a long shadow on Latin America's ability to make up ground and move ahead in the 1990s.

However, there is a positive counterpoint in the establishment of democracy throughout Latin America in the 1980s. Brazil, Argentina, and Uruguay installed democratic governments. In Chile, the 1988 plebiscite signaled the end of military rule. In Mexico, a hotly contested presidential election that same year made it plain that political opening must take place. Democracy today stands up in the face of extraordinary challenges. In Argentina, economic distress led the Alfonsín government to leave office early, allowing the next team to have a try. The transition was peaceful and democratic, without a putsch.

Democracy does not make it easier to run a tight economy. On the contrary, it lends voice and power to those left out for decades. Building an economic democracy is tricky, and the temptations of populism are always close at hand. The support of the industrialized countries can help Latin America build the economic foundations of stable democratic rule. There is an important role for the outside world in helping foster the return of capital flight. Without this capital, growth cannot be financed, and without a coordinating mechanism capital will not return. We are mesmerized by events in Eastern Europe, but we are blind to the extraordinary risks in Latin America today.

The pendulum in Latin America has swung from populism to favoring conservative candidates: Brazil's President-elect Fernando Collor de Mello and Peruvian front-runner Mario Vargas Llosa are promising a retreat from statism and a return to prosperity. If they fail, the pendulum will swing back very far.

We have an urgent interest in stabilization and measured reform. Unless growth returns and living standards start rising, massive social confrontation becomes inevitable.

Arnold C. Harberger

We have been asked in this panel discussion to draw some lessons from the crisis that befell Latin America in the 1980s. It is hoped that by paying more attention to certain basic fundamentals of economics we can avoid repeating the same mistakes in the future. The lessons that I will draw relate primarily to problems that arose in the banking and financial area, but I will also have some comments on exchange rate management and privatization.

We have seen in the past decade a lot of countries in which the banking systems have gone bad. This happened in Argentina, Chile, Mexico, and Uruguay—and in the United States as well with the savings and loan debacle. All of these crises were a consequence of bad loans. In my view, one of the important lessons from this experience is that if the government is going to be responsible for bailing out the banking system when it overextends itself, then the taxpayers deserve a seat on the board. What that means in practice is that we should have an adequately regulated banking system to help prevent the excesses that gave rise to the banking failures of the past. I feel that even this simple lesson has not yet been fully digested by the economics profession, particularly that part of the profession concerned with finance. We must be willing to pay the price for financial stability in terms of forcing banks to maintain prudence and security, to prevent them from running wild and to make sure that bad loans do not occupy a dangerously large share of the banking system's portfolio. Even when a breakdown of the system is avoided, bad loans that have to be renewed period by period are noxious. Whatever part of the banking system's portfolio they occupy is simply money that is unavailable to be lent for positive, productive, dynamic purposes.

I do not really know whether bank credit belongs in the production function or not, but I do know that it would be very costly for any country to try to do without it. It has already proved costly in those countries where, because of inflation and other sources of reduction in the size of the financial sector, bank credit is reduced to a small fraction of what it is in more normal and better circumstances. Credit greases the wheels of the economic machine, and we should not forget that.

Problems with credit have emerged both within the countries of Latin America and internationally in the form of the debt crisis. To me, the solution to the latter was fairly obvious from the beginning: each individual creditor

Arnold C. Harberger is Professor of Economics at the University of California, Los Angeles, and the University of Chicago. He has written extensively on economic policy problems and has served as consultant to the governments of Argentina, Bolivia, Brazil, Chile, Colombia, Costa Rica, El Salvador, Honduras, Mexico, Paraguay, Uruguay, and Venezuela.

bank should have gotten together with each individual debtor, and between them they should have arrived at their own solutions to the problem under the prevailing laws. Instead we have the rather anomalous situation in which the international banks that have not sold off on the secondary market are still clinging to the fiction that they are ultimately going to get repaid 100 cents on the dollar. I don't think they are going to get 100 cents on the dollar, nor should they. The international banks' debt has to be written down; the only question is to what level. Once that debt is written down, say to a half or two-thirds of what it is today, there will still be the problem of servicing that written-down debt (table 7.3). The debt is not going to disappear, and at prevailing interest rates as well as any we are likely to see in the future, it seems pointless to talk about significant positive net resource transfers from the developed world to the major debtors among the developing countries.

Some people believe that if the net resource transfer to the developing countries is not positive, then something is terribly wrong. The principal message that I want to convey here is that this is not so, that a well-functioning financial system, with loans greasing the wheels of economic progress, is one in which new loans are constantly being made to new borrowers. The whole idea is that, in principle at least, loans should be used for highly productive purposes. Interest and amortization can then be paid out of the proceeds of each project, and the borrowing entity (or nation) can still benefit because the projects yield a surplus above and beyond debt-service payments. Good loans are still benefiting the receiving country (because of their productivity) even during the stage when they are being paid off.

In a healthy capital market, a debtor country is simultaneously receiving "old" debt, with funds generated by the productivity of "old" projects, and also incurring new debt—not for the purpose of rolling over old loans, but rather in order to finance new, highly productive investments. In a sense, the payments on old loans can be thought of as the fuel that is recycled to make new loans.

What really worries me is the thought that, with a reduced level of international debt in the wake of the prospective writedowns, we are once again going to start rolling over the amortization payments on the written-down debt. Those amortization payments should come out of taxes, to the extent the original projects financed by the loans were not sufficiently productive. I agree with Rudiger Dornbusch that we need fiscal strengthening for this purpose as well as for others. This is the way in which the international credit system can be brought back to health.

This picture that I have drawn of a two-way street in which debt service on old loans goes one way, and new funds for new projects go the other way, will surely entail a net resource transfer very different from what it was in 1979–80. It is consequently going to require significantly higher real exchange rates (in the sense of a higher peso price for the dollar). I happen to believe that almost any

Table 7.3 Prices of Latin American bank debt in the secondary market
(cents per dollar of face value)[a]

Country	July 1985	July 1986	July 1987	November 1988	November 1989
Argentina	60	63	47	22	13
Brazil	75	73	57	45	21
Colombia	81	80	71	59	64
Mexico	80	56	54	47	40
Peru	45	18	11	7	6
Venezuela	81	80	75	45	36

a. Bid price.

Source: Shearson Lehman Hutton and Salomon Brothers, Inc.

exchange rate system is right for some patient at some time. One has to fit the system to the circumstances. Most countries in Latin America have seen a gyration of real exchange rates in recent years. The variability of real exchange rates was low in the 1950s. It increased moderately from the 1950s to the 1960s, then dramatically from the 1960s to the 1970s. As a result, exporters in these countries have recently been seeing signals that change crazily from year to year. What is needed in such cases is something similar to what one would prescribe for a patient who has had a nervous breakdown. You need sedatives; you need a stable environment, to calm the patient. This is the sort of remedy that can be provided by high real exchange rates that are more or less stable and to which the government is more or less firmly committed. Their function is to provide the positive signals for long-term allocation of resources. When people invest in real productive capacity, they invest for 10 or 20 years, or even more. One important role of the real exchange rate is to provide sensible price signals to guide such investment decisions.

Brazil in the 1968–79 period maintained a virtually constant real exchange rate and provides a fascinating illustration of this point. I always subtract 5 percentage points from any given Brazilian growth rate, as a kind of handicap, because of Brazil's natural advantages. Even so, Brazil performed quite well in that period compared with other countries that did not maintain stable real exchange rates.

To maintain a real exchange rate within a range one needs policy instruments. The exchange rate is a price, the solution of a supply-and-demand problem. The Brazilians found a way to maintain that price. They set the real exchange rate high and announced that they would keep it there and accumulate reserves. They further announced that when reserves got so high as to threaten to force the currency to appreciate, they would liberalize imports. That is what they did, as economists applauded and said that what they were doing was wonderful. Then came the 1973 oil crisis, and Brazil started to lose reserves. The policy response was to reimpose the same restrictions that had been previously removed. The economists stopped applauding. A better policy for Brazil at that time would have been to allow a real devaluation to ensue, as the natural outcome of the oil shock.

In any case the Brazilian situation illustrates perfectly that if one tries to fix the real exchange rate one needs at least one instrument to serve as the balance wheel; in Brazil's case it was import restrictions. However, import restrictions are not the best instrument, certainly not for the 1990s. Instead, the massive levels of debt in nearly all the Latin countries offers a much better mechanism: by varying the rate at which that debt is paid off, one can offset the other forces that are operating on the real exchange rate. One chooses a range for the real exchange rate that one would like to see prevail for a long time, and one allows the rate of payoff of the debt to be a little slower or a little faster, depending on whether other market forces are operating to make the real exchange rate rise or fall. This may require some consensus on the part of the lending authorities and the banks, but in the present atmosphere, it seems to me, such a consensus would not be difficult to obtain.

Central America provides another interesting example. In the 1970s, during the heyday of the monetary approach to the balance of payments, Dick Zecher and Donald McCloskey studied the Central American countries and showed how rapid their adjustment to disturbances had been under their traditional fixed exchange rate systems, say from 1860 to 1930. Their evidence on the speed of adjustment helped buttress the monetary approach. Central America indeed had very stable real exchange rates for a long period, and one has to wonder looking at the present circumstances how that was accomplished. Why did we not observe real exchange rate gyrations in those early years?

I think I now understand how such great stability was achieved, and I checked these ideas on a recent trip to Central America. Economists from the developed world now regularly counsel the government of developing countries experiencing balance of payments bonanzas—Venezuela and Mexico during the oil boom, Guatemala in the coffee boom—to prudently park the extra foreign-exchange proceeds abroad. This would help them avoid the Dutch disease, and later they could bring the money back as it was needed to finance productive investments when good opportunities arose. Unfortunately, recent governments receiving such advice have always agreed but never followed through. This is part of the reason why real exchange rates have recently been so variable. So what kept the exchange rate stable in earlier years in Central America? The answer is that the individual coffee growers acted on the advice that their governments of recent years failed to follow. Growers left their money abroad when prices and profits were high, and took it back when the bad years came.

I've checked this theory with at least 10 different coffee growers in at least three different countries, and they confirm that that was the way their fathers did it. My proposal of varying debt repayments as a way of stabilizing the real exchange rate—not rigidly fixed but within a range—is a way for modern governments to do something like what the old Central American coffee growers did, with good results, for many decades.

I could not agree more that fiscal discipline is absolutely fundamental to the adjustment proces. It is clearly the source of the problems Argentina has had for so many years, and in general the countries that are now suffering most are the ones that have had the most difficult time with the fiscal side, whereas the countries that have been doing well are all countries that in one way or another have faced the fiscal issue.

I think we should recognize openly that we do have a lot of good stories to tell about Latin America. Colombia has distinguished itself over the years. It stands out as a model of macroeconomic prudence in the region; it doesn't do flamboyant things, but neither does it allow itself to get trapped in some crazy extreme. Bolivia, Chile, Costa Rica, Mexico, and Uruguay are all countries that in recent times have shown the way to make positive and sensible decisions.

Finally, I want to comment on privatization. Privatization is not something to be sought for its own sake. Rather it should be seen as a potential solution to a problem. The problem arises when government enterprises are not working well. There is no urgent reason to privatize the enterprises that do work well, as has been the case with many electric utilities all over Latin America for a long time, least of all if they are natural monopolies. Privatization should be seen as a remedy for those public enterprises that are causing problems, particularly fiscal problems. In such cases the costs and benefits of the situation should be analyzed, and where the enterprise has every likelihood of doing better in private hands, one should privatize there.

It is essential when privatizing not to give away the store but to find a good buyer at a good price. On the other hand, where state enterprises are generating huge current losses, it may be better to sell them off immediately rather than wait for an improved economic situation to raise their value. In Chile in the mid-1970s, the first post-Allende privatization took place in a recession. At that time the money supply was expanding at the rate of 20 percent a month, mainly to cover a fiscal deficit, three-fourths of which came from the losses of state enterprises. I feel it was definitely prudent in the face of that difficult choice to sell those enterprises, even though the price might have been higher two years later, because the economy would have suffered a great deal had monetary expansion gone unchecked in the interim.

In the end the best approach, which I think of as the modern approach to economic policy, is one that weighs the costs and the benefits of every action under consideration, whether it is setting the exchange rate, privatizing, or regulating the credit and banking system. This cost-benefit approach may not be as flashy and flamboyant as some of the nostrums that get bandied about in our debates and discussions, but in the end it seems to be what sound economic management is all about, and it certainly is where we as professional economists can make the greatest contribution.

Victor L. Urquidi

As its subtitle states, this volume asks "How Much Has Happened?" in the countries of Latin America and the Caribbean that are supposed to have carried out adjustment programs. We have learned from the papers submitted, and from the comments and discussion, that quite a lot has happened—some countries have adjusted fairly successfully, after many ups and downs and deviations from their original plans that were caused by events out of their control. Consequently, one of the conclusions that emerges from this discussion is that, given the difficult circumstances, some remarkable adjustment has in fact been accomplished in quite a number of countries. Yet on various occasions something has occurred, such as a sharp fall in oil prices or some serious crisis on the domestic front, to upset the adjustment process.

At the same time I am tempted to argue how little progress has been made in the policy-relevant discussions in the creditor countries, including the international agencies, which have been behind the times in many respects. It seems that the whole approach of the regions' creditors to the issue of adjustment has been to say to the countries of Latin America, "You have got yourselves into this mess. Now you must get out of it. And you are not going to get much help from the outside. You are going to have to keep on paying a very high level of debt service." We have some evidence that this policy has recently changed somewhat, but the changes have not been fundamental. Although the purpose of this conference was to examine domestic adjustment policies and not the external debt, the debt is a basic issue that cannot be left out of the picture. There is an obvious interaction; the problems are interdependent.

One point that was not covered in John Williamson's background paper (chapter 2) but that other participants mentioned is the decline in the terms of trade that the Latin American countries have suffered. This decline was not an act of God but a consequence of the policies of the developed countries. The recent collapse of the International Coffee Agreement, to mention only one case, is the result of a policy decision instigated by the consumer countries. The OPEC countries likewise made such a policy decision when in early 1986 they pushed the price of crude oil down to $8 a barrel, and the developed countries seemed delighted with the result. We are still faced with the old problem of whether or not the prices of basic products can be reasonably stabilized or not, within

Victor L. Urquidi is Research Professor Emeritus at El Colegio de México. He has worked at the Bank of Mexico, the World Bank, United Nations Economic Commission for Latin America and the Caribbean, and the Ministry of Finance of Mexico and has taught throughout Latin America. He was formerly President of the International Economic Association.

certain ranges. Whatever may be the final judgment on that issue, the terms of trade have moved against the Latin American countries, except for some sudden and temporary jumps in the price of a few commodities, such as copper in 1988 or coffee in 1986. These developments made many people euphoric, but now the "normal" situation has returned. The terms-of-trade issue is one that, in my view, cannot be left out of these discussions and is indeed an issue of world economic policy.

I agree entirely with Williamson's emphasis on the need to reduce the budget deficit, however defined, to manageable proportions, and I am very much in sympathy with Rudiger Dornbusch's comments on the subject in this panel, for fiscal discipline is the key to everything else. Laxity in managing public finance has been at the root of many of the problems of Latin America, not only in the 1980s but indeed ever since the early 19th century.

I also agree that a carefully equilibrated real rate of exchange is important in the realignment of exports, in their expansion toward new markets, and in changing the export structure. But I would have liked to see a little more emphatic distinction between basic products, which do not necessarily react to a depreciation, and nonbasic products, particularly manufactured goods, which have been shown to react quite favorably to undervaluations or to corrections of gross overvaluation of the real rate of exchange. Venezuela has faced that dilemma for many years, as Ricardo Hausmann (chapter 5) showed very clearly, and many other countries have had similar experiences. A country does not export more basic products when it depreciates, given current world market conditions.

These considerations lead me to the question of how to stimulate nontraditional exports. Williamson makes too ready an assumption that by maintaining the appropriate rate of exchange—in other words, appropriate relative prices—one sets off a whole new process of successful export promotion. There are some good examples of this happening, for example, Brazil's long-term mini-devaluations and its measures and incentives to promote exports. A more recent example is that of Mexico. We conducted a study in Mexico at the firm level to find out what it is in the whole menu of export promotion policies and measures that firms react to (Urquidi et al. 1988). We found, for example, that the multinational corporations are not very interested in the export promotion measures adopted in Mexico, because they have their own policies and long-term investment strategies. In one case in Mexico, a US automobile company had clearly decided, long before the debt crisis, that Mexico was a good place to increase capacity to manufacture vehicles for the US market. Many others decided later to do the same, German and Japanese companies among them. Firms such as these are not greatly impressed by the lower real wages in Mexico or by specific export promotion measures, because their overall strategy has more to do with the possibility of introducing new technologies in time, having good transportation available, counting on ready-made external distribution outlets, and so on.

We also learned that the chemical firms in Mexico considered that the arbitrary pricing of basic petrochemicals by Pemex, the state-owned oil corporation, and its control of supply were the main obstacles to exports, and so they were not interested in other things such as tax incentives. In some industries the chief obstacle to exporting turned out to be uncertain deliveries and an uneven quality of inputs from local suppliers. But we also found that other manufacturers did respond to export incentive measures.

Thus, we have a rather mixed picture. I believe that in judging the growth in Latin American nontraditional exports, especially of manufactures, one should not look at the aggregates only, but instead perform a detailed breakdown by industry and analyze the effects of specific measures.

This inevitably raises some broader issues: What is the world market for automotive vehicles and parts, electronic goods, chemicals, and other products? Can multinationals operating in Mexico, Brazil, and other Latin American countries compete indefinitely with the Far East? One must also recognize that not all countries in Latin America have a short- or even a medium-term capability to develop exports of manufactures.

There seems to be a ready assumption among economists, in Mexico at least, that there is a great deal of idle capacity available in the region, and that all one has to do is put it to work. But what might have been idle capacity eight years ago is no longer "available" capacity today. It is no longer, for the most part, economically idle. It has been left behind technologically and probably managerially as well. If exports of nontraditional products are to be increased, new investment is needed. It will not be enough to turn a key and get the motors running in the old factories to bring about a rapid resurgence in exports of manufactures.

I agree very much with what Williamson and others have said about privatization. Presented in simple terms, privatization is a bit of a myth, and it has been pushed too far both ideologically and in terms of policy. Liberalization of trade has also gone ahead too quickly and too far—in Mexico, for example— and is promoted in much too simple terms in a number of countries—again, certainly in Mexico. This subject needs looking into in a much more detailed fashion.

I am surprised, on the other hand, that Williamson, in addressing the reallocation of resources in the public sector, seems to favor primary over university education. I can understand the emphasis on primary education, but expenditure in this area consists mostly of wage payments and is one of the major current problems in achieving fiscal discipline. I would not argue against raising the presently miserable wages of teachers, but given the general constraints, what has happened to university education, and to science and technology, is even worse and represents a real disinvestment. It would cost much less to at least maintain real expenditure on universities and research institutes than to raise substantially the salaries of primary school teachers.

On the matter of tax reform, it is very difficult to carry out a sensible restructuring in the midst of general economic stagnation. Even in Brazil, the modest average increase in GDP per capita reported by Cardoso and Dantas (chapter 4) is not really growth but a sign of stagnation. How much tax reform can take place under these conditions? What sectors are to be taxed? There are indeed glaring gaps in the tax system; however, the taxation of income on capital flight is only a remote possibility. On the other hand, we have let holders of substantial *domestic* liquid assets earn high real rates of interest tax-free. In Mexico in late 1989, for instance, a 22 percent real rate of interest could be earned on a current (money market) bank deposit, the bulk of it tax free (a purely nominal tax is collected at the source). This net income is not treated as cumulative to other sources of personal income for tax purposes, and therefore the holders of these accounts do not get pushed into the high tax brackets. Governments should take a serious look at inequities such as these and reconsider whether a 22 percent real rate of interest is a needed incentive to prevent capital flight. (Needless to say, the spread leads to borrowers having to pay over a real rate of over 30 percent.) This is a technical problem that also has its political aspects, naturally.

I can appreciate the arguments that many governments have advanced against debt-equity swaps: for instance, their inflationary potential. However, much depends on other factors, that is, on the impact of the rest of the macrofinancial situation. Swaps need not lead to inflationary expenditures; indeed, they can serve to attract additional foreign investment, to increase exports of goods and services, and, of course, to save on interest payments in the short run. Large interest payments translate into a high ratio of interest to exports of goods and services, and this is the main problem. For Latin America as a whole, aggregate exports since 1982 have been essentially stagnant. The recent small increase may not be permanent. In fact, since world trade has risen in dollar terms at a rapid pace in the last few years, Latin America's aggregate exports, despite the growing component of nontraditional goods, especially manufactures, clearly represent a shrinking percentage of the world total. In other words, Latin America's participation in the world economy has declined. The lack of export incentives arises not only from the problems of the adjustment programs themselves, and from practical difficulties in penetrating new markets, but also from international protectionism through nontariff barriers.

Finally, there are clear limits to what weak economies can do. This comes out clearly in the experience of the Central American and Caribbean economies (discussed by Saborio and Worrell, chapter 6), and we should perhaps pay more attention to these cases. But it is also true of the more powerful Latin American economies—even in the larger regional economies per capita income is not very high. The real problem is that the magnitude and intensity of the external and domestic shocks have been so great that the Latin American economies, which are basically rather weak and poorly structured, have not been able to face them adequately without external assistance. If there is no prospect of a renewed net positive flow of resources to Latin America, or at least to the major countries, it is going to be extremely difficult to carry out the adjustments. This is particularly true of countries that have suffered violent changes in external and domestic variables for which they were not prepared and with which they have not been able to cope institutionally or politically. A related problem is the preference among the financial authorities in the Latin American countries, especially the central banks, for carrying out only short-term adjustments in financial management, with no medium-term perspective.

In conclusion, Latin America is not doing well. No one in Latin America thinks any more about development, but only in a limited way about how to recover some growth. One hears high officials boasting that GDP has increased over the last few months a few tenths of a percent above the rate of population growth.

So what is the next phase? I believe there are clear limits to the renegotiation of the external debt. What will be the outlook post–Brady Plan? The time will come when no more countries will qualify under the Brady initiative. A limited debt reduction may be clearly insufficient, even though it is necessary. Where do we go from here? There must be some means of recycling all this net negative transfer back into the countries, not necessarily on a large scale, but on a moderate one that will help countries carry out their adjustment policies and programs, assuming they know what they want, that they have the required domestic political backing, and that they can exercise the responsibility to do things well.

In the last few years we have heard the Economic Commission for Latin America and the Caribbean repeating lamentations about the "lost decade," so that we seem to be at the end of the line. Will another year of zero growth or a few tenths of a percentage point up or down be conducive to starting up development? It has been said that we must redefine development. But the problem is greater than that: we must learn how to recover the loss of infrastructure, the loss in human resources capability, and the deterioration of our economies in the last 10 years, and stop thinking only of the adjustment and of refinements in the adjustment procedures.

Maréchal Bosquet, who witnessed the charge of the Light Brigade in 1854, said, *C'est magnifique, mais ce n'est pas la guerre.* Similarly we could say about what is now going on in Latin America, *C'est magnifique, mais ce n'est pas le développement!*

Discussion

William Cline queried Rudiger Dornbusch's appraisal of Mexican exchange rate policy. He, too, had worried about the peso again becoming overvalued, but how did Dornbusch reconcile that concern with his warnings about the inflationary consequences of a renewed devaluation? Dornbusch explained that the solution he had in mind was a faster crawl rather than a maxi-devaluation: this would indeed mean postponing the day when inflation fell to the Swiss level, but it could leave the bulk of the inflation decline intact.

Cline also suggested that Dornbusch's characterization of the IMF as the banks' debt policeman was outdated: the Fund had backed Mexico in its recent debt-restructuring negotiation. Was Dornbusch implying that it would have been better if Mexico had broken with the banks when it found that it could not get its original target of a 55 percent debt reduction (or equivalent concessions)? Dornbusch replied that all that would have been required for Mexico to get that discount was for the World Bank or the IMF to conditionalize its cash contribution on its achievement. In the absence of that support, Mexico's determination to avoid confrontation meant that it had ended up with only a 35 percent discount, which left it in financial disarray. Washington had let Mexico down.

Alain Ize argued that a part of the explanation for the rebound in Mexican interest rates lay in the economy's starting to overheat. He drew attention to the reintroduction of dollar-indexed debt instruments aimed at reducing the interest bill. He expressed the opinion that Mexico would have been better off with another new money package, since the country needs the money now rather than in 5 or 10 years' time, but with some contingent provisions to assuage concerns about an increasing debt–GDP ratio.

Peter Hakim sought other panelists' reactions to the Dornbusch thesis that something like a Marshall Plan is essential to foster economic recovery. Is it really true that all the pain and sacrifice will be wasted without massive outside help? Are there no examples of countries that recovered through their own unaided efforts? If so, what would a Marshall Plan for Latin America look like? And does the United States have a compelling national interest in funding such a plan comparable to that which motivated the Marshall Plan or, before it, the Dawes Plan?

Victor Urquidi responded that Latin America could not rely on a Marshall Plan, since the region was not a serious threat to anyone. It had to look to self-reliance. Given the modest importance attached to the region nowadays by the industrial countries, it would have to learn to live with a zero, or at best a very small positive, net transfer. The region would have to reorder its investment priorities and decide how to insert itself into the world economy.

John Williamson suggested that one obvious counterexample to Dornbusch's thesis that recovery requires massive external inflows was Korea at the beginning of the 1980s, but Dornbusch countered that Korea's difficulties at that time were no more than a hiccup. Williamson thought that the bigger fall in output in Latin America could be expected to create the conditions for a subsequent rebound, rather than ruling out the possibility of recovery. Another counterexample, suggested by Shafiqul Islam, was Chile.

Dragoslav Avramović attributed the one-third decline in gross investment in Latin America (which may have reduced net investment to near zero) overwhelmingly to the negative transfers that have resulted from the continuing failure to come up with a coherent debt plan. The Inter-American Development Bank's seminar held two weeks before the conference had suggested widespread resignation to the prospect of continued stagnation that this implied. He argued that the only way to improve the region's prospects was a six-year "quasi-moratorium," aiming to cut the negative transfer from some $30 billion to perhaps $6 billion per year. This would be done by suspending (or paying in local currency) interest payments as well as amortization on both private and intergovernmental debts, and even on debts to international institutions that did not disburse more than the debt-service payments they received. After six years, investment should have recovered, stabilization should have been achieved, and, if the real interest rate has by then fallen to its historical norm, countries should be able to service even a somewhat increased level of debt.

Richard Webb discussed the case for a Marshall Plan or the sort of "economic time out" mentioned by Susan Collins (Chapter 6). He agreed with Victor Urquidi that such ideas were unrealistic, but argued that, more crucially, they were undesirable. It is desperation that will cause adjustment. Any breathing space will just lead to more postponement. One can always try to design highly conditional programs with careful phasing, but the restrictions are typically evaded. Perhaps there is some danger that, faced with a clear option between sinking and swimming, some countries will not respond. He nonetheless believed desperation to be the one chance of a turnaround.

Once decent policies are in place, the danger is one of too much rather than too little money. In the case of Peru, M2 consisted of about $3 billion worth of local currency in 1986. Today it consists of $2 billion worth of dollars and maybe $0.5 billion of local currency. Those $2 billion will be reconverted and become available to the central bank, perhaps too quickly, as a consequence of any really good program. Massive remonetization has happened elsewhere. Moreover, Peru has excess capacity that can come back into production quickly, it has unused taxable capacity, and it has the potential to attract a sizable proportion of the flight capital now held abroad—far more than any conceivable Marshall Plan might offer in new borrowing opportunities. Finally, there is now a backlog of good projects that have been researched and that could be launched quickly once confidence returns.

Richard Webb's argument that "desperation is our best hope" was reformulated by Ricardo Hausmann. Economists designing policy tend to assume that they have a free hand, subject to an exogenously determined store of political will. This leads them to what may be termed the equilibrium approach to adjustment, in which some markets are equilibrated first and then policy proceeds to tackle another disequilibrium. A different path, which might be termed the Machiavelli-Hirschman approach, follows a disequilibrium trajectory, in which one asks what type of disequilibrium could gain political support for the next reform. For example, in Venezuela trade liberalization is anathema to both business and trade unions, and consumers are unorganized. The protection breeds monopolies, and then price controls are introduced to control the monopolies. Prices were freed in 1989 to counter a collapse in supply, despite opposition from ministers who feared that monopoly rents would result. But this liberalization so accentuated the conflict that it created the political will to reform trade policy.

Another example is the following: in an oil-based economy, devaluation provides a transitory solution to the fiscal problem, which thereby makes it difficult to gain political support for tax reform. It seems strange that a society faced with a choice between extremely high real interest rates on the one hand and devaluation and inflation on the other should be unable to muster the political will for tax reform, but the Machiavelli-Hirschman approach suggests that the key may be to confront society with a sufficiently painful short-run choice in order to induce adoption of policies, like tax reform, that offer a way out in the long run. Hausmann wondered how the panelists would choose to sequence their preferred set of policy reforms so as to maximize political support.

Shafiqul Islam asked what explained why former colleagues, students, and teachers who work at the IMF support policies that Dornbusch had labeled "crazy," for example, pushing Mexico to liberalize imports irrespective of the circumstances, ignoring Argentine overvaluation, or writing handbooks for debt buybacks rather than tax reform. What explains the behavior of the IMF?

Referring back to the Mexican debt deal, John Underwood suggested that the amount of debt reduction that had been achieved was about what should have been expected, given that $7 billion was available and given the secondary market price. Banks had sold the amount of debt reduction that the international institutions had been prepared to buy.

DeLisle Worrell reminded the conference of the context in which the Marshall Plan proposal had been developed, namely, that of getting investment moving again. This is a serious problem, and one that arrives *after* the authorities are committed to a stabilization program. When the sacrifices have been made and short-run reforms are in place, it is necessary to deal with the "wait and see" attitude of private investors. Perhaps a Marshall Plan—a large-scale official commitment—is just what is needed to convince the private sector that stabilization is going to stick. Did anyone have a better alternative to suggest?

Juan Cariaga noted that Bolivia had indeed been desperate in 1985. It had to overcome its problems by its own efforts. The international institutions had initially been highly skeptical: their first disbursements took a year to arrive, and in the interim Bolivia had survived by capital repatriation. Cariaga challenged Dornbusch's assertion that the IMF was trying to collect the debt for the banks: rather, the IMF insisted on its customary practice of closing the external financing gap. Bolivia escaped the need to agree with the banks first by showing that it could manage without new money.

In replying to the discussion, Rudiger Dornbusch asserted that Jeffrey Sachs had to dissuade the IMF from demanding a Bolivian devaluation a month after the hyperinflation had been stabilized: the Fund had regarded devaluation as the only way to get the current account numbers to match the debt-service numbers. The fuss that Sachs had made succeeded in getting the Fund to change its policy. Dornbusch confirmed that DeLisle Worrell had pinpointed the circumstances that he thought justified a Marshall Plan. Mexico provides a prime case in point. Mexicans have $80 billion abroad. What are the circumstances in which they might bring a substantial part of that sum back? A key condition is that the exchange rate not be a major risk factor. But how can that be when the choice is between a wage explosion caused by devaluation and a major recession caused by an attempt to restore external balance? Given such a choice, asset holders wait. This waiting will cause the stabilization program to unravel, which will confirm the asset holders in their conviction that it was indeed better to leave their money abroad. A Marshall Plan for Mexico could finance a surge in investment and provide the needed reassurance that the peso is not going to undergo a sudden devaluation. Mexico needs to do its part by introducing a value-added tax, in addition to what it has already done, so as to reinforce fiscal conservatism. Dornbusch dismissed the thesis that hope is to be found in desperation: Bolivia still suffers declining per capita income. It is the best proof that stabilization is not sufficient to restore growth.

Arnold Harberger expressed a perennial suspicion of panaceas. A prudent approach would be to identify those investments that have a proven payoff, and make sure they get done. The passage of time and the evolution of the economy will lead to a revival of the growth process. Those who call for a Marshall Plan should recall the huge flow of capital into Latin America in 1979–81, which was the origin of the debt crisis. Wasn't that a Marshall Plan? Are more new loans really advisable even before the first debt crisis has been overcome?

Victor Urquidi regarded talk of a Marshall Plan as unrealistic. He recalled that the original Marshall Plan, unlike Dornbusch's variant, provided money that did not have to be repaid. Latin America, in contrast, is paying reparations as though it had lost the war against underdevelopment (and at a higher rate than Germany had paid after World War I). If only Latin America could get even the *interest* on its flight capital back, that might be enough to turn the corner. The attempt to attract capital repatriation now is the source of the very high real interest rates in Mexico, and thus one of the main problems the country is facing.

8

From Policy Consensus to Renewed Economic Growth

From Policy Consensus to Renewed Economic Growth

Enrique Iglesias

The beginning of a new decade is an excellent time to reflect on the evolution of the adjustment process in Latin America. We are already in the eighth year of adjustment, and it is very interesting to see the direction in which things are moving. But how do we proceed from here, and what will be the final outcome? These are questions for which I do not have easy answers.

We at the Inter-American Development Bank (IDB) recently held a seminar that addressed some of the same issues that have been discussed at this conference. After so many years of debating the issues surrounding adjustment, on which ones have we finally reached a consensus, and on which ones is consensus still far away? What have been the results of the policies that have been implemented and what have we learned from them? And in what areas do we need to continue working to get Latin America out of the mess that it is now in?

First of all, I think that we do have a consensus on the nature and origins of the crisis. We may disagree on certain details, but with respect to the basic thrust the consensus is there. I think we also have a consensus on the short-term and the long-term impact of the crisis, and on the nature of the agenda for structural adjustment. I think we must be optimistic about the eventual results. In spite of all the nuances and limitations that apply in specific countries, my general view is that the region is moving in a positive direction.

After many years of following developments in the region from the Economic Commission for Latin America and the Caribbean (ECLAC), from my own country, and most recently from the IDB, my conclusion is that the crisis in the region grew out of a combination of two problems. The first problem, a deeply rooted one, has to do with the structural management of the Latin American economies over the last 30 years. The second is of course the debt issue.

Enrique Iglesias is President of the Inter-American Development Bank and a former Executive Secretary of the Economic Commission for Latin America and the Caribbean. He has served as the President of the Central Bank of Uruguay and as its Minister of External Relations.

My diagnosis of the first problem focuses on three critical errors. One is the distortion of the price system in the mixed economies that characterize practically all of the countries in the region. There was too much tolerance of inflation, and there were too many ill-conceived policies aimed at redistribution of income. This inflationary trend has been accelerating in recent years and today in many countries has become the most important issue.

The second error is one that dates back to the 1950s, namely, an overreliance on policies of import substitution. Of course, we are all generals after the battle, and at the time the question was hardly raised whether this policy was right or wrong. Yet the result was that the Latin American countries became closed economies. This closedness meant the loss of some valuable opportunities for trade in the 1970s and 1980s. Latin America is now starting to emerge from its isolation, but the cost of our past mistakes has been increased inefficiency in our economies, and for this we have no one to blame but ourselves.

Last but not least is the question of voluntarism. Our generation was one that believed strongly in the role of the state. I continue to think the state has a major role to play, but perhaps we went too far and asked governments to do too many things. I remember Albert Hirschman saying to us at ECLAC that one of the major mistakes we in Latin America have made is that we asked more of our governments than they could deliver. The recent history of the region shows that we were unable to build efficient, stable, and equitable economies. There is a great irony in this, in that many of the inefficiencies were the result of policies implemented in the name of the poorer classes that ended up benefiting the upper classes and the bureaucrats.

Of course, superimposed on this already critical situation is the debt syndrome. The 1970s was an era of permissiveness, and we must remember how easy it was to get money in those days to understand why there must be clear co-responsibility between debtors and lenders.

Since 1982 Latin America has transferred to the developed countries a net flow of resources amounting to $203 billion—that is nearly half of the region's total debt. The debt overhang remains a major problem, externally and internally, as we all know. The implications of the debt for our internal accounts is very clear, particularly in those countries (the majority) where the private debt was guaranteed or transformed into public debt, so the debt became a public problem, not a private one. This transfer of resources has generated enormous pressures not only on the balance of payments, but also on the internal allocation of resources between the private and the public sector.

The situation has two important additional elements. They are matters about which we in the region can do very little, but nevertheless they are part of the problem. One is the very high interest rates of recent years. The other is the decline in the terms of trade, which dropped by some 21 percent in the 1980s. This second external shock, over which we had no control, cost Latin America an additicnal $30 billion in 1989. My purpose in mentioning these important factors is not to assign blame but simply to complete the picture.

With respect to the impact of the crisis I think we again have a consensus. The economic decline of Latin America in the 1980s is truly sad when you compare it with the record of the 1960s and 1970s. Those decades witnessed sustained growth of 5 percent to 6 percent annually—a brilliant achievement. In contrast, during the 1980s, the region's average per capita product declined at the rate of nearly 1 percent per year. By the end of the decade, GDP per capita for the region as a whole was 8.1 percent lower than in 1980. And as we know very well, many of the countries in the region also suffered crippling rates of inflation.

Some other unfavorable trends were mentioned at the IDB seminar, and I think they are crucial in assessing the impact of the crisis. One is the lack of investment, which as a share of GDP has fallen by one-third, from nearly 24 percent in 1974–80 to 16 percent in 1983–89. This means the region's investment gap is on the order of 8 percent of GDP, or $70 billion in 1989. And this happened in spite of the fact that internal savings kept up at a very good pace. This lack of investment has a tremendous negative effect on the current and future development of the region.

Another important consequence of the crisis is the institutional damage. When I was at ECLAC, working closely with the governments of the region, there was a lot of activity going on in the various public institutions. The deterioration of these institutions in the 1980s across Latin America, with exceptions, is enormous. Central banks, planning ministries, economic ministries, public enterprises—all have been affected, not to mention the deterioration of public infrastructure, which for us at the IDB could become the main agenda in itself. If we devoted all the Bank's money to helping restore and rehabilitate infrastructure, we would barely scratch the surface.

I think there is also fairly broad agreement on the targets of an agenda of structural adjustment, although we may not agree on the instruments. Marcelo Selowsky (1989) has written an interesting paper about the stages of structural adjustment. In the first stage, according to his scheme, the most important thing is to stop inflation. This requires primarily reduction of the deficit, bringing order to the fiscal accounts. In the second stage one addresses the incentive system and public-sector reform, including efforts to increase competition through deregulation. The third stage sees the restoration of sustained growth through increased investment. I think that these stages are very widely accepted. Today when we ask how the reforms should be addressed, most will agree that the first step is a shock approach to deal with inflation, and that this implies a tremendous attack on the primary fiscal deficit.

Everyone would also agree that the second front is public-sector reform, which implies not only prudent budget policies—obviously a major conclusion of history—but also an efficient allocation of resources, efficient deregulation of productive activity, and reducing the administrative cost of raising revenues. To achieve these ends, one of the major reforms that I see happening in the future is the decentralization of government; indeed it is already happening in countries like Colombia, Brazil, and Chile. This very positive trend has implications far beyond the economic ones. I see it as a question of the consolidation of democracy. The centralized Latin American state is a legacy of colonial times. Reorganizing the state and the execution of power through decentralization is one of the major issues on which I think we must concentrate in the coming years. The other element on which we all agree is that the opening of the economy will have to continue in the future. These elements constitute probably the basic elements of any agenda of structural reforms.

Most of the real progress that Latin America has made in the last eight years is not yet reflected in the official statistics. Indeed the statistics are rather stingy in terms of giving an accurate account of what is going on. Those who have been working in the region for many years will acknowledge that there has been a major change in attitudes, and that this change in attitudes is spreading everywhere. Moreover, this is a change that was started by the region's political leaders—something that was unimaginable some years ago. Politicians who used to promote populistic policies are now taking a very tough and architectural approach to economic solutions. I perceive a change in attitude toward and a willingness to confront issues that were traditionally taboo, such as the role of the state, interest rates, and exchange rates. These things are evidence of the maturing of the region, and that increasing maturity is to me the important harvest of this dramatic crisis we are living through.

We cannot yet demonstrate many unqualified successes, it is true. One can speak of Chile, a special political case. One can mention Uruguay, and one can mention other countries such as Bolivia, Colombia, Costa Rica, Mexico, and Venezuela where reforms are moving forward. And that is something we can put on the table.

There are some specific areas in which one can point to major successes across the region. One of these is macroeconomic control. What was being done only in Colombia for so many years we are now seeing almost everywhere. There has also been significant progress toward opening up the region's economies. The expansion of exports that one sees in countries like Mexico, Brazil, Uruguay, or Chile is really very impressive.

The same is true with respect to the reform of the state. We are seeing revolutionary changes in attitudes toward the state, the role of public enterprises, and the need for deregulation, privatization, and opening to foreign investment. We must acknowledge that many things are happening in the realm of structural adjustment in the region.

Where do the problems now lie? Clearly we cannot be completely satisfied with and complacent about the adjustment that is going on. Latin America has a very tough time ahead of it. There are going to be internal problems, external problems, and political problems along the way.

Looking first at the internal situation, we do not have a consensus on the amount of time that the adjustment measures need to mature, or on the proportions and the sequencing of the instruments with which we are working. The timing question is a very important one, as the success stories in Latin America and in the rest of the world show.

The timing question is also closely linked to the question of expectations. The postponed expectations and aspirations of the public are a major political problem. It is very difficult to explain to governments starting a major program of adjustment that the process is going to take years. The political process is clearly oriented toward having results in one or two years, which is not enough time for lasting results to be seen. Hence there is a potential incompatibility between the time that is necessary for structural adjustment and the social and political tolerance left in our countries after seven or eight years of sustained reduction in the standard of living.

The second question has to do with the proportions and sequencing of the instruments we are using. There are still differences of opinion on this issue, some of which Selowsky mentioned. When we speak about the need to go through stages, we must be careful not to fall into certain traps. The stages must be adapted to different situations; in the final analysis it is the individual case that counts. For example, some economies, like Brazil, have a positive trade balance but a huge fiscal imbalance. The result of this sort of dichotomy is accelerating inflation, because the need to service the debt increases the fiscal imbalance. Analogous difficulties arise in other economies where a good fiscal situation is combined with a very tight external situation. Such imbalances in the sequencing of adjustment give rise to additional problems.

The third question is the role of external finance. A few days ago, Michel Camdessus, Managing Director of the IMF, Shahid Husain, Vice President for Latin America at the World Bank, and David C. Mulford, Assistant Secretary at the US Treasury, all said—in different words but the message was the same—that unless there is now a clear response from the international side in terms of providing the necessary financing, the whole adjustment process will encounter serious problems. I too believe strongly that debt relief and new money are important components of the structural adjustment process. Unless external financing comes in at the right moment and in the right amounts, the prolongation of this process is going to become a major source of instability.

I am worried about the time these negotiations take and about the signals that are sent by these delays in a situation that is already very nervous both internally and externally. It is crucial in organizing these processes to be mindful of the external reaction. The Brady Plan is itself a recognition that debt relief and new money are essential parts of this fragile adjustment, and unless they come together as part of the package, the process is going to experience serious problems.

There is an increasing recognition that structural adjustment is also a major political problem that requires tremendous commitment on the part of political leaders. We are still in the process of consolidating our democratic institutions. The political leaders of Latin America are being confronted with rising expectations engendered by the transition to democracy. I see this in my own country. And of course there is the normal resistance of vested interests—in the business community, the trade unions, and elsewhere. Last but not least, the institutional weaknesses I mentioned above are an obstacle to implementing reforms.

It is therefore essential that we put this question of the debt behind us as soon as possible. That is easy to say but very difficult to do. Nevertheless the slow progress of the debt negotiations is becoming a real deterrent to getting things accomplished in other areas of adjustment. The question of the pace and sequencing of adjustment thus becomes a major issue. In the case of Mexico, the mere fact that the agreement was reached—and despite all its limitations it was a very good agreement—sent a major signal to the markets. The agreement sent new signals to actors in the private sector, and it is they after all who are going to solve the adjustment issue in the final analysis. The repatriation of their capital will play an important role in solving the problem.

My final assessment of the situation in Latin America is one of optimism. I am optimistic, first, because of the new realism that is evident in the political leadership of the region. Another reason for optimism is that I think the international organizations are more than ever before conscious of their obligation to play an active role. The support of institutions like the IDB, the World Bank, and the IMF is crucial at this moment, and they should be in the front line of action. Latin America itself has the resources and the experience, and now I think we have the political will. Taking all these positive developments into consideration I can only be optimistic that Latin America will continue moving ahead.

9

The Progress of Policy Reform in Latin America

9

The Progress of Policy Reform in Latin America

John Williamson

As early as 1983, the 1980s were being labeled a "lost decade" for Latin American economic development. This gloomy prognosis has been more than justified by events: it is now estimated that per capita output in the 1980s for the region as a whole will show a decline of almost 10 percent (Economic Commission for Latin America and the Caribbean 1989b, table 9.1), compared with increases of almost 40 percent through the 1970s and about 30 percent through the 1960s. As the decade ended, the region remained mired in stagflation, burdened by foreign debt, disfigured by the world's most inegalitarian income distribution, and crippled by a continuing lack of confidence on the part not only of its foreign creditors but also of its own entrepreneurs, manifested in low domestic invest-ment and massive holdings of flight capital.

All this is true, and yet there are reasons to hope that the decade of the 1990s may be very different. First and foremost, in recent years there has been a remarkable transformation in the attitudes of Latin American policymakers. Michel Camdessus, Managing Director of the International Monetary Fund (IMF), recently remarked that whereas his predecessor Jacques de Larosière used to spend all his time trying to persuade ministers what they ought to be doing, he himself found that now they all *want* to do the right things.[1] The content and scope of this change are reviewed in the pages that follow, and have been documented in detail in the earlier part of this volume.

A second reason for hope is that democracy in Latin America has not merely survived economic tribulations that conventional wisdom doubted it could withstand, but has spread ever wider. In March of 1990 every Latin country in South America has, for the first time in history, a democratically elected

---

1. At a meeting of "Face to Face" at the Carnegie Endowment for International Peace (Washington, DC) on 29 June 1989.

This chapter was published separately as *The Progress of Policy Reform in Latin America* POLICY ANALYSIS IN INTERNATIONAL ECONOMICS 28 (Washington: Institute for International Economics, January 1990).

president. Nor is it just that democratic forms have been preserved: the democratically elected leaders of the region have begun to show a willingness to accept short-run risks in order to implement policies that they believe are needed for long-run economic revival. In doing so they have demonstrated a political courage that puts their counterparts in some developed countries to shame. They are also challenging the contention of some political scientists, alluded to by Barbara Stallings (chapter 3), that only authoritarian regimes are capable of imposing the sacrifices required to pursue structural adjustment.

Yet another reason for hope is that the developed countries are at last trying (through the Brady Plan) to reduce the debt overhang of those debtor countries that have helped themselves (through policy reform). A number of participants at the conference held that the help currently on offer is unlikely to be adequate to the needs of the situation,[2] but the fact that some help is available is unquestionably progress.

The chapter starts by a personal recollection of a visit to La Paz that in retrospect begins to look as though it may have involved witnessing a turning point in history. It proceeds to examine 10 areas of policy reform that have been urged on the debtor countries, seeking to illuminate how much agreement there is on the desirability of each objective and to what extent policies actually have been reformed in Latin America, and in some cases whether the results of those reforms justify the expectations held of them. The chapter then turns to a country-by-country examination of the state of Latin American economic thought, policy, and performance. It concludes by discussing whether the reforms being implemented are appropriate and adequate to the situation, and what else needs to be done. The material used is drawn primarily, although not exclusively, from the Institute's November 1989 conference.

La Paz, August 1985

In early 1985 I was invited by the local office of the Instituto Latinoamericano de Investigaciones Sociales to visit La Paz to lecture on exchange rates and stabilization policy. It was proposed that I schedule my visit for the next occasion when my travels took me sufficiently close to La Paz to bring the additional airfare within my hosts' budget constraint. Since economists with an interest in monetary economics do not pass up their first opportunity to visit a country being ravaged by hyperinflation, I accepted with alacrity. Chance resulted in the conditions for a visit being satisfied on 10–14 August 1985.

---

2. It should be noted, however, that debt was not supposed to be the topic of the conference, and accordingly no substantial discussion of the debt problem is presented until the very end of this chapter.

Bolivia had voted for a new president on 15 July. Hugo Banzer, a former general who had seized power in a coup in 1971 and then governed comparatively competently until 1978, had won a plurality of the vote. Victor Paz Estenssoro, who had been president three times before, had come in second. But since Banzer had not obtained a majority, the Bolivian constitution provided that the new president should be elected by the Congress. On 6 August the parties whose candidates had come in second and third had combined forces to defeat Banzer and give Paz a fourth term. This seemed an ominous portent, for in his earlier terms Paz had established a decidedly populist[3] reputation. In contrast, Jeffrey D. Sachs, a professor of international economics at Harvard, had been working with some of Banzer's advisers to design a coherent stabilization program, emphasizing that hyperinflation had historically been stopped suddenly rather than by a gradual deceleration.

The need in Bolivia for some kind of stabilization program was overwhelming. Prices had risen about 24,000 percent over the preceding year and at the time of my visit were doubling every two weeks or less. The mechanism responsible for the inflation was simple: tax revenue had eroded to 3 percent of government expenditure (1 percent of GDP), with around 75 percent of expenditure financed by the central bank. The bank's emissions were immediately converted by their recipients into dollars, which drove the parallel exchange rate and with it virtually all prices upward.[4] When I was there a dollar bought about a million pesos on the parallel market (the official rate was 75,000); the change given my host when he paid the toll on the superhighway (built courtesy of the commercial banks during their lending binge) up to the altiplano where the airport is located consisted of four wads of 1,000-peso bills. A dollar also bought two or three tankfuls of gasoline. Miners with access to the privileged stores (the "comissariat system") on a day when stocks were on hand could buy over a kilogram of prime beef for the equivalent of 1 US cent, since the price had not been raised since the 1950s. Per capita income had already fallen by more than 25 percent from its (unimpressive) peak in the early 1980s and was still declining.

---

3. "Populism" is something that is easier to identify than to define. The best definition I know is that offered by Ricardo Hausmann (chapter 5): redistribution not disciplined by a budget constraint. It would have been more accurate to speak of distribution rather than redistribution, inasmuch as the prefix implies that one takes away from X to give to Y, but the sense of the term would then have been obscure. Note that populism is not inherently left-wing: some of us, for example, would describe President Reagan's 1981 tax cuts as distinctly populist.

4. Throughout this study, exchange rates are described in the characteristic Latin way as the price of one unit of foreign exchange: this means that the exchange rate is said to *increase* when the local currency depreciates.

I gave my first lecture on stabilization policy on the morning of 12 August. I talked of the need for a program to be consistent, comprehensive, and credible, assuming that I was whistling in the dark. When the session ended I was whisked off to lunch with the six-man team that President Paz had charged with designing a comprehensive stabilization program in two weeks. I listened, scarcely able to believe my ears, as they outlined what they had in mind. It was far indeed from the combination of a half-hearted increase in public utility prices, devaluation, and a wage and price freeze that usually passes for a program when a populist finally realizes that he can no longer do things that will make him popular.

Paz's team planned to unify the exchange market and ensure a realistic, competitive exchange rate, while at the same time depoliticizing the process of depreciation by instituting a system of auctions controlled by the central bank. They proposed abolishing all import restrictions and replacing the entire complicated tariff structure with a uniform import tariff of 20 percent. All consumption subsidies and price controls were to disappear. The labor market was to be liberated from crippling restrictions on hiring and firing. The banking system was to be largely deregulated. State enterprises would be decentralized or liquidated. Pending tax reform, the fiscal deficit was to be limited by increasing the price of gasoline to the world market level. In short, Paz's advisers planned the equivalent of about five GATT rounds, six Gramm-Rudmans, and more deregulation than had been accomplished by the Carter and Reagan administrations together, all overnight.

I am not quite sure whether I would have enthused over such a program had I first learned of it in a World Bank seminar, but since I had spent the morning urging boldness on the assumption that it would be in short supply, I could hardly do other than applaud. I went on to my afternoon seminar still not quite sure that the Paz administration would really try to implement such a program, and suspecting that even if they did it would never be accepted. How unjustified my skepticism proved to be can be appreciated by reading the account of Juan Cariaga (one of the team that hosted the lunch where I got my glimpse of history in the making) in chapter 3. My lecture schedule was completed the following morning at the central bank, whose employees were notorious for going on strike to prevent the implementation of policies (such as devaluation) of which they disapproved. There I expounded the virtues of a competitive exchange rate.

Just over a week after I left Bolivia, President Paz made his now-famous "Bolivia is dying" speech in which he launched his New Economic Program, the provisions of which were contained in a single 170-article decree. Bolivia had been an extreme case of all the policy errors that have afflicted Latin America in the postwar years: inward-looking import substitution, an inability to say no to requests for favors from special interests, an ever-accommodating central bank to finance the resulting deficits, an overvalued exchange rate to fight inflation, a bloated public sector lacking incentives to economize, hostility to direct investment from abroad, and so on. President Paz and his administration recognized that this model had reached the end of the road. They swept it away with a program that combined stabilization and the most radical liberalization since Ludwig Erhard's 1948 reforms that launched the German economic miracle.

The program succeeded in stopping the hyperinflation and (eventually) arresting the decline in per capita income. Bolivia has repaired its relations with the international financial institutions and eliminated most of its debt overhang with the commercial banks. But no one can claim that the program has launched a Bolivian economic miracle. True, the country suffered a series of stunning external shocks in the months after the program was launched. In October 1985, the bottom fell out of the market for Bolivia's principal legitimate export, tin (its price fell by 54 percent from mid-1985 to mid-1986). In January 1986, the oil price collapsed, carrying down with it the price of what had by then replaced tin as Bolivia's major legitimate export, natural gas. Some months later, Argentina, Bolivia's only customer, suspended payment for its gas purchases altogether. Even the price of cocaine fell. Perhaps, given terms-of-trade shocks that in total cost the country as much as 10 percent of GDP, Bolivia did well to avoid a further reduction in per capita income. Be that as it may, the reward for Bolivia's brave policy reforms has so far been meager.

For several years after Bolivia launched its program, it was generally regarded—by those who knew of it at all—as an aberration in a continent that remained chronically incapable of adopting the policies that had led to prosperity in other parts of the world. True, Chile had done many of the same things Bolivia was now doing; indeed, it had done many of them back in the 1970s. But Chile had then spoiled it all by maintaining a system of 100 percent *ex post* wage indexation, failing to supervise the newly deregulated financial system, and adopting an exchange rate policy inspired by the monetary approach to the balance of payments, which assumed (counterfactually) that the price level was determined by arbitrage from abroad so that inflation would stop once the exchange rate was fixed. In any event, Chile was run by a rather unsavory dictator and therefore was deemed not relevant to what was likely to happen elsewhere. Mexico seemed to be changing course, but what was the chance of that surviving beyond the term of President Miguel de la Madrid? Prime Minister Edward Seaga of Jamaica had been doing things of which Ronald Reagan approved ever since 1981, but again with sufficiently meager results that he seemed unlikely to survive the next general election. Costa Rica had adopted many reforms, but, skeptics noted, it didn't even service its debt properly. Colombia had made a successful adjustment, but any success it had must be due to its toleration of the drug trade. Rumor had it that Uruguay was behaving sensibly, but Uruguay is so tiny it hardly mattered.

In 1989, however, a series of developments occurred that made it increasingly difficult to continue dismissing the reform movement gaining momentum in Latin America. The newly elected President of Mexico, Carlos Salinas de Gortari, quickly proved himself every bit as committed to economic reform as his predecessor, and put together possibly the strongest economic team in the world to further the process. As Chile approached its first democratic elections since 1970, the opposition voiced its determination to maintain the thrust of the military regime's economic policies, which were at last clearly producing results. Costa Rica's failure to service its external debt in full looked less damning after the Brady Plan was launched. Colombia's efforts to tackle the drug trade indicated that perhaps its presence was not quite the unalloyed boon that had been assumed. Above all, politicians with a populist reputation began winning elections—first in Jamaica, then in Venezuela, then in Argentina—and immediately proceeded to confront their supporters with the need for drastic stabilization and liberalization measures. The Bolivian program of 1985 suddenly began to look like a historic turning point rather than an aberration.

It was in this context that the Institute for International Economics decided to convene its November 1989 conference. The conference brought together economists from each of eight Latin American nations—Bolivia, Chile, Peru, Argentina, Brazil, Mexico, Colombia, and Venezuela—to report on the changes occurring in their countries. In addition, five countries in the Caribbean and five in Central America were discussed in papers devoted to those regions, for a total of 10 papers covering 18 countries. The authors of the country papers were asked to examine the new realism in Latin American economic policy. What do the policy reforms in their countries consist of? How widely are they supported? How extensively have they been implemented? What are the results of the reforms so far? Are additional measures needed? These are the questions that were posed to the conference and are taken up in the following pages.

Ten Areas of Policy Reform

My background paper for the conference (chapter 2) identified 10 areas where policymakers and scholars in "Washington" could arguably muster a fairly wide consensus as to the character of the policy reforms that debtor countries should pursue. "Washington" was defined for these purposes as encompassing "both the political Washington of Congress and senior members of the administration, and the technocratic Washington of the international financial institutions, the economic agencies of the US government, the Federal Reserve Board, and the think tanks." The authors of the 10 country studies presented at the conference were asked to try to give some idea of the extent to which local views on those topics coincided with what I termed the "Washington consensus," as well as to describe what reforms had been implemented and with what results. (Inevitably some authors treated these guidelines less deferentially than others!)

One danger of this approach is that it may rekindle memories of a Washington that tries to dictate to its neighbors what they should be doing. Perhaps it is no coincidence that the two authors assigned to write about small countries neighboring the United States (Sylvia Saborio on Central America and DeLisle Worrell on the Caribbean) both went out of their way to emphasize in their remarks at the conference that national consensus, not Washington pressure, is what is needed to sustain successful policy reform.

I could not agree more. Once again, Bolivia provides a textbook case in point. The six members of the team that designed the program could among them command knowledge not just of economics but of a broad sweep of history, from the German hyperinflation of the 1920s to Bolivia's own stabilization program in 1956 and Seaga's liberalization in Jamaica. They were also aware of the climate of opinion in Washington and the proposals that Jeffrey Sachs had been developing with the Banzer team (they had available a paper of his on the shock treatment needed to stop hyperinflation). As recorded in Juan Cariaga's paper (chapter 3), the team did meet with missions from the IMF and the US Agency for International Development (AID), but these missions seem to have been as skeptical of whether anything would materialize as I was. The Bolivian team designed their own program, bearing in mind the need to overcome this foreign skepticism. The fact that the program was homemade is surely one reason why it survived the brutal external shocks that followed and was endorsed by 70 percent of the electorate in 1989.

The purpose of trying to delineate what Washington thinks countries ought to do and then asking how much they have in fact done is not to encourage the habit of browbeating debtors into following foreign orders, but rather to establish whether views on desirable policies have tended to converge. In the final section of this chapter I shall offer my general judgment on that and develop what I see as the policy implications. The remainder of the present section is devoted to presenting the evidence on which that general judgment is based.

Fiscal Discipline

Almost everyone in Washington at least pays lip service to the need for fiscal discipline, despite the failure of the US government to master its own fiscal deficit. My background paper (chapter 2) argued for a double test of whether a deficit was undisciplined: *either* if it was supporting an excessive pressure of demand manifested in increasing inflation or an unsustainable payments deficit, *or* if it was leading to a secular increase in the ratio of government debt to GNP.

The latter criterion implies that except in a cyclical downturn an inflation-adjusted budget deficit in excess of around 1 percent to 2 percent of GNP is evidence of policy failure.

The conference appeared to endorse the contention that large and sustained fiscal deficits are a primary source of macroeconomic dislocation in the form of inflation, payments deficits, and capital flight. Interestingly, not a single speaker fretted about the Keynesian dangers of creating a recession as a result of cutting budget deficits. This does not necessarily mean that everyone would dismiss the usefulness of an expansionary Keynesian fiscal policy under all circumstances, or would want to tell policymakers that fiscal consolidation has no cost in terms of lower output, but it does perhaps reflect widespread agreement on one or possibly two propositions.

The first is that the recessionary (expansionary) effects of fiscal contraction (expansion) are short-lived, especially under conditions of financial crisis. The second and perhaps more controversial proposition is that, except in the very short run, it is quite possible that crowding out will be more than complete: a bigger budget deficit so undermines confidence that private investment falls by more than the direct stimulus to demand. This was of course the argument used by Germany to defend its refusal to reflate in the mid-1980s. It may have been unpersuasive in the German context, but it looks entirely plausible in Latin America.

Many of the country papers indicated a major change in the attitudes of politicians as well as economists, from a pervasive indifference to the size of the budget deficit at the beginning of the decade to heroic efforts to reduce the deficit after the debt crisis brought home the need for adjustment. Perhaps the major exceptions to this generalization are Chile, which had already come to value fiscal discipline (and had a budget surplus) in the early 1980s; Brazil, where government savings have declined by about 9 percent of GDP during the decade without most politicians showing undue concern; and Peru.

Table 9.1 attempts to summarize fiscal performance in 10 of the 18 countries covered by the conference. The 10 countries whose performance is reported in table 9.1 (and in tables 9.2 through 9.9) are the eight for which individual papers were presented plus Jamaica and Costa Rica, the major debtors in the Caribbean and Central America, respectively.

Six of the 10 countries have achieved substantial fiscal consolidation (at least 6 percent of GDP from the primary deficit): Bolivia, Chile,[5] Mexico, Colombia, Jamaica, and Costa Rica. To give some idea of what a fiscal consolidation of 6

---

5. Chile's fiscal consolidation over 1984–88 was only 3.7 percent on the primary measure, but its fiscal position is so solid (and its improvement was achieved in the face of social security reform that cost the government 3 percent to 4 percent of GDP—see Meller, chapter 3) that it would be paradoxical to exclude it from the list.

Table 9.1   Latin America: fiscal performance in the 1980s

Bolivia	Nominal deficit of 27 percent of GDP in 1984 reduced to 6 percent in 1988.
Chile	Nominal surplus in 1978–81; deficit reached peak of 3.6 percent of GDP in 1985; surplus restored by 1987.
Peru	Primary surplus of 1.4 percent of GDP in 1984-85 converted to primary deficit of 6.5 percent in 1988.
Argentina	Decline of primary deficit from average of 8 percent of GDP in 1980–82 to 3 percent in 1985–88. New effort to reduce deficit under Carlos Menem in 1989.
Brazil	Government savings fell by about 9 percent of GDP from 1981 to 1988; borrowing requirement of public sector exploded to almost 50 percent of GDP in 1988; inflation-corrected measures of deficit show no clear trend.
Mexico	Primary deficit of 7.4 percent of GDP in 1982 converted to surplus of 7.4 percent in 1988 (target of 6 to 7 percent).
Colombia	Nominal deficit of 6.3 percent of GDP in 1984 reduced to 2.1 percent in 1988. Primary deficit of 3.7 percent converted to surplus of 2.4 percent.
Venezuela	Violent gyrations in 1981–88; new effort to reduce deficit under Carlos Andrés Pérez in 1989.
Jamaica	Reduction of nominal deficit from 16 percent of GDP in 1980–84 to 7 percent in 1987, but with rebound to 11 percent in 1988.
Costa Rica	Nominal deficit reduced from 14 percent of GDP in 1982 to expected 2.8 percent in 1989. Primary deficit of 7.9 percent of GDP in 1980–82 converted to surplus of 7.4 percent in 1988.

Sources: Country studies in preceding chapters; personal communications with authors; Selowsky (1989, table 9.2).

percent of GDP means, recall that the revised Gramm-Rudman-Hollings legislation aimed to reduce the US fiscal deficit by 3 percent of GNP over six years—an aim that looks increasingly unlikely to be achieved. It is true that when inflation is brought down the nominal deficit gets a double bonus: interest payments on the public debt decline, and the real value of tax collections increases, since accrued tax obligations are not eroded by inflation before the payments reach the treasury (the Olivera-Tanzi effect). It is also true that fiscal accounting is very unsatisfactory, both because of the distortions that arise in the absence of monthly accounting under conditions of high inflation and because the losses of the central bank are often not included in the fiscal deficit (chapter 4 discussion). When all is said and done, however, fiscal performance in these six countries is impressive.

Two of the remaining four countries, Argentina and Venezuela, launched major reform programs including a drive for fiscal consolidation after the election of new presidents in 1989. The remaining two, Brazil and Peru, will have new administrations taking office early in 1990.

In sum, the transformation in attitudes toward fiscal discipline has been profound. There are still lively debates as to how the phrase "fiscal discipline" should be interpreted, and there are still political arguments about who should bear the burden of fiscal consolidation, but, in sharp contrast to the position a decade ago, the importance of fiscal discipline is now widely accepted in Latin America. Although most countries need further fiscal consolidation and a few have not yet started the process, a great deal has already been achieved.

Public Expenditure Priorities

Washington, especially parts of political Washington, tends to regard expenditure cuts as a better way of reducing budget deficits than revenue increases. Prime candidates for economies include subsidies, especially indiscriminate ones,[6] and (although this is politically sensitive) military expenditure and public administration. Some areas of expenditure are regarded more charitably, notably those having the character of investment rather than consumption and those expected to benefit the poor disproportionately. Thus, there is fairly broad agreement that infrastructure investment, expenditures on health and education, and subsidies that are carefully targeted to protect vulnerable groups should be cut back less or should even be increased. Policy reform consists of

---

6. Subsidies are said to be "indiscriminate" when they benefit all the consumers (or occasionally all the producers) of the subsidized good, as opposed to a subset who merit support by virtue of some characteristic like low income. The opposite of an indiscriminate subsidy is a "targeted" one.

keeping a tight rein on public expenditure and shifting its composition to benefit the future and the disadvantaged.

A summary of the record of the 1980s in terms of the control and composition of public expenditure in the 10 countries appears in table 9.2. Only four countries—Bolivia, Chile, Mexico, and Jamaica—seem to have succeeded in reducing public spending as a proportion of GDP. And only five countries—the same four, plus Colombia—achieved a large part of their expenditure reductions at the expense of subsidies. In Venezuela high-income mortgage borrowers were protected against increased interest rates in 1989 by a new subsidy costing some 2 percent of GDP. Only in Bolivia and Jamaica was spending restructured from the current to the capital account; the opposite happened in Colombia and Costa Rica. Health and education seem to have been squeezed at least as hard as other items of spending virtually everywhere.

The record in this area is a lot less impressive than that on fiscal discipline. This relative weakness of policy reform parallels, even if it was not caused by, substantial divergences of views within Washington. Thus, the IMF has a principle of *not* trying to tell countries the form that their expenditure cuts should take, although in practice it is distinctly hostile to subsidies. In contrast, the World Bank is inextricably involved in decisions on certain items of public expenditure, notably public-sector investments for which it lends. It has in recent years "carried out numerous reviews of public investment, and in some cases public expenditure. . . to strengthen the Bank's advice and conditionality" (World Bank 1988, 41). But even the Bank does not seem to have made the reordering of public expenditure priorities a central focus of its structural adjustment lending. DeLisle Worrell (chapter 6) suggests that the perception that Washington has any social concerns at all is rather recent and perhaps the result of its past unfortunate experiences in countries like Jamaica. The country papers make it clear that spending priorities is not an issue on which opinion has coalesced in Latin America. It is surely one that deserves more attention.

Tax Reform

Although many politicians in Washington still cannot resist the temptation to seek a tax break for some favored interest group, there is a very general consensus that an efficient tax system is one with a broad base, sufficiently simple rules to permit effective enforcement, and moderate marginal tax rates. Many of those who worry about an inegalitarian income distribution now seem to believe that base broadening is a more effective mechanism for securing a degree of progressivity than very high marginal rates, although views certainly

Table 9.2   Latin America: control and composition of public expenditure in the 1980s

Bolivia	Current expenditures cut by about 10 percent of GDP. State-owned tin mines closed, subsidies eliminated, investment increased.
Chile	Constraint on public expenditures (especially salaries and subsidies) imposed during 1970s was intensified in 1980s, including squeeze on health and education—but not defense.
Peru	Spending sharply increased in 1986–87; subsidies rose by 7 percent of GDP as inflation was combated by repressing public-sector prices. Cutbacks and price adjustments in September 1988.
Argentina	Some decrease in noninterest expenditures in 1980s, more than offset by increased interest payments.
Brazil	Current spending plus transfers rose by 2 percent of GDP between 1982 and 1988, largely because of increased interest costs. Health and education spending is poorly targeted.
Mexico	Over 50 percent of budget preempted by interest payments in 1988. Extreme austerity elsewhere, including health, education, and investment as well as subsidies.
Colombia	Little change in overall public spending as percentage of GDP, but switch from capital to current spending, including increased interest payments. Share of spending on education fell sharply. Efforts to cut subsidies.
Venezuela	Sharp swings in investment in state enterprises. New subsidy to high-income mortgage borrowers of 2 percent of GDP in 1989. Three-year program initiated in 1989 to align public-sector prices with border prices (for tradeables) or long-run marginal costs (for nontradeables).
Jamaica	Interest costs increased but other expenditure cuts severe, including health and education. Subsidies cut and targeted. Infrastructure restored.
Costa Rica	Shift from capital to current expenditure, and from social and development outlays to debt service.

Sources: Country studies in preceding chapters and personal communications with authors.

still differ on the importance of maintaining progressivity in the tax schedule (see, for example, Sachs 1989b, 118).

Such tax reforms also seem to be increasingly popular among Latin economists and policymakers. Table 9.3 reveals that four countries—Bolivia, Chile, Colombia, and Jamaica—have undertaken tax reforms directed at simplification and base broadening, usually in association with lower marginal rates and sometimes embodying a major shift toward reliance on indirect taxation. Mexico has closed loopholes in its corporate tax regime and has recently legislated further changes. Plans for tax reform are also under consideration in Argentina and Venezuela (and in Ecuador). Peru has suffered severe erosion of its tax revenue as a result of inflation (in contrast to Brazil, where taxes are indexed so that the Olivera-Tanzi effect has been unimportant).

A particular issue raised in the background paper (chapter 2) was the taxation of interest income from flight capital. In practice this income is everywhere untaxed, which has a series of pernicious effects, most notably in worsening income distribution and encouraging capital flight. A remedy would require *both* legislation to make such income legally liable to tax *and* information-exchange arrangements to permit tax obligations to be enforced (Lessard and Williamson 1987).

Too few authors responded to the request for information on this topic to justify its presentation in a table, but the situation in the four main source countries of flight capital is as follows. Argentina in the past has not sought to tax foreign investment income but is now contemplating changing that law. Brazil in principle does tax such income but makes no effort to enforce the law. Mexico also taxes foreign investment income in principle; moreover, since the conference was held, it has signed a tax-information-sharing agreement with the United States, under which the US Internal Revenue Service will on request furnish the Mexican tax authorities with information on the receipts of a specified individual from a specified source. Since the agreement does not provide a mechanism for routinely furnishing the Mexican authorities with information on the receipts of all Mexican residents, it is unlikely to end tax evasion, but it does at least represent a first step in attempted enforcement. Venezuela introduced legislation to tax foreign investment income in 1987, but in the absence of any enforcement mechanism the tax yielded no revenue, and in the interest of tax simplification it was abolished in 1989 (at the urging of the IMF).

Rudiger Dornbusch (chapter 7) complained that Washington has failed to produce a manual explaining how to do a tax reform. The complaint is legitimate. Nonetheless, tax reform is an issue that made substantial progress in the 1980s, in Latin America as in the United States. More is likely to happen in the near future in several countries (table 9.3); still more is needed, especially to reverse the erosion of the tax base caused by capital flight.

Table 9.3 Latin America: tax reform in the 1980s

Bolivia	Drastic simplification of tax system in 1986 to value-added tax, gasoline tax, other indirect taxes, and a tax on inferred wealth. Revenue increased from 2 percent of GDP in 1984 to 9 percent in 1987.
Chile	Major simplification of indirect tax system in 1975. Reform in 1984 broadened tax base and cut marginal rates, probably making system more regressive.
Peru	Revenue eroded by Olivera-Tanzi effect.
Argentina	Reform under discussion.
Brazil	Significant income tax reforms in 1985 and 1987 geared to perfecting indexation and anticipating tax collection on income from financial assets.
Mexico	Elimination of corporate tax loopholes. Tax revenue rose by 1 percent of GDP over 1982–88, during a period when revenue from oil taxes fell by 5 percent of GDP. Further reforms of income taxation recently passed by Congress.
Colombia	Reforms in 1983 and 1986 aimed to broaden base, strengthen enforcement, and rationalize structure. Revenue increase of about 1 percent of GDP by 1987.
Venezuela	Plans for a value-added tax and for income tax reform to broaden the base and lower marginal tax rates were presented to Congress in October 1989, but their approval is still doubtful.
Jamaica	Major income tax reform in 1986 aimed at base broadening, simplification, and a single low marginal rate of 33⅓ percent.
Costa Rica	Twin tax reforms in 1987: expanding base of indirect taxation and shifting tax burden from production to consumption, and simplifying income tax structure while reducing marginal tax rates.

Sources: Country studies in preceding chapters and personal communications with authors.

Financial Liberalization

My background paper suggested that Washington favors market-determined interest rates and also that it looks with disfavor on both negative and (because of the discouragement of investment and the implications for government and corporate solvency) excessively positive real interest rates. There is a potential conflict between those objectives, inasmuch as market-determined interest rates can be very high during a period of crisis involving incipient capital flight.

Several people, including Stanley Fischer (chapter 2), have suggested that my focus on interest rates was too narrow. It is certainly true that one of the objectives sought by a number of World Bank structural adjustment loans has been liberalization of the financial system, accompanied by a strengthening of prudential supervision. Such liberalization will involve eliminating preferential interest rates to favored borrowers and will thus tend to lead to interest rates being market-determined. It has also been argued that where there is a conflict between market-determined and low interest rates, the former should take precedence: insistence on maintaining subequilibrium rates will provoke capital flight. Rather than treating the real interest rate as a policy variable to be set at a positive but moderate level, the achievement of a moderately positive interest rate should be taken as a symptom of policy success.

Financial liberalization is interpreted here as applying to the domestic financial system and not necessarily implying the abolition of exchange controls. The minimal attention given to this subject in the latest *World Development Report* (World Bank 1989b), the focus of which is the role of the financial system in economic development, is symptomatic of a tendency to treat the abolition of exchange controls as a desirable but low-priority objective. However, it should be noted that Stanley Fischer (chapter 2) questioned the thesis that most of Washington places little priority on liberalization of the capital account.

Table 9.4 attempts to summarize progress in financial liberalization in Latin America. Interest rates were already primarily market-determined in six countries—Chile, Argentina, Brazil, Mexico, Colombia, and Costa Rica—at the beginning of the decade. They have since been freed in three more, although in Venezuela the courts forced the central bank to decree maximum rates at which the banks could lend and minimum rates they had to pay on deposits, while in Jamaica a supposedly free rate has got stuck. In Colombia interest rates tend to be set oligopolistically, and the government is now seeking to increase competition by allowing the entry of foreign competitors. Another important reform has involved strengthening the supervisory system in Bolivia and Chile. Little seems to have been done to eliminate credit subsidies except in Bolivia and to some extent Brazil.

Financial liberalization would seem to be another issue on which the intellectual consensus is still incomplete. Rudiger Dornbusch (chapter 7)

Table 9.4   Latin America: financial liberalization in the 1980s

Bolivia	Interest rates freed and preferential rates abolished in 1985.
Chile	Interest rates freed in 1970s. Abolition of capital controls and poor prudential supervision of financial system contributed to 1982 crisis, whose resolution required sundry subsidies. New supervisory system established in 1980s.
Peru	Banks were nationalized in 1987 and interest controls have been extended.
Argentina	Interest rates free since 1977. Fluctuations somewhat diminished in recent years, until the end of 1989.
Brazil	Some credit subsidies phased out. Large fluctuations in (market-determined) real interest rates.
Mexico	Interest rates freely determined but recently maintained high to deter capital flight.
Colombia	Interest rates largely free of government control but set oligopolistically. Some reduction in extensive subsidized credit that is principally directed to large, wealthy borrowers. Law under consideration to increase competition by liberalizing regulations on foreign investment in financial sector.
Venezuela	Government tried to free interest rates in February 1989, but courts obliged central bank to impose limits, and Congress gave a countervailing subsidy to those with old mortgages.
Jamaica	Interest rates raised and freed in 1984, but nominal rates remained largely unchanged as inflation fell, producing high real interest rates.
Costa Rica	Some deregulation of interest rates and credit allocation although pockets of subsidized credit remain for special categories of borrowers. High real interest rates.

Sources: Country studies in preceding chapters and personal communications with authors.

continues to warn against the dangers of excessively high real interest rates, and he has argued elsewhere that the only conclusion justified by the empirical evidence is that strongly negative real rates are dangerous (Dornbusch 1989a). At the other extreme, Allan H. Meltzer (chapter 2) includes an absence of exchange controls among the basic institutional requirements for an efficient economy. In between lies the sort of position recommended in the 1989 *World Development Report*, namely, the elimination of financial repression and of directed, subsidized credit flows, subject to adequate financial supervision and first achieving enough macroeconomic balance to prevent liberalization from leading to astronomical real interest rates. Table 9.4 suggests that Latin America has been making progress, albeit of a rather spotty character, toward this middle position.

Exchange Rates

There is now a very wide consensus in Washington that export-led growth is the only kind of growth Latin America stands any chance of achieving in the next decade. There is equally little controversy over the proposition that the first key prerequisite to export-led growth (or "outward orientation") is a competitive exchange rate. By that is meant one that will promote a rate of growth of exports that will allow the economy to grow at its supply-side potential. It is also fairly widely accepted that, in order to invest in production for the export market, business needs assurance that the exchange rate will remain competitive in the future. And it is taken for granted that a unified exchange rate is preferable to a system of multiple rates.

The only recent influential challenge to this view of which I am aware is that of Sachs (1989b, 114), who expresses "profound doubts" about the wisdom of a devaluation when the exchange rate is unified and the budget under control and the purpose is simply to raise the profitability of tradeables production. It is easy to agree with him that such a devaluation is pointless unless it changes the real exchange rate, and policymakers always need to ask themselves whether the target real exchange rate they seek to maintain through a crawl is one that is compatible with equilibrium of the real economy. But to oppose devaluation because it involves "deliberate redistribution . . . which can gravely undermine political support for the government" is to encourage governments to place a quiet life ahead of the long-run national good. This is the argument that was used to oppose devaluation in Chile in 1982 (chapter 3).

The importance of a competitive exchange rate also seems to be widely accepted in Latin America these days. Occasions may still arise in the course of stabilization programs when an exchange rate should be pegged to provide a "nominal anchor" even at some risk of overvaluation developing, but this is a risk of which most policymakers are now acutely aware. There is concern today in Mexico over the moderate loss of competitiveness sustained under the 1987 Economic Solidarity Pact, which has reduced inflation to about 20 percent; this contrasts strikingly with the indifference of Martinez de Hoz to a much larger overvaluation of the Argentine peso at the beginning of the 1980s.

Table 9.5 summarizes exchange rate policy during the 1980s in the 10 countries under study. Nine of the 10 are ending the decade with substantially more competitive exchange rates than they had before the debt crisis, the exception being Peru. Peru is also the only country that still retains a system of multiple exchange rates, although parallel markets with significantly different rates continue to exist in Brazil and Colombia (and existed until December 1989 in Argentina). Half the countries—Chile, Brazil, Mexico, Colombia, and Costa Rica—operate an explicit crawling peg, whereas in Bolivia, Argentina, Venezuela, and Jamaica the exchange rate floats or is "managed flexibly" (it is not clear whether these two descriptions amount to a substantive difference). Only Peru still has an old-fashioned jumping peg.

The reward for these more realistic exchange rate policies (which have in some cases been complemented by fiscal incentives and streamlined administrative procedures, e.g., for drawbacks) has been quite impressive growth in nontraditional exports in five of the countries: Chile, Brazil, Mexico, Colombia, and Costa Rica. In Argentina and Venezuela the record is less impressive, but the commitment to maintain competitive exchange rates has in the past been far weaker, and there have been episodes of overvaluation. Performance has been disappointing in Bolivia and Jamaica. In Peru, exports have stagnated, which is hardly surprising.

The present dominant view that a competitive exchange rate is a basic essential for restored economic growth (let alone for external balance) represents a sharp break with much past thought. Richard Webb (chapter 3) recounts how as recently as 1980 a member of the IMF staff tried to convince him that devaluation was pointless because it would inevitably be totally offset by inflation. The view that the exchange rate should provide a nominal anchor and that competitiveness should be allowed to take care of itself was represented at the conference by Meltzer (chapter 2) but very much as a minority viewpoint. The consensus says that the exchange rate should be managed primarily to ensure competitiveness.[7]

---

7. What then provides a nominal anchor? A fiscal-monetary policy geared at a nominal income target is what I have recommended elsewhere for the G-7 countries (Williamson and Miller 1987), and I see no reason why it should not serve for the larger Latin American countries too.

Table 9.5   Latin America: exchange rate policy in the 1980s

Bolivia	Rate unified in 1985 and set daily in a currency auction strongly influenced by central bank. Massive initial devaluation of official rate; some concern that present rate may not be sufficiently competitive.
Chile	Devaluation (45 percent in real terms since 1982) is main tool of structural adjustment. Strong export growth since 1986.
Peru	Real appreciation of more than 50 percent since 1985; multiple rates.
Argentina	Gross overvaluation disappeared after abandonment of *tablita* (1978–81), but large variations in real exchange rate persist. Supercompetitive rate in April-September 1989.
Brazil	Rate was 20 percent more competitive in 1983–88 than in 1977–82; maintained relatively constant by crawling peg (although with some recent slippage). Strong growth of manufactured exports in 1980s.
Mexico	Large real depreciation since early 1980s (at least 20 percent), but some concern over real appreciation during anti-inflation pact (since end-1987). Strong growth in manufactured exports, although weaker in 1989.
Colombia	Real devaluation of 34 percent since 1984. Long-standing relative stability of real exchange rate through crawling peg. Nontraditional exports have grown 14 percent per year since 1984.
Venezuela	Unification of exchange market in 1989; adoption of floating rate and substantial real devaluation in consequence.
Jamaica	Flexible management of exchange rate since 1983, used to achieve substantial real devaluation.
Costa Rica	Real devaluation of 35 percent to 40 percent since early 1980s; 27 percent per year growth in nontraditional exports.

Sources: Country studies in preceding chapters and personal communications with authors.

Trade Liberalization

The complement to a competitive exchange rate on an outwardly oriented policy agenda is trade liberalization. The consensus in Washington is that import licensing is a particularly counterproductive form of trade restriction that should be replaced by tariffs, without delay. Similarly, imports of inputs needed for export production should be liberalized immediately, with exporters entitled to drawbacks on any remaining tariffs on imported inputs. It also seems to be widely accepted that tariffs should be reduced gradually over time. However, differences persist over the priority to be accorded to tariff reduction, with Eliana Cardoso (chapter 6), Rudiger Dornbusch (chapter 7), Shafiqul Islam (chapter 7 discussion), and Victor Urquidi (chapter 7) expressing strongly the view that import liberalization has been over-hasty in countries like Mexico. In particular, there is still disagreement over whether it is advisable to set a timetable for tariff reduction in advance, or whether it is wiser to specify the objective of tariff reduction and then implement it in stages, the timing to be determined by the balance of payments situation.

Anyone who still thinks that Latin American attitudes are frozen in the doctrines of import substitution propagated by the Economic Commission for Latin America and the Caribbean (ECLAC) in the 1950s and 1960s should study the country papers from the conference. There may still be less messianic zeal for free trade in Latin America than in parts of Washington, but there is nonetheless a general acceptance that import substitution was pushed much too far and that countries will benefit in the long run by opening up their economies and trading more. The qualifications to support for freeing trade are similar to those voiced elsewhere in the world: the fear that import liberalization may create unemployment, especially in the short run, and the fear that if all countries try to sell more of their traditional exports they will end up worsening their terms of trade rather than increasing foreign-exchange earnings. The first fear may be addressed by timing import liberalization with an eye to macroeconomic conditions, and the second by looking to nontraditional exports, but neither implies abandoning trade liberalization. Doubtless parts of industry (as well as the bureaucracies of these countries) remain strongly opposed to import liberalization for less public-spirited reasons, but they tend not to articulate their views.

Table 9.6 records the remarkable progress that has been made in liberalizing Latin American import regimes over the course of the decade. In 1980, only 2 of the 10 countries—Chile and Argentina, both of which had eased their import restrictions under the Chicago-inspired Southern Cone liberalization of the late 1970s—had reasonably open import regimes. Both countries raised their levels of protection again in response to the debt crisis, but in the case of Chile this retreat was moderate and temporary. Bolivia, Mexico, and Jamaica have all

Table 9.6   Latin America: trade liberalization in the 1980s

Bolivia	Overnight replacement of complex, highly protective system by single uniform tariff of 20 percent in 1985; subsequently reduced gradually to 10 percent. Not a member of GATT.
Chile	Trade liberalized in 1970s. Tariffs increased to 35 percent in response to 1982 crisis, but subsequently reduced in stages to 15 percent.
Peru	Multiple exchange rate system used to provide high level of protection against inessential imports. Widespread import licensing.
Argentina	Liberalization in 1976–81, followed by new protection in response to crisis; intent to reliberalize since 1987. Tariffs reduced to maximum of 40 percent in 1989.
Brazil	Rationalization of tariff structure and reduction of tariff rates in 1988, but import licenses remain binding for many products.
Mexico	Import licensing almost universal in 1982 and still covered 92 percent of production in 1985, but abolished by 1989. Phased but rapid reduction of tariffs as well. Joined GATT in 1986.
Colombia	Gradual and reluctant import liberalization, reversing increase in protection in 1980–84. Proposal to reduce prior licensing under discussion.
Venezuela	Radical import liberalization program initiated under Carlos Andrés Pérez in 1989: most import prohibitions already abolished and tariffs reduced to maximum of 80 percent. Negotiating for GATT membership.
Jamaica	Quantitative import restrictions eliminated and tariffs lowered to 20 percent to 30 percent for most items.
Costa Rica	In 1986 Central American Common Market countries rationalized their common trade regime by converting specific to *ad valorem* tariffs, etc., and reduced mean external tariff from 53 percent to 26 percent. In 1987 Costa Rica (alone so far) agreed to further reduce average external tariff to 16 percent. Due to join GATT in 1990.

Sources: Country studies in preceding chapters; personal communications with authors; GATT, *Basic Instruments and Selected Documents*, including supplements (Geneva: GATT).

accomplished dramatic liberalization since the early 1980s. Colombia and Costa Rica have also made significant progress. Argentina and Venezuela have recently committed themselves to radical liberalization. Only Peru and Brazil remain locked in the old protectionist mode.

Another sign of the change in attitudes toward trade policy is the rising membership in the General Agreement on Tariffs and Trade (GATT). At the end of the 1970s (after Colombia joined in 1979), 4 of the 10 countries were still nonmembers. Of these, Mexico joined in 1986, Costa Rica is expected to join in 1990, and Venezuela is currently negotiating to join, leaving only Bolivia as an outsider.

Foreign Direct Investment

Outward orientation also implies a willingness to welcome foreign direct investment rather than to resist it on nationalistic grounds. Such investment can bring needed capital as well as skills and know-how, and most of Washington regards it as very silly to resist such benefits. However, there is considerable disagreement about whether it makes sense for debtor countries to subsidize foreign investment through debt-equity swaps.

Nationalistic hostility to foreign investment has waned in Latin America over the last decade, and this was reflected at the conference. Doubtless this change of attitude is in part attributable to recognition that the replacement of direct investment by bank loans in the 1970s in an effort to "maintain independence" backfired, as the ensuing debt crisis brought with it a far more drastic impingement on sovereignty. Many countries seem to have learned from history and have adopted a more welcoming policy, as table 9.7 shows. Once again, it is only in Peru and Brazil that neither policies nor attitudes have eased.

As in Washington, however, the merits of debt-equity swap programs are highly contentious in Latin America, with attitudes varying from strong support (by the government, although not the opposition) in Chile to considerable skepticism in most other countries. Even countries like Brazil and Mexico that have had extensive swap programs in the past have now drawn back, motivated partly by a conviction that the programs are either excessively inflationary or else add to the fiscal deficit by swapping cheap foreign debt for expensive domestic debt, and partly by the calculation that they involve a "fire sale" of domestic assets. Most participants in the conference seemed to find these arguments convincing, although William Cline (chapter 4) did question whether much of Brazil's inflation acceleration in 1988 could legitimately be attributed to debt-equity swaps, and Victor Urquidi (chapter 7) did argue that swaps might have a legitimate role under certain circumstances. Indeed, of the various complaints that Rudiger Dornbusch (chapter 7) voiced to justify his charge that

Table 9.7   Latin America: foreign direct investment in the 1980s

Bolivia	Signed agreements with Overseas Private Investment Corporation, Multilateral Investment Guarantee Agency (MIGA), etc., to permit foreign guarantees intended to promote direct investment.
Chile	Permitted freely since 1970s. Extensive debt-equity swap program.
Peru	Nationalization of major foreign oil producers in 1985. Remittances blocked.
Argentina	Removal of legislative barriers.
Brazil	Large stock of foreign investment in place. New (1987) constitution expresses hostility, although this has not led to concrete new barriers. Large and highly inflationary program of debt-equity swaps in 1988.
Mexico	Sweeping liberalization of regulations restricting foreign investment in 1989. Substantial increase in commitments (to $2 billion by October 1989). Program of debt-equity swaps in 1986–88; resistance to resuming swaps under Carlos Salinas administration, although a swap program will be included under Brady Plan debt reconstruction.
Colombia	Discussion of relaxation on restrictions, starting with financial sector.
Venezuela	Attitudes have become more welcoming. A substantial program of debt-equity swaps ($600 million per year) has been announced; first auction took place in November 1989.
Jamaica	Government has welcomed, but response has been modest.
Costa Rica	Welcomes foreign investment, which gets same treatment and incentives as domestic investment. Restrictions apply only to communications and a few other "strategic" industries. Recently signed MIGA protocol.

Sources: Country studies in preceding chapters and personal communications with authors.

Washington was guilty of "malpractice" in its relations with Latin America, this was the one that appeared to attract the most sympathy.

The more welcoming attitude toward foreign direct investment has not yet been rewarded by increased inflows, except perhaps in Mexico. Debt-equity swaps led to an accounting increase in several countries in 1988, but the terms of these swaps make this a doubtful benefit.

Privatization

Since the launching of the Baker Plan in 1985 both the US government and the World Bank have taken an active role in pressing developing-country governments to divest themselves of state enterprises. The principal motivation is the belief that private ownership sharpens the incentives for efficient management and thereby improves performance. A subsidiary objective, however, is that of easing the strain on public finances, both by the cash received from the sale itself and by elimination of the need to finance new investment and often ongoing deficits. Considering that state versus private ownership was for many years the litmus test of one's position on the political spectrum, support for privatization (at least where it promises to increase competition) has become surprisingly broad.

A similar transformation in attitudes seems to have taken place in Latin America (table 9.8). Mexico nationalized its banks in 1982, and around the same time several countries (e.g., Chile and Venezuela) acquired additional state enterprises reluctantly as a result of bailouts. But since 1985 only one country has deliberately undertaken a major nationalization: Peru nationalized its banks in 1987. Meanwhile privatization has come onto the political agenda in one country after another and is apparently a rather popular cause. Pedro-Pablo Kuczynski (chapter 3) cites a recent public opinion poll that found 49 percent of the Peruvian public in favor of privatization and only 35 percent against. Actual sales have been modest so far except in Chile, Mexico, and Costa Rica (and perhaps Colombia and Jamaica), but the trend is unambiguous and quite strong.

Not everyone at the conference was convinced that the emphasis placed on privatization is merited. Patricio Meller (chapter 3) was extremely critical of the speed of privatization in Chile and of some of the techniques that have been employed to further the process, which he argues have further aggravated inequality in wealth ownership. This may undermine the legitimacy of the operation and could thus threaten the efficiency benefits that it was hoped would result. Felipe Larraín (chapter 5) also expressed concern that ill-prepared privatization could discredit a program with important potential benefits. Cardoso and Dantas (chapter 4) and Cline (chapter 4) are other participants who expressed the view that privatization is being treated as too much of a

Table 9.8 Latin America: privatization in the 1980s

Bolivia	State enterprises decentralized or had their functions transferred to unsubsidized regional public-sector bodies, but were not privatized.
Chile	Already extensive in 1970s. State forced to take over many enterprises, especially financial intermediaries, in 1982–83; these have since been reprivatized (partly by debt-equity swaps). Large program to privatize traditional state enterprises begun in 1986.
Peru	Limited to a few cases where plants were handed over to employees. Banks nationalized in 1987, but several remain under effective private control.
Argentina	A few enterprises privatized successfully after 1983. Plans to privatize TV stations, telecommunications, and national airline in 1990.
Brazil	Since 1980, 17 out of over 300 state enterprises have been privatized; a bill currently before Congress would permit privatization of another 19.
Mexico	About 130 mostly small state enterprises have so far been privatized, and only 496 of 1,155 state enterprises existing in 1983 are still state-owned. The process is proceeding, with telephone company a forthcoming candidate. Limited private competition now allowed in some petrochemicals.
Colombia	Modest in extent. Reprivatization of industrial assets of Grupo Grancolombiano, a troubled bank taken over by the government. State development bank has sold its holding in the local car assembly plant to Renault, is selling a paper mill, and plans to divest all its holdings in productive firms.
Venezuela	Plans announced in 1989 to privatize commercial banks, cement companies, sugar mills, hotels, and other assets taken over in earlier years. Further privatization is under consideration.
Jamaica	Privatization of a range of state corporations including sugar estates and banks, and leasing of agricultural enterprises. Deepened state involvement in bauxite-aluminum industry, however.
Costa Rica	State holding company has been essentially dismantled and its companies privatized, liquidated, or relocated.

Sources: Country studies in preceding chapters and personal communications with authors.

panacea. I have some sympathy with this skepticism, even though I also suspect that this is the one reform of the ten that is more popular with the public in Latin America than with the governments or the intellectuals.

Deregulation

Another popular cause in Washington since the days of the Carter administration has been deregulation. The United States has deregulated its own airlines, trucking, natural gas, telecommunications, and (partially) banking over the last 12 years, to generally beneficial effect. There is also a perception that Latin America suffers from excessive regulation far more than the United States ever did. One might therefore have expected to find deregulation high on the list of policy reforms sought by the international agencies when they negotiate structural adjustment programs with Latin countries. In fact the topic does not seem to have received a great deal of emphasis, nor has it attracted very much research on what could usefully be done.

It would also seem that opinion within the economics profession, let alone public opinion, in Latin America has not yet jelled on this issue. Juan Carlos de Pablo (chapter 3) actually called deregulation the most important issue facing Argentina; but authors of two other country studies did not judge it of sufficient significance to merit comment at all. Only Bolivia and to some extent Mexico undertook extensive deregulation in the 1980s (although Chile had already done so in the 1970s); some movement has also occurred in Colombia and Costa Rica, and recently in Argentina (table 9.9). Brazil has gone the other way, or at least has adopted a constitution with Alice-in-Wonderland regulations that may not have much effect on how the economy works in practice.

It should be stressed that deregulation is quite compatible with prudential supervision of financial institutions; indeed, it makes such supervision all the more essential, as the US experience with the savings and loan industry has demonstrated.

Property Rights

My list of policy reforms that Washington could agree on recommending to Latin America was rounded out by the proposition that well-entrenched property rights are a basic prerequisite for efficient operation of a capitalist system, and one generally lacking in Latin America. I suppose that I was provoked into adding property rights to the list by an article (Bethell 1989) that derided me as a "hydraulic economist" (this was presumably intended to be an abusive term for a macroeconomist) who was indifferent to such legal institu-

Table 9.9 Latin America: deregulation in the 1980s

Bolivia	All price controls and restrictions on hiring and firing eliminated in 1985. Banking system largely deregulated.
Chile	Prices deregulated in 1970s; regulation not perceived as major problem any more.
Peru	No action, although chronically needed.
Argentina	Petroleum sector deregulated in 1989. Expectation of more measures as part of current round of reforms.
Brazil	New constitution contains additional regulations, including a 12 percent ceiling on real interest rates and restrictions on firing, of doubtful effectiveness.
Mexico	Trucking already deregulated, resulting in 10 percent increase in capacity. Process of removing entry barriers under way. Price controls still pervasive as part of anti-inflation social pact; concern about how they can be removed without jeopardizing price stability.
Colombia	Some government decentralization and simplification, but conflict between powerful pro-regulation lawyers' lobby and deregulating private sector and technocrats leaves prospects at best limited.
Venezuela	Price controls for all except 10 items were removed in 1989.
Jamaica	Most price controls removed in 1981, with prices regularly adjusted on those items (e.g., fuels) that remain subject to control. Deregulation not seen as major issue.
Costa Rica	Some deregulation of prices, wages, and financial variables.

Sources: Country studies in preceding chapters and personal communications with authors.

tions as private property, which the author was convinced were at the core of Latin America's problems. Since I did in fact believe the question to be an important one but had little idea of which countries confront a major security-of-property issue, it seemed that adding the issue to my list would be an efficient way to repair my ignorance.

In this I turned out to be mistaken. Only 2 of the 10 country studies commented on the issue at all (which is why the answers are not summarized in a table). Juan Carlos de Pablo (chapter 3) agreed with the proposition that property rights tended to be insecure in Latin America and that this was a significant problem. But Rudolf Hommes (chapter 5) argued that, at least in Colombia, property rights are already well entrenched and defended with tenacity, to the point where they constitute a major obstacle to both agrarian reform and urban development.

Although the responses in the country papers did not suggest that the issue of property rights is perceived as a critical one in Latin America, the topic was taken up by two of the discussants of my introductory paper. Allan Meltzer (chapter 2) welcomed its presence and stressed its importance. He also emphasized that property rights were merely one of a series of institutional requirements of a capitalist system, along with "a legal framework, a commercial code, and removal of exchange controls." Stanley Fischer (chapter 2) argued along similar lines:

> One of the most difficult intellectual challenges the Washington consensus faces is how to encourage private-sector development, how to create an enabling environment that is conducive to the development of an efficient private sector. The issue goes well beyond property rights, to the creation of legal, accounting, and regulatory systems, and the need for efficient government administration.

It would have been better if my focus on property rights had been broadened to include the enabling environment, and it is encouraging to find that the World Bank regards the interpretation of what this fine phrase should mean as one of its major intellectual challenges. But it is fairly clear that at this stage no consensus has been established on the substance of the issue.

A Country-by-Country Survey

In principle the purpose of the conference was conceived as being to fill in the cells of an $n \times 10$ matrix, where n is the number of countries under study. The previous section presented nine tables, each of which may be thought of as a 10-row column vector for one of the 10 policy instruments under consideration (as noted, there was insufficient discussion of property rights for this subject to merit a table), with each row representing a country. If all these tables were laid side by side, one would have a 10 × 9 matrix summarizing the results of the conference for the seven major countries of Latin America, plus Bolivia, Jamaica, and Costa Rica. In fact, table 9.10 (page 405) consists of a highly condensed summary of that matrix.

The present section looks across the rows of the matrix to discuss the situation in each of the countries. The order in which these countries are treated follows (almost) the order of the rows in each of the tables in the last section. That is, we start off with the three countries that can be taken as involving strong policy experiments: Bolivia, Chile, and Peru. We then turn to the three largest countries of the region: Argentina, Brazil, and Mexico. The two major countries that this classification omits, Colombia and Venezuela, are treated next. (In retrospect, it might have made sense to treat Colombia as a fourth policy experiment, in continuity, and Venezuela as the fourth major debtor, but this idea suggested itself only after the conference had been held and the discussants had presented their comments on the groupings as they are treated here.) The five Caribbean countries (including Jamaica) treated in DeLisle Worrell's paper come next, followed by the five Central American countries analyzed by Sylvia Saborio. The list is completed by a brief treatment of each of three countries— Ecuador, Paraguay, and Uruguay—that were, regrettably, not discussed at the conference. The countries entirely omitted from the survey are thus only Belize, Cuba, French Guiana, Haiti, Panama, Suriname, and the smaller Caribbean islands.

Bolivia

Bolivia is perhaps the most extreme case of adoption of the policies that constitute the "Washington consensus;" certainly it is so in terms of the speed with which it implemented its reforms. Tax reform required approval by the Congress and was therefore delayed for almost a year, and tariffs were reduced gradually from their interim level of a flat 20 percent to the final goal of a flat 10 percent. But everything else—restoration of fiscal discipline, elimination of subsidies, deregulation of the banking system and freeing of interest rates, unification of the exchange market and adoption of an auction system (which devalued the official rate drastically), elimination of trade controls and implementation of a uniform tariff, decentralization of state enterprises, and abolition of price controls and restrictions on hiring and firing—was achieved overnight with a single decree promulgated by President Paz Estenssoro just three weeks after he took office.

The Bolivian plan looks almost like a laboratory experiment of everything that Washington preaches—one that is all the more convincing because, as Juan Cariaga (chapter 3) emphasizes, it was designed by a group of Bolivians constrained only by what they perceived as the logic of their situation and the need to mobilize national support, with no pressures from Washington. The results, as noted above in my account of my 1985 visit to Bolivia, have been mixed. Hyperinflation was arrested and per capita income had stopped falling by 1988, and Bolivia has reestablished its credentials with the international financial community and has been helped in buying back most of its commercial bank debt very cheaply. Yet, at least as measured by the standard macroeconomic indicators like per capita GDP, the economy is stagnating rather than booming.

Perhaps things would have been quite different but for the severe external shocks (collapsing prices of tin and natural gas, and Argentina's suspension of payment for its gas imports) that afflicted Bolivia after the stabilization program had been put in place. If those factors were indeed critical, Bolivia should do better in 1990 now that Argentina has resumed payment. Perhaps the Bolivians have made a mistake in not seeking a more competitive exchange rate (Morales 1988, Mann and Pastor 1989). Or perhaps Bolivia should feel satisfied that things are going in the right direction at last, with savings, investment, and nontraditional exports at least creeping up (from negligible levels in the mid-1980s) each year. Bolivia, after all, is classified as a least-developed country; its task of diversifying into new activities, now that it can no longer rely exclusively on its traditional resource-based exports, is more similar to that facing sub-Saharan Africa rather than to the problems confronting its Latin neighbors. To demand policy changes just because a miracle has failed to materialize may be to jeopardize the chance of long-run recovery.

Chile

Chile implemented most of the "Washington" policy reforms in the 1970s: fiscal discipline (the budget was in surplus prior to the debt crisis), reduction in subsidies, tax reform, liberalization of financial markets and freeing of interest rates, unification of the exchange market, trade liberalization, welcoming of foreign investment, privatization, deregulation. For a long time the adoption of those policies by the Chilean government threatened to give them the kiss of death, partly because of the political odium the Chilean regime had earned by its ruthless seizure of power and by the authoritarian way in which it subsequently governed. But skepticism was also reinforced by the fact that the many sensible polices Chile pursued were combined with three disastrous errors. One was the lack of prudential supervision of the newly deregulated financial system. The second was the maintenance of 100 percent *ex post* wage indexation. The third was the decision to fix the nominal exchange rate, in the belief that this would lead to a rapid decline in inflation to the international rate.

In fact the fall in inflation was slow (partly because of the wage indexation) and left the Chilean peso vastly overvalued, but the resulting massive current account deficit was willingly financed for a while: those who followed Chile at that time got a preview of Nigel Lawson's argument that there is no need to worry about a current account deficit provided it is the counterpart to private- rather than public-sector borrowing. When the debt crisis came, Chile was dragged down along with all its fiscally undisciplined neighbors, its problems greatly magnified by the associated collapse of its unsupervised financial system.

Patricio Meller's conference paper (chapter 3) describes the Chilean government's response to the new crisis. He undertakes a pioneering calculation of the costs that the chosen adjustment strategy incurred; in 1982–83 absorption was over 30 percent below its 1981 level, and was still 5 percent below 1981 levels in 1988 (output recovered its 1981 level in 1986, and per capita GDP in 1989). In addition there has been a large redistribution of wealth from the public in general to the creditors of the financial institutions that had to be bailed out by the public sector, and to the new owners of the privatized concerns that were sold rather cheaply (with a double subsidy going to those lucky foreign buyers who exploited debt-equity swaps).

Nevertheless, although the Chilean adjustment was costly, it has at least been effective. This time around the Chilean authorities completed their microeconomic reforms by deindexing wages and installing arrangements to supervise the financial system. They complemented these with a major devaluation and a crawling peg to keep the exchange rate competitive. Aided by good luck with copper prices, Chile has now enjoyed four years of solid (over 5 percent per year) economic growth. It has worked its external debt down to $17.8 billion (from a peak of $20.7 billion in 1986) and its interest-exports ratio from a peak of nearly 50 percent to under 25 percent, while keeping inflation below 20 percent and reducing unemployment to under 7 percent. The thrust of current Chilean policy has been explicitly endorsed by the political opposition, which will take power in March 1990.

Before enthusing too much over the policy experiments of the past few years, however, one should remember that Chilean per capita GDP is still about 13 percent below what it would have been on the basis of the pre-1970 trend. Indeed, until 1989 one might reasonably speak of the Chilean economy "recovering" rather than "growing." And 1989 bore all the marks of an unsustainable preelection boom that will one day be cut off by a fall in the copper price if it is not reined in first by a return to more responsible macro policies. The Chilean debt-equity swap program has involved shifting much of the debt burden to the future (Meller chapter 3; Larraín and Velasco 1989). Nevertheless, once a democratic government takes office, Chile should be in a good position to negotiate a debt restructuring under the Brady Plan that will allow it to put the debt crisis behind it. It is presumably not a coincidence that

Chile was the first country to implement the bulk of the "Washington consensus."

Peru

Until 1985 Peru followed a more or less conventional adjustment strategy, attempting to continue servicing its debt in the absence of new lending. In 1985 Alan García was elected president, committed to seeking an alternative path to the austerity recommended by the despised orthodoxy. The alternative he chose was the conventional populist path: increased government spending, wage increases, price controls, subsidies to state enterprises to keep prices down, a multiple exchange rate system, suspension of debt service, and, in 1987, nationalization of the banks. With the possible exception of the suspension of debt service, a policy that might find some pockets of support in Washington, this is the antithesis of the Washington consensus. Yet in 1985 it inspired great hopes in Latin America that at last one country was attempting to find a less costly response to the debt crisis.

Some of us at the time recalled the prophetic words on populist economics of that great Latin exponent of "eclectic economics and centrist politics" (his own description), Carlos Díaz Alejandro (1981, 121–22):

> The early stages of populist governments are likely to [witness] substantial expansion in government expenditures not financed by tax collections, either because the opposition blocks efforts to raise taxes or because the government regards fiscal and monetary management as less important than structural reforms. Fiscal deficits are more likely to be financed by borrowing from the central bank than from either the domestic or foreign private sectors. Increased public expenditure will be channeled more toward consumption than investment, although in human capital formation important advances may be registered. Across-the-board massive wage increases also accompany the early stages of populist governments. Because these measures will be felt in output expansion, especially of wage goods, rather than an acceleration of inflation (which may even decline during the early stages of populism), the government will be confirmed in the wisdom of its heterodoxy. Pressure on the balance of payments in those early times can be handled by strengthening administrative import-repressing mechanisms, drawing down reserves, and seeking foreign loans. Even sympathetic observers warning of future dangers due to excesses in fiscal, monetary, exchange rate, and income policies will be dismissed by the remark that "now the economy works differently." Under those euphoric circumstances concern for economic efficiency, export promotion and a minimum of concern for fiscal and monetary prudence will be regarded as prima facie evidence of "reactionary positions" not only by most populist politicians, but also by government economists giving top priority to achieving structural reforms, or seeking a rapid transition to a centrally planned economy, or simply believing that economic efficiency, export promotion, and prudent fiscal and monetary policies are of little consequence for the welfare of most people in the country.
>
> External events may or may not add to the euphoria of the early stages of populism but frequently add to its closing troubles. The external shocks may come from a

deterioration in the terms of trade, or from hostile foreign governments intending to "make the (populist) economy scream." Even when the external shocks (or an exogenous domestic one, such as a drought) are relatively minor, they can seriously destabilize an economy already weakened by the consequences of populist economic policies.

During the last stages of populism there will be general agreement that "things cannot go on like this" and that something must be done. Within the populist coalition, some will argue for a bold move toward centrally planned socialism, thus further encouraging capital flight and a slump in private investment. Moderate populist technocrats may be able to attempt their own stabilization plans, which will come too late. The opposition will move for the kill, culminating in a military coup.

Mercifully, the (political) times have changed in Latin America, and the García presidency looks like ending with a democratic election rather than a military coup. But the economic consequences of populism have changed little, except that nowadays the disasters—documented for Peru in Pedro-Pablo Kuczynski's conference paper (chapter 3)—are on a hyper scale. In commenting on Kuczynski's paper, Richard Webb invited the conference to contemplate the reaction that would have been provoked if, in September 1988, a Peruvian government had announced that, with the aim of building up reserves by $1 billion and slowing inflation, it planned to introduce an orthodox program that would halve current government expenditures and the real wage, and practically eliminate public investment. He then remarked that anyone looking at the actual numbers for Peru a year later would be able to claim that the program had been completely successful! Without any precipitating external shock, real wages have indeed been halved and real GDP has fallen by 20 percent.

Kuczynski concludes his paper by sketching some of the steps that a new government will need to take. Here we are back on ground familiar to the Washington consensus. One can only hope that if and when a Peruvian government does implement such measures they will prove both more effective than those in the typical stabilization plan that Díaz Alejandro went on to sketch, and less costly than they were in Chile. One reason for optimism on that score is the emergence in recent years of an authentic Peruvian movement in support of bootstrap capitalism, spearheaded by Hernando de Soto. But even under the worst scenario, the outcome is unlikely to rival the disaster that has befallen Peru under populism.[8]

---

8. On the disastrous results of populist policies, see also Sachs (1989a) and Dornbusch and Edwards (1989).

Argentina

Argentina made several attempts at reform during the tenure of President Raúl Alfonsín, who replaced the discredited military dictatorship amid high hopes in 1983. The exchange rate continued to oscillate, but it was highly competitive at times and never became grossly overvalued as it had under the *tablita*, Argentina's preannounced crawling exchange rate system that prevailed from 1978 to 1981. In addition, an important drive to liberalize trade was initiated in 1987; restrictions on foreign investment were relaxed; and a few small privatizations were undertaken.

Attempts were also made to stabilize prices under the Austral Plan (1985) and the Primavera Plan (1988). In some ways, such as the attempt to ensure that prices were frozen near equilibrium levels, these plans were rather sophisticated. But they were undermined by continued fiscal deficits. What seems to have happened is that the abrupt halt to inflation through the imposition of wage and price controls put the Olivera-Tanzi effect sharply into reverse: tax revenues rose sufficiently to let the politicians procrastinate in implementing plans for tax reform and expenditure cuts and in controlling the losses of state enterprises. (The latter are truly awesome: the railway system alone loses some 1 percent of GDP, two australes for every austral it earns.) Such tax increases as actually occurred were usually temporary (typically involving export taxes), and before long the public realized that the fiscal deficit had not changed fundamentally, whereupon credibility collapsed. By the time the Alfonsín government left office, Argentina was experiencing true hyperinflation.

Carlos Menem was elected president in May 1989 in the first democratic transition in Argentina since 1930. He had inherited the leadership of a party (the Peronistas) with a long populist tradition, and he had sounded quite populist himself in his former role as a state governor (although during the presidential campaign he had scrupulously avoided giving hostages to fortune). This populist image made Argentina ungovernable for the six-month interregnum foreseen by the constitution, so Alfonsín resigned early and Menem took office on 8 July.

The new government announced a sweeping program of policy reforms one day after it assumed office, setting what is perhaps a record for prompt action. These reforms included:

- The promise of a monthly cash budget intended to produce small surpluses after debt service payments are made, backed by an undertaking that the central bank (which is to be made independent) will end all finance to the public sector and expand the money supply only as the counterpart to reserve accumulation

- A cut in public spending achieved through temporary suspension of industrial promotion schemes and rises in the prices charged by public enterprises

- A broadening in the base of the value-added tax and a serious drive to collect income taxes due

- A steep devaluation of the austral to a new fixed exchange rate

- Easing of "Buy Argentina" legislation prohibiting importation by the public sector where a domestic substitute exists

- A privatization program starting with two television companies and the state telecommunications concern.

In most countries such a sweeping program could be expected to transform expectations. But, as Juan Carlos de Pablo emphasizes in his conference paper (chapter 4), governmental credibility in Argentina has long since vanished. A program can restore hope, as this one did, but its credibility has to be earned the hard way. It must be shown that the finances of the public sector have indeed been transformed, that wrecking wage demands will be resisted, and that the exchange rate and public-enterprise prices will not be held frozen in a vain attempt to provide a "nominal anchor" at the cost of unsustainable distortions in relative prices.

By the end of 1989 the initial stabilization attempt, which had looked so hopeful when the Institute's conference was held in early November, had already collapsed. Before writing off Carlos Menem's attempt to arrest Argentina's long decline, however, it is worth remembering that the initial attempts to stop many of the interwar hyperinflations also failed. When the Menem team tries again, it will need to take to heart de Pablo's warning (chapter 4) that the orthodox portion of the initial stabilization program was allowed to lag. If Argentina finally gets the balanced budget it was promised, many of the other reforms will have a chance to prove their worth.

Brazil

A decade ago any economist in the contemporary Washington mainstream attempting a comparative evaluation of economic policies in the Latin American countries would surely have put Brazil at or near the top of the class, along with Colombia and perhaps (depending on how he or she evaluated the freeze on the exchange rate versus the microeconomic liberalization) Chile. Such high marks for Brazil are not conceivable today. Of the 10 countries whose policy reforms are summarized in tables 9.1 to 9.9, only Peru has moved more decisively away from the policies Washington regards as appropriate.

Although some measures of the fiscal deficit show no clear trend, government savings (revenue minus current spending) have clearly fallen. Expenditure is poorly targeted, both among and within sectors, and this has probably got worse rather than better. There has been no major tax reform (although tax revenues have held up well under the acceleration of inflation, aided by further refinements of indexation). Some credit subsidies have been phased out, but real interest rates remain highly variable. Apart from some rationalization of the tariff structure, protection has remained unchanged or even increased: import licenses are often binding. Privatization has come on the political agenda, but it has been slow, half-hearted, and modest. The new constitution expresses hostility to foreign investment and specifies regulation of the unregulatable. About the only offset to all this (an important one, admittedly) is that Brazil has throughout maintained a competitive exchange rate, which became even more competitive after 1983.

Even so, as Eliana Cardoso and Daniel Dantas emphasize (chapter 4), in terms of economic performance Brazil has done relatively well over the decade. Per capita income has more or less stagnated, but even this means that Brazil was unambiguously outperformed only by Colombia and Chile in all of Latin America. The social indicators (life expectancy, infant mortality, literacy, etc.) are distressing, but they are slightly less appalling now than a decade ago. The value of exports has almost doubled. The trade balance has gone from a slight deficit to a massive $16 billion surplus. For a few months in 1986, during the Cruzado Plan, there were even hopes that inflation might be tamed, until it became clear that the orthodox part of the program was totally lacking.

Does this record suggest that it is better to "accommodate" to the disappearance of external finance by printing money and borrowing domestically (as Cardoso-Dantas suggest) than to adjust to it? Is the Washington consensus wrong after all? I think not. Today Brazil stands on the brink of hyperinflation, the latest monthly rate of 55 percent ready to shoot into the stratosphere should the holders of the substantial internal debt (average maturity 24 hours plus a few minutes) suffer a jolt to their confidence. Capital flight is already estimated to be running as high as $12 billion per year. Sooner or later stabilization will have to be undertaken, and at that time some of Brazil's income gain relative to the other Latin countries is likely to be lost. Perhaps the resilience of the Brazilian private sector will permit that ground to be recovered speedily. But the longer stabilization is resisted, the greater the danger that it will be preceded by hyperinflation and a collapse of the private sector that will prevent a quick rebound.

Even if the disaster of hyperinflation is avoided, one has to worry how much longer the Brazilian private sector can retain its resilience in the face of the unreformed depredations of its government. Perhaps the most depressing feature of Brazil today is not the threat of hyperinflation, for at least everyone recognizes that this is a threat, but the widespread indifference to the failure of Brazil to start liberalizing its economy. Brazilians have for years joked that "Brazil is the country of the future, and always will be." One wonders how much longer even the limited optimism implicit in that joke will be able to survive if the winds of change that have brought such welcome revolutions in the Iberian peninsula, Eastern Europe, and the Soviet Union, and that are now rustling through Spanish-speaking Latin America, continue to pass Brazil by.

A great deal clearly hinges on the initiatives taken by President-elect Fernando Collor de Mello. He is still largely an unknown quantity, although his platform did contain some elements—notably a reordering of public expenditure priorities and privatization—that are consistent with the Washington agenda. He will face some distinct difficulties if he does decide to attempt a comprehensive set of policy reforms: the costs of protection are smaller for a large economy like that of Brazil, and up to now Brazil has managed to live off the capital bequeathed by its relatively sensible policies of the 1970s, so that the public may not perceive changes to be urgent. Moreover, policy reform will need to acquire an authentic Brazilian character if it is to be endorsed by a country with such prickly nationalism. But if Collor fails to rise to the challenge, Brazil may one day wake up to find that it has been left behind.

Mexico

It was the inability of Mexico to continue servicing its external debt that set off the regionwide debt crisis in August 1982. The immediate reaction of the Mexican government was to deflate, devalue, intensify import restrictions, impose exchange controls, and nationalize the banks (although it was not clear what the last measure was likely to accomplish). This is the opposite of the Washington consensus, as Javier Beristain and Ignacio Trigueros remark (chapter 4). By 1984–85 some relaxation was possible, and modest per capita growth was reestablished, but at the cost of real appreciation, a deterioration of the fiscal position, and accelerating inflation. Concern about that slippage combined with two brutal new shocks, the Mexico City earthquake and the fall in the oil price, to induce an intensification of fiscal austerity and a new real depreciation of the peso. Nontraditional exports responded impressively, but at the cost of acute stagflation, involving a recession in 1986 and further acceleration of inflation. It was this development that stimulated adoption of the Economic Solidarity Pact, which has remained in place from December 1987 to the present. This program, which included wage and price controls and an initial freeze (followed by a gradual crawl) of the exchange rate, has brought inflation down to about 20 percent per year.

Although macroeconomic policy has oscillated from year to year, the underlying trends are unmistakable. The primary fiscal balance went from a deficit of 7 percent of GDP to a surplus of equal size. Public-sector prices were raised to realistic levels. The real exchange rate is still at least 20 percent to 25 percent more competitive than at the start of the decade (and, using a wage deflator, substantially more competitive than that). Even more impressive than the macro adjustment is the revolution in micro policy that got under way after the initial panic reaction. Mexico has joined the GATT, progressively eliminated the near-universal import licensing that prevailed at the beginning of the de la Madrid administration in 1983, and reduced tariffs to a maximum of 20 percent. It has greatly liberalized restrictions on foreign direct investment. It has undertaken a substantial privatization program. And it has deregulated trucking and dismantled some entry barriers.

In July 1989, Mexico reached agreement with its commercial bank creditors on a comprehensive debt reconstruction under the terms of the Brady Plan, achieving some reduction in both its total indebtedness and the cash flow needed to service its debt. The terms were not as good as those originally sought by the Mexican negotiators (which was doubtless not a surprise to them), but evidently the private sector found them sufficiently reassuring to repatriate a significant sum of flight capital. This in turn gave the Mexican authorities the chance to push interest rates down no less than 22 percentage points in a single month. The return of flight capital combined with a significant pickup in investment suggested that entrepreneurial confidence was reviving and growth was coming into sight. There remained the nontrivial problems of dismantling the wage-price controls imposed under the Pact and securing the real depreciation of 10 percent or so needed to ensure continuing rapid export growth without rekindling the inflationary fires. But in August 1989 it was reasonable to hope that Mexico might at last be about to put the debt crisis behind it.

Recent months have been less encouraging. It seems that the banks' choices from among the options available to them under the debt-restructuring agreement are proving so different from those expected as to complicate finalization of the deal. This has eroded confidence again and tended to push interest rates back up. With luck these difficulties will soon be resolved, and the reward for Mexico's sacrifices will be a period of substantial growth. But the current delicate state of Mexico serves to remind one of the truth of a proposition that many delegates to the conference succeeded in voicing, despite the insistence of the organizers that this was not what this particular conference was about, namely, that the most zealous reforms on the part of the debtor countries will need some cooperation from their creditors in order to bear fruit.

Colombia

Had Colombia been included among the countries undertaking policy experiments, it would have been as an experiment in continuity. It was the only one of the larger Latin American countries that even tried to resist the temptation to exaggerate its transitory good fortune in the late 1970s through heavy borrowing, but instead tried to save for a rainy day. This is surely the main reason why Colombia is the only major borrower in Latin America to have avoided rescheduling. To prevent the destruction of its nontraditional export industries during the easy years, it maintained exchange controls and allowed the dollar to go to a discount on the black market. In the end Colombia overoptimistically tried to spend its way through the 1980–82 recession, and by 1983 the country found itself with an excessive budget deficit (6 percent of GDP) and a moderately overvalued currency. But over the years that followed it reestablished fiscal discipline without a crisis and devalued the peso by 34 percent in real terms without abandoning the crawling peg that has now operated uninterrupted for over 22 years.

Avoidance of the drastic policy lurches that the rest of Latin America has suffered is presumably the main reason Colombia is ending the decade with the region's best growth record.[9] But even 1.5 percent per capita per year is hardly a brilliant performance. One possible explanation is that Colombia has maintained continuity of its microeconomic as well as its macroeconomic policies, and these have been less benign. It continues to offer subsidized credit to privileged (usually rich) borrowers, to allow an oligopolistic banking cartel to set interest rates, to impose extensive import controls, to discourage foreign direct investment, and to maintain many regulations and a large state sector. The traditional Latin statist model has begun to be nibbled away at the edges—Colombians have been given a taste of privatization, there has been discussion of allowing new (foreign) competition in banking, and there has been some gradual and reluctant import liberalization—but no sharp break has happened yet or is being contemplated. Perhaps, then, it is not surprising that per capita growth is only 1.5 percent per year despite competent macroeconomic management.

Could a critic of the Washington consensus turn this argument around and claim that the preservation of positive growth in Colombia is due to its retention of the statist model, while its modest rate reflects the unreasonable caution of its

---

9. An alternative explanation might point to the boom in narcotics exports, but if that is the main factor, it is difficult to explain why Bolivia and Peru—both of which earn a larger proportion of their export income from drugs—have had such a disastrous decade. Indeed, some Colombians claim that the costs of combating the drug trade exceed the income it yields, so that it is a net drag on the economy.

macro management? I do not think so. On that hypothesis Peru should have outperformed Colombia, not sunk to the other end of the achievement scale.

The consistency of Colombia's macro policy has much to teach the rest of Latin America (and countries more distant). But its micro policies badly need reform. Rudolf Hommes's conference paper (chapter 5) indicates that many Colombian economists share that view. Let us hope that they get a chance to make their voice heard when Colombia can once again turn aside from its present preoccupation with battling the drug barons to plan new economic reforms.

Venezuela

Venezuela's statist, oil-driven economy had already run into stagflationary problems before the first oil price decline in 1981–83 created a need for adjustment. From then until the beginning of 1989 policy was rather erratic. The fiscal deficit gyrated as cuts in public investment in the name of fiscal discipline were succeeded by increases in public investment in the name of growth, and devaluation was achieved half-heartedly under a multiple exchange rate system instituted to prevent sensitive sectors from suffering too much.

In January 1989 Venezuela was surprised to discover that the first action of its new president, the former populist Carlos Andrés Pérez, was to implement a drastic, comprehensive program embracing both stabilization and liberalization. Fiscal policy was tightened; public-sector prices were raised sharply; plans for tax reform were drawn up; an attempt (circumscribed by judicial support for a constitutional challenge to the new policy) was made to free interest rates; the exchange market was unified and the bolivar floated, resulting in a large real devaluation; a radical trade liberalization program was announced, starting with the tariffication of quotas; privatization was put on the agenda; attitudes toward inward direct investment became more welcoming.

Venezuelans, however, did not welcome the program. The initial announcement provoked bloody riots in the streets of Caracas. Ricardo Hausmann (chapter 5) reports that public support for the program, especially for projects like tax reform, remains weak. He recounts a particularly depressing incident in which the Congress passed a law shielding high-income mortgage borrowers from the consequences of the rise in interest rates, at a cost of about 2 percent of GDP. Populism is bad enough when its favors are directed at the poor, but populism for the privileged can only make one despair.

The Pérez government has made a brave attempt to institute the sort of policy reforms that "Washington" thinks are needed. But it is too early yet to be sure that it is going to succeed in making those reforms stick. In the final session of the conference, Richard Webb ruminated on how a major reform program often comes about only as a response to desperation. Before Pérez, Venezuelans (in dramatic contrast to the Bolivians) had been experiencing not a crisis, but an artificial prosperity maintained by huge subsidies financed from fast-depleting currency reserves. The situation was indeed unsustainable, but the absence of an open crisis made it difficult for the public to accept the need for drastic corrective measures (Larraín, chapter 5). Discouraging as the thought is, one cannot help wondering whether Venezuela has yet suffered enough to shake it out of a complacency built on years of easy oil money and to allow a radical set of reforms to take root.

Barbados

Barbados has managed its affairs conservatively in the 23 years since independence. With an economy fueled primarily by tourism, it has become a high-income developing country, although growth faltered in the 1980s. Perhaps because it never embraced populist statism, it has not inaugurated a major program to implement policy reforms. The Barbadian government agrees that large budget deficits should be avoided, although it does not always succeed in keeping them as small as might be desired. Its expenditure priorities broadly match those of the Washington consensus. It has lowered the burden of direct taxation and shifted it to indirect taxation. The financial sector is oligopolistic but has, at least until recently, produced moderately positive real interest rates. The government would like its fixed exchange rate to become more competitive, but it has not yet decided that the margin of overvaluation is large enough to justify the risks of destabilization that a nominal devaluation would entail. Trade liberalization is under study. Foreign investment is welcome. Deregulation is not an issue, save for the need to strengthen prudential supervision in the financial sector. Privatization is acceptable in principle but has not yet been implemented.

It all sounds rather like a typical OECD country in an earlier decade. Yet a number of those countries did at times get into trouble when they attempted to combine central bank financing of budget deficits that were rather larger than intended *ex ante* with a commitment to a fixed exchange rate that gradually became uncompetitive. Unless timely action is taken, the day may come when Barbados is faced with the need for a stabilization program.

Dominican Republic

The Dominican Republic was forced by adverse external developments to adopt a stabilization program in 1982. For the next three years the government moved, if rather indecisively, toward selective implementation of the Washington agenda. But its efforts brought recession in 1985, and this doubtless contributed to the opposition's victory in the 1986 election. The new government was much less sympathetic to the Washington agenda. Modest progress has been made toward reducing the fiscal deficit, but subsidies remain large, subsidized credit remains available for favored activities, the exchange rate was pegged and exchange controls were reimposed in 1987, and the closest the country got to trade liberalization was the establishment of some free trade zones. The replacement of a miscellany of indirect taxes by a modified value-added tax is the only policy reform that the Dominican Republic has enacted since 1986. After a temporary growth surge in 1987, per capita income has again declined while inflation has accelerated and public utility services have deteriorated (manifest particularly in an erratic electricity supply).

Guyana

Guyana is a country reduced to penury by past statist mismanagement. Power outages are chronic, transport and communications are unreliable, social services have declined, the country has been suspended by the IMF for failure to service its debt to the Fund, and GDP per capita has fallen perhaps 35 percent over the decade. A recent report cited by DeLisle Worrell (chapter 6) warns that—in a country originally colonized by the Dutch, where most of the settled land is below sea level—the sea defenses are in an alarming state of disrepair. The fiscal deficit equaled 37 percent of GDP in 1988.

In this desperate environment a government committed to policy reform took office in 1988. It has reduced employment in the public sector and sought to privatize or close loss-making state enterprises. Interest rates are now being managed to secure a positive real rate, and the exchange rate is adjusted regularly to keep it competitive. The extensive system of trade and price controls is being dismantled. Foreign direct investment is welcome. Worrell's paper reports a lack of public enthusiasm for the new direction of policy, and it is too soon yet to know what results it may bring. The change of policy has, however, stimulated the creation of an international support group intended to restore Guyana to eligibility to borrow from the IMF.

Jamaica

Jamaica undertook extensive if reluctant adjustment actions under the tutelage of the IMF in the late 1970s. When Edward Seaga replaced Michael Manley as Prime Minister in 1980, much the same macroeconomic policies were pursued, but out of conviction as well as necessity, and were combined with microeconomic liberalization. Trade has been significantly liberalized, privatization has been attempted, subsidies are now targeted, foreign direct investment has been welcomed, and tax reform has been introduced. The payoff for these policy reforms has so far been mixed: inflation has fallen to single digits, and per capita growth was positive in 1986-87, but the social indicators have deteriorated, investment remains low, the payments position is still fragile, and in 1988-89 per capita income edged down again. Jamaica is another country where the benefits from a determined program of policy reform are still modest. Nevertheless, when Manley turned the tables and beat Seaga in the 1988 elections, his first act was to promise to maintain and deepen, rather than reverse, Seaga's policy reforms.

Trinidad and Tobago

The easy years for Trinidad and Tobago, an oil-exporting country, ended when the oil price began to decline in 1982. Adjustment policies were rather indecisive from then until 1986, when the major oil price fall made further procrastination impossible. A new government took office later that year and introduced a comprehensive program of stabilization and liberalization in 1987. The fiscal deficit is being tackled by reducing employment and wages in the public sector, imposing user charges, increasing public utility prices, implementing tax reform, and cutting subsidies to state enterprises. The exchange rate is now managed to preserve competitiveness, the currency having been devalued sharply at the end of 1985. Trade is being liberalized, and there has been some deregulation of the financial markets. The government is now seeking private-sector partners for new investments rather than further expansion of the state enterprises, which are being pruned back through rationalization, divestiture, and closure. However, this program has not yet succeeded in arresting the fall in income that has persisted through the whole decade (a cumulative decline of over 40 percent in per capita terms), let alone in securing a renewal of growth.

Costa Rica

Costa Rica encountered its own debt crisis in 1980–82, some time before the rest of Latin America. The government of Luis Alberto Monge initiated a serious stabilization plan in 1983, and it and its successor subsequently undertook a series of liberalization policies. The country has achieved an impressive reduction in the fiscal deficit; has reduced subsidies; has implemented a tax reform; has achieved and maintained a competitive exchange rate; has undertaken a significant liberalization of trade; and has privatized a series of enterprises formerly owned by the state holding company. The results have been positive: growth has averaged 4.5 percent per year for the last four years, and inflation has remained under 20 percent, while nontraditional exports have grown at an average rate of 27 percent per year. Nevertheless, both the fiscal position and the balance of payments remain vulnerable. Too many of the economies in government expenditure have been temporary, and the courts have begun awarding large wage increases to workers in the public sector, so that the ability to consolidate the fiscal improvement is open to doubt. Moreover, full servicing of Costa Rica's debt would not have permitted the growth rates actually realized. The Brady Plan debt restructuring recently agreed upon with the commercial banks is intended not to reduce the negative transfer from Costa Rica, but to provide a legal basis for the cut that has already occurred, in the hope that this will reinforce confidence and permit the consolidation of growth.

El Salvador

The economy of El Salvador has stagnated for the past decade, buffeted by the internal insurrection and cosseted by the indiscriminate subsidies that Washington (the AID in particular) was provoked into providing. In 1989 the new administration did, however, announce what sounded like a standard set of "Washington" plans for reform. These envisage a reduction in the budget deficit, to be achieved by eliminating subsidies, cutting expenditure, increasing taxes, and improving tax administration; monetary restraint and positive real interest rates; a two-tier foreign exchange market that gives some role to market forces (a devaluation has already occurred); a measure of trade liberalization; and the deregulation of most prices. The program aims to protect the poor and to reduce absolute poverty. However, as Sylvia Saborio (chapter 6) implies, it is unrealistic to expect El Salvador to give high priority to long-term economic reform at a time when its security is threatened by the insurrection that resurfaced in November 1989.

Guatemala

In the first half of the 1980s Guatemala sought to combat adverse shocks (declining terms of trade and internal insurrection) by fiscal expansion and the maintenance of an overvalued currency financed by foreign borrowing. This strategy ceased to be viable in 1985, and the following year a new administration introduced a short-run macroeconomic stabilization program. This met with substantial success in cutting the fiscal deficit and achieving a real devaluation, and since then nontraditional exports have grown at a rate of 18 percent per year. More important in easing the foreign-exchange constraint in the short run was the flow of foreign credits that the program unlocked. Guatemala has seen a return of modest growth, and investment has been reviving, but recovery remains precarious. The country has not undertaken any substantial liberalization.

Honduras

Honduras, like El Salvador, has experienced a decade of near stagnation, with no severe crisis that might have exercised a cathartic effect. Some rather half-hearted reforms have nevertheless been undertaken. Austerity measures have been adopted to reduce the fiscal deficit. Nontraditional exporters earn transferable certificates that can be used to buy imports as well as local currency, thus achieving a partial, disguised devaluation of the lempira (which has been fixed at 2:1 against the dollar since 1918, doubtless helping explain the continuing hang-up about devaluation). These measures have not sufficed to satisfy the World Bank or the IMF, and indeed the Fund has declared Honduras ineligible to borrow because of a buildup of arrears. The new president, Rafael Leonardo Callejas, has declared his openness to reform and his intention of restoring good relations with the Bretton Woods institutions.

Nicaragua

Nicaragua ended its first decade after the Sandinista revolution in a state of economic collapse, with a 40 percent fall in GDP per capita since 1980 and inflation of 14,000 percent per year. The civil war and the hostility of the United States must go far to explain this lamentable outcome. (One factor that cannot be blamed, however, is the denial of access to external credit: Nicaragua has had by far the largest positive resource transfer, relative to GDP, of any Latin American country.) These difficulties were compounded by the destruction of incentives and the willingness to accommodate large public-sector deficits through the printing press. An orthodox package was adopted in early 1989, involving significant cuts in public expenditure, rises in interest rates to the point where they are positive in real terms, unification of the exchange market involving a large effective devaluation, reduced subsidies and increased taxes, and deregulation of many wages and prices. Even if this package qualifies as an incomplete "policy reform" rather than a temporary tactical retreat, it can hardly get a fair test until peace returns to the region.

Ecuador

Ecuador, an oil-exporting country, first faced the need to adjust to the twin squeeze of lower oil prices and high interest rates in 1982. Its initial reaction was to combine a conventional stabilization program of fiscal restraint and devaluation with an intensification of import controls. After León Febres-Cordero was elected president in 1984, the government set out to liberalize the economy. The exchange rate was floated, interest rates were freed, trade and payment restrictions were reduced, and the regulations governing foreign investment were relaxed. However, the opposition gained a clear congressional majority in 1986 just after the oil price decline had created a need for further retrenchment. An earthquake severed the trans-Andean oil pipeline the following year, intensifying the recessionary trend. The government allowed policy to drift in the run-up to the 1988 presidential election. A large fiscal deficit emerged, and the exchange rate remained frozen in the face of accelerating inflation.

The new government that took office in August 1988 moved promptly to implement a stabilization program. The fiscal deficit was tackled by raising the ridiculously low domestic price of petroleum derivatives, and many public-sector charges were also increased. Tax collection was improved and expenditures cut. The financial system was reliberalized, reversing the backsliding of the previous two years. The currency was devalued and put on a preannounced crawl. Tax reform involving broadening the tax base and cutting the marginal rates of the income tax, as well as closing loopholes in the corporate tax and substituting a value-added tax for the existing turnover tax, is currently before the Congress. However, the new government initially reintroduced trade restrictions, although it has recently made some moves in a liberalizing direction again. It also reintroduced payments controls and extended regulation. Ecuador has not had a privatization program, although it never had such an extensive network of state enterprises as to make this an urgent issue.

Inflation continued to accelerate for a time after implementation of the stabilization program, to a peak of close to 100 percent per year. It has since begun to fall back. Output is more or less stagnant. Although the present government has been serious about stabilization, it seems to be of a mixed mind about the virtues of liberalization.

Paraguay

There was a period during construction of the Itaipu hydroelectric dam in the early 1980s when Paraguay had the fastest growth rate, around 8 percent per year, in South America. Since 1982, however, per capita income has stagnated, with the recessions of 1982–83 and 1986 (a drought year) offsetting the intervening recovery. Paraguay did not experience any significant policy reform until recently: the recorded fiscal deficit remained moderate (or the accounts have even been in surplus), but the public sector suffered from the usual statist ills, and there was a multiple exchange rate system with the main exporting rate overvalued.

Matters began to change after the overthrow of President Alfredo Stroessner, Latin America's longest-surviving dictator, in early 1989. The new government made a serious attempt to collect taxes and to cut public expenditures by firing superfluous employees and raising the prices charged by public enterprises. The recorded fiscal deficit may nonetheless rise, since unification of the exchange rate made transparent a deficit previously hidden by the ability of public enterprises to import at an unrealistic exchange rate. The unified exchange rate has been floated, and the currency has depreciated substantially in real terms.

The new government is also talking of substantial liberalization of the economy. The financial system, which is still subject to interest controls and is heavily distorted, may be liberalized. A tax reform package is in preparation. There is talk of a low uniform tariff to replace the existing complex system involving many relatively high tariffs that are selectively enforced. The government is aiming to privatize its steel and cement plants. The new regime seems to be respecting property rights and to have abandoned the demands for kickbacks on threat of peremptory takeover that had deterred enterprise, including foreign direct investment, under Stroessner.

Inflation continued to rise immediately after introduction of the stabilization program but is now declining again. Per capita growth has been positive in 1988-89. Recorded exports have responded strongly to unification of the exchange rate. It remains to be seen just how many of the present good intentions will be implemented and sustained, but it is just conceivable that the Paraguayan economy, which can draw on a largely literate labor force, might respond to the removal of its shackles in the same way that the Filipino economy seemed to be doing before the December 1989 coup attempt in Manila.

Uruguay

Uruguay, like Chile, undertook a wide-ranging liberalization of its economy in the 1970s, but threw away the benefits by implementing a preannounced crawling devaluation that was supposed to decelerate inflation faster than was consistent with the fiscal deficit. A severe depression followed abandonment of this *tablita* system in November 1982. Uruguay's final years under military dictatorship were characterized by drift in economic policy and acute stagflation in economic performance.

The democratic government that took office in early 1985 embarked on a program of policy reform. This included virtual elimination of a primary fiscal deficit of about 3 percent of GDP, achieved by increases in the prices charged by public-sector enterprises, a tax reform package, and improved tax administration. Interest rates were freed in 1985, and prudential supervision of the financial system has been strengthened. The floating exchange rate has been maintained at a competitive level. Import tariffs have been reduced to a maximum of 45 percent, although these are supplemented by strict restrictions on the import of vehicles and a few other products. Some state enterprises have been closed, as have some railway lines, and there have been scattered modest privatizations, including ongoing reprivatization of financial institutions rescued after the 1982 financial crisis. Foreign direct investment is welcome, though scarce. Deregulation has been notable by its absence in the labor market, where firing is almost impossible, payroll taxes are heavy, and trade unions remain strong.

Growth picked up in 1986–87, reducing unemployment from 13 percent to under 9 percent, but inflation has remained high at over 60 percent per year. Most recently, output has stagnated again and the trade balance worsened. Investment remains low, under 10 percent of GDP. Uruguay seems to be another country whose policy reforms have not been rewarded by a return to sustained growth. One possible explanation is that the process of liberalization remains incomplete, especially in the labor market.

Assessment

This section takes up four broad themes that arise from the preceding discussion. First, is there indeed a consensus on desirable policy reform in Latin America, who shares it, and what does it amount to? Second, how much have policies actually been reformed? Third, what have been the results of policy reform? Finally, what is the agenda now? The last question is subdivided into issues facing Latin America and those facing Washington.

How Much Consensus?

Richard Feinberg (chapter 2) argued that one could not expect to find consensus on anything much, let alone on the list of 10 economic policy instruments discussed above, if one interprets "Washington" as embracing the American political spectrum "from Jesse Jackson to Jesse Helms." But, he suggested, if one thinks of Washington slightly less all-embracingly as constituting primarily those individuals and institutions with a professional concern for events in Latin

America, there would seem to be, if not complete consensus, at least a great deal of convergence. Moreover, the convergence extends to Latin America itself: this was manifest at the Institute's conference, just as it had been at another conference held two weeks earlier by the Inter-American Development Bank (Iglesias, chapter 8). Indeed, Stanley Fischer suggested that the convergence extends to practically the whole community of development economists worldwide. It seems it would have been more accurate to call the "Washington consensus" the "universal convergence."

There are different ways of describing the intellectual position that is being converged upon. Enrique Iglesias (chapter 8) spoke of macroeconomic control, opening up the economy, and reforming the role of the state. Stanley Fischer described its content as a sound macroeconomic framework, an efficient and smaller government, and an efficient and expanding private sector, to which he added policies aimed at poverty reduction—a topic excluded from my list, for reasons discussed below.

My list consisted of 10 policy instruments. Agreement on the importance of one of these, fiscal discipline, now appears to be universal. It was not always so, as Juan Carlos de Pablo (chapter 4) notes. The need for a competitive exchange rate was also very generally endorsed, although a few qualifications must be made to allow for possible use of the exchange rate as a nominal anchor. Once again, this was not always so: Richard Webb (chapter 3) recounted how in 1980 he had been advised against even imagining that devaluation might help. For a long period Latin populists made at least partial common cause with the Chicago adherents of the monetary approach to the balance of payments, and subsequently with the supply-siders, to deride the orthodox stabilization package of fiscal discipline and a devaluation to restore competitiveness. Now there seems to be wide agreement that the orthodoxy of the 1960s—long the core of IMF conditionality—is right.

Opening up the economy, involving trade liberalization and a welcome to foreign investment as well as a realistic exchange rate, also meets with very general approval. This marks a striking change from the attitudes that prevailed as recently as 1986, when the emphasis on this theme in the Institute's study *Toward Renewed Economic Growth in Latin America* (Balassa et al. 1986) still encountered considerable resistance. Such reservations as persist concern the speed of import liberalization and (even more widely questioned) the wisdom of subsidizing direct investment by debt-equity swaps.

Tax reform is another subject on which there seems to be wide agreement that action is desirable.

After that, one gets to the subjects that, in the words of Rodrigo Botero (chapter 7), touch on "redefinition of the development model," namely, the reordering of public expenditure priorities, financial liberalization, privatization, deregulation, and creation of an enabling environment. Botero notes that there is a good deal less agreement in this area, which covers various aspects of the role of the state in the economy. This is really not surprising when one reflects on what is at stake.

Spanish-speaking Latin America, in particular, has a long tradition, going back to the practice of the Spanish crown of granting economic privileges to its colonists, of regarding the state as a dispenser of concessions rather than an impartial arbiter. In such a system political struggle is an attempt to gain control of the state apparatus so as to redirect privileges to the advantage of oneself and one's friends. This nurtured a private sector that was both weak and dependent. Postwar reformers, whether concerned to accelerate development or to attack privilege, found it natural to seek a solution in an expanded economic role for the state.

For a time this worked reasonably well, but it has become increasingly clear that there are inherent limits to the ability of the state to compensate for the weakness of the private sector by taking on entrepreneurial functions that in the developed countries are left to private enterprise. As Balassa et al. (1986, chapter 4) pointed out, the control capabilities of the state became overloaded, and attention was diverted away from creation of a healthy policy environment and provision of basic public services, roles that the private sector is much less capable of filling. Moreover, the private sector was further weakened, and this weakness then "justified" further state intervention.

What the World Bank refers to by the anodyne term "structural adjustment" is perhaps best interpreted as an attempt to break out of this vicious circle. To the uninitiated, "structural adjustment" might suggest that the problem is perceived as one of having a productive structure biased toward the production of too many nontradeables and too few exportables to be compatible with the restoration of simultaneous internal and external balance. The remedy suggested by this diagnosis is to invest more in exportables-producing industries, a process that can be facilitated by foreign borrowing. But in fact this has almost no connection with the content of structural adjustment loans as these have been developed by the World Bank (1988b). Rather, structural adjustment is about opening the economy plus reordering public expenditure priorities, financial liberalization, privatization, deregulation, and the provision of an enabling environment for the private sector. A more descriptive term for the process is obviously "liberalization."

Structural adjustment, then, aims at the replacement of a traditional statist system by a market system. The essential feature of a market system is that individual rewards are determined primarily by success in producing something that can be sold on an impersonal market, rather than by gaining privileges ("rent seeking"). Widespread private enterprise may be a necessary condition for a market system, but it is certainly not sufficient: a series of private monopolies that gain their market position at the pleasure of the state still constitute a statist system.[10] Nor need one equate the market system with a capitalism red in tooth and claw in which Michael Milken is a corporate hero: the West European model of a social market economy and the Japanese variant of corporations that recognize long-term social obligations to employees, suppliers, and customers are as legitimate as the caricature of the American version.

The 1989 revolution in Eastern Europe suggests that a market system may be a more natural complement to political democracy than we have been accustomed to recognizing. One reason for this complementarity would seem to lie in the need to be able to accommodate economic change. An authoritarian state may be capable of managing the economy with tolerable efficiency, at least as long as the economy itself is reasonably simple (i.e., underdeveloped), because of its ability to override the protests of the losers. A democratic state, on the other hand, requires the impersonal market mechanism as a social institution for deflecting the wrath of those who suffer from economic change, as well as for offering them the chance to search out alternative opportunities elsewhere.

A democratic state that inherits a statist economy may be in a particularly difficult situation. Barbara Stallings (chapter 3) mentions that cases she has examined give little assurance that democratic regimes are capable of accomplishing much structural change; this finding is consistent with the previous argument. Once they have succeeded in making the transformation to free markets, liberal democratic regimes may be just as able to absorb change as those that rely on statist authoritarianism (indeed, the contrast between Western and Eastern Europe suggests that they may be more capable of accommodating change). But that initial transformation is singularly difficult, since it involves long-term losses by those who recognize that their services will no longer be required or protected in the leaner state of the future.

The Bolivian liberalization would seem to provide a counterexample to the argument that democratic regimes are incapable of structural change, although it is one that arose out of such desperate circumstances that one has to hope that the precedent is of limited relevance. Costa Rica and Jamaica offer more encouraging precedents. But at this stage the jury is still out on whether Latin America will succeed in making the historic transformation from statism to free markets to match the replacement of its former authoritarian regimes by democracy.

---

10. See Hernando de Soto (1989) for the already-classic development of this point.

How Much Has Happened?

Table 9.10 provides a summary view of which countries have reformed and in what ways, drawing on tables 9.1 through 9.9. Inevitably some of the entries are judgment calls on which it is possible for reasonable people to differ. For example, Chile's zero score on public expenditure priorities reflects a judgment that its effective restraint of spending on salaries and subsidies was offset by an excessive squeeze on health and education and excessive spending on defense. Argentina's plus score on fiscal discipline reflects the fact that the deficit has fallen, even though it obviously has not fallen enough. Those who distrust my judgments should go back to tables 9.1 through 9.9 to invent their own scores for table 9.10.

The judgments expressed in table 9.10 in fact seem to be generally consistent with the views expressed by those conference participants who explicitly tried to answer the question of which countries had implemented major programs of reform. For example, Arnold Harberger (chapter 7) listed six reformers: Bolivia, Chile, Colombia, Costa Rica, Mexico, and Uruguay. Enrique Iglesias (chapter 8) mentioned the same six and also added Venezuela as a recent reformer. Argentina might be added as another recent reformer, despite the collapse of its first stabilization attempt after the conference was held. Three English-speaking Caribbean countries—Guyana, Jamaica, and Trinidad and Tobago—would also seem to qualify.

The rows of table 9.11 show a classification of countries according to the extent of their policy reforms, with the period in which the main reforms were implemented being indicated in parentheses. The first row contains those among the countries just named that initiated reforms prior to 1988, less Colombia. Colombia is excluded despite its exemplary record of macroeconomic management—effective and relatively prompt stabilization following a much smaller deterioration than that experienced elsewhere—because of its very limited implementation of microeconomic liberalization measures (Rudolf Hommes, chapter 5). Uruguay has been allowed to remain in the first row, despite some misgivings about the extent of its liberalization.

The second row of table 9.11 contains those countries classified as having undertaken partial policy reform prior to 1988. Colombia and Guatemala are placed in this row, as countries that have implemented determined stabilization policies but very limited liberalization. Barbados is also placed there because, although its microeconomic policies would have earned it a place in the first row ever since independence, its current macro policy of clinging to what looks like an overvalued exchange rate is building up the danger of a future stabilization crisis.

The third row contains six countries that have undertaken policy reforms only recently (during or after 1988). In Argentina, Venezuela, and Guyana, the

Table 9.10 Latin America: summary of policy reform in the 1980s

Country	Fiscal discipline	Public spending priorities	Tax reform	Financial liberalization	Competitive exchange rate	Trade liberalization	Foreign direct investment	Privatization	Deregulation
Bolivia	++	++	++	++	+	++	+	0	++
Chile	+	0	+	++	++	++	+	++^a	+
Peru	–	–	0	–	–	–	–	–	0
Argentina	+	0	0^a	0	+	0^a	+	+^a	+^a
Brazil	0	–	+	0	+	0	–	+	–
Mexico	++	0	++	0	+	++	++	++	+
Colombia	++	0	+	+	++	+	0^a	+	0
Venezuela	0	0	0^a	+	+	++	+	+^a	+
Jamaica	+	0	++	+	+	++	+	+	++
Costa Rica	++	0	++	0	++	+	+	+	+

++ substantial reform

+ some reform (or no need to reform)

0 no significant change (or mixed changes)

– retrogression

a. More action expected shortly.

Sources: Tables 9.1 to 9.9.

Table 9.11 Latin America: policy reform and economic performance

Policy reform	Growth	Stagnation	Decline
Yes	Chile (1974–84) Costa Rica (1983–87)	Bolivia (1985) Mexico (1983–88) Jamaica (1983–86) Uruguay (1974–86)	Trinidad and Tobago (1987)
Partial	Colombia (1983–84)[a] Barbados	Guatemala (1986)[a]	
Recent	Paraguay	Venezuela El Salvador Ecuador	Argentina Guyana
No		Brazil Dominican Republic Honduras	Peru Nicaragua

Note: Years in parentheses denote period of principal reforms.

a. Major reforms in macroeconomic policy only.

Source: See table 9.10 and text for rows, table 9.12 and text for column classification.

reform effort has been fairly comprehensive. Paraguay has made a quiet and encouraging start to reform, although it is not yet clear that this will be extended and followed through. El Salvador has announced a comprehensive set of reform plans, but it is difficult to believe that a country facing its internal security problems will be able to implement many reforms effectively. Ecuador's latest reform effort is largely concentrated on macroeconomic stabilization (although it went through an aborted liberalization attempt in 1983–85).

The final row, of nonreformers, contains five countries. None of them can be accused of total indifference to the need for reform, but in each case the reforms have been modest or half-hearted. Brazil has combined grotesquely ineffective stabilization policies—periodic freezes undermined by fiscal profligacy—with very little liberalization. Honduras has not attempted much serious reform yet. Both Peru and Nicaragua have made recent efforts to stabilize and even, in the latter case, to liberalize, but there is no evidence that their governments have experienced a change of heart comparable to that of the countries in the top row. The Dominican Republic went through a period of moderate policy reform in 1983–85, but this went into reverse after the election of a new government in 1986.

The title of the Institute's conference was "Latin American Adjustment: How Much Has Happened?" The answer suggested by tables 9.10 and 9.11 is the same as that given by Victor Urquidi (chapter 7): quite a lot.

The Results of Policy Reform

Has policy reform paid off in restoring sustainable growth? This, after all, is the test of policy reform: however strongly one may believe that it is a shortsighted error to accommodate inflation or to tolerate an unsustainable balance of payments deficit, the main reason to avoid both is that beyond some point they threaten the maintenance of growth. The only serious qualification to treating growth as the test of whether policy reform has succeeded is if there is some reason to expect a trade-off between growth and a more equitable income distribution: the "big trade-off" identified by Okun (1975). However, since there is no reason to believe that the countries with poor growth performance have compensated for this failure by improving their income distribution, it seems legitimate to concentrate on growth as the measure of success.

Table 9.12 therefore shows estimates of per capita GDP growth rates for the periods 1981–89 and 1988–89. The latter set of figures is used as the primary basis for classifying countries among the columns of table 9.11, which indicate whether countries are growing, stagnating, or declining. The countries classified as growing have all experienced a rise in per capita GDP of at least 2 percent in 1988–89, and all except Costa Rica have recovered the level of GDP with which they started the 1980s. The countries classified as stagnating typically show recent changes of less than 2 percent in either direction and a cumulative decline of around 10 percent (with a wide variance) through the decade. The declining countries have all experienced recent falls in GDP of over 5 percent and cumulative falls in excess of 20 percent.

Most of the countries fall naturally and unambiguously into the category to which they have been assigned, but three marginal cases in the stagnation category call for an explanation. The first is Venezuela, where per capita GDP fell by almost 11 percent in 1989 after its stabilization measures were introduced. To get a measure of Venezuela's performance prior to policy reform, it is more appropriate to focus on its growth in 1987–88, on which basis it belongs in the stagnation category. The second country, El Salvador, is a marginal candidate between stagnation and decline. Third, and apparently most paradoxical, is Ecuador, which is here denied classification as a growing country because its jump in GDP in 1988 was simply a rebound caused by the reopening of the trans-Andean oil pipeline after its rupture in 1987.

A number of countries doubtless have reason to hope that their future performance will improve on that shown in table 9.12. One of the most hopeful

Table 9.12 Latin America: growth in the 1980s (percentages)

Country	Growth in GDP per capita[a]	
	1981–89	1988–89
Growing countries		
Chile	9.6	12.0
Costa Rica	−6.1	2.4
Colombia	13.9	2.5
Barbados	8.1	4.8
Paraguay	0.0	6.2
Stagnating countries		
Bolivia	−26.6	−0.4
Mexico	−9.2	−0.3
Jamaica	−5.8	−1.5
Uruguay	−7.2	−0.5
Guatemala	−18.2	1.6
Brazil	−0.4	−1.5
Dominican Republic	2.0	0.0
Honduras	−12.0	0.0
Venezuela	−24.9	−8.7[b]
El Salvador	−17.4	−3.5
Ecuador	−1.1	12.1[c]
Declining countries		
Trinidad and Tobago	−40.8	−10.2
Peru	−24.7	−23.3
Nicaragua	−33.1	−17.5
Argentina	−23.5	−11.1
Guyana	−33.1	−8.2

a. Cumulative.

b. 1.6 percent in 1987–88.

c. −2.0 percent in 1989.

Source: Economic Commission for Latin America and the Caribbean (1989c, table 9.3).

is Mexico, where per capita GDP already edged up in 1989 and is expected to increase further in 1990, as its policy reforms finally begin to bear fruit. Similarly, the two countries that have departed furthest in recent years from prudent macro and liberal micro policies—Peru and Nicaragua—presumably hope that they have bottomed out since the implementation of stabilization programs.

How much support does this classification provide for the hypothesis that the key to economic growth is to embrace the set of policy reforms being recommended by "Washington"? That hypothesis suggests that one should expect to find a preponderance of countries on the principal diagonal of the 3 × 3 matrix formed by consolidating the two final rows of table 9.11. In fact, one finds 7 out of 21 countries on that diagonal, of which 6 are in the two corners, whereas only 2 countries are found in the opposite (off-diagonal) corners. Countries like Chile and Costa Rica that undertook the costs of policy reform in the early 1980s are now starting to benefit, whereas those that adopted a populist path (Peru) or that failed to come to grips with their fiscal deficits (Argentina) are now paying the price.

Consider also the 14 countries not located on the principal diagonal. Colombia and Barbados have succeeded in growing despite doubts about their micro and macro policies respectively; they would probably have grown faster had those policies been better conceived. Brazil, the Dominican Republic, and Honduras are stagnating, whereas Venezuela and El Salvador stagnated before they attempted policy reform: the fact that they are or were not collapsing scarcely constitutes a case against reform. Ecuador experienced a strong fluctuation associated with the interruption of oil production, but after allowing for that its production would also seem to have been at best stagnant. Trinidad and Tobago can perhaps still be disregarded as a country whose reforms are so recent as not to provide a fair test. Paraguay is an interesting case of a country that was doing reasonably well even before policy reform.

The disturbing feature of table 9.11 is, however, the existence of four countries that instituted serious programs of policy reform before 1988 but are nonetheless still stagnating. Of these four, Mexico looks the closest to resuming growth. Indeed, it looked set to resume growth once before, when the 1986 oil price shock intervened. The critical question is whether the private sector can be convinced that Mexico is going to have enough foreign exchange to allow investment to expand and to avoid a new maxi-devaluation of the peso that would wreck the stabilization program (Dornbusch, chapter 7). Such a conviction would prompt repatriation of enough flight capital to support the resumption of growth and end Mexico's debt crisis.

Bolivia is different. It has already settled most of its debt to the commercial banks through a buyback on favorable terms, and there is little reason to think that the remaining debt overhang is the factor preventing the resumption of growth. (And bankers should note that the inability to borrow "new money" to finance a part of the interest that no longer has to be paid cannot be blamed either!) In view of recent terms-of-trade shocks totaling some 10 percent of GDP and the extremely narrow base of Bolivia's traditional export sector, perhaps the best that one should hope for is stabilization of per capita income while the investment rate gradually rises: gross investment has so far edged up from under 8 percent of GDP in 1986 to over 12 percent in 1989. Nontraditional exports are rising year by year, from a negligible base. One can reasonably ask whether a somewhat more competitive exchange rate might be capable of accelerating the process of recovery without igniting a new surge of inflation, but even without that, one can argue that today Bolivia looks more hopeful than it has for a long time.

Jamaica and Uruguay are both cases where the benefits of policy reform have so far been disappointingly meager. Both, especially Uruguay, had a period of positive per capita growth in 1986–87, but have since experienced renewed stagnation. Uruguay suffers from its geographic location, dwarfed by two neighbors flirting with hyperinflation, and its microeconomic liberalization seems to have been incomplete. Jamaica may have suffered from uncertainty as to whether policy reform would survive an electoral defeat for Edward Seaga. Both are heavily indebted countries that have not yet been recognized as deserving candidates for Brady-style debt reconstructions.

Policy reform has not yet succeeded in its primary objective of promoting the resumption of robust growth, except in Chile and to a lesser extent in Costa Rica and Colombia. Nevertheless, there are signs of hope elsewhere, notably in Mexico and, on a longer time perspective, in Bolivia. There is nothing in the record of the 1980s to suggest that the thrust of the policy reforms urged on Latin America has been misconceived.

The Agenda for Latin America

The first task facing Latin America in the 1990s is to complete the transition from the statist populism of the past to the new realism on which the region embarked in the 1980s. Those countries that have not yet faced the challenge of stabilization and liberalization should not delay further. The best time to start is after a new president takes office, preferably one with a mandate to modernize and not one who has to spring the program on his supporters by surprise.

Efficient stabilization normally involves more than balancing the budget. Dornbusch asserted (chapter 7): "Without budget balancing a stabilization will not last; without incomes policy it may not even start."[11] The possible use of a "heterodox shock" as a *supplement* to an orthodox stabilization program is no longer particularly controversial—problems have arisen when it has been treated as a *substitute*. Where inflation has got completely out of control, however, some stronger "nominal anchor" may be needed in the short run, like a stable exchange rate or even dollarization.

A question raised by several speakers at the conference was the proper sequencing of economic reforms. A significant literature has grown up on this topic, sparked initially by the failure of the Southern Cone liberalization attempts at the end of the 1970s, and the contention of some that this failure owed much to premature liberalization of the capital account. Marcelo Selowsky (1989) recently presented a stylized description of the process of policy reform in Latin America: reform starts off with fiscal stabilization (stage I), proceeds to structural reform of the incentive system (stage II, consisting of trade liberalization, deregulation, and acceptance of foreign direct investment), and finally leads to stage III where rates of return are high and recovery follows. That all sounds very sensible, until one starts reflecting that Bolivia undertook stages I and II simultaneously rather than sequentially, whereas Mexico pressed ahead with opening its economy even while the fiscal deficit persisted and inflation accelerated.

Much of the literature on sequencing is still highly inconclusive, but Sebastian Edwards (1989) argues that some robust guidelines can be offered with respect to the liberalization of both domestic capital markets and international capital flows. As far as the domestic capital markets are concerned, liberalization needs to be preceded by the restoration of fiscal discipline, the establishment of a system of prudential supervision, and the adoption of a time-consistent exchange rate regime. Restrictions on international capital flows should be maintained until after the domestic capital market has been liberalized and trade reform has been largely completed. To those rules I would add the proposition that there is no reason to delay the tariffication of import controls. Beyond that, however, the best sequence would seem to be a function of political realities, administrative capacities, and country-specific economic circumstances, rather than being subject to general regularities that economic analysis can hope to establish.

---

11. I disagree strongly with Dornbusch, however, that the IMF committed malpractice in taking "almost a decade to come to grips with the concept of inertial inflation and the resulting need for incomes policy," with reference to its discussions with Brazil in the early 1980s. Had Dornbusch accused the Fund of being slow to accept the need to use an inflation-adjusted concept of the budget deficit, there would be some truth in his charge. But the IMF pressed Brazil, unsuccessfully as it turned out, to modify its wage indexation formula in 1983 so as to permit a gradual reduction of inertial inflation without an excessive cost in terms of recession. The Fund has never been dogmatically opposed to incomes policy.

A second general issue, emphasized by Dornbusch (chapter 7), is how to reestablish growth once stabilization has been achieved. Too often it is blithely assumed that private investment will be crowded in as soon as the fiscal deficit is brought down. Dornbusch points to those countries that have implemented determined policy reforms but not reestablished growth, and argues that the problem arises because the entrepreneurs are "waiting." If they bring back their flight capital to make an investment now, they risk losing all if the stabilization collapses. Better to wait a few months until it is clear that the stabilization program will stay the course and that it will succeed—the cost is only a few months' lost profits. When will it be clear that stabilization has succeeded? When other entrepreneurs have started repatriating and investing. So everyone waits for everyone else, and the economy meanwhile stagnates.

How can one provide a signal that might induce a simultaneous commitment on the part of a critical mass of entrepreneurs? Dornbusch's own suggestion is to launch a Latin "Marshall Plan." One danger of speaking in those terms is that a Marshall Plan suggests funds for the region as a whole and therefore invites Richard Webb's protest that "desperation is our only hope" (chapter 7): policy reform capable in the long run of lifting the region out of its state of underdevelopment may never get under way if bailouts are always on hand to keep the old model afloat. DeLisle Worrell was correct in pointing out that what Dornbusch had actually argued for was financial support for countries like Mexico that had implemented comprehensive policy reforms, but that idea is surely conveyed more naturally by calling for definitive debt settlements than for a "Marshall Plan."

A key question for Latin America is whether it should try to achieve debt settlements through the medium of the Brady Plan, rather than by unilateral (or joint) moratoria or repudiations on the one hand, or by demanding a new debt strategy on the other. The unilateral strategy appears unpromising—not primarily because it risks jeopardizing the goodwill of the commercial banks (the Chilean experience suggests that their goodwill is of regrettably little cash value; see chapter 3), but because it is incompatible with the restoration of domestic confidence. There is a basic incongruity between denying the property rights of foreigners and reassuring national capitalists that their property rights are so secure that they can prudently lend to the government at a low interest rate and invest in the domestic economy. Recognizing that incongruity does not require that continued full servicing of external debt become the overriding objective of national economic policy. However, if and when a country lacks the foreign exchange both to sustain an acceptable growth rate and to service its foreign debt in full, prudence suggests that any necessary partial suspension of interest payments be announced in as nonconfrontational a way as possible and accompanied by continued negotiation with the banks aimed at achieving a settlement that will permit future debt service according to the revised contractual obligations.

Nor does the beginning of the new decade seem a propitious time to seek another new debt strategy. Past experience, from Volcker and de Larosière to Baker, and from Baker to Brady, indicates that there is a delay of over three years from the introduction of one debt strategy to the recognition that it has failed and that a new strategy is needed. Given that the Mexican restructuring under the Brady Plan has already come so close to success, and may still succeed when it is finalized, it seems altogether more sensible to work within that framework than to guarantee a further two or three years of debt crisis by demanding something more generous. Since possible improvements in the Brady Plan are more the responsibility of Washington than of Latin America, however, discussion of how present arrangements might be improved is delayed until the next section.

Apart from lifting the debt overhang in a way calculated to build rather than erode confidence, restoration of growth requires persistence in the policies of stabilization and liberalization that have been discussed at length above. Rather than searching for some macroeconomic panacea, Latin America needs the patience to endure the hard slog of building up savings, making sure they are invested rationally, and devoting additional resources to human capital formation and the refurbishment and improvement of the infrastructure. That could usefully be supplemented by following the Mexican example in negotiating tax-information-sharing agreements so as to have some chance of beginning to collect revenue from the interest income on flight capital that is not attracted back home. Anything that politicians can do to increase confidence that the policy reforms will be sustained rather than capriciously abandoned or reversed could also be helpful.

At least two topics that were not included in my "Washington agenda" are going to demand the attention of Latin American policymakers in the coming years. The first concerns an omission from my list that provoked strong complaints from both Stanley Fischer and Patricio Meller in chapter 2 of the conference volume: the subject of income distribution and poverty reduction. One reason why I did not include this topic is that the list was intended to cover policy instruments, and income distribution is not a policy variable.[12] Suppose that one does indeed share a concern for a more egalitarian income distribution: what *policies* does one then recommend? A progressive tax system, which in the Latin context means first and foremost effective enforcement and the abolition of loopholes that allow the privileged to escape taxation; public expenditure that

---

12. The same comment applies to complaints voiced by de Pablo (chapter 4) that credibility was omitted from the Washington agenda: its omission was not occasioned by dismissal of the subject's importance.

benefits the poor disproportionately, like basic health and education, and carefully targeted subsidies; deregulation and an extension of property rights so as to allow the informal sector to compete; and land reform, or perhaps land value taxation. All these things except the last (which seems to command no interest whatsoever in Washington) are included in the Washington agenda.

In the second place, it is not clear that a high priority is in fact attached to egalitarianism in parts of Washington, despite some tempering of the rather shocking indifference to distributional issues that characterized the early years of the Reagan administration. Nor should this occasion surprise, given that a very important part of Washington, namely the US executive branch, is run by self-proclaimed conservatives. Colin Bradford complained (chapter 2 discussion) that if the economists form a consensus on everything, the Latin politicians who achieve power by their hard-won democracy will end up having nothing left to decide. Surely the priority to be attached to egalitarianism is the issue par excellence that divides left from right, and on which the politicians therefore should be expected to make the substantive decisions. Not only is it hopeless to expect consensus on this issue; such a consensus would be a denial of democracy.[13]

However, if the Washington consensus also is (or becomes) a Latin American consensus, the terms of the battle between left and right over distribution will be fundamentally changed. Too often in the past a progressive concern for income distribution has gone along with idiot economics, in the form either of Marxist gobbledegook (in Eurasia) or of populist statism (in the Western Hemisphere).[14] Through the good works of Roger Douglas of New Zealand, Felipe González, Mikhail Gorbachev, Bob Hawke, and Lech Walesa, it looks as though that equation may finally have been broken in the Eastern Hemisphere in the 1980s. The embrace of policy reform by Patricio Aylwin, Victor Paz Estenssoro, Michael Manley, Carlos Menem, and Carlos Andrés Pérez should—if their reforms succeed—do the same thing in the Western Hemisphere. That would clear the ground for a political battle over income distribution in which the left is no longer burdened by fears that it threatens to ruin society as a whole in the process.

Stanley Fischer (chapter 2) also complains that my statement of the Washington agenda contains nothing about the environment, which is now high on Washington's list of concerns. I agree that a consensus has now jelled in Washington on the importance of this issue, although it is very recent: recall that

---

13. Consensus may extend to agreeing that such egalitarian measures as are introduced should be efficient in the sense of sacrificing the least possible output for a given redistribution (as the Washington consensus essentially does), but it cannot be expected on the issue of where to draw the line on the efficiency frontier (Okun's big trade-off).

14. As noted before, not all populists have been on the left wing, but the majority have.

James Watt was Secretary of the Interior as recently as 1983. It is not clear that such a consensus already extends to Latin America.

If Fukuyama (1989) turns out to be correct in having proclaimed the "end of history," in his strictly limited sense of the definitive victory of liberalism over its various totalitarian challengers of the last two centuries, it is plausible to expect that the next great episode of history (in the more general sense) will be the battle to save the planet on which our species evolved from environmental disaster. If Latin America joins the rest of the world in ending history in Fukuyama's sense, it too will be able to give environmental concerns the priority they merit. But that is, at best, a battle for the 1990s and beyond; it is not what the policy reforms of the 1980s were about.

Washington's New Agenda

Whether and when Latin America recovers will depend primarily on its own efforts, and in particular on the vigor with which it pursues the policy reforms discussed in this chapter. Whether it uses recovery to begin servicing its immense "social debt" and to preserve and restore the environment will likewise depend primarily on the course of its own domestic political debate.

Nevertheless, "Washington" is not without influence or responsibility on these issues. The international institutions have a clear responsibility to help Latin America restore growth, and to help the countries of the region reduce poverty and care for the environment—at the very least to the extent that the countries themselves decide they want to pursue those objectives. And while the geostrategic interest of political Washington in ensuring that free-market democracy triumphs is less overwhelming in Latin America than in Eastern Europe, it is a not-inconsequential matter whether the likes of Sendero Luminoso start taking over.

If Washington is to take these responsibilities toward Latin America seriously, what does it need to do differently?

First, Washington (meaning in this context primarily the World Bank) should think more deeply about those items on the Washington agenda that the earlier discussion suggested were still unclearly or unsatisfactorily defined. These include the reordering of public expenditure priorities, financial liberalization, research on what could advantageously be deregulated, and thought on the concrete steps needed to create an enabling environment.

Second, Washington (meaning in this context perhaps the Fiscal Affairs Department of the IMF) should accept Rudiger Dornbusch's challenge of preparing a manual on how to design and implement a tax reform. Although the primary emphasis should be on broadening the tax base, the potential role of progressivity in the rate structure in ameliorating the region's appalling income inequalities also deserves attention.

Third, Washington (meaning the US Treasury and its sister institutions in the other developed countries) should do what it can to assist Latin countries in extending effective tax coverage of interest income earned on flight capital. The tax-information-sharing agreement recently signed with Mexico is an encouraging first step in this regard, but much more needs to be done.

Fourth, Washington (meaning primarily the US Treasury and the Institute of International Finance) should take a more balanced approach toward debt-equity swaps. It is understandable that the banks should press for such swaps, but it needs to be recognized that only when the debtor gets a substantial share of the discount can it also expect to gain. That may still leave a useful role for debt-equity swaps—for example, as a concession to the banks as part of a comprehensive debt-restructuring agreement, on the Mexican model. But it is quite unjustified to condemn a debtor country for seeking to limit swaps to the level that it can afford and to circumstances where it achieves worthwhile debt reduction.

Fifth, Washington (meaning here the environmental think tanks in the first instance) needs to consider carefully just what policy changes Latin countries should make in order to reflect the sort of environmental concerns that are now prevalent in Washington. So far about the only relevant policy that Washington has agreed on is that the World Bank and the Inter-American Development Bank (IDB) should stop subsidizing destruction of the environment in the fulfillment of their primary duty of aiding development. There needs to be a far clearer vision of the role that might be played by changes in land tenure, by reduced subsidies on pesticides, by the introduction of taxes on environmentally harmful products, by stricter regulation of chemicals, by comprehensive land-use planning, and so on. Of course, recommendations on such subjects (e.g., for taxes on harmful products) will have a hollow ring if pressed before the industrial countries are themselves prepared to act on them. And once a consensus on what needs doing has been established, Washington (meaning now the administration and the Congress as well as the World Bank and the IDB) will need to decide whether it is prepared to put its money where its mouth is. It could make an immediate down payment by resuming US support for birth control programs in the Third World.

Finally, there was a very widespread feeling at the Institute's conference that Washington needs to do something more on debt. Although debt was not the focus of the conference, it is impossible to conclude a discussion of what needs to be done to support Latin American policy reform without some consideration of the topic.

It was argued in the previous section that Latin America would be well advised to work within the framework of the Brady Plan, which has three key features. The first is a theme endorsed by Enrique Iglesias (chapter 8): that policy reform and debt relief[15] are complements. In this view debt relief without policy reform amounts to throwing good money after bad, even permitting the perpetuation of harmful policies beyond what would otherwise be possible, while policy reform without debt relief is liable to come to naught for lack of the financial wherewithal to get the economy moving again.

The latter view is occasionally challenged, a notable recent challenger being Clive Crook (1989, 55). He argues that the debt relief potentially available from the Brady Plan is quite marginal compared with the benefits that can be expected from a determined program of policy reform. But even if one accepts that this is true, it neglects an important point of political economy made by Felipe Larraín (chapter 3), namely, that it is not obvious to a large part of the populace in the typical country being invited to stabilize and liberalize that these actions are indeed in their best interest. (Things may be different when a country has suffered as much as Bolivia, but one hardly wants to make such misery a precondition for achieving free markets.) A definitive debt reconstruction may be just the type of reward needed to make a program of policy reform politically sustainable during the interregnum before it starts showing substantial results in terms of growth. And the example of other countries getting such benefits may also help persuade countries that have not yet embarked on serious policy reform to take the plunge.

Moreover, there are abundant and persuasive historical examples where external support has played a key role in sustaining a program of stabilization, or liberalization, or both. These include some (although not all) of the interwar cases where hyperinflation was stabilized, through the Marshall Plan in the 1950s and Indonesia in the late 1960s, to cases in the 1980s like Turkey, Israel, Costa Rica, and even Chile (which enjoyed a positive transfer until 1986). The most elementary economics tells one that (except when an economy has developed considerable excess capacity in a recession) the restoration of growth requires investment, and a negative transfer siphons resources out of the economy, making investment that much more difficult. It is therefore no great surprise to find historical cases where external support has proved worthwhile.

Perhaps the most compelling argument of all, however, is provided by recent events in Mexico. The evidence of the market shows that a marginal difference in external support can make a critical difference in the revival of confidence and the resumption of growth.

---

15. "Debt relief" is the natural umbrella term to use for what official jargon describes as "debt reduction and debt service reduction": it means any reduction in the present value of contractual future debt-service obligations, whether it is the principal or the interest rate that is reduced, or both.

For these three reasons, therefore, the Brady Plan was right to offer external support, and right to condition it on a determined and effective program of policy reform.

A second key feature of the Brady Plan is that, in the attempt to persuade banks to participate at least semi-voluntarily, it aims to offer the banks a range of options from which to choose rather than to compel all banks to give the same concessions. This is a feature that many participants at the conference probably disapprove of, but one that seems to me quite defensible. If the next US Secretary of the Treasury feels obliged to introduce a successor to the Brady Plan, it may well abandon all pretense of a voluntary framework, but it seems sensible first to try and sidestep the difficulties and risks that compulsion would entail. Those who have attacked the Brady Plan for allowing some banks to provide new money rather than debt relief should note that the Mexican agreement ran into trouble because too *few*, not too many, banks chose the new money option.

The third key feature of the Brady Plan is the decision to use the international financial institutions to provide the cash that will "buy" debt relief from the banks. It was rather brave of the official community to modify its former refusal to contemplate any shift of risk from the private to the public sector, since this is in fact a highly cost-effective way of helping the debtors while leaving the position of the banks largely unchanged, but it is easily misrepresented as a bank bailout.

Within the constraints imposed by those three key parameters, what could the official community do to make sure that countries like Mexico are able to convince the market that their Brady-style restructurings are, at last, definitive?

The most obvious step would be to provide more cash: in any voluntary or even semi-voluntary scheme, more cash will buy more debt relief. A shortage of cash for enhancements has been one of the factors holding up finalization of the Mexican deal.

A more modest step could also help. At the moment, the Bank and the Fund both earmark the funds they lend in support of debt relief for either debt reduction (buybacks or principal collateralization) or interest support (interest collateralization). Like most earmarking, this is prone to lead to inefficiency: it may prevent a country from making use of a given sum of money in the way that best satisfies the mutual interests of debtor and creditor. The country that has so far suffered most from this petty restriction is the Philippines, but sooner or later it will doubtless inconvenience some Latin debtor too. This earmarking should be abandoned forthwith.

It remains a difficult and time-consuming task to persuade all banks to participate in debt restructurings. Stephany Griffith-Jones (1989) has recently proposed changes in the rules for tax relief that would address this problem. At present European banks are generally eligible for tax relief on their provisions against nonperforming loans, whether or not these provisions are used to grant relief to the debtor; American banks, on the other hand, get tax relief only when debt relief is granted. The European practice encourages provisioning but provides no incentive to translate this into debt relief, whereas the American practice gives no incentive to provisioning and therefore leaves banks in a less favorable position to grant debt relief. It would be possible to get the best of both worlds by granting contingent tax relief on provisions, the relief being withdrawn retroactively from any bank that fails to participate in an agreed debt restructuring.

The time also seems to have come for developed-country governments to ask themselves whether they have done as much as they should with respect to their own loans. At the moment only the commercial banks are expected to provide debt relief; the Paris Club merely reschedules bilateral debt owed to the public sector. A lot of this debt is owed to export credit agencies, and there seems to be no very convincing reason why these creditors should be treated less stringently than the commercial banks. The simplest approach would be to forgive the same proportion of this debt as the banks choosing debt reduction agree to forgive. Alternatively, that proportion of the debt could be converted into local-currency terms, to be spent in future years on projects in the environmental, educational, or social fields that are agreed to be of mutual interest to creditor and debtor. The Export-Import Bank of the United States has already started provisioning, so it has some cushion that would allow it to participate in debt reduction.

In addition to reducing their own claims as part of a Brady-style debt restructuring, official creditors need to show a greater willingness to extend additional public-sector loans where the circumstances justify it. A good historical precedent, which one hopes will be highly relevant in the near future, is the provision of stabilization loans to countries undertaking a serious attempt to halt hyperinflation. Another situation that may arise in Mexico in the early 1990s is lending in support of economic recovery. If one takes the view that flight capital is likely to return if and only if there is enough alternative financing in place to make capital repatriation dispensable, it would be inexcusable to jeopardize Mexico's future by a failure to provide an adequate volume of contingent finance.

Finally, Washington needs to make sure that other countries that have earned a Brady-style debt restructuring get the opportunity for an early negotiation. The candidates are essentially the countries in the first row of table 9.11, plus Colombia, on account of its quite exemplary record of macroeconomic management. The candidates for Brady-style restructurings are clearly not exhausted by Mexico, the Philippines, and Costa Rica: within the Western Hemisphere one needs to add at least Chile (just as soon as a democratic government takes office), Jamaica, and Uruguay. Bolivia also needs help in completing the process of buying back its debt.

Concluding Remarks

A profound movement of policy reform is under way in Latin America. Few countries have undertaken comprehensive reforms and some have undertaken few reforms at all, but a lot more is happening than Latin America is being credited with in the industrial countries. The substance of the reforms amounts to emulating the policies of macroeconomic prudence, outward orientation, and domestic liberalization that have so benefited the developed countries and later the East Asian NICs during the postwar era. Latin America, like Eastern Europe, is now attempting the transition from statist authoritarianism to free-market democracy that Spain and Portugal made successfully in the last two decades.

The success of this historic effort is by no means assured. It is therefore important that the industrial countries do what is needed to increase the probability that policy reform will succeed. By far the most important contribution they can make at the present time is to ensure that countries with a solid record of policy reform get a definitive restructuring of their debt. The Brady Plan provides an adequate framework to achieve that, but its prospects would be much improved by more cash, an abandonment of earmarking, a tax incentive for banks to participate, and parallel treatment of debt owed to export credit agencies, as well as more generous public-sector loans where the circumstances justify them. Thus strengthened, the prospect of a Brady-style debt restructuring could provide an effective incentive to countries to persevere through the difficult early stages of reform.

The policy reforms now being attempted have relatively little to say about social issues and income inequality, and almost nothing to do with the environmental question. These are issues of critical importance in the current Latin American context, on which "Washington" should be prepared to offer helpful advice. But whether they are addressed more satisfactorily in the future than they have been in the past will be a test of Latin America's restored democratic institutions rather than something that Washington can expect to determine.

References

Amsden, Alice H. 1989. *Asia's Next Giant: South Korea and Late Industrialization.* Oxford: Oxford University Press.

Arellano, J. P. 1983. "De la liberalización a la intervención. El mercado de capitales en Chile: 1974–83." *Colección Estudios CIEPLAN* 11 (December): 5–50.

———. 1986. "La literatura económica y los costos de equilibrar la balanza de pagos en América Latina." In R. Cortázar, ed., *Políticas macroeconómicas. Una perspectiva latinoamericana*, 61–96. Santiago: Ediciones CIEPLAN.

———. 1988. "Crisis y recuperación económica en Chile en los años 80." *Colección Estudios CIEPLAN* 24 (June): 63–84.

Arellano, J. P., and M. Marfán. 1986. "Ahorro-inversión y relaciones financieras en la actual crisis económica chilena." *Colección Estudios CIEPLAN* 20 (December): 61–93.

———. 1987. "25 años de política fiscal en Chile." *Colección Estudios CIEPLAN* 21 (June): 129–62.

Arrau, P. 1986. "Series trimestrales del producto geográfico bruto revisado, 1974–85." *Notas Técnicas* 89. Santiago: CIEPLAN (December).

Balassa, Bela, Gerardo M. Bueno, Pedro-Pablo Kuczynski, and Mario Henrique Simonsen. 1986. *Toward Renewed Economic Growth in Latin America.* Mexico City: El Colégio de Mexico; Rio de Janeiro: Fundação Getúlio Vargas. Washington: Institute for International Economics.

Barandiarán, Edgardo 1988. "The Adjustment Process in Latin America's Highly Indebted Countries." Washington: Latin American Region, World Bank (March, mimeographed).

Bernal, Joaquin. 1989. "Política fiscal." In E. Lora and J. A. Ocampo, eds., *Introducción a la macroeconomia colombiana.* Bogota: Fedesarrollo, Tercer Mundo Editores.

Bethell, Tom. 1989. "Third World Hydraulics." *The American Spectator* (June).

Blejer, Mario, and Ke Young Chu. 1988. "Measurement of Fiscal Impact. Methodological Issues." *IMF Occasional Paper* 59. Washington: International Monetary Fund.

Brecher, Richard A., and Carlos F. Díaz Alejandro. 1977. "Tariffs, Foreign Capital, and Immiserizing Growth." *Journal of International Economics* (November).

Bruno, Michael, Guido Di Tella, Rudiger Dornbusch, and Stanley Fischer. 1988. *Inflation Stabilization: The Experience of Israel, Argentina, Brazil, Bolivia, and Mexico.* Cambridge: MIT Press.

Buiter, Willem H. 1988. "Some Thoughts on the Role of Fiscal Policy in Stabilization and Structural Adjustment in Developing Countries." *NBER Working Paper* 2603. Cambridge, MA: National Bureau of Economic Research (May).

Cardoso, Eliana. 1989. "From Inertia to Megainflation: Brazil's Macroeconomic Policies in the 1980s." Medford, MA: Fletcher School of Law and Diplomacy, Tufts University (mimeographed).

Cardoso, Eliana, and Rudiger Dornbusch. 1987. "Brazil's Tropical Plan." *American Economic Review* 77, no. 2: 288–92.

Cariaga, Juan L. 1985. "Bolivia's Hyperinflation (1982–1985). Causes and Effects." In J. R. Ladman and J. A. Morales, eds., *Redemocratization in Bolivia: A Political and Economic Analysis of the Siles Zuazo Government, 1982–1985.* Tempe, AZ: Center for Latin American Studies, Arizona State University.

————. 1988. "How Stabilization Was Achieved in Bolivia." In J. R. Ladman and J. A. Morales, eds., *Bolivia After Hyperinflation: Political, Economic and Social Perspectives.* Tempe, AZ: Center for Latin American Studies, Arizona State University.

————. 1989a. "Curing Hyperinflation: The Bolivian Experience." In A. P. Drischler, ed., *The United States and the World Economy.* Washington: The Johns Hopkins Foreign Policy Institute, School of Advanced International Studies (forthcoming).

————. 1989b. "The Bolivian Stabilization Program 1985–1988." Presented at the Western Economic Association International 64th Annual Conference, 22 June 1989, Lake Tahoe, NV.

Ceara-Hatton, Miguel. 1989. "La economia dominicana: crisis y reestructuración." Santo Domingo: Centro de Investigación Económica (mimeographed).

Cline, William R. 1987. *Informatics and Development: Trade and Industrial Policy in Argentina, Brazil, and Mexico.* Washington: Economics International.

Corbo, Vittorio. 1982. "Inflacíon en una economía abierta: el caso de Chile." *Cuadernos de Economía* 56 (April): 5–15.

————. 1985. "Reforms and Macroeconomic Adjustments in Chile During 1974–84." *World Development* 13, no. 8: 893–916.

Corbo, Vittorio, and J. de Melo. 1989. "External Shocks and Policy Reforms in the Southern Cone: A Reassessment." In G. Calvo et al., eds., *Debt, Stabilization and Development.* Oxford: Basil Blackwell.

Corden, W. Max. 1988. "Macroeconomic Adjustment in Developing Countries." *IMF Working Paper* 88/13. Washington: International Monetary Fund (February).

Cornia, Giovanni Andrea, Richard Jolly, and Frances Stewart. 1987. *Adjustment with a Human Face.* Oxford: Clarendon Press on behalf of UNICEF.

Coutts, K.J., H.G. Cury, and F. Pellerano. 1986. "Stabilisation Programmes and Structural Adjustment in the Dominican Republic." *Labour and Society* 11, no. 3 (September): 361–78.

Crook, Clive. 1989. "Poor Man's Burden: A Survey of the Third World." Supplement to *The Economist* (23 September).

Cuddington, John. 1986. *Capital Flight: Estimates, Issues, and Explanations.* Princeton Studies in International Finance 58. Princeton: Princeton University.

Cumby, Robert, and Richard Levich. 1987. "On the Definition and Magnitude of Recent Capital Flight." In Donald R. Lessard and John Williamson, eds., *Capital Flight and Third World Debt.* Washington: Institute for International Economics.

de Macedo, Jorge Braga. 1982. "Exchange Rate Behavior with Currency Inconvertibility." *Journal of International Economics* 12 (February): 65–81.

de Pablo, Juan Carlos, and Alfonso José Martínez. 1989. *Argentina: A Successful Case of Underdevelopment Process.* Washington: World Bank.

de Pablo, Juan Carlos, and Miguel Angél Manuel Broda. 1989. "Política económica en paises increíbles." *Meeting of the Econometric Society,* Santiago (August).

de Soto, Hernando. 1989. *The Other Path: The Invisible Revolution in the Third World.* New York: Harper & Row.

De Walle, Nicolas Van. 1989. "Privatization in Developing Countries: A Review of the Issues." *World Development* 17, no. 5: 601–15.

Díaz Alejandro, Carlos. 1981. "Southern Cone Stabilization Plans." In W.R. Cline and S. Weintraub, eds., *Economic Stabilization in Developing Countries.* Washington: Brookings Institution.

Dornbusch, Rudiger. 1974. "Real and Monetary Aspects of the Effects of Exchange Rate Changes." In R. Z. Aliber, ed., *National Monetary Policies and the International Financial System,* 64–81. Chicago: University of Chicago Press.

————. 1980. *Open Economy Macroeconomics.* New York: Basic Books.

————. 1986. "Special Exchange Rates for Capital Account Transactions." *The World Bank Economic Review* 1, no. 1 (September): 3–33.

————. 1989a. "From Stabilization to Growth." Presented at a conference on the Economic Reconstruction of Latin America at the Fundação Getúlio Vargas, Rio de Janeiro (7–8 August).

————. 1989b. "Real Interest Rates, Saving, Investment and Growth." Cambridge: Massachusetts Institute of Technology (mimeographed).

Dornbusch, Rudiger, and Sebastian Edwards. 1989. "Macroeconomic Populism in Latin America." *NBER Working Paper* 2986. Cambridge, MA: National Bureau of Economic Research.

Dornbusch, Rudiger, and Stanley Fischer. 1986. "Stopping Hyperinflations Past and Present." *Weltwirtschaftliches Archiv.*

Dornbusch, Rudiger, and Mario Henrique Simonsen. 1988. "Inflation Stabilization: The Role of Incomes Policy and Monetization." In Rudiger Dornbusch, ed., *Exchange Rates and Inflation,* 439–66. Cambridge: MIT Press.

Economic Commission for Latin America. 1989a. "Magnitud de la pobreza en ocho paises de America latina en 1986." Santiago: CEPAL (June, mimeographed).

————. 1989b. *Balance preliminar de la economia de America latina y el Caribe 1989.* Santiago: CEPAL.

Edwards, Sebastian. 1989a. *Real Exchange Rates, Devaluation, and Adjustment: Exchange Rate Policy in Developing Countries.* Cambridge: MIT Press.

————. 1989b. "The Sequencing of Economic Reform: Analytical Issues and Latin American Experiences." Presented at a conference on US–Korea Economic Relations at the Institute for International Economics, Washington (12 December).

Edwards, Sebastian, and Alejandra Cox-Edwards. 1987. *Monetarism and Liberalization: The Chilean Experiment.* Cambridge, MA: Ballinger.

Erickson, Kenneth. 1985. "Brazil." In Howard J. Wiarda and Harvey F. Kline, eds., *Latin American Politics and Development.* Boulder, CO: Westview Press.

Evans, Peter. 1989. "Declining Hegemony and Assertive Industrialization: U.S.–Brazil Conflicts in the Computer Industry." *International Organization* 43, no. 2 (Spring):207–38.

Ffrench-Davis, Ricardo. 1982. "El experimento monetarista en Chile: una síntesis crítica." *Colección Estudios CIEPLAN* 9 (December): 5–40.

————. 1989. "El conflicto entre la deuda y el crecimiento en Chile: tendencias y perspectivas." *Colección Estudios CIEPLAN* 26 (June): 61–90.

Fishlow, Albert. 1972. "Brazilian Size Distribution of Income." *American Economic Review* 62 (May): 391–402.

Fontaine, John A. 1987. "The Chilean Economy in the Eighties: Adjustment and Recovery." Presented at the Central Bank Symposium, Viña del Mar, Chile (December).

Foxley, Alejandro. 1982. *Latin American Experiments in Neoconservative Economics.* Berkeley: University of California Press.

Fukuyama, Francis. 1989. "The End of History?" *The National Interest* (Summer).

Garay, L. J., and A. Carrasquilla. 1987. "Dinamica del desajuste y proceso de saneamiento." *Ensayos Sobre Política Económica* 11 (June). Bogota: Banco de la República.

Glade, William. 1989. "Privatization in Rent-Seeking Societies," *World Development* 17, no. 5: 673–82.

Goldstein, Morris, and Peter Montiel. 1986. "Evaluating Fund Stabilization Programs with Multicountry Data: Some Methodological Pitfalls." *IMF Staff Papers* 33, no. 2.

Griffith-Jones, Stephany. 1989. "European Banking Regulations and Third World Debt: The Technical, Political, and Institutional Issues." *Institute for Development Studies Discussion Paper* 21. Brighton, England: Institute for Development Studies.

Guisarri, Adrián. 1989. *La Argentina informal*. Buenos Aires: Emecé.

Hachette, D., and R. Lüders. 1988. "El proceso de privatización en Chile desde 1984." *Boletín Económico* (March): 4–11. Santiago: Universidad Católica.

Harberger, Arnold. 1985. "Observations on the Chilean Economy, 1973-1983." *Economic Development and Cultural Change* 18 (April): 451–62.

Hausmann, Ricardo. 1981. "State Landed Property, Oil Rent and Capital Accumulation in the Venezuelan Economy." Ph.D. diss., Cornell University.

———. 1988. "Venezuela en 1987." *Coyuntura Económica* 18, no. 2 (June): 241–78.

———. 1990. *Shock externo y ajuste macroeconómico*. Caracas: Ediciones IESA (forthcoming).

Hemming, Richard, and Ali Mansoor. 1988. "Privatization and Public Enterprises." *Occasional Paper* 56. Washington: International Monetary Fund.

Hirschman, Albert O. 1965. "Out of Phase." *Encounter* 25, No. 3 (September).

Hoffmann, Helga. 1989. "Poverty and Prosperity: What Is Changing?" In Edmar L. Bacha and Herbert S. Klein, eds., *Social Change in Brazil, 1945-1985: The Incomplete Transition*. Albuquerque: University of New Mexico Press.

Hommes, Rudolph. 1988. "La ineficiencia del sector financiero colombiano." *Estratégia* no. 128.

Hung, L., and R. Piñango. 1985. "Crisis de la educación o crisis del optimismo y del igualitarismo?" In M. Naím and R. Piñango, eds., *El caso Venezuela: Una ilusión de armonía*, 422–51. Caracas: Ediciones IESA.

Hwa, E.C. 1989. *Colombia: Country Economic Memorandum: Productivity Growth and Sustained Economic Development* (report no. 7629-CO). Washington: World Bank.

Instituto Nacional de Estadísticas. 1989. *IV encuesta de presupuestos familiares* (December 1987–November 1988), vols. 1 and 2. Santiago: INE.

International Monetary Fund. 1988a. *Government Finance Statistics Yearbook*, vol. 12. Washington: International Monetary Fund.

———. 1988b. *International Financial Statistics Yearbook* 1988. Washington: International Monetary Fund.

Jadresic, E. 1985. "Formación de precios agregados en Chile: 1974–83." *Colección Estudios CIEPLAN* 16 (June): 75–100.

———. 1986. "Evolución del empleo y desempleo en Chile, 1970–85." *Colección Estudios CIEPLAN* 20 (December): 147–94.

Kaldor, Nicholas. 1967. *Strategic Factors in Economic Development*. Ithaca, NY: Cornell University Press.

Khan, M., and Malcolm Knight. 1985. "Fund-Supported Adjustment Programs and Growth." *IMF Occasional Paper* 46. Washington: International Monetary Fund.

Kuczynski, Pedro-Pablo. 1977. *Peruvian Democracy Under Economic Stress: An Account of the Belaunde Administration, 1963-1968*. Princeton: Princeton University Press.

———. 1988. *Latin American Debt*. New York and Baltimore: Twentieth Century Fund and The Johns Hopkins University Press.

Kume, Honorio. 1989. "A reforma tarifaria de 1988 e a nova política de importação." Rio de Janeiro: Fundação de Comercio Exterior (mimeographed).

Larraín, Felipe. 1988. "Public Sector Behavior in a Highly Indebted Country: The Contrasting Chilean Experience." Santiago: Universidad Católica (September, mimeographed).

Larraín, Felipe, and Andres Velasco. 1989. "Can Swaps Solve the Debt Crisis? Lessons from Chilean Experience." *Princeton Studies in International Finance* (forthcoming).

Larrañaga, O. 1989. "El déficit del sector público y la política fiscal de Chile, 1978–87." Santiago: CEPAL (September, mimeographed).

Lessard, Donald R., and John Williamson, eds. 1987. *Capital Flight and Third World Debt.* Washington: Institute for International Economics.

Lora, E., and José Antonio Ocampo. 1988. "Estructura económica, políticas de ajuste y distribución del ingreso: la experiencia de los ochentas." In E. Lora, ed., *Lecturas de macroeconomia colombiana.* Bogota: Fedesarrollo, Tercer Mundo Editores.

Mann, Arthur J., and Manuel Pastor, Jr. 1989. "Orthodox and Heterodox Stabilization Policies in Bolivia and Peru, 1985–1988" (mimeographed).

Marcel, M. 1989. "Privatización y finanzas públicas: el caso de Chile, 1985–88." *Colección Estudios CIEPLAN* 26 (June): 5–60.

Meller, Patricio. 1989. "Economic adjustment and its distributive impact." Paris: Organization for Economic Cooperation and Development (June, mimeographed).

Meller, Patricio, and A. Solimano. 1984. "El mercado de capitales chileno: laissez faire, inestabilidad financiera y burbujas especulativas." Santiago: CIEPLAN (mimeographed).

Mendes, J.C. 1987. "Uma analise do programa brasileiro de privatização." *Conjuntura Economica* 41, no. 9 (September): 11–24.

Merrick, Thomas. 1989. "Population since 1945." In Edmar L. Bacha and Herbert S. Klein, eds., *Social Change in Brazil, 1945–1985: The Incomplete Transition.* Albuquerque: University of New Mexico Press.

Meyer, Arno, and M. Silvia Bastos. 1989. "A fuga de capital no Brasil." Rio de Janeiro: Fundação Getúlio Vargas (mimeographed).

Meyer, Arno, and Maria Silvia Marques. 1989. "Implicações macroeconômicas de conversões da dívida externa." Rio de Janeiro: Fundação Getúlio Vargas (unpublished).

Morales, Juan Antonio. 1988. "The Cost in the Bolivian Stabilization Program." In J.R. Ladman and J. A. Morales, eds., *Bolivia After Hyperinflation: Political, Economic and Social Perspectives.* Tempe, AZ: Center for Latin American Studies, Arizona State University.

Morán, C. 1989. "Economic Stabilization and Structural Transformation: Lessons from the Chilean Experience, 1973–87." *World Development* 17, no. 4: 491–502.

Morandé, F., and Klaus Schmidt-Hebbel, eds. 1988. *Del auge a la crisis de 1982.* Santiago: ILADES.

Moreira, Heloisa, and Renato Baumann. 1987. "Os incentivos ás exportações brasileiras de produtos manufaturados." *Pesquisa e Planejamento Econômico* 17, no. 3 (August): 575–98.

Naím, M., and R. Piñango. 1985. *El caso Venezuela: una ilusión de Armonía.* Caracas: Ediciones IESA.

Nelson, Joan M., ed. 1989. *Fragile Coalitions: The Politics of Economic Adjustment.* Washington: Overseas Development Council.

———. 1990. *Economic Crisis and Policy Choice: The Politics of Adjustment in the Third World.* Princeton: Princeton University Press.

Nogales, J. 1989. *Bolivia: la nueva política económica y las elecciones de 1989.* La Paz: Los Amigos del Libro.

Ocampo, José Antonio. 1989a. "El desarrollo económico." In E. Lora and J. A. Ocampo, eds., *Introducción a la Macroeconomia Colombiana.* Bogota: Fedesarrollo, Tercer Mundo Editores.

————. 1989b. "Colombia and the Latin American Debt Crisis." In Sebastian Edwards and Felipe Larraín, eds., *Debt, Adjustment and Recovery: Latin America's Prospects for Growth and Development*. Oxford: Basil Blackwell.

Okun, Arthur. 1975. *Equality and Efficiency: The Big Trade-off*. Washington: Brookings Institution.

Ortega, Francisco. 1988. "Discurso de clausura." Paper presented at a symposium on Capital Markets sponsored by the Asociación Bancaria, Cali, Colombia (September).

Palma, P. 1986. *1973–1983: Una década de contrastes*. Caracas: Academia Nacional de Ciencias Económicas.

Paredes, Carlos. 1989. "Exchange Rate Regimes, the Real Exchange Rate, and Export Performance of Latin America." Washington: Brookings Institution (mimeographed).

Pazos, Felipe. 1978. *Chronic Inflation in Latin America*. New York: Praeger.

Piorkowski, Anne. 1985. "Brazilian Computer Import Restrictions: Technological Independence and Commercial Reality." *Law and Policy in International Business* 17, no. 3: 619–45.

Planning Institute of Jamaica. 1989. *Economic and Social Survey of Jamaica 1988*. Kingston: Planning Institute of Jamaica.

Polak, Jacques J. 1989. *Financial Policies and Development*. Paris: Organization for Economic Cooperation and Development.

Resende, Fernando, et al. 1989. "A questão fiscal." In *Perspectivas da Economia Brasileira*. Rio de Janeiro: Instituto de Pesquisa Econômica e Social.

Rocha, Sonia, and Hamilton Tolosa. 1989. "Pobreza metropolitana e políticas sociais." In *Perspectivas da economia brasileira*. Rio de Janeiro: Instituto de Pesquisa Econômica e Social.

Rodriguez, Miguel A. 1987a. *La política económica para el crecimiento*. Caracas: Academia Nacional de Ciencias Económicas.

————. 1987b. "Consequences of Capital Flight for Latin American Debtor Countries." In Donald R. Lessard and John Williamson, eds., *Capital Flight and Third World Debt*. Washington: Institute for International Economics.

————. 1990. "Public Sector Behavior in Venezuela: 1970–85." In Felipe Larraín and Marcelo Selowsky, eds., *The Public Sector and the Latin American Crisis*. San Francisco: International Center for Economic Growth, ICS Press.

Rodriguez, Flavia. 1987. "Recession and Adjustment: The Dominican Case 1983-1985." Mexico City: Centro de Estudios Monetarios Latinoamericanos (mimeographed, January).

Roett, Riordan. 1985–86. "Peru: The Message From Garcia." *Foreign Affairs* 64, no. 2 (Winter): 274–86.

Rosende, F. 1987. "Ajuste con crecimiento: el caso chileno." *Documento de Investigación* 32. Santiago: Banco Central (December).

Sachs, Jeffrey D. 1986. "The Bolivian Hyperinflation and Stabilization." *NBER Working Paper* 2073. Cambridge, MA: National Bureau of Economic Research.

————. 1989a. "Social Conflict and Populist Policies in Latin America." *NBER Working Paper* 2897. Cambridge: National Bureau of Economic Research.

————. 1989b. "Strengthening IMF Programs in Highly Indebted Countries." In C. Gwin and R.E. Feinberg, eds., *The International Monetary Fund in a Multipolar World: Pulling Together*. Washington: Overseas Development Council.

Sargent, Thomas, and Neil Wallace. 1981. "Some Unpleasant Monetarist Arithmetic." *Federal Reserve Bank of Minneapolis Quarterly Review* 5, no. 3 (Fall): 1–17.

Scheetz, Thomas. 1987. "Public Sector Expenditures and Financial Crisis in Chile." *World Development* 15, no. 8: 1053–77.

Sedlacek, Guilherme Luis. 1989. "Evolução da distribuição de renda entre 1984 e 1987." In *Perspectivas da Economia Brasileira*. Rio de Janeiro: Instituto de Pesquisa Econômica e Social.

Selowsky, Marcelo. 1989. "Preconditions Necessary for the Recovery of Latin America's Growth." Presented at the World Economic Forum, Geneva (22–23 June).

Shleifer, Andrei. 1989. "Externalities as an Engine of Growth." Presented at a conference on The Economic Reconstruction of Latin America at the Fundação Getúlio Vargas, Rio de Janeiro (7–8 August).

Solimano, A., and A. Zucker. 1988. "El comportamiento de la inversión en Chile 1974–87: aspectos conceptuales, evidencia empírica y perspectivas." Santiago: PREALC (August, mimeographed).

Stallings, Barbara, and Robert Kaufman. 1989. "Debt and Democracy in the 1980s: The Latin American Experience." In Barbara Stallings and Robert Kaufman, eds., *Debt and Democracy in Latin America*. Boulder, CO: Westview Press.

Tanzi, Vito. 1989. "Fiscal Policy and Economic Restructuring in Latin America." Presented at a conference on The Economic Reconstruction of Latin America at the Fundação Getúlio Vargas, Rio de Janeiro (7–8 August).

Taylor, Lance, et al. 1980. *Models of Growth and Distribution in Brazil*. New York: Oxford University Press.

Thomas, Clive Y. 1989. "Foreign Currency Black Markets: Lessons from Guyana." *Social and Economic Studies* 38, no. 2 (June): 137–84.

Thorpe, Rosemary. 1987. "La opción del APRA." *El Trimestre Económico* (September).

Urquidi, Victor, Francisco Giner, Alfonso Mercado, and Taeko Taniura. 1988. "Export Promotion of Manufactures in Mexico." *Joint Research Program Series* 71. Tokyo: Institute for Developing Economies.

Velasco, A. 1988. "Liberalization, Crisis, Intervention: The Chilean Financial System, 1975–85." *IMF Working Paper* 88/66 (July).

Webb, Richard C. 1977. *Government Policy and the Distribution of Income in Peru, 1963–1973*. Cambridge: Harvard University Press.

Williamson, John. 1985. *The Exchange Rate System*. POLICY ANALYSES IN INTERNATIONAL ECONOMICS 5. Washington: Institute for International Economics.

Williamson, John, and Marcus H. Miller. 1987. *Targets and Indicators: A Blueprint for the International Coordination of Economic Policy*. POLICY ANALYSES IN INTERNATIONAL ECONOMICS 22. Washington: Institute for International Economics (September).

World Bank. 1985. "Structural Adjustment Loan" (report no. P-4131). Washington: World Bank.

―――. 1987. *Chile: Adjustment and Recovery* (report no. 6726). Washington: World Bank (December).

―――. 1988a. *Brazil: Public Spending on Social Programs; Issues and Options* (report no. 7086-BR). Washington: World Bank.

―――. 1988b. *Adjustment Lending: An Evaluation of Ten Years of Experience*. Washington: World Bank.

―――. 1988–89. *World Debt Tables*, vol. 2. Washington: World Bank.

―――. 1989a. *Peru: Policies to Stop Hyperinflation and Initiate Economic Recovery*. Washington: World Bank.

―――. 1989b. *World Development Report 1989*. Washington: World Bank.

Worrell, DeLisle. 1987. *Small Island Economies: Structure and Performance in the English-Speaking Caribbean Since 1970*. New York: Praeger.

Appendix

Conference Participants
6–7 November 1989

Jeffrey Anderson
Institute of International Finance

Michael Atkin
International Finance Corporation

Dragoslav Avramovíc
Bank of Credit and Commerce

Norman A. Bailey
Norman A. Bailey, Inc.

Thomas O. Bayard
Institute for International Economics

Joel Bergsman
International Finance Corporation

C. Fred Bergsten
Institute for International Economics

Sterie T. Beza
International Monetary Fund

Rodrigo Botero
Harvard University

Colin Bradford
World Bank

Lawrence Brainard
Bankers Trust

Ernst A. Brugger
Swiss Chapter

Eliana Cardoso
Tufts University

Juan L. Cariaga
Inter-American Development Bank

Steve Charnovitz
Democratic Steering and Policy
    Committee

Peter Chase
Office of Senator Bill Bradley (D-NJ)

William R. Cline
Institute for International Economics

Donald V. Coes
University of Illinois

Michaela Collins
Swiss Bank Corporation

Susan Collins
Harvard University and Council of
    Economic Advisers

Vittorio Corbo
World Bank

Juan Carlos de Pablo
Centro de Estudios Macroeconómicos
    de Argentina

Celso de Souza
Embassy of Brazil

Guido Di Tella
Embassy of Argentina

Rudiger Dornbusch
Massachusetts Institute of Technology

Sebastian Edwards
University of California, Los Angeles

Jessica Einhorn
World Bank

Kimberly Ann Elliott
Institute for International Economics

Guy F. Erb
Erb and Madian

Richard Erb
International Monetary Fund

Richard E. Feinberg
Overseas Development Council

C. David Finch
Bethesda, Maryland

Stanley Fischer
World Bank

Kim Flower
Americas Society

George Folsom
US Department of the Treasury

Henry Fowler
Goldman, Sachs and Co.

B. Brooks Frazar
Citibank

Diana Gregg
US Department of the Treasury

Martine Guerguil
United Nations Economic Commission
   for Latin America and the Caribbean

Richard Haas
International Monetary Fund

Peter Hakim
Inter-American Dialogue

Arnold Harberger
University of Chicago

Ricardo Hausmann
Instituto de Estudios Superiores de
   Administración

C. Randall Henning
Institute for International Economics

Daniel Hofmann
Neue Zürcher Zeitung

Ann L. Hollick
Foreign Service Institute

Rudolf Hommes
Estrategia

Nancy Hunt
Industrial Bank of Japan

Enrique Iglesias
Inter-American Development Bank

Shafiqul Islam
Council on Foreign Relations

Alain Ize
International Monetary Fund

Fred Z. Jaspersen
World Bank

Walter K. Joelson
General Electric Canada

Patrice Franko Jones
Colby College

Alexandre Kafka
International Monetary Fund

Christopher Kennan
Rockefeller Family and Associates

Miguel Kiguel
World Bank

Bill Knepper
Council of the Americas

Charles Kovacs
Chase Manhattan Bank

Pedro-Pablo Kuczynski
First Boston International

Carol Lancaster
Institute for International Economics

Felipe Larraín
Harvard University

William Lowther
IFT Investment Corporation

Luis Luis
Institute of International Finance

Sandra Masur
Eastman Kodak

Steve Maybee
General Electric

William J. McFadden
US Department of the Treasury

Patricio Meller
Corporación de Investigaciones
   Económicas para Latinoamerica

Allan H. Meltzer
Carnegie-Mellon University

Allan Mendelowitz
US General Accounting Office

David Miller
Institute for International Economics

Ann Misback
Arnold and Porter

Bailey Morris
Institute for International Economics

Helga Mramor
Austrian National Bank

Masayuki Nakao
Matsushita

Joan Nelson
Overseas Development Council

Jack Norman
Dow Jones Economic Report

Gastón Pacheco
Embassy of Bolivia

David Paul
IFT Investment Corporation

Jacques J. Polak
Per Jacobsson Foundation

Carlos Quijano
World Bank

Alfred Reifman
Congressional Research Service

Rita M. Rodriguez
Export-Import Bank of the United
States

James L. Rowe, Jr.
Washington Post

Sylvia Saborio
Overseas Development Council

Enrique Sánchez
General Motors

Jennifer Schlauffler
Industrial Bank of Japan

Horst Schulmann
Institute of International Finance

David Sevigny
World Bank

Paul Simon
US Department of State

Dorothy M. Sobol
Federal Reserve Bank of
New York

Paulo Sotero
O Estado de São Paulo

Barbara B. Stallings
University of Wisconsin

Louellen Stedman
US Department of the Treasury

Larry Stoerrs
Congressional Research Service

John Stremlau
US Department of State

Manuel Suarez-Mier
Embassy of Mexico

Alain Thery
International Science and Technology
Institute, Inc.

Michael Treadway
Institute for International Economics

Ignacio Trigueros
Instituto Tecnológico Autónomo de
México

Peter P. Uimonen
Institute for International Economics

John Underwood
World Bank

Victor L. Urquidi
El Colegio de México

Joseph Wargo
Texaco Latin America/West Africa

Richard Webb
Lima

Helmut Weixler
Vienna

Gary Welsh
Bankers Association for Foreign Trade

Peter J. West
Institute of International Finance

Sweder van Wijnbergen
World Bank

Denise Williamson
World Bank

John Williamson
Institute for International Economics

Barry D. Wood
Voice of America

DeLisle Worrell
Central Bank of Barbados and Institute
for International Economics

Nancy Worth
International Monetary Fund

Index

Birth control. *See* Population growth
Bolivia, 41–53
adjustment program, 41–53, 95, 104,
358
Comibol (state-owned mining
company), 44–45
deregulation, 49, 378–79
economic status of, 356–57
election of May 1989, 41
exchange rate policy, 47–48, 370–71
financial liberalization in the 1980s,
367–68, 403
fiscal performance and, 43–47,
360–61, 363–64
foreign direct investment, 49–50, 375
General Labor Act of 1939, 47
hyperinflation, 45, 48, 53, 95, 100,
106
interest rate policy, 48–49
need for stabilization program, 355
privatization, 49–50, 377
stabilization, 19, 98, 100, 312
structural change, 403
tax reforms, 45–46, 53, 250, 365–66
trade policy, 48, 372–74
and Washington consensus policy
reforms, 381–82
and World Bank, 50–51
Bosquet, Maréchal, 337
Botero, Rodrigo, 309–11, 401
Bradford, Colin, 36
Bradley, Bill (Senator), 12
Brady Plan, 354, 412, 414–18
in Costa Rica, 396
debt crisis and, 349, 383
launching of, 358
in Mexico, 390
Brazil, 129–51, 170–73, 181–82,
190–94
adjustment program, 170–73
balance of payments, 132, 137
bank debt prices in secondary market,
329
central bank of, 146, 184
computer industry, 134–36
debt-equity swaps, 145–47, 171
decentralization of government, 348
deregulation in the 1980s, 378–79
exchange rate policy in the 1980s,
370–71
export performance, 136, 348
financial liberalization in the 1980s,
367–68
fiscal performance and, 129–30, 138,
314–15, 360–61, 364

fiscal policies, 140–44
foreign direct investment, 139–140,
375
growth rate in, 329
health care in, 149–50
import performance, 132–34
income distribution, 147–50
inflation, 129–51, 170–73
and International Monetary Fund
(IMF), 9
Law of Similars, 135
monetary policy, 144–47
poverty, 147–50
privatization, 143–44, 377
public sector borrowing requirement
(PSBR), 141–42
real exchange rate in, 330
stabilization in, 313
tax reforms in 1980s, 366
trade policy, 131–40, 373
transitional democracy, 99
and Washington consensus, 387–89
and World Bank, 132, 149
Bresser Plan, 129
Broda, Miguel Angél, 113
Brookings Institution, 21
Budget balancing, 313
cyclical versus annual, 29
Budget deficits. *See* Fiscal deficits
Buiter, Wilhelm H., 66
Bush, George, 23
Buybacks, 321–22

C
CACM. *See* Central American Common
Market
Callejas, Rafael Leonardo, 300, 397
Camdessus, Michel, 11, 349, 353
Capital flight, 12, 19, 23, 323–24
Capital gains taxation, 23
Cardoso, Eliana, 105, 129–52, 170–73,
181–82, 190–94, 372, 388
Cariaga, Juan L., 41–53, 98, 100–101,
105, 341, 356, 359, 381
Caribbean, 257–60, 303–06
economies of, 336–37
fiscal discipline and, 360
international financial institutions
(IFIs) and, 260
and Washington consensus, 264–73
CARICOM, 272
Carrasquilla, A., 213
Carter, Jimmy, administration on
deregulation, 16–17
Cauas, J., 78

and Washington consensus, 391–92
and World Bank, 201, 219
Comibol (Bolivia), 44–45, 47
Comissão de Política Aduaneira (Brazil), 133
Commerce Department, US, 22
Comparative advantage, 112
Competitive exchange rates, 13–14, 26, 34
Computer industry, of Brazil, 134–36, 171–72
Conable, Barber, 11
Convergence, versus Washington consensus, 22, 24, 37, 401
Corbo, Vittorio, 95–97, 106
Corden, W. Max, 64
CORFO (Chile), 81–82
Cornia, Giovanni Andrea, 11
Corporate state, 311
Corruption, 8, 17, 321
Costa Rica, 285, 287–88, 292–94, 303–06
  adjustment programs, 105, 250
  central bank losses in, 314
  democracy in, 99
  deregulation in the 1980s, 378–79
  economic performance, 296–97
  exchange rate policy in the 1980s, 370–71
  external debt in, 358
  financial liberalization in the 1980s, 367–68
  fiscal performance and, 360–61, 363–64
  foreign direct investment in the 1980s, 375
  privatization in the 1980s, 376–77
  tax reforms in 1980s, 366
  trade liberalization in the 1980s, 373–74
  and Washington consensus, 395–96
Coutts, K. J., 261
Cox-Edwards, Alejandra, 106
Crawling peg, 131, 136, 239
  and Costa Rica, 296
Credibility, of stabilization program, 323
  in Argentina, 113
  in Peru, 93
Credit subsidies, 136
Cruzado Plan, 129, 190, 388
Cuddington, John, 138
Currency. See Exchange rate
Currency boards, 30
Current account
  in Brazil, 191

in Chile, 59–60
in Colombia, 199, 214
in Mexico, 186
Cury, H. G., 261

D

Dantas, Daniel, 129–52, 170–73, 181–82, 388
Data Resources, Inc., 138
de Hoz, Martínez, 124
de la Madrid, Miguel, 158–59
de Melo, J., 97
de Pablo, Juan Carlos, 111–28, 169–70, 177–79, 188–89, 378, 380, 387
de Soto, Hernando, 385
De Walle, Nicolas Van, 143–44
Debt crisis
  in Bolivia, 42
  in Brazil, 129–30, 138, 149
  in Chile, 54, 106
  in Colombia, 248
  in Costa Rica, 395–96
  in Jamaica, 262
  Latin American, 328, 346–47
  in Mexico, 155–59
  in Peru, 107
  in Venezuela, 248
Debt relief, 349, 418–19
  in Caribbean nations, 278
  importance of, 183
  and US Treasury, 23
Debt relief. See also Brady Plan
Debt strategy, advantages of, 321–22
Debt-equity swaps, 15–16, 30, 34, 105, 236, 252–53
  in Argentina, 120
  in Bolivia, 50
  in Brazil, 145–47, 171
  in Chile, 83
  in Jamaica, 272
  in Venezuela, 236
Debt-equity swaps. See also Privatization
Debt-GNP ratio, 9
Decontrol of prices, 54
Deficit reduction, 30
Deindexation, 73–74
Democracy, 36, 99
  and adjustment programs, 105
  in Argentina, 114
  in Latin America, 325–26, 353–54
  "Pact for Democracy," 106
Democratic Party, 22
Deregulation, 16–17, 22, 30, 34–35, 278, 378
  in Argentina, 122–24, 127

External debt. *See also* Debt crisis
External sector policies, 33–34
External shocks, and Central American
economy, 281
Exxon Corporation. *See* Standard Oil of
New Jersey

F

FDI. *See* foreign direct investment
Febres-Cordero, León, 398
FEER. *See* Fundamental equilibrium
exchange rate (FEER)
Feinberg, Richard, 21–24, 37, 400
Ffrench-Davis, Ricardo, 70
Financial liberalization, 367–69
Financial reforms, 320–21
of Central American countries,
288–92, 311
Fiscal deficits, 8–10, 21–22, 33
of Argentina, 169
of Bolivia, 43–46
of Brazil, 141–43, 181–82
of Chile, 55, 59
of Colombia, 201–04
debt-GNP ratio, 9
International Monetary Fund (IMF)
and, 8–9
of Jamaica, 259, 270–71
of Mexico, 163
of Peru, 103
of Venezuela, 230–32
Fiscal deficits. *See also* Public-sector
deficit
Fiscal discipline
interpretation of, 362
for policy reform, 359–60
Fiscal policy, 22–23, 26–27, 32–33
of Brazil, 140–44
Fiscal policy. *See also* Macroeconomic
policy
Fiscal reform,
in Argentina, 114–15
in Central American countries,
285–88
in Chile, 54
Fischer, Stanley, 25–28, 37, 367, 380,
413
Fixed exchange rates, 18, 313
Flight capital. *See* Capital flight
Fondo de Garantías de las Instituciones
Financieras (Colombia), 208, 216
Fontaine, John A., 69
Foreign direct investment, 15, 277
in Argentina, 120
in Bolivia, 49–50

in Brazil, 139–40
in Chile, 83
in Colombia, 214–16, 252–53
in Jamaica, 272
in Latin America, 374–76
role of, 322
in Venezuela, 236, 251–52
Foxley, Alejandro, 81
Fundamental equilibrium exchange rate
(FEER), 14

G

Garay, L. J., 213
García, Alan, 86, 90, 99–100, 105, 325,
384–85
GDP
fiscal consolidation and, 360–61
of Latin America, 312
per capita, 347
General Agreement on Tariffs and Trade
(GATT), 31
trade policy and, 374
General Labor Act of 1939, of Bolivia,
47
Germany, 171
Glade, William, 144
Government, decentralization trends in
Latin America, 348
Government spending. *See*
Expenditures, Fiscal deficits, Fiscal
policy, Public-sector policies
Gramm-Rudman-Hollings Act
enactment of, 8
suspension of, 9
Great Britain, *See* United Kingdom
Guatemala, 285, 287–88, 292, 294
economic performance, 298–300
and Washington consensus, 396–97
Guisarri, Adrián, 125
Guyana, 261–62
and Washington consensus, 268–70,
394

H

Hachette, D., 81
Hakim, Peter, 338
Harberger, Arnold, 36, 188, 327–32,
341
Hausmann, Ricardo, 245, 247, 334,
340, 392
Hawke, Bob, 414
Health expenditures,
in Brazil, 149–50
in Colombia, 201–04
and education expenditures, 11–12

Heterodox policies, versus orthodox, 27, 127, 161
Hirschman, Albert O., 36, 346
  "unbalanced growth" theory, 123
Hommes, Rudolf, 105, 199–223, 246–47, 380
Honduras, 285, 287, 292
  economic performance, 300
  and Washington consensus, 397
Hong Kong, 30
Hung, L., 233
Hyperinflation,
  in Argentina, 113, 115, 126–27, 169–70, 178, 189
  in Bolivia, 45, 48, 53, 95, 100, 106
  in Mexico, 157, 184, 190
  in Peru, 189
  stopping of, 357

I

IDB. *See* Inter-American Development Bank
IFIs. *See* International financial institutions
Iglesias, Enrique, 343–50, 401
IMF. *See* International Monetary Fund
Imports
  of Argentina, 124
  of Bolivia, 48
  of Brazil, 132–37
  of Chile, 55
  of Colombia, 215, 218
  of Costa Rica, 282
  of Jamaica, 272
  liberalization of, 14, 27, 33–34, 320
  licensing, 14–15
  of Mexico, 159, 162
  of Peru, 87
  substitution policies, 29, 346
  of Venezuela, 229
  World Bank view on liberalization of, 15
Imports. *See also* Liberalization, Trade policy
Income distribution, 413–14
  in Brazil, 147–50, 172–73
  in Caribbean nations, 258
  in Colombia, 211
  and reduction of inequality, 32
Income distribution. *See also* Poverty
Income tax
  in Argentina, 179
  in Barbados, 265
  in Bolivia, 45
  in Brazil, 184

in Chile, 80
in Colombia, 209–10
in Costa Rica, 287–88
in Dominican Republic, 267
in Jamaica, 271
in Mexico, 184
in Peru, 91
in Venezuela, 235, 250
Incomes policy, and inflation, 317
Indexation, role of, 318–19
Industrial policy, 22
Inflation, 21, 26, 29, 32, 95, 312–13, 346
  in Argentina, 125–27
  in Bolivia, 45, 48, 53
  in Brazil, 129–51, 170–73, 388
  in Chile, 96, 99
  Cruzado Plan and, 388
  incomes policy and, 317
  in Mexico, 155, 157–58, 161, 180–81
  in Peru, 86–87, 91, 103–04, 107
  problem of, 312–13, 346
  in Venezuela, 224, 233, 238
Inflation. *See also* Hyperinflation
Informal economy. *See* Parallel market
Informatics. *See* Computer industry
Institute for International Economics, 21, 358
Institute of International Finance, 15
Instituto de Fomento Industrial (Colombia), 216
Instituto Nacional de Estadísticas (Chile), 77, 101
Inter-American Development Bank (IDB), 350
  adjustment and, 345
  and Bolivia, 50–51
  and Central America, 279
  and Chile, 70
  conference at, 21, 112
  and Peru, 89
Interest rates, 13, 30, 276
  in Argentina, 119
  in Bolivia, 48–49
  in Brazil, 144–45
  in Chile, 56
  in Colombia, 211–12
  in Costa Rica, 291
  international real, 96
  in Jamaica, 271
  in Mexico, 166–68
  in Peru, 91
  in Venezuela, 236–38
  subsidies, 207–08

Paz Estenssoro, Victor, 106, 381
Pazos, Felipe, 192, 239
Pérez, Carlos Andrés, 229, 247, 392–93
Pechman, Joseph A., 12
Pellerano, F., 261
Peru, 86–95
  adjustment measures, 91–93, 99–100,
    104
  Andean Pact leadership, 89
  bank debt prices in secondary market,
    329
  central bank of, 102
  deregulation in the 1980s, 379
  economic policy in the 1980s, 86–89
  exchange rate policy in the 1980s,
    370–71
  financial liberalization in the 1980s,
    368
  fiscal performance and, 360–61, 364
  foreign direct investment in the
    1980s, 375
  inflation, 86–87, 91, 103–04, 107,
    189
  interest subsidies, 103
  multiple exchange rate system, 87
  privatization, 92–93, 377
  public confidence in, 93–94
  Sendero Luminoso, 89–100
  stabilization in, 313
  tax reforms in 1980s, 366
  tax revenues in, 314–15
  trade liberalization in the 1980s, 373
  transitional democracy, 99
  and Washington consensus, 384–85
  and World Bank, 88–89
Piñango, R., 233
Polak, Jacques J., 13, 192–93
Policy instruments, definitions of, 7–8
Policy reform, 1–2, 7–38, 407–10
  areas of, 358–80
  deregulation, 16–17
  exchange rate, 13–14
  fiscal deficits, 8–10
  foreign direct investment, 15
  interest rates, 13
  privatization, 16
  property rights, 17
  public expenditure priorities, 10–12
  summary of 1980 changes, 404–08
  tax reform, 12–13, 36
  trade policy, 14–15
Political stability, 35
Political systems, and economic policy,
  99
Population growth, in Brazil, 148

Populism, definition of, 355
Poverty, 27, 32
  in Brazil, 147–50
  in Guyana, 394
  in Nicaragua, 301
Poverty. See also Income distribution
Price controls, 30
  elimination of Bolivian, 49
Primary deficit. See Fiscal deficits
Primavera Plan, 126, 318, 386
Privatization, 16, 30, 34–35, 100–101,
  277–78, 335
  in Argentina, 127, 170, 178
  in Bolivia, 49–50
  in Brazil, 143–44
  in Central America, 294–95
  in Chile, 80–84, 101
  in Colombia, 216–17, 251–52
  in Costa Rica, 295
  in Jamaica, 272
  in Latin America, 376–78
  in Mexico, 160
  in Peru, 92–93
  resolution of fiscal crisis, 316–17
  role of, 331–32
  in Venezuela, 235, 251–52
Privatization. See also Debt-equity swaps
Programa de Reordenamiento
  Económico y Social de Corto Plazo
  (Guatemala), 299
Property rights, 17
  in Colombia, 217
  in Latin America, 378–79
Protectionism, 224
PSBR. See Public-sector borrowing
  requirement
Public choice theory, 30
Public-sector borrowing requirement
  (PSBR), of Brazil, 141–42
Public-sector deficit. See Fiscal deficits
Public-sector noninterest expenditures,
  of Mexico, 160
Public-sector policies
  of Argentina, 115
  of Chile, 77–80
  U.S. versus Latin America, 33
  of Venezuela, 234–35
Public-sector policies. See also Fiscal
  policy
Puerto Rico, 271

Q
Quasi-fiscal deficit, 314

POLICY ANALYSES IN INTERNATIONAL ECONOMICS

1 **The Lending Policies of the International Monetary Fund**
John Williamson/*August 1982*
$8.00   0–88132–000–5   72 pp

2 **"Reciprocity": A New Approach to World Trade Policy?**
William R. Cline/*September 1982*
$8.00   0–88132–001–3   41 pp

3 **Trade Policy in the 1980s**
C. Fred Bergsten and William R. Cline/*November 1982*
(Out of print)   0–88132–002–1   84 pp
Partially reproduced in the book *Trade Policy in the 1980s*.

4 **International Debt and the Stability of the World Economy**
William R. Cline/*September 1983*
$10.00   0–88132–010–2   134 pp

5 **The Exchange Rate System**
John Williamson/*September 1983, 2nd ed. rev. June 1985*
$10.00   0–88132–034–X   61 pp

6 **Economic Sanctions in Support of Foreign Policy Goals**
Gary Clyde Hufbauer and Jeffrey J. Schott/*October 1983*
$10.00   0–88132–014–5   109 pp

7 **A New SDR Allocation?**
John Williamson/*March 1984*
$10.00   0–88132–028–5   61 pp

8 **An International Standard for Monetary Stabilization**
Ronald I. McKinnon/*March 1984*
$10.00   0–88132–018–8   108 pp

9 **The Yen/Dollar Agreement: Liberalizing Japanese Capital Markets**
Jeffrey A. Frankel/*December 1984*
$10.00   0–88132–035–8   86 pp

10 **Bank Lending to Developing Countries: The Policy Alternatives**
C. Fred Bergsten, William R. Cline, and John Williamson/*April 1985*
$12.00   0–88132–032–3   221 pp

11 **Trading for Growth: The Next Round of Trade Negotiations**
Gary Clyde Hufbauer and Jeffrey J. Schott/*September 1985*
$10.00   0–88132–033–1   109 pp

BOOKS

Dollar Politics: Exchange Rate Policymaking in the United States
I. M. Destler and C. Randall Henning/*1989*
$11.95   0–88132–079–X   192 pp

Foreign Direct Investment in the United States
Edward M. Graham and Paul R. Krugman/*1989*
$11.95   0–88132–074–9   182 pp

SPECIAL REPORTS

1 **Promoting World Recovery: A Statement on Global Economic Strategy**
by Twenty-six Economists from Fourteen Countries/*December 1982*
(Out of Print)   0–88132–013–7   45 pp

2 **Prospects for Adjustment in Argentina, Brazil, and Mexico: Responding to the Debt Crisis**
John Williamson, editor/*June 1983*
(Out of Print)   0–88132–016–1   71 pp

3 **Inflation and Indexation: Argentina, Brazil, and Israel**
John Williamson, editor/*March 1985*
(Out of Print)   0–88132–037–4   191 pp

4 **Global Economic Imbalances**
C. Fred Bergsten, editor/*March 1986*
$25.00 (cloth)   0–88132–038–2   126 pp
$10.00 (paper)   0–88132–042–0   126 pp

5 **African Debt and Financing**
Carol Lancaster and John Williamson, editors/*May 1986*
$12.00   0–88132–044–7   229 pp

6 **Resolving the Global Economic Crisis: After Wall Street**
Thirty-three Economists from Thirteen Countries/*December 1987*
$3.00   0–88132–070–6   30 pp

7 **World Economic Problems**
Kimberly Ann Elliott and John Williamson, editors/*April 1988*
$15.95   0–88132–055–2   298 pp

Reforming World Agricultural Trade
Twenty-nine Professionals from Seventeen Countries/*1988*
$3.95   0–88132–088–9   42 pp

8 **Economic Relations Between the United States and Korea: Conflict or Cooperation?**
Thomas O. Bayard and Soo-Gil Young, editors/*January 1989*
$12.95   0–88132–068–4   192 pp

FORTHCOMING

The United States as a Debtor Country
C. Fred Bergsten and Shafiqul Islam

Equilibrium Exchange Rates: An Update
John Williamson

Global Oil Crisis Intervention
Philip K. Verleger, Jr.

The Debt of Low-Income Africa: Issues and Options for the United States
Carol Lancaster

Economic Sanctions Reconsidered: History and Current Policy,
Revised Edition
Gary Clyde Hufbauer, Jeffrey J. Schott, and Kimberly Ann Elliott

The Uruguay Round: What Can Be Achieved?
Jeffrey J. Schott, editor

Pacific Area Developing Countries: Prospects for the Future
Marcus Noland

Financial Intermediation Beyond the Debt Crisis, Revised Edition
Donald R. Lessard and John Williamson

Economic Policy Cooperation: Reflections of a Practitioner
Wendy Dobson

Reciprocity and Retaliation: An Evaluation of Aggressive Trade Policies
Thomas O. Bayard

The Greenhouse Effect: Global Economic Consequences
William R. Cline

The Costs of US Trade Barriers
Gary Clyde Hufbauer and Kimberly Ann Elliott

Energy Policy for the 1990s: A Global Perspective
Philip K. Verleger, Jr.

A GATT for Investment
C. Fred Bergsten and Edward M. Graham

International Adjustment and Finance: Lessons of 1985–1990
Paul R. Krugman

TO ORDER PUBLICATIONS PLEASE WRITE OR CALL US AT:

Institute for International Economics
Publications Department
11 Dupont Circle, NW
Washington, DC 20036
202-328-9000